Hayner Public Library District-Alton

0 00 30 0257181 2

Honey Island

By Julius Hunter

No Longer the Property of
Hayner Public Library District

D1213357

Edited by Kay Freilich

HAYNER PUBLIC LIBRARY DISTRICT
ALTON, ILLINOIS

OVERDUES .10 PER DAY. MAXIMUM FINE
COST OF BOOKS. LOST OR DAMAGED BOOKS
ADDITIONAL $5.00 SERVICE CHARGE.

BRANCH

Copyright © 1999 by Julius Hunter

All rights reserved. No part of this book may be reproduced in any form or by
any electronic or mechanical means, including information storage and retrieval
systems, without permission in writing from the author, except by a reviewer,
who may quote brief passages in review.

ISBN 1-891442-10-4

Library of Congress Catalog Number: 99-071328

Virginia Publishing Company
4814 Washington Blvd.
St. Louis, MO 63108
(314) 367-6612

29.2
HUN

ADK-9130

Table of Contents

Dedicated to the memory of my great-great-grandparents, Ellen & Ned Rounds

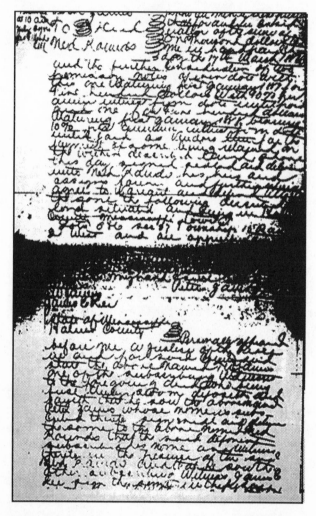

A weathered copy of the deed granting Ned Rounds 216 acres of Mississippi land in 1886 for $1,000 cash.

Acknowledgments

One of the most challenging elements of writing a book is the often futile attempt by the author to thank every single person who has made a significant contribution to the creative effort. But here it goes, with extra special thanks to any and every contributor who has been inadvertently omitted:

To my late grandmother, Hattie Coats; my mother Atlener "Lena" Hunter Outlaw; my aunt Willetta Perkins, who allowed me to chronicle her trials and triumphs as a teenage girl in St. Louis during the end of the "Roaring '20s" and beyond; and my late cousin Pearline Scales for her loving kindness and unflagging support of all my endeavors.

To Ann Fleming whose genealogical expertise and inspiration sparked my interest, guided my initial roots pursuits, and patiently propelled my research efforts in such an extraordinary way; to Jennifer P. S. Plaat for editing aid, research assistance, and for continuous moral support from start to finish of this project; to my sister, Carol Hunter, for accompanying me to Mississippi, helping me interpret what turned out to be a totally foreign environment for me in the Magnolia State and helping with the courthouse research; and to The Rev. M. L. Houston and the Congregation of Jones Chapel Missionary Baptist Church of *Honey Island* for keeping the faith of our fathers.

To family members previously known and those newly-discovered; and to completely new friends for sharing memories and for their invaluable help in compiling the materials in this tome: to Savannah Miller Young for helping me with Mississippi orientation; John H. Quinn, Esq.; W. C. Trotter, Esq., of Belzoni; Cousin Bessie Burton of Chicago; Annie West Rounds; Mattie Straughter and The Honorable Rufus Straughter of Belzoni; Mattie Burns Williams of Belzoni; Thaddeus Rounds of Chicago; Thelma Lee Rounds of Memphis; Joe Nathan Turner; Sally Turner; Fannie Scott and Lue Annie Scott of Isola; Rev. Jodie Thurman of Belzoni; Warren "Red" Baker of Belzoni; Herbert Fullilove of *Honey Island*; Lois Jackson, Belzoni; and to Barbara Hunter Millner of Carlisle, Massachusetts, for frequent reviews of the drafts and for ongoing moral support.

To friends, librarians, and researchers for help with locating records and facts: Jill Barge for research assistance; Craig Scott of Washington, D. C., for archival research; Charles Brown of the Mercantile Library for research aid; Megaera Ausman, Archivist of the U. S. Postal Service in Washington, D. C.; Genealogist Ruth Land Hatten of Jackson; Joyce Loving of the St. Louis County Library; to St. Louis Zoo Director and my good friend Charles Hoessle for providing more information about the snakes on *Honey Island* than anybody else in the world could have possibly known; to Genealogist Emory Webre; Jane Julian, Kentucky State Archivist in Frankfort; Larry Banks, Hydraulics Chief of the Army Corps of Engineers in Vicksburg; Mayor Tom Turner of Belzoni; Phillip Chauvin Jr., President of the Terrebonne, Louisiana, Genealogical Society; Sybil McCann of the Houma-Terrebonne Louisiana Tourist Commission; and Jennifer Taft at the Bureau of Land Management in Springfield, Virginia; Peter Rexford for locating stamps from the *Honey Island* post office era; and Dr. G.H. Tichenor Antiseptic Company of New Orleans.

And thanks to those who helped with the technical aspects of producing this book: Jack Byrne, Ph.D., for editing assistance; Alan Gorman for computer consultations—especially during the wee hours of the morning when the darned computer decided to act up; Tom Ackerman for word processor and editing assistance; and Brooks Dyer for early draft review in basically suggesting that I cut some of the material he and future readers might find extraneous.

To my wonderful and inquisitive daughters, Jennifer and Julia, for whom I've written all my books, and whose thirst for knowledge about their ancestors has fueled my ongoing investigation of the Rounds Family story.

I also want to thank my colleagues at KMOV who have had to listen to my daily discoveries about my roots for more than two years now.

And finally, I want to thank all the Rounds Family members from around the nation who, at the Rounds Family Reunion in Memphis in September 1999, gave me hearty encouragement to dig deeper.

Honey Island
Cast of Characters

To help you keep track of some of the principal people who are part of the *Honey Island* story, and to give you a quick reference to their relationships to each other and to the author, please accept this little guide.

Baker, Warren "Red": our affable guide on our historic 1998 visit to *Honey Island*.

Byrd, George Jr.: husband of Ninnie Rounds, son-in-law of Westly, first *Honey Island* postmaster (appointed 1907); my great-uncle.

Coats, Rhoda Hattie Rounds Williams: daughter of Westly and Hager Rounds, married (1) Anderson Williams and (2) John Coats, always called Hattie or "Mama"; my grandmother.

Coats, John: second husband of my grandmother, Rhoda Hattie Rounds.

Johnson, Gertrude "Lovie" Williams: daughter of Hattie Rounds and Anderson Williams, granddaughter of Westly Rounds and Hager, my mother's sister; my aunt.

Johnson, Pearline "Pearl": see Pearline Johnson Scales.

Johnson, Walter: husband of Gertrude Williams, father of Pearline and Evarine; my uncle.

Outlaw, Atlener "Lena" Williams Hunter: daughter of Hattie Rounds and Anderson Williams, granddaughter of Westly Rounds and Hager; my mother.

Perkins, Willetta "Singie" Williams: daughter of Hattie Rounds and Anderson Williams, granddaughter of Westly Rounds and Hager; my aunt.

Rounds, Ambrose: son of Westly and Hager, called "Bud" or "Uncle A"; my great-uncle.

Rounds, Annie West: wife of Jesse Rounds, daughter-in-law of John Rounds, niece by marriage of Westly Rounds.

Rounds, Ellen: wife of Ned Rounds, original surname unknown, mother of Lucy, Westly, George, Martha, John, and Eddie; my great-great-grandmother.

Rounds, Hager: (sometimes spelled Hagar), original surname unknown, mother of Kimmie, Ninnie, Hattie, Ambrose, Carrie, Henry, and Lillie B.; my great-grandmother.

Pfeiffer, Lillie B. Rounds: daughter of Westly and Hager Rounds, aunt of Willetta Williams, wife of Wes Pfeiffer; my great-aunt.

Rounds, Mary Hughes Lewis: second wife of Westly Rounds, mother of Minnie, John, Willie and Robert Lee Lewis and of Inez, Annette, Eva, Elmer, Perry, and Benjamin Rounds; my step-great-grandmother.

Rounds, Ned: the earliest identified ancestor, former slave, purchaser of hundred of acres of *Honey Island* farmland, "banker," entrepreneur; my great-great-grandfather.

Rounds, Ninnie: daughter of Westly and Hager Rounds; wife of George Byrd Jr.; my great-aunt.

Rounds, Rhoda Hattie: see Hattie Rounds Williams Coats.

Rounds, Rufus: son of Jesse and Annie West Rounds; great-grandson of Ned and Ellen Rounds; my second cousin, once removed.

Rounds, Thaddeus "Ted": son of John and Luthisha Syfax Rounds, grandson of Ned Rounds; my great-uncle.

Rounds, Westly: son of Ned and Ellen Rounds, husband of (1) Hager and (2) Mary Hughes Lewis; my great-grandfather.

Rounds, Will (Lewis): son of Mary Lewis Rounds and her first husband, often used the name of his step-father Westly Rounds; my step-great-great-uncle.

Scales, Pearline "Pearl" Johnson: daughter of Gertrude Williams and Walter Johnson, a great-great-granddaughter of Ned Rounds; my cousin.

Simmons, Tom: husband of Martha "Mattie" Rounds, son-in-law of Ned and Ellen Rounds; my great-great-uncle.

Straughter, Mattie: Belzoni educator and wife of Humphreys County State Representative Rufus Straughter; our dynamic and cordial guide to *Honey Island*.

Williams, Anderson: first husband of my maternal grandmother Rhoda Hattie Rounds, father of Atlener (my mother), Gertrude and Willetta; my grandfather.

Williams, Atlener: see Atlener Williams Hunter Outlaw.

Williams, Gertrude: see Gertrude Williams Johnson.

Williams, Willetta: see Willetta Williams Johnson.

Williams, Mattie Burns: daughter of Mary Simmons and Porter Burns, granddaughter of Martha "Mattie" Rounds and Tom C. Simmons; my second cousin, once removed.

Prologue

Please God...don't let her die. It was a simple prayer we family members and all her friends sent up to a higher authority. As we launched our collective petition heavenward we realized the Almighty's response might not be to our liking. Isn't it always easier, though, to ask for something from somebody more powerful than we than it is to accept that person's answer? Members of the Rounds family have learned to relinquish power over life and death to the Omnipotent. "Not my will, but Thine," we've yielded in our Baptist, Methodist, Lutheran, Catholic, and other churches for as long as any family member can remember, going back at least 140 years. Roundsfolk even helped found a little Mississippi Baptist church a century ago.

It was hard to let go of my dear cousin Pearl—Pearline Johnson Scales. We had lost her mother, my mother's sister Gertrude, just the year before. My family didn't seem quite willing to mouth the mantra about our will versus His will so soon again. Some of Pearl's kinfolk scoured medical data hoping to help her doctors try to find a miraculous cure. A few who knew her began to fabricate diagnostic nonsense about her ailment. It was even whispered that a friend of hers from the Caribbean had put a voodoo hex on her. Some—particularly the Rounds family members who had already lived full lives—would have offered themselves in her place. We would have held onto one of her arms and played tug of war with God to keep her. But the mysterious illness which put her under virtual arrest in the hot St. Louis summer of 1998 appeared to be dragging her slowly, slowly, ever so slowly, to God's side of the line.

The team of doctors who tried to rescue her from the jaws of death were baffled as she began to slip away from us in her room at Barnes-Jewish Hospital. She was now a shadow of the robust woman she once was. Her seventy-one-year-old frame began to gnarl. Her back curled into a pitiable curvature. With assistance from at least one person, she managed to walk, but only at great risk of tumbling forward. Her skin darkened to a shade that was unrecognizable even to those of us who knew her well. Her face, though, did not wrinkle one bit. The faces of members of the Rounds family never seem to wrinkle. There were family jokes about how the Yazoo River drinking water in our Mississippi heritage kept crow's feet and wrinkles away. Surely when Pearl was a *Honey Island* girl she must have gulped enough river water to protect her countenance from the aging process.

Despite that quirk, there were many other graphic signs of her body's deterioration. Her voice began to take on a raspy quality. Or lack of quality. Her weight began an involuntary and incredibly rapid plummet. More than forty pounds in three weeks! She had lost her ability to swallow, a simple feat the able-bodied take for granted. She choked on mere morsels of food.

They tried feeding her a liquid supplement pumped through a tube down her throat. But she could neither tolerate the procedure nor hold onto the tiny amounts of supplement that managed to trickle into her stomach.

The diminishing smiles she managed to radiate gave undeniable clues to the fact that she was often in a great deal of excruciating pain.

Pearl loved to smile and we loved her radiance. She was not one to trade a grimace or a furrowed brow for a smile. She was never willing to let us hear a groan or whimper as a substitute for a good laugh. That was and is a trait of my family. No matter how bad one's health is, an inquiry about how we are doing elicits the historic and unique Rounds family response: "Right good!" I can't begin to count the number of times that was Pearl's response as she wasted away before our eyes.

She had inherited the mantle of Associate Matriarch of our family after my Grandma Hattie passed in 1978. (Black people of southern heritage, even after they have moved north, never "die" or "pass away." We pass.) Pearl shared the position with my Aunt Willetta. The two women had to be artists...painting a sometimes rosier picture of how things were in our family than they actually were to any outsider who dared ask. They were plasterers...patching up petty squabbles and major rifts in the family. They sat as judges who could handle small claims or they addressed the charges of family members who wanted to make a federal case out of it. They were shepherdesses who regularly checked on our flock. Even the black sheep. They were nurses...caring for the sick and suffering. The two were hospitable hostesses who made sure that there were never too many months allowed to pass without all members and branches of the family sitting down to break bread as well-bred and well-fed families should. It's the way things were done in the Rounds family for more than a century since the family patriarch, Ned Rounds, donned suit and tie to preside over *Honey Island*, Mississippi, breakfast, lunch, and supper feasts.

I had been particularly drawn to Cousin Pearl since the time she took care of me and read to me as my babysitter fifty years before she needed twenty-four hour hospital attention for herself. She had always harbored an inordinate interest in my career through the years. She actually kept a scrapbook of my every accomplishment from my grade school days at Cole School. In the most recent versions of her chronicles, she could recite every quip I made on my television newscasts since 1970 that made her chuckle or grit her teeth or feel peeved. She could always tell me which suit, shirt, and tie I wore on which evening. Many evenings when I got home after a late newscast, I would find the Call Notes light blinking and a message like this when I checked:

"Hello, Julius. This is Pearl. Just wanted you to know that you guys really cracked me up with that story about the burglar who got stuck in the chimney."

Or:

"Hi, Julius. This is Pearl. Wow, were we looking sharp tonight! I just love that suit and tie you wore. Really didn't want anything else. Just wanted to let you know you looked good tonight. 'Bye."

Or:

"Hi, Julius. This is Pearl. Hope everything is alright with you. You looked a little tired or upset or something tonight. Give me a call when you can. Bye now."

Right after the Fourth of July, I phoned Pearl's physician, Dr. Wald. He expressed frustration and dismay and acknowledged that he and his associates were still flat out baffled by Pearl's condition. He told me he was expecting more neuro-muscular test results the very next day, and he promised to call me with that information.

Dr. Wald's tone was grave when he reported back to me the next day as he had promised.

The confirmed diagnosis by the medical team? Lou Gehrig's Disease. Amyotrophic lateral sclerosis. A vicious killer. He asked me to help break the news to family members who weren't familiar with ALS—specifically Pearl's daughter and son, my cousins Theresa and Michael. ALS is a ruthless death sentence. Absolutely incurable. The doctor, who sounded almost like he was fighting back tears, estimated that Pearl would have a maximum of six months to live. And the pain she would experience, he said, would make her not want to live that long.

When I phoned Pearl after that devastating conversation with Dr. Wald, she was completely coherent and able to muster up the intelligence for which she was well-known. She told me in a low, hoarse whisper that she was fully aware of the diagnosis and the prognosis. But, she told me, doctors weren't always right and she knew that God would help her beat the death sentence. The faith she expressed along with her quiet resolve, convinced me that it was possible that she would, indeed, walk out of there.

When I spoke with her the next day, she had slipped into what I hoped was only temporary insanity.

"Julius, do you know about those people?"

"What people?" I asked gingerly.

"You know. Those people. They can help you get well. They've got the secrets. You have to know who they are. They look different. You know who I'm talking about. You have to get in touch with them because they're the only ones who can get me out of here. And I'm ready to go whenever you can find them."

My heart sunk. I choked up. What incredible deterioration of a good mind.

The next day produced a remarkable transformation in her mental state. And in her physical strength. Her voice was stronger. Her resolve was bolder. Even Dr. Wald was taken aback. Pearl insisted that she get out of what was supposed to be her death bed. She demanded her street clothes. My mother noticed that the laces on her canvas shoes were dirty and put them in her handbag to take them home to launder. That morning the patient had ordered her son to bring her a hamburger with all the trimmings. She devoured the burger like she hadn't eaten in weeks. And she hadn't. She even put in an order for our Aunt Willetta to bring her a piece of fried chicken for dinner that night. She got it. And ate it. All of it.

When I spoke with her, I choked up once again. This time it was because I thought I was hearing and witnessing a true miracle. Maybe even the first one that I had ever seen.

Since I knew she was interested in every project I had ever tackled, I told her that I planned to write a book about our family's once prosperous life in Mississippi and eventual flight to points north. She was, as anticipated, excited. She confirmed that she had left *Honey Island*, Mississippi, at an early age, but since she was an inquisitive child she had asked her mother lots of questions. She had asked our Grandmother Hattie a whole passel of questions, too. Pearl confessed that she knew a lot she had never talked about to anyone before.

When I asked her if she knew how her father, my Uncle Walter, was able to buy the one-way train tickets to St. Louis to get his little family away from the hard life in Mississippi, Pearl let out a little chuckle that would, without its raspiness, have been the laugh we all would recognize as her unique outpouring of happiness. She remembered that her father had to "appropriate" a small truckload of coal to buy those train tickets to freedom. We even had a laugh about whether Uncle Walter had ever thought about returning to Mississippi to pay for the "appropriated" coal.

"Not on your life, child," she chortled. "My daddy wasn't any dummy. Man, they would have strung him up by the highest pine tree in the county!"

"Isn't part of that coal story the fact that the white man whose coal it was owed Uncle Walter some money anyway?" I asked the invigorated patient.

"That's what I heard. Daddy had done some work for the man and then when pay up time came, the man called Daddy the "n" word and refused to give him what he had promised to pay."

What a marvelous story. Since the guy owed Uncle Walter money, Pearl's father comes off as a hero and not as a criminal. He had only taken the coal. Stealing the entire truck would have put Uncle Walter in a category the family could not have recorded as laudable. And theft of the truck would have made this hard-working black man who just wanted to get his family out of Mississippi the honored guest at an old-fashioned "necktie party." Uncle Walter, according to the stories I had heard, was even clever enough to get somebody else to buy the train tickets to St. Louis so a posse wouldn't be able to track down the fugitive and his family.

Pearl's improved health punched the bright rays of hope through what had seemed to be an impenetrable veil of darkness just the day before. I could tell she was really enjoying this conversation about the only subject we had never talked about before in the myriad chats we'd had over the years. Mississippi. She had never brought up the ancestral home in the Magnolia State. Aunt Gertrude was particularly tight-lipped about any memories of Mississippi. It just occurred to me after this latest talk with my hospitalized cousin that perhaps my aunt had been particularly mum about Mississippi because she had harbored deep fears for all those years that some sheriff from Humphreys County might some day knock on the door and haul Uncle Walter away. Even after his death in 1975, she might have been paranoid about losing the comfortable lifestyle Uncle Walter had set up by the sweat of his brow for his wife and daughters.

Now, with both her parents gone, and with her unexplained resurrection from the depths of near-death, Pearl and I would be able to talk freely. It might even be therapeutic, I thought, for Pearl to move beyond the traditional and impregnable code of silence about the family's life in Mississippi. I even imagined in the rush of the moment that I might enlist a revitalized cousin as a research assistant on my roots-tracing project. What deep, dark family secrets did she know? What had she heard about our illustrious great-great-grandfather, Ned Rounds, who by all accounts weighed three-hundred pounds? What about his son, our great-grandfather Westly? Had her mother or our Grandmother Hattie confided any juicy tidbits about how Ned became a banker of sorts on idyllic *Honey Island* and how he managed to come up with hundreds of dollars in cash as a down payment for the hundreds of acres he owned? Whatever happened to all that land anyway?

If only this ever-inquisitive cousin of mine who was such an ardent keeper of scrapbooks and I had started logging the Rounds family saga twenty, even thirty years earlier! We would have had one helluva story to put down on paper for generations of Rounds descendants who are entitled to know a colorful story that had only been leaked out over the years in stingy, laconic whispers. It was as if the Mississippi expatriates in our family—the *Oldtimers*—had fled an oppressive foreign country and had religiously conspired to keep their northern-born children from ever learning the mother tongue. But all that would change now.

"Tell you what I'd like to do, Cousin Pearl," I gleefully offered. "I'd like to check with you every morning with a little quiz about *Honey Island* and everything you know about our family's life in Mississippi. I've never figured out why we've never talked about that."

"Well, you know, the old folks never liked to talk too much about life down there."

"Were they ashamed or scared or what?"

"I think a little of both. Life was tough for them down there."

"Not always."

"No, they lived pretty high on the hog for a long time. But then they lost it all. Everything."

"Let's talk about it tomorrow. I don't want to tire you out too much."

"No...no...I'm not tired at all. In fact, I going to try to see if I can get somebody around here to take me for a little walk down the hall."

"Well, take it easy now. Don't overdo it. Talk to you tomorrow morning. Same time, same station. Get your thinking cap on about Mississippi."

"I'll be ready."

"Bye now. Love you."

"Love you, too. Bye."

Hallelujah! That old Rounds family tenacity was kicking into full gear again. And that old-time religion. I anxiously began trying to figure out exactly what I'd talk to Pearl about in our next conversation. Were there any old photos her mother and father might have from their life on *Honey Island*? What stories had she heard fifty or sixty years ago while memories were fresher? Did she know anything about any old family records or family Bibles?

As the family member designated to stay in touch with Pearl and Dr. Wald, I happily reported Pearl's miraculous improvement to all the family members who anxiously awaited word from me. Some of them were sure that their fervent prayers were being answered by a God who was not quite ready to take Pearl yet. Maybe a God who wanted Pearl and me to link up and dig up the story of "The Rounds Family of *Honey Island*, Mississippi," I thought to myself. I could hardly contain my excitement on the drive to the newsroom. Over nearly three decades of reporting good news and bad news on the evening newscasts, I, of course, preferred the glad tidings. On this day I had nothing but good news to tell my caring colleagues about the dramatic upswing on Cousin Pearl's medical chart.

Dr. Wald telephoned me just before eight that evening. He didn't have to tell me what motivated his call. I could hear tears in his voice. He was choked with obvious emotion.

"Your Cousin Pearl has lapsed into a Code Red condition. Her breathing has stopped. And her heart has stopped. The crash team is doing everything they can to revive her. To be honest with you, though, I don't think she's going to make it."

I thought about my mother cheerfully washing those dirty shoe laces, getting them all ready to take them back to Pearl the next morning so her newly-energized niece could take more walks down the hall. Maybe Pearl wouldn't have to wash those laces for a very long time after she had begun to take walks around her block and all over town once she got home.

Just minutes before I was to start down to the studio to deliver the ten o'clock news that night, Dr. Wald phoned me again. It was now official. Pearl was gone. Dead. One of the most beloved lights in the lives of so many people was snuffed out by an unrelenting disease named after a baseball player. As I hung up the phone and started the walk down the block-long hallway to the studio, I was struck by a resolution I had avoided making for my entire life. I would now go to Mississippi. I would now find out all I could about my family's southern heritage. I would find the *Honey Island* of Pearl's birth. I would make the journey in her name and in her memory.

She would want me to do that. I would not let her down.

Very early the very next day I phoned my travel agent and ordered my first plane tickets to a not-so-far-away place I had avoided all my life. I had shunned this place like the plague my relatives had, by their collective silence, suggested it was.

I would go to Mississippi.

 Digging for Mississippi Roots

My great-great granddaddy was a big shot! If ever it could be said that somebody lived "high on the hog," it could be said about Ned Rounds and his large family. He owned more prime farmland land in the late 1880s than most folks around him did. Hundreds of acres of rich Mississippi Delta property. He was a gentleman farmer, a prosperous banker, an enterprising entrepreneur, a respected community leader, and a good Christian family man. And, did I mention that he was black?

My great-great-grandpa couldn't read nor write…if one believes the census reports in the late 1800s. Quite frankly, I don't believe them. When he bought all those big clumps of land around his beloved *Honey Island,* Mississippi, he plunked down hundreds of dollars of hard, cold cash on the barrel head. An incomparably brilliant feat for an illiterate black former slave in 1886! Old Ned never got any of those government grants for free or cheap land that all the white folk who owned the land before him got. But he did inscribe any official papers that had to be signed with a big, fat "X." I personally think that was some kind of ruse he put on to throw off those who were out to thwart a black man's bold adventures into a cold, capitalistic world. We're still trying to figure what happened to all his land. Why don't those of us who are his natural heirs still own any of that land down there in Mississippi? Well, I mentioned that Ned Rounds was black, didn't I?

Now that my Cousin Pearl was dead and unable to tell me any tales or help me with my research, I had decided to go to *Honey Island* to find out everything possible about our family's life there. It wasn't going to be easy, though. My family didn't talk much about those Mississippi years. Some good stories and some wonderful memories were lost when all that land slipped through the hands of Ned's descendants. I eventually gathered over the years that there was at least a latent embarrassment about blowing the land ownership. I reasoned rather late in my life that even though my kinfolk mostly lived in peace and prosperity on *Honey Island,* they were ashamed of their relative lack of education, social sophistication, and cultural breadth. It was a real effort to get anybody in my family who had actually lived on *Honey Island* to talk about Mississippi. There was a great deal of muddied Mississippi mystery about the Rounds family roots.

What the *Honey Island* refugees *would* admit to is that they had no handed-down stories about Ned Rounds or his family living under the dark cloud of slavery. They all have tales of praise about how clever and resourceful Old Ned was. But I had to take their word—or their lack of word—for what our family was like a long, long time ago in Mississippi.

During my entire childhood and beyond, nobody in the family ever packed up his/her bags and piled into a car or caught a plane or a train for a *Honey Island* visit or vacation. We went to Memphis or Chicago or Detroit when we took trips. As a kid I never traveled any farther south than South St. Louis. I always thought it was odd that we didn't go back to Mississippi. Why didn't we? I'm sure now a lot of the reason for avoiding Mississippi was that shame I just talked about. But I never asked.

That shame poignantly but vividly showed up in one of the most popular, potentially excruciating, and possibly devastating street games played by black kids my age and older for many, many decades. It was variously called *"jonin',"* *"joinin'"* or *"snaps"* or *"playing the dozens."* The idea of this game of verbal assaults was for two or more contestants to square off and hurl insults at the mother of the other. The form was to begin each attack with *"Yo' mama..."* The mothers were, of course, nowhere near these jousts for the jugular. Had either mother suddenly appeared at the scene of the bout, the match would have been shortened considerably. While a crowd gathered—usually in the schoolyard before or after school or during recess—the winner was declared when one opponent broke into tears, threw in the towel, or threw a punch to turn the game into a fistfight. The best *"joner"* could link his insult to a previous one and capitalize on the segue. Laughter, hoots, jeers, cheers, whistles, and whatever we called the predecessor of the "high five" were the reward the best man got.

Mothers were particularly beloved in the ghetto. They were so very often the strong force around which the black family evolved. To have one's mother publicly denigrated was all even the biggest bully could take. Mississippi was very often thrown into the exchange of insults to rub salt into the wounds. Typical of the mother/Mississippi insult was:

Contestant #1: *"Yo' mama got a house in Mississippi so small the roaches gotta walk in single file!"*

Contestant #2: *"Oh, yeah? Well, yo' mama's house down in Mississippi is so small they couldn't paint the walls. 'Cause if they did, they'd stick together!"*

I've wondered since my youth why kids with roots in Alabama, Louisiana, Arkansas, Tennessee, or other southern states didn't take anywhere near the amount of verbal ridicule as kids with Mississippi heritage did. Adults didn't treat Mississippi any better.

Movie maker John Sayles once declared of the Magnolia State:

"I would rather be a cockroach in New York than emperor of Mississippi."

After a recent return tour of the south with his camera, acclaimed African American photographer Herbert Randall said in a July 1999, article in *People* magazine:

"I promised myself when I left Mississippi in '64, if I could get out without being maimed or killed, I would never come back."

The author and chronicler of life in Mississippi, Anthony Walton, notes in his book, *American Journey,* that his father, Claude, who left Mississippi two decades after most of the Rounds clan had fled their homeland, was fond of saying:

"I call it 'sippi' 'cause I don't Miss it."

Shame. Fear. Ignorance. Misgivings. Misinformation. No information. Headlines. Shadows. All worked in concert to keep me from feeling good about taking a trip down south to check out my roots, to claim a heritage of bittersweet memories.

I should have gone to Mississippi a long, long time ago to find out what happened to the more than three hundred acres of Rounds land. Guess I was afraid to go. Ashamed to go. Too busy with other things to go.

It's a pity and perhaps a true shame that when I was a child I never learned anything in school about Mississippi except for the awful stuff I heard about the state in those animated schoolyard insult matches. Even though I lived with and around relatives who had suffered the awful pain inflicted by Jim Crow, I never heard any first-hand stories from them about the blatant, brutal, ugly form of Mississippi racism. My relatives who experienced *Honey Island* weren't at all eager to share their Mississippi past lives with those of my generation born up north. For some reason, many *Oldtimers* clammed up in an almost conspiratorial way about the lives they led in the south.

It is still as if they were afraid those of us who lost our Mississippi accents and became better groomed, better educated, more acculturated, more urbanized, and a bit more sophisticated might laugh at them. The famous *Rounds Selective Memory* almost always kicked into overdrive whenever we northern-born whipper-snappers have tried to extract information from the *Oldtimers* about life on *Honey Island*. We have learned only those little tidbits from our elders that they have deemed non-condemning, non-threatening, and non-incriminating.

In my fifty-plus years of occupying a minuscule—and perhaps ultimately insignificant—space in the relatively safe, fairly secure, and generally comfortable patch of Earth called St. Louis, Missouri, I have never harbored any real yearnings to leave the womb to journey to an ancestral land whose sheer name evokes so many haunting mysteries, tragedies, fears, and uncertainties. Mississippi. There is a dark uneasiness which emanates from the mists of Mississippi's swamp lands, a musty mystique which rises with the vapors of its bayous, and there's that veil of smoke which covers some of Mississippi's more sinister secrets.

As an inquisitive young boy, I was baffled about why my loved ones who had fled or deserted Mississippi and the land of milk and honey that was once *Honey Island* would not talk freely about their lives as residents of the Magnolia State. In fact, getting them to open up about life in Mississippi was like—like pulling hen's teeth—an expression they had inadvertently packed in the luggage they brought with them to Missouri and other points north.

My relatives, who probably didn't read statistics and newspapers regularly or well, were expatriates of a state which appeared, long before the time of their mass exodus—and to this very day still appears—at the very bottom of almost all charts on education, health care, lifestyle, culture, infrastructure, and matters socio-economic. There was, and still is, unabashed shame, embarrassment, and latent fear cloaked in much of everything my Mississippi-born relatives are willing to share. Those of us who ask questions of their past lives can only assume there are more than sufficient grounds for their reluctance to talk about life in Mississippi. They learned at early ages not to make uncensored comments to plantation owners, overseers, strangers, law officers, politicians, or ultimately to Yankee offspring, about their state's deficiencies or the state of any of their personal deficiencies. They cradled in their guts fears only they could know from indelible experiences as slaves and sharecroppers and freedmen.

In Mississippi, my ancestors and their African American neighbors were never any more than a subdominant, beaten-down segment of a society—subservients of a government which once allowed them to be kidnaped from their African homelands, transported across an ocean, sold like cattle, chained, beaten, humiliated, and strung up to die for sometimes minimal infractions of the laws written and administered by Whites. My Mississippi-born kinfolk learned that from the cradle to the grave they dared not gaze directly into the eyes of their oppressors—whether my folks called them "Master" or "Mister"—to challenge the duties or sentences handed them. The Rounds family members, no matter how proud and independent they were, knew to step off Mississippi sidewalks when a white person approached. My kin knew their place at washrooms, lunch counters, and on public conveyances from birth to the Public Accommodations Act of 1964 and beyond.

So it is not at all strange that the *Oldtimers* who enjoyed Mississippi at its best and survived Mississippi at its worst were, at least initially, so reluctant to tell the stories about their lives in the Old South. The tales they painstakingly doled out in small portions over years and decades are more than just fables. In most cases the mouth-to-mouth recitation of their anecdotes can be corroborated by official documentation and on-site inspection.

There are the stories about Old Ned being a bona fide Mississippi Delta landowner during a time in which *Negroes* were still being lynched by the dozens—each year. There are family memories of George Byrd Jr., serving as a proud, sophisticated, and dignified postmaster of the all-black *Honey Island's* very own post office more than nine decades ago. And, there are accounts of little Jones Chapel from which they were baptized, schooled, married, spiritually inspired, and buried. When prodded, they remember the railroad's names and numbers for the trains which transported them to and from *Honey Island* as many as ninety years ago. Their memories of the prosperity in which they lived a century ago are independently substantiated by story-tellers who are neither in the same room, the same state, nor the same age at the time of the telling.

Members of the Rounds family who left the once-idyllic prosperity of *Honey Island* have, perhaps, more reason than their black and white neighbors who lived in less comfort, to talk about their past lives. The pride, boldness, enterprise, independence, and affluent standards set by Old Ned Rounds was stripped from his immediate descendants by the vagaries of the times and by the inability of Ned's heirs to roll with the cruel and relentless punches he somehow survived for most of his life. In a matter of less than thirty years after Old Ned's death, a family which had ginned its own cotton, processed its own sugar cane, shepherded its own livestock, and shared the supper table bounty with family and neighbors had virtually lost it all.

In one case, a young Rounds descendant's father had to ship the winter coat of the daughter he had brought with him to St. Louis back down to *Honey Island* so that the second daughter would be warm enough on the wintry journey to join her family in St. Louis. That sad story is in sharp contrast to the flourishing family over which Ned Rounds had presided. Here was a man who, in 1886, had the wherewithal to fork over a thousand dollars in cash as partial payment for a big parcel of *Honey Island* farmland. The year of one of Ned's *Honey Island* land purchases—1886—was a year in which there were seventy-four *reported* incidents of Blacks being lynched in the United States. It may also have been the year in which the Rounds family and their neighbors began to be reluctant about telling anybody outside the perimeters of *Honey Island* what wonderful bounty was being enjoyed in the island's isolation.

Something terribly earthshaking happened in my little world in 1955 that helped me begin to understand some horrible things about Mississippi and the reasons we didn't go there. I was twelve years old and had just entered eighth grade at Cole Elementary School. I had been allowed to skip second grade so I was younger than most of the other students in my class and already beginning to get a bit nervous about going on to Sumner High School at thirteen.

One day in late October 1955, after the Cole School bell had dismissed us students for the day, I headed straight for the barbershop, in the Old West End Waiter's Club complex on Vandeventer Avenue not far from my home on Windsor Place. Whenever I went to get my hair cut, the first thing I would do would be to snap up a copy of *JET* magazine, a weekly edition printed by Johnson Publications of Chicago. My family couldn't afford the magazine's subscription fee, but I loved that little magazine! *JET* featured a lot of pictures and news blurbs—all oriented to a black readership. Easy reading. Comprehensive. Well done. It was like an early *People* magazine tailored to the black community. I can never forget that the cover of the October 13th edition blared:

NATION HORRIFIED BY MURDER OF KIDNAPED CHICAGO YOUTH

October 13, 1955, the date of that jarring *JET* issue, was my twelfth birthday.

I quickly flipped through the pages to find the story just before Red the barber called me to his chair. My heart stopped. Then started to pound. Fast. I was actually shaking! My eyes riveted on the most indelible and incredible photographs I had ever seen in my twelve years of life. The photos were blatantly horrific. Terrifying. Nauseating. I looked away from it. I breathed harder and harder. I looked back at it. I looked away again. I didn't want Red or any of the customers to see that I was sick.

Here on two full pages of the little tabloid were the pictures of a bloated, battered, bruised, wrinkled corpse whose eyes looked like they had been sewn shut. It was the grotesque visage of a fourteen-year-old black boy. Emmett Till. Murdered by vigilante action in **MISSISSIPPI**. Emmett was only two years older than I. I choked back tears. I felt hot. I wanted to throw up. I read on reluctantly and quickly and by compulsion as I took my time getting to the barber's chair on wobbly legs.

"Shame about that boy down in Mississippi," Red intoned. *"But that's the way white folks like to deal with Negroes down there,"* he continued. *"It's a goddam shame."*

I couldn't respond. I was torn up inside.

Here are the points of that article that I shall never forget for the rest of my life:

• Emmett Till had been shot through the head at close range.

• The left side of his skull had been crushed.

• His nude body was weighted down by a 200-pound mechanical fan of some sort before it was thrown into the Tallahatchie River.

Emmett Till was born and raised in Chicago. He was a chubby, free-spirited soul. He liked to talk a lot even though he stuttered. He loved to play little jokes on his schoolmates and the kids in his neighborhood. Some might have even called Emmett brash. Cocky. Perhaps he adopted that image to overshadow his stuttering. In August of 1955 his mother, Mamie Till Bradley, allowed her son to visit some cousins in Money, **MISSISSIPPI**, about forty miles northeast of the site that was once the Rounds family *Honey Island* homestead.

To show his country cousins in Money that life was very different in Chicago when compared to the oppressed lives they led in their southern circumscription, young Till, nicknamed "Bobo" by his kinfolk and friends, reportedly showed the boys a photo he carried in his wallet of a white girl he claimed was his girlfriend. Emmett's cousins were amazed. That kind of thing—a black boy in Mississippi dating a white girl and carrying her picture around in his wallet— crazy! Stupid! Dangerous! Unheard of! In fact, some of his kin were so incredulous that there was interracial dating in the Windy City that they decided to put Emmett's claims to the test. They dared him—in fact they *"double-dog"* dared him—to go into a little grocery store in the heart of town and ask Carolyn Bryant, the white female clerk, to go out with him. A dare is one thing, but among black kids of that era a *"double-dog"* dare was a put up or shut up forever proposition. Emmett couldn't pass up the challenge. He should have.

They watched as he entered the store on a pretext of buying some bubble gum. The boys were amazed at "Bobo's" boldness. Or his stupidity. This guy hadn't been in town two weeks and he was taking them up on the wildest, most outlandish escapade they had ever seen in their lives. After a short while, Till's cousins went into the store to haul Emmett out and get him home. Carolyn was quick to tell her husband that an uppity black kid from Chicago had actually flirted with her and asked her for a date. When he left her store, she claimed, he let out an insulting wolf-whistle. As the boys ran away, one of them yelled that they thought Carolyn Bryant was getting a gun. She would have had to be a good shot to hit the fleeing young boys. Who knows? Maybe she threw in a couple of things in her story that Emmett didn't even do. Maybe she told Roy Bryant that the *nigger* kid had even fondled her or tried to kiss her or tried to rape her. Exaggerations by white females with ulterior motives had caused many lynchings in the south and a few up north, too.

In the dead of night, around two in the morning of August 28, 1955, Roy Bryant and his half-brother J. W. Milam pounded on the front door of Moses Wright's house. The sixty-four-year-old Wright was Emmett's great-uncle and a man who knew enough about white rage to put up no resistance to the two inflamed white men. Cursing loudly, the invaders ordered Moses Wright to stand back and his wife to go back to bed if she knew what was good for her. They found the room where the fourteen-year-old Chicagoan was sleeping and dragged him out of the house. As head of the house, Moses Wright put up absolutely no resistance. If he had put up a fight against the invaders, he reasoned from what he had seen and heard in Mississippi, he and his entire family could be the next victims swinging from a rope. Emmett Till was never seen alive again. His body was found three days later. The bloated pulp that had been fished out of the river was so unrecognizable Till's Uncle Moses and the boy's mother could identify the body only by a ring on young Till's finger.

The condition of the body caused an outrage and uproar around the country when Tallahatchie County Sheriff H. C. Strider audaciously suggested that the grossly disfigured body retrieved from the Tallahatchie was not even that of Emmett Till. Strider went on to claim that the NAACP had actually "planted" the body. What's more, the sheriff made the wild claim that he had heard that a thousand carloads of Chicago Blacks were on their way to Mississippi to avenge Emmett's murder.

As preposterous as the sheriff's ruminations were, he may have thought it incredible if not alarming to learn that more than 100,000 family members, friends, neighbors, and other mourners filed by Till's open coffin during the three days the body lay in its frighteningly grotesque state.

Ironically and sadly enough, many members of the Rounds family who were not members of the Jones Chapel congregation on *Honey Island* were members of the Sweet Home Missionary Baptist Church. They were baptized in the very same body of water in which Emmett Till's mutilated body was thrown, the Tallahatchie River.

Mattie Straughter is now a Belzoni elementary school counselor and wife of a Mississippi state legislator. She still remembers that she was a teenager picking cotton in her grandfather's field near Deovolente, Mississippi, when she got the news of Emmett Till's brutal murder. Deovolente is one of the unique all-Black communities in Mississippi like Mound Bayou and *Honey Island* where independence and industry were a matter of town pride. As Mattie and her relatives worked frantically to bring in the cotton crop, her father appeared with a copy of *JET* magazine. It wasn't at all easy for black folks to get their hands on a copy of *JET* in the Mississippi of the 1950s.

Copies of *The Chicago Defender*, *JET*, and *Ebony* magazines and other printed materials aimed at enlightening and updating the African American community nationwide were regularly and mysteriously destroyed at the Belzoni post office in the 1950s and 1960s. Some Blacks who lived in Belzoni, Yazoo City, and other little Mississippi towns feared having the postal clerks turn their names over to the local sheriff if they were on the subscription list of the "radical, Yankee, Communist nigger" newspapers and magazines. Others feared intimidation from Ku Klux Klan members or from the local alcohol-fueled "rednecks" who wanted to get drunk and raise hell with local Blacks on a Friday or Saturday night. Those beatings, kidnapings, rapes, and lynchings remembered by Mattie Straughter and many of the *Oldtimers* were almost always carried out in the heat of the night...and in the wee hours.

Mattie's father, in his spare time and on weekends, was a "runner," one of the brave souls who smuggled black-oriented periodicals and literature to his family and other Blacks in Mississippi communities. A runner had to move in absolute secrecy, sometimes speak and write in code, change his pickup times regularly, and move with the stealth of the panthers that once roamed the region.

Long before Mattie's father risked his life to get contraband reading materials to Mississippi Blacks, my great-uncle George Byrd Jr., and his father before him were conduits for smuggled flyers, magazines, and newspapers. The man who married my great-aunt Ninnie was a natural for the clandestine work. He was *Honey Island's* first postmaster forty-eight years before Emmett Till was lynched not too far away from my family's Mississippi homestead.

Mattie Straughter's father would drive into Mound Bayou, Mississippi, where a certain black physician would, in the utmost secrecy, mete out news publications from the outside world of particular interest to Blacks. Located between Hollandale and Rolling Fork, northwest of *Honey Island* by sixty-five miles or so, Mound Bayou today is a progressive town of more than two thousand residents. It has been a fertile field for progressive thinking among its African American residents since its founding in 1887. The little town once hosted the then quasi-popular Booker T. Washington as a speaker at a town hall lecture. Author Chalmers Archer Jr., a Mississippi native and former resident of Holmes County, remembers that his well-read father was quite unimpressed with the speech of the co-founder and president of Tuskegee Institute. Archer writes:

"Papa said, 'I agreed with most of what Booker T had to say that day, but disagreed with his philosophy of casting down one's bucket wherever one was. This smacked of the white's man idea that black people should be satisfied with what they had, rather than make any attempt to better themselves.'"

Mrs. Straughter also remembers how shattered, but angry, she was when she, in a Mississippi cotton field, first saw the same shocking *JET* magazine photo of Emmett Till in that coffin that I had seen in a St. Louis barber shop.

"When my daddy handed me that magazine with Emmett Till's picture in it, I got sick of my stomach. I felt that I had to throw up. I just sat down in my granddad's cotton field and cried. The awful murder wasn't all that far from where I was when I read the JET *article and saw that horrible picture. And I had a whole flash of boys my age who I knew and loved who could have been in that magazine picture instead of Emmett Till.*

"Then from the shock and sickness I felt, I moved on to anger. It seems a little bit strange now, but I blamed it all on Till's uncle. As a teenager I felt his uncle shouldn't have given him up so easy. But it soon settled in with me that there was really nothing the old man could have done to stop the killers. They would have just killed him, too, if he had put up any resistance. And maybe they would have butchered his entire family, too. But I blamed Till's uncle at the time."

Mattie Straughter and those closest to her did not believe that Till had made a pass at the white store clerk. They couldn't believe, she says, that Till would be stupid enough—even coming from a northern city where things might be different—to whistle at a married white woman.

"And I don't necessarily believe he had a picture of a white woman in his wallet. We all felt that was just part of some trumped-up stuff the media was given to help justify the lynching."

Bryant and Milam were brought to something less than justice. They swaggered into court knowing that the all-white jury would never convict a white husband whose wife had been insulted by a black teenager. Just as certainly, they knew the half-brother would not be found guilty of murder when all he was doing was help his kin defend Carolyn Bryant's honor.

The trial—the first charging whites with the murder of a black victim in Mississippi in sixty-five years—was a travesty of law. The two defendants sauntered into the courtroom with a smug grin on their faces when the trial began on September 19. Under examination and cross-examination they all but admitted they had killed Emmett. There were witnesses who claimed they had heard Emmett emit a wolf whistle aimed at Carolyn Bryant. Till's mother explained that to help her son overcome a serious stuttering problem, she had told him that when he reached the point of stammering, *"If you get hung up on a word, whistle, and go ahead and just say it. It's funny. It really worked."* His mother suggested that her son was trying to tell someone what he had bought in the store, and whistled to stop himself from stuttering.

The all-white jury members had obviously made up their minds long before they even began a very brief deliberation. They came back with a "not guilty" verdict for both men.

Mamie Till Bradley had demanded that her son's body be returned to Chicago where she insisted on an open-casket funeral. She wanted the world to see the ugly, scary side of Mississippi justice. No doubt about it, this brave woman was going for shock effect. It worked. It scared the living hell out of a twelve-year-old black boy in St. Louis. It scared a teenage black girl picking cotton in her grandfather's field near Deovolente. And, no doubt, this grotesque story terrified every other black child across the entire nation who saw the newspaper and magazine pictures of Emmett Till's bloated and severely damaged remains lying in that open coffin. Strangely enough, the horror generated by the *JET* magazine spread also produced the desired effect relished by both Emmett Till's mother and the killers.

Annie West Rounds, the wife of one of Ned's grandsons, remembers the reign of terror in Mississippi directed against Blacks immediately following Emmett Till's brutal murder. She was particularly afraid as a mother of seven boys.

"We couldn't get any news of what was going on about the lynching. The radio stations didn't say anything about it. The local television news programs didn't even touch on the Till lynching. And the colored people all around us were scared to death and we all talked about it in whispers. Never in public.

"You couldn't even buy a newspaper in Greenwood or Tchula at any of the stores. There would be a whole pile of newspapers stacked up in those stores and if we colored folks who were absolutely hungry for news tried to buy one, the white clerks would tell us that the newspapers had already been spoken for; already sold... already been taken. The man who used to deliver the newspaper to us every day just stopped delivering after the Till murder. No explanation. Just stopped delivering. He was faithful before then.

"If you got JET magazine or anything like Ebony, you just stopped getting them. I heard they were holding them up at the post office. Destroying them at the post office and recording the names of the subscribers for the Klan.

"My son, Rufus, liked to dance and party. He loved jazz music and liked to go into Greenwood and Lexington to find parties on a Friday night or a Saturday night. It really scared me to death when he went into Lexington. That was a bad place for colored folk back then. That's where the Klan hung out and acted up all the time. But Rufus had found a pretty little girlfriend in Lexington. When I would beg Rufus not to go into Lexington, he would say 'Aw, Mama, I'll be careful. Nothin's gonna happen to me.' But I was scared to death somethin' would happen to him... somethin' bad like what happened to Emmett Till. We finally read about what happened in a newspaper somebody got a hold of. I think the paper was out of Chicago. We passed that newspaper with the Emmett Till story in it until it was completely wore out. And we all got scared."

As irony would have it, two of the men implicated in the Till murder but never punished for it, Malcolm Witte and Leon Turner, moved to Greenwood and set up a little store near the plantation where Annie Rounds and her sons worked. Mrs. Rounds remembers:

"We would sometimes pass that store in Greenwood and we would try to sneak a peek at those two white men in their store. We wouldn't want them to know we were looking at them 'cause, Lord knows, we could be next for something horrible. So we would mostly hold our eyes down when we passed that store."

Chalmers Archers, a descendant of Holmes County slaves just like I am, remembers that Lexington, Mississippi, the same place young Rufus Rounds loved to go to dance, was a dangerous place in the 1940s and 1950s for socially-active, carefree young Blacks. Archer writes:

"Lexington in the early 1940s was a separate and unequal place. This was a place where Blacks could not even approach the front door of a white person's home without being screamed at or even harmed. Back doors were for Blacks. This was a town where there were "colored only" and "white only" signs on the courthouse bathroom doors and where certain restaurants were known to be off limits to Blacks even without signs to say so."

It was certainly understandable that Jesse and Annie Rounds stayed up until the wee hours of the morning until their prone-to-party son was safe and sound again at home after one of his sorties into Lexington. The ultimate fear was too much for Jesse and Annie. With all those boys in the family, they appeared to their parents to be just so many potential Emmett Tills. In 1956, just a year after the Emmett Till murder, Jesse and Annie Rounds packed up and moved their family off the Lucas plantation and out of Mississippi. They moved to a house at 4545 North Market in the safer confines of St. Louis.

****

Emmett Till's murder was just one of three lynchings recorded in Mississippi in 1955. There may have been more, of course. The Rev. George W. Lee was murdered in Belzoni—so very close to my family's enclave on *Honey Island*. He had led a voter registration drive that enlisted 400 of the 16,000 Blacks in Humphreys County to sign up to vote. There were 7,000 Whites in that county in 1955. Another black man, Lamar Smith, was lynched in 1955 at Brookhaven, Mississippi.

Less than a decade after the Till murder, the state of Mississippi created a Legal Action Advisory Committee which was set up to thwart the efforts to integrate systems, customs, and institutions in the state. Among the committee's recommendations: all out-of-state lawyers had to get clearance from the Mississippi bar—a law to discourage anybody from filing civil rights litigation; repeal of the compulsory law requiring school attendance; and, to block the civil rights investigations of the FBI, the Committee recommended that individual rights guaranteed by the state could not be violated under the umbrella of Federal law.

In 1955, Mississippi's White Citizens Council launched a campaign to punish Blacks who tried to vote or integrate schools. Violators were threatened with the loss of their jobs and the denial of any bank or store credit. The tactics of intimidation, along with the lynchings, caused the number of Blacks registered in Mississippi to drop in 1955 from 22,000 to 8,000. Nearly 100 bills were submitted in the nation's 84th Congress that year to guarantee civil rights. Not one of them passed.

When I was nineteen years old and still in a state of fear and denial about my ancestral association with the state of Mississippi, black civil rights worker Medgar Evers was gunned down in front of his house in Jackson. I marked June 12, 1963, in my mind's diary as yet another reason not to go down to Mississippi on my next vacation—or any other vacation. Self-proclaimed white supremacist Byron De La Beckwith was finally convicted of Evers' murder in 1994, more than thirty years after the killing and after two all-white hung juries.

A heinous crime committed in August 1964 helped neither the promotions of Mississippi's Chamber of Commerce's efforts to lure tourists and conventions nor my interest in ever going to my ancestral state. The summer of 1964 was a tense time in the South. Racially-charged incidents lit up the front pages of the nation's newspapers and burned the broadcast wires feeding radio and TV news coverage. Hundreds of college students, many of them White, began to board buses, trains, and planes headed for the Deep South to sign up Black voters. Among the so-called "freedom riders" were three Northerners: James Earl Chaney, Andrew Goodman, and Michael Schwerner. Chaney, a 21-year-old black man, was familiar with the ways of the South. He was from Meridian, Mississippi. Goodman, age 20, was from New York City, the son of a building contractor and a student at Queens College. Schwerner was a 24-year-old native of Pelham, New York, and a graduate of Cornell University. The three young activists, part of a team of 400 volunteers, disappeared on June 21 from Philadelphia, Mississippi, about eighty miles northeast of the Rounds homestead on *Honey Island*.

Civil rights activists became alarmed, but there was a strange nonchalance about the disappearances from some southern stalwarts and opponents of integration. President Lyndon Johnson telephoned Mississippi's senior senator, James Eastland, the day after Goodman, Chaney, and Schwerner vanished, to report his presidential fears.

"Jim, we've got three kids missing down there. What can I do about it?" the President asked.

"Well," replied Eastland, *"I don't believe there's three missing."*

Five weeks after their mysterious disappearance, the worst fear of their parents, other loved ones, colleagues, and empathizers were realized. *Time Magazine* reported it this way:

"In 101 degree heat, FBI agents swarmed over an earthen dam on Olen Burrage's Old Jolly Farm, six miles southwest of Philadelphia, Miss. Through the scrub pines and bitterweed, they bulldozed a path to the dam, then brought up a lumbering dragline whose huge bucket shovel began chewing a V-shaped wedge out of the 25-foot-high levee. Twenty feet down, the shovel uncovered the fully clothed, badly decomposed bodies of three young men lying side by side in a pocket of red clay."

I had taken part in a number of civil rights demonstrations that steamy summer. We picketed the Howard Johnson restaurant at Kingshighway and Natural Bridge boulevards, the Jefferson Bank, Famous-Barr department store, and even a White Castle hamburger shack on Natural Bridge. But all our efforts were in the safety of the quietest of the nation's towns, St. Louis. Some of our number were arrested at the Jefferson Bank—including my friends Marian Oldham, Ron Glenn, and a man who would later become a U.S. Congressman, Bill Clay. These three were among those who did some real jail time, something that most of us didn't have to give as a sacrifice.

I have often wondered if I could have spent real jail time. Of course I was committed to the cause—but short of giving one's life, time in the city jail would be a horrible punishment. None of us were beaten, fire-hosed, bitten by dogs, or murdered. But, all of us St. Louis demonstrators—Black and White—were resolute in making life in St. Louis better for minorities than life had been for many hundreds of thousands of Blacks in Mississippi and millions of African Americans in the Old South even in the years after slavery officially ended.

Then came June 1966. I had just finished my first year of teaching eighth grade at the then all-black Hamilton Elementary School in St. Louis. That's when James Meredith, the first Black to integrate the University of Mississippi, was seriously wounded on a narrow road in northern Mississippi by a blast from a 16-gauge shotgun loaded with buckshot. The shooter was a white out-of-work hardware contractor. Meredith was the son of a farmer from the tiny town of Kosciusko sixty miles directly east of *Honey Island*. I realize now I had begun to plot on a map in my mind where all these Mississippi atrocities were relative to my family's old stomping grounds.

The images of Till and Evers and Chaney and Schwerner and Goodman and Meredith and all the other victims of Mississippi hate began to fade slightly in my mind in the decades that followed. Like many other African Americans of my era, I began getting so caught up in the pursuit of personal life, liberty, and happiness and comfort that I started sublimating the facts of my ancestry. There were many others like me who began to forget the fact that the shackles of slavery still bound so many of our people. Our ancestors—many of them—had folded under the physical, mental, and emotional pressures of trying to stay afloat and alive. The Rounds family members were certainly among them. They fled Mississippi in droves in the 1920s and '30s and they never looked back—except perhaps in their dreams and nightmares. My kinfolk with Mississippi roots virtually refused to talk about their past. It took a real effort to get any of them to talk about their proud, free, and independent past lives on idyllic *Honey Island*. As they allowed their past to fade, I was an accomplice in obliterating my heritage. It was really not so much a sin of commission. It was, however, a sin of omission.

I made several ineffectual efforts to record the stories my dear grandmother would recount if, and only if, she were asked the right questions in the right setting at the right time. But then I'd drop the effort in pursuit of other preoccupations. When I launched my latest feeble effort in the summer of 1998, a strange string of circumstances picked me up, shook me violently, and hurled me across time and miles and slammed me down on Mississippi soil. It was an epiphany that will never allow me to return to the complacency and genealogical ignorance of the past.

Cousin Pearl's death would change my life. Cousin Pearl was actually born in Belzoni, Mississippi, but her mother was born on *Honey Island* as my mother and

AuntWilletta had been. During that last phone call to her in her hospital room, I thought I would try to tweak her memory and give her a bit of mental exercise by asking her about an incident that happened when she was just eleven years old. An appendicitis attack. She rose to the challenge and remembered the entire episode in vivid detail. I added her memories to this work. Seven hours after I talked with Pearl, she was dead.

I needed to go to Mississippi as soon as I could get away from my job. As I arranged that trip, I decided to take Carol, the youngest of my three sisters, with me. She works for the St. Louis City Development Agency and has experience in reading maps and plats. She also has a personality that does not take "no" for an answer easily, a trait that would be extremely valuable in a region in which I anticipated we would find official reticence in helping us trace our roots.

I was so entranced by this epiphany, this metamorphosis in my thinking, that I gave up a bit part in a Hollywood movie that was being shot in St. Louis. Director George Hickenlooper, a former St. Louisan, had asked me if I would play myself—a television newscaster who reveals the turning point of *The Big Brass Ring,* starring William Hurt and Amanda Richardson. The shoot was originally scheduled for August 6, but a production delay had pushed the film session in which I would get my big movie break to August 11. Hickenlooper phoned me to tell me about the change, but I told him that I would be in Mississippi on the eleventh. He asked if I could change my schedule and I did not hesitate for a second to tell him I couldn't do it. I was leaving for my ancestral state on Friday, August 7, and was not scheduled to return to St. Louis until late in the evening of August 11. I **had** to be in Mississippi that day and I could not cut short my mission. The director expressed his disappointment. I expressed mine. But there would be no changes.

Like a mad man I began racing to try to set up an itinerary for the trip so that I could maximize my five days in Mississippi. I needed maps. I called Triple-A and had a clerk there prepare a package showing the roads Carol and I would have to travel once we left our hotel in Jackson each day. The maps arrived the next day. I telephoned the U. S. Geological Survey in Rolla, Missouri. They sent a map that showed *Honey Island* barely peeking up above the map's border in the lower right corner. I phoned the Survey office back and was told that in order to get a better picture of *Honey Island* I would have to order four maps. So be it. I sent them my second check. They sent me the other three maps.

I telephoned the Mississippi Highway Patrol. In two days of calling I never got anywhere with that office. I frantically placed several calls in the days before the trip to the Mississippi State Highway Department. A clerk, who sounded like I had awakened her, promised me that if I faxed her a copy of my check for seven dollars she would send by overnight mail a map showing the precise location of *Honey Island* and I would get it the next day. I phoned her back about four hours after our initial conversation just to check to see if the fax had arrived. She told me: *Oh, I don't know if it's come in or not. The fax machine is upstairs and I haven't had a chance to get up there yet."*

> **cunctation**, *n.*, Procrastination; delay; the act of putting off until at least tomorrow... or next month that which could be done right now. A true art form in Mississippi.

I wondered, mindful of my hyperactive composition, how it would take anybody four hours to go upstairs to check for a fax when *immediate* response had been promised. Welcome to "Dealing with Mississippi!" Or maybe it was dealing with any state office. I didn't know, but I blamed it on Mississippi. I hadn't heard good things about Mississippi, after all. The map I was expecting on Tuesday arrived the following Monday—a full week from the original order date on which I was assured the map would be rushed to me. A week *is* "next day" in Mississippi, I would learn. In fact, the map a courthouse official in Belzoni had sworn up and down he would send me right away had not arrived in three months. Sometimes "right away" means three months or more in Mississippi, I would learn.

Eventually I got some specific information about the ancestral homeland. For those with cartographic interests, it is located at 330735N latitude and 0902238 longitude, at the place where the Yazoo River reigns. It's about as far north as the northern border of Louisiana. Old maps indicate that *Honey Island*, probably quite unbeknownst to anybody in the Rounds Family, lies 110 feet above sea level in Mississippi's lowlands. The biggest city near it is Belzoni; the distance was measured by the earliest residents of *Honey Island* as *"a five hour wagon ride."* That was before their Model-T Fords replaced their horses and mules and cut the travel time into town by one or two hours. Yazoo City to the south of the island is also near *Honey Island*. So, in fact, are Greenwood, Greenville, Vicksburg, and Jackson—if one has good transportation. I wouldn't want to travel to either of these cities by mule-drawn wagon from *Honey Island*. I guess I would have had to if Ned or West had asked me to "run over to Greenwood" or any of those other towns to pick up something or other. Talking to the *Honey Island Oldtimers* about those big towns would have been just like talking to them about London, Paris, or Rio. Sure, they'd heard about Greenville and Vicksburg and Jackson. They might have even known a person or two who had traveled that far. But Belzoni or Yazoo City to many of the *Oldtimers* were all that they'd ever personally know, see, or care to know about big cities.

I started calling the local courthouses. Clerks in the Humphreys County Courthouse referred me in my phone inquiries to the Holmes County

Courthouse, and clerks I spoke with in the Holmes County Courthouse passed me off to the Yazoo County Courthouse where I was referred back to either Holmes or Humphreys Counties in a dizzying exercise of numbers no longer in service, voice-mails, e-mails, busy signals, and notices that key clerks were variously at lunch, out of the office on sick leave, on vacation, or in a meeting. Whew! Frustrating as hell! But it was a real indication that an in-person visit was the only way to find out anything at all significant about *Honey Island*.

The search for courthouse information on the Rounds homestead through telephone inquiries was complicated by the fact that the land mass that was *Honey Island* was, at one time or another, a part of not one, but three, Mississippi counties which are contiguous. When Mississippi was first surveyed the island was assigned to Yazoo County. Then it became a part of Holmes County. Today, what remains of *Honey Island* records are buried in the Humphreys County Courthouse. Inquiries to the Holmes County Courthouse in Lexington are now forwarded to the Humphreys County Courthouse in Belzoni and vice versa.

Clerks in either of those offices who don't want to be bothered are sometimes likely to refer a caller to the Yazoo County Courthouse in Yazoo City, knowing full well that venue has had nothing to do with any place near *Honey Island* for more than a hundred years. Since *Honey Island* has been located in each of these three counties, it was absolutely necessary to get information from all three.

The Rounds family members never had any contact with Yazoo County. They settled on their homestead when it was an official part of Holmes County. In 1918, the community that was *Honey Island* moved into the hands of the Humphreys record keepers.

The quickest and most positive response I got was from Meg Ausman, the historian for the U. S. Postal Service in Washington, D.C. I had phoned her to find out about the *Honey Island* post office my grandmother, mother, and aunts had told me about. It was, they had proudly told me, operated by my great-uncle, George Byrd Jr. Sure enough, this delightful and knowledgeable woman rushed me the first concrete indication that my kinfolk had not imagined this story. Great-Uncle George had, indeed, been *Honey Island*'s first postmaster. He was commissioned in 1907. Yes!!! Something tangible to grab onto and give me fuel to push on. God bless you, Meg Ausman!

In sharp contrast to this remarkable success in talking to an actual "live" person in a Washington, D.C., office and then getting a prompt and courteous return on my investment of a phone call, I was later to experience some heartbreaking developments on the eve of my journey to Mississippi.

It occurred to me that if I could get in touch with some Baptist preachers in Humphreys or Holmes County, I might be able to find out if Jones Chapel still stood. Through a series of referrals, I got the telephone number of a woman who managed several funeral homes. I assumed from my end of the phone that the woman I talked to was an elderly white woman. My assessment of her race was borne out when she offered me the telephone number of one Baptist preacher. But then, she told me:

"Scratch that number."

"Why?" I asked.

"Oh, that's colored," she replied. "You'll never get anything out of colored."

I was stunned. Startled. Speechless for a moment until I mustered up a voice to say: "I don't understand why I couldn't get anything out of colored folks, ma'am. You see, I'm colored."

She laughed a nervous little laugh, and said: "You gotta be kiddin' me. Right?"

I assured her of my race, and out of a natural consequence of her embarrassment and my loathing of further conversation with this racist woman, the conversation ended abruptly.

The next series of phone calls hurt even more. It also occurred to me that with so few leads on the virtual eve of my Mississippi mission, I might try to solicit some help from my colleagues in the news business. One of my co-workers referred me to the news director at a Jackson, Mississippi, television station. Bob Thomas, who heads up the news operation at WVJX, told me that he didn't have any reporters on his staff who were familiar with the area around Belzoni and *Honey Island*, but a reporter who had once worked for him grew up in the area of my interest. The reporter was now working for a TV station in Memphis, and Thomas supplied the phone number.

When I reached him, the reporter turned out to be an affable colleague who told me he had, indeed, grown up around the area near where Jones Chapel stood. He told me that his mother still lived in Louise, Mississippi—very close to the area I had targeted for investigation. Yes, he told me, he could get me some names and leads. It was nice to know that this spirit of collegiality was in full effect here. We chatted about things Mississippian and St. Louisan and about our careers. I told him, after feeling comfortable with him, the story of the woman who ran the mortuaries. Then I gave him the punch line. " I am African American," I assured him. "Despite my apparent lack of a regional or racial accent."

My almost-would-have-been new friend appeared to take the information in complete shock. I could almost literally hear his jaw drop and although he had promised professional courtesies, I never heard from him again. I phoned his office five more times and left messages on his voice-mail on four of the five occasions. I left a message with his news director the other time. No response. I could only suppose that the reporter, who is white, came to the realization that his kinfolk and sources in the area around Louise, Mississippi, wouldn't or couldn't be of much help to me given the incredible chasm which exists unto this day in Mississippi between Blacks and Whites. There's a chasm between the races in St. Louis, too, though it's a wee bit more subtle here. Conversations like

I had with the mortuary lady and the TV reporter were to prove typical, I'd find, in my pursuit of information about my ancestors.

A call to a service station in Belzoni got me in touch with an old guy I was told would know "every wrinkle in the road" about the area around the *Honey Island* property and Jones Chapel. This white man runs an auto body shop in Belzoni. Our brief conversation, punctuated by the sound of hammer on metal, went this way:

"Mr. Brazelton, my name is Julius Hunter. Got a minute?"

"Just about that."

"I'm trying to find out if a church in Humphreys County called Jones Chapel still exists. It's on some land called Honey Island."

"Hmmmm…That a colored church?"

"Yes, it is. Know anything about it?"

"Yep. Think I do. Think that's offa 12—Highway 12. It you go north on 49 to 12. Then you go about eight or nine miles west on 12. Take the second black top road after you get off 49 and follow it to the gravel road. I think you'll find that lil church. It's pretty deep into some pretty tall cotton. You may have to take a lil dirt road, too if I'm recollectin' right. But can I ask ya somethin'?"

"Yes, sir."

"What's your interest in a colored church?"

"Oh, I'm just interested in old colored churches. They're kinda my hobby."

"Okay. Call me if you get lost. Gotta go."

"Okay. Thank you."

Something happened to me in that conversation that would kick in every now and again as I prepared to go to the Magnolia State and after I got to Mississippi. In a quick flush of reasoning that I needed to push the "subterfuge" button, I decided that I would not tell this stranger, this white guy in an auto body shop, who I was. I certainly wasn't about to tell him when and why I was coming to Mississippi. I could have stood up proudly and told this old gentleman about my race and my great-great-grandfather's hundreds of acres on *Honey Island* and how he might have gotten screwed out of all of it. But if this guy happened to be the local Grand Gizzard of the KKK, I would not be giving this stranger any critical information about my identity or itinerary.

Since finding out information about *Honey Island* and the old Rounds homestead by telephone turned out to be almost as intriguing as it must be to try to find the Lost City of Atlantis from a phone booth, I was confident I had made the right decision to go to Mississippi for face-to-face interaction despite the frustrations.

I continued to make my phone attempts to line up an itinerary that would bear fruitful information. My batting average was—putting two incongruous words together—mighty low. My next series of phone queries taught me that one must be careful about how and when one makes inquiries in person, in written form, or by telephone.

First of all, Yankees, Black or White, who demand information or maps or other documents in a hurried, rude, manner are likely to think they have landed in a foreign country where the language, pace and general attitude are altogether different. On the other hand, if in person, by letter, fax, or on the phone one takes on a slower, more charming, even courtlier approach, one is likely to get much more assistance from a Mississippi office. But never faster assistance. Those who are inquisitive about courthouse information also must never give the operator, clerk, or recorder the idea that one is digging up information for a grand jury probe. Furthermore, while mention of the author's association with a St. Louis television station opens doors and files in big northern cities, television affiliation seemed to turn on caution lights all over Mississippi—the rural areas in particular.

Here's more advice to northerners making cartographical or statistical inquiries of Mississippi Delta courthouse staffers: check the clock before showing up or phoning. One should not make calls too early in the morning. Some Mississippi clerks seem to enjoy a gearing-up period. They don't generally seem to want to be shoved into their file cabinets before they've hung up their coats in their closets. It's also a wise decision to avoid any inquiries when the big hand on the clock begins to pass the half-hour mark and is beginning its descent upward to the noon hour. Remember, too, that lunchtime can be slow and leisurely for courthouse workers. Remember that some Mississippi official offices are actually closed from noon to one. Those who leave their posts a little before noon are not likely to return to their desks and be ready for business until after 1:30 PM.

Then I also learned that there seems to be an afternoon period that brings sluggish responses until 3:30 PM or so. Keeping in mind how important the office clock is in Mississippi, please note that it seems almost impolite to call within a half hour of going-home time. Clerks seem to be concerned that efforts to help you after that time might tie them up beyond the time they ordinarily leave the office for home. With these caveats in mind, I usually made my courthouse inquiries from 10:30 and 11 AM and between 3:30 and 4:00 PM. Maybe I shouldn't generalize, but that's the way it seemed to me.

Always address the Mississippi clerk on the first face-to-face, phone or written encounter, by the formal title of *Mr.* or *Mizz So-and-So.* Slip in the Christian name only after some degree of familiarity is established, along with the assurance that the clerk or official can feel comfortable calling you by your first name, too. Even if you get a clerk to acquiesce to the use of your first name once or twice, he or she will almost certainly revert back to calling you by your last name with the title *Mizz* or *Mr.* affixed.

Another thing I learned is that it never hurts to take the time to chew the fat and shoot the breeze a little bit when seeking information from a Mississippi clerk or office staffer. Ask about the weather, the weekend plans, sports scores, or news items that are not too controversial. Or ask how long they've been doing whatever it is that will take them a long time to do for you. No matter how hurried one is—never *appear* to be in a hurry. It also help if you can affect a not-too-transparent honey drippin' southern drawl as you make your inquiries.

****

It was only two days before my scheduled trip to the ancestral homeland and I didn't have a single concrete contact in Belzoni or Yazoo City. Every lead had fizzled and I had begun to feel like a failure as an investigative reporter. In a strange kind of way I was actually excited about going to Mississippi! I had gotten over my fears and apprehensions; my memories of Emmett Till, James Meredith, and the three slain civil rights workers were vivid, but I had convinced myself that kind of violence couldn't happen to me. Surely, that kind of ugly thing didn't happen in 1998. The really pressing issues was: with whom would Carol and I talk when we got there? We would, of course, spend some time at the courthouses in Belzoni and Lexington, and perhaps take a trip to the courthouse in Yazoo City. We didn't have a clue, though, as to whether the old family church, Jones Chapel, was still standing. If it were still around, where was it? With few verifiable phone directions to the little chapel, we could really waste a lot of time and gasoline trying to find it. Of one thing I was certain: if Jones Chapel were alive and well, we would have to travel two-lane to one-lane highway, blacktop road, gravel road, and dirt road to find it. Would there be any road signs? I feared there would not be.

I had heard from some of the officials and clerks and other basically uncooperative sources that there is not today a single highway or road sign with the words **HONEY ISLAND** on them. The place had just mysteriously disappeared from many memories and many maps. How sad that a place that had at one time or another been home to at least eighty-two relatively prosperous and independent black families was a part of ancient history.

The Wednesday before our Friday departure date was rather bleak. My eighty-year-old Cousin Bessie in Chicago phoned to say that all her leads had dried up on *Honey Island* and there was a disconnected phone number for the one woman she was trying to reach on the island. My Aunt Willetta, who is a few years older than Bessie, phoned to tell me that she had also failed to line up any contacts. Add those disappointing reports to all the others I had experienced and I wondered if I should delay the trip. That would have been a different big hassle. I probably could have reclaimed my cameo role in George Hickenlooper's movie. I got quite depressed.

Then an incredible thing happened! I received a phone call—quite by surprise—from my good friend, Savannah Young. She is an outstanding, dynamic, St. Louis educator whose husband was a deputy superintendent of the St. Louis school district and a fraternity brother of mine in Sigma Pi Phi. Savannah said she hadn't heard from me for awhile and was just calling to see how I was. I told her about my Mississippi Project and poured out my frustrations and disappointments regarding contacts in the Delta. She reminded me that she is a graduate of Tougaloo College right outside Jackson and near Belzoni. She volunteered, in her inimitable energetic style, to peruse her college yearbook and find some names of contacts in Belzoni or Jackson. She said she'd get back with me. And knowing Savannah Young, I knew she would! Promptly! I thanked her. Even though it was a promise from a true human dynamo, I had had such a string of bad luck that I harbored doubts that there was anything even Savannah Young could do.

Next day as I sat at my desk in my study still trying to find out by phone if anybody could tell me anything at all about a Jones Chapel or a *Honey Island* or any members of the Rounds Family—dead or alive—my fax machine issued a ring to let me know there was a message incoming. Could it be? Would it be? A fax from Savannah? Or could it be any of the dozens of pieces and loaves of bread I had cast upon the waters hoping for a bountiful return of information? I couldn't wait for the machine to spit out the fax; tried to read it as it was cranking out of the machine. Finally, and as quickly as I could safely snatch the sheet of paper out of the machine, I scanned the message. It was, in fact, from Savannah. Bingo! She had struck gold! She gave me the names of two of her sister alums from the Tougaloo College annual. She really didn't know them personally, she told me, but she knew enough about each to think I could get help from them. This dear friend included a thumbnail sketch of the two names she had found. Mattie Straughter was one of them. Her husband, the representative, was Rufus Straughter. Rufus—the same name as Savannah's husband! Sheer irony or the beginning of some Providential Guidance of the First Order? Savannah also listed the name of Mrs. Crystiana Randle, a retired school librarian, another Belzoni resident. Savannah's message indicated she had spoken to Rufus and Mattie Straughter and Mrs. Randle and all three knew where Jones Chapel is and were ready, willing, and eager to be of help. They were awaiting a phone call from me. Hosanna, Savannah! Hooray and hallelujah! Thank God!

I called Savannah back and thanked her profusely and promised dinner for her and Rufus to show my thanks. Now to call my brand new contacts who knew the territory Carol and I would be visiting as pilgrims in a new land for us St. Louisans.

I telephoned Mrs. Randle first:

"Hello, Mrs. Randle. This is Julius Hunter in St. Louis."

"Yes."

"Savannah Young just talked with you and told you about me and my upcoming trip to Mississippi."

"Yes."

"She told me you might be able to help me find a Jones Chapel and the old Rounds homestead on Honey Island."

"Yes."

"My sister and I are coming down on Friday."

"Yes."

"You did say you could help us?"

"Yes. Who did you say your people were?"

"The Rounds Family of Honey Island. Right near where you live in Belzoni."

"Well, I know a lady named Rounds, but you better talk to my husband. He knows more about what you're looking for."

"Your husband?"

"Yes."

"Is he there now? May I speak to him?" I had begun to panic, thinking I had struck out again, hit another snag, run into still another Mississippi brick wall.

"He won't be back for another hour or two."

"But he will talk to me. You think he can help?"

"Yes."

"Well, thank you," I said with disappointment dripping from my words. "Thank you. I'll call back in a couple of hours."

"Okay."

"Goodbye."

"Goodbye."

My heart plummeted to some low point in its chamber and hit with a "thunk" when I heard that receiver click on the other end. There must have been some mistake. This was not a woman who was excited, eager, or enthusiastic about talking to me. Savannah must have given me a wrong number, I thought. Or maybe I had caught Mrs. Randle at a bad time: just out of the shower or just as she was putting a cake in the oven or just as she was rushing off to a doctor's appointment or just as she was racing out to pick up a grandchild from the nursery. I came up with a dozen possibilities. If Savannah had just talked with this very same woman, how could Mrs. Randle sound so distant and laconic?

I was crushed. I've got some of the toughest skin in the world, but I was absolutely crestfallen. If my brief conversation with Mrs. Randle had been any of the hundreds of interviews I've filmed and taped on television and radio over the last thirty years, it would not have made it to the airwaves. I phoned Savannah back:

"Savannah, dear. Did you give me a wrong number?"

"Why? What do you mean?"

"Well, I just spoke with a woman who sounded as if she had never heard of you, me, or anybody else."

"Really? What did she say?"

"Nothing. Absolutely nothing. I mean, Savannah, this lady was like an iceberg. She was polite, but really tight-lipped."

"Well, Julius, there are some things you've got to learn before you head off to Mississippi. Mississippi is not Missouri or like any place you've ever been. First of all, black folks have learned for centuries not to talk to strangers. It's gotten them in trouble from the days of slavery right up until today."

"Yes."

"And you gotta realize, honey, you may not sound very black to somebody you're talking to on the phone. Mrs. Randle was just sounding you out, and frankly she may not be comfortable talking to somebody she's never seen who sounds like a white boy from the North."

"I've run into that before. I mean, when I've talked to folks in Mississippi. Maybe I should try to develop more of a drawl."

"Wouldn't hurt. And in Mississippi and other places in the Deep South, women don't talk to men on any kind of equal basis. The menfolk do the talking; their womenfolk do the listening, unless their husbands ask them to speak.

"That's pretty chauvinistic, isn't it?"

"It would be here in St. Louis. But you've got to understand where you're going to be. And I hope you didn't call her by her first name, Crystiana."

"No, I didn't commit that sin. I figured she was much older than I, and I wouldn't ever call an older woman by her first name unless I knew her well and had her permission."

"Where do you think you got that custom? Probably got that from your grandmama and mama, from the Mississippi they grew up in."

"Probably."

"I'll bet when you get down there you won't find anybody comfortable in calling you by your first name, even when you tell them it's okay to do so."

"What'll they call me?"

"Mr. Hunter! And if they know you have a doctorate in something or other, in anything, they'll call you 'Dr. Hunter.' And if you're a teacher or educator of any kind they're likely to call you 'Professor Hunter.' Or 'Fessa Hunter.' They'll even call you 'Brother Hunter' before they'll dare call you just 'Julius.'"

"Well, I do have two honorary doctorates," I said with a chuckle.

"When I talked to them down there I didn't bother to tell them that so you wouldn't be saddled with being called 'Doctor Hunter.' I didn't even tell them that I have a real Ph.D. because Mrs. Randle and Mrs. Straughter would never call me Savannah. They'd call me 'Dr. Young.'"

"Got it."

My lesson in the etiquette of the South continued.

"I hope you didn't just jump into what you were trying to find out. You know, about the church and Honey Island *and everything."*

"What do you mean?"

"I hope you spent some time making a few little warm-up pleasantries first."

"Well, I didn't want to waste a lot of her time, and you know I'm not much for beating around the bush and chewing the fat."

"Well, brother, you had better slow it down and cool your jets when you talk on the phone to anybody in Mississippi and when you get down there Friday. Just slow it down. You should have asked Mrs. Randle how the weather was down there. Tell her a nice little story or two about your great-great granddaddy or your grandmama. That would have broken the ice a lot more."

"Okay, maybe I blew it. But would you mind calling her back just to find out if she really wants to talk to me and help me out."

"No problem. I'll call her back right now. Then I'll call you right back."

"Thanks. You're a sweetheart. I owe you."

"Don't get too frustrated. It's going to all work out, I guarantee you. Just remember the things I told you about dealing with Mississippi folk. And it wouldn't hurt to say a little prayer."

"I will. And I took notes. Thanks."

After we hung up, I took a few minutes to reflect on all that dear Savannah had taught me in this crash course. I'd like to think I'm a fairly quick study. But I realized that I had, in fact, violated every tenet of *"How to Talk Effectively with Mississippians by Telephone, 101"* in my brief conversation with Mrs. Randle. I waited on pins and needles for Savannah to get back to me.

When she called back, I snapped up the phone handset and waited for the reply. Mrs. Randle was perfectly cordial with Savannah again, was glad to have heard from me so quickly, wanted Savannah to ask me to bring one of the four books I've written for her to see. She was excited about Carol and me coming to Mississippi. Wait a minute, I thought. We must be talking about two different women. But I remembered all the things Savannah had imparted and realized that she had taken all the right approaches. Plus, this was a woman talking to a woman. Mrs. Randle even wanted Savannah to send her Savannah's father's obituary since Mrs. Randle had known him.

Wow! Amazing! Incredible!

With much more confidence now, I phoned the Straughters. By now, I had dialed the 601 area code many dozens of times. But I now felt like a veteran solicitor/inquisitor. I got Mattie Straughter on the phone and she immediately deferred to her husband, the state legislator for Humphreys County. Rufus Straughter was polite, but reserved. He thought he and his wife could help me find the church. He had visited Jones Chapel recently, he told me, and it was still standing and had an active church program even though he thought only a couple of black folks still actually lived on *Honey Island*. He would only call me "Mr. Hunter" even though I had invited him to call me "Julius." After a brief and rather formal conversation, he told me that his wife was really the activist and talker in the family and he said he would put her back on the phone.

This delightful and gregarious woman began to open up just a little bit now that the formality of deferring to her husband was satisfied. She told me she had even done some homework and found a cousin of mine that I didn't know I had. In fact, she had found a number of people who wanted to talk with me. Fantastic! She had only spoken to Savannah a couple of hours before and she already had lined up some interviews. My kind of contact! Mattie must be just like Savannah. And me! I thanked her profusely and told her I would contact her once Carol and I had reached Jackson.

I could not believe how my luck had changed in just a matter of a few hours and after weeks of duds and dead-in leads. I phoned Carol to tell her that we would soon be "dancing in high cotton." I didn't know how unbelievably prophetic that little folksy aphorism would turn out to be. Must have been the prayer.

What followed in my pursuit of my family's history would make even the most devout agnostic believe in a Divine Hand.

 *You <u>Can</u> Go Home Again!*

We were on our way! We were headed to *Honey Island*.

Carol and I left St. Louis in a driving rain on an early morning Delta Airlines flight. We were disappointed that there was no breakfast offered on the flight in this Age of Economy in which all the airlines fly. Cranberry juice, orange juice, or water were all we were offered for the hour and five minute flight to a layover in Atlanta. Why the hell would we have to stop over in Atlanta to get to Jackson? I thought. We were wise to grab a bagel and coffee in Atlanta because the fifty-five minute flight from Atlanta to Jackson would offer no more than the first leg of the journey, except those little bags containing about eleven peanuts.

As we sat in the busy Atlanta hub I could not help but reflect on the conditions under which my kinfolk had made the trips back and forth between St. Louis and Belzoni by train before the mid-1930s. A number of my relatives in St. Louis and in Chicago had told me how the Illinois Central train made a stopover in Memphis each way. Sometimes they had to wait at the Memphis train station for four or five hours. They didn't dare try to sit and grab a snack in the coffee shop or restaurant in the terminal in the Tennessee town because Mr. Jim Crow patrolled the station. All my relatives had to bring a little sack meal and eat in the "COLORED" section of the seating area. Here on this August day in 1998, Carol and I could have our choice of sitting and dining in any of the restaurants in the vast food court or at eateries in any of the other airport concourses. I guess some things have changed for the better.

As our plane dropped through the cloud cover on its approach into Jackson, Carol and I began to comment on how green and lush the countryside below appeared. It looked like a very plush green carpet with lumps under it. As soon as we touched down for our first visit to the homeland state, we noted that the Jackson airport was surprisingly small and there was very little activity. We rented a gold-colored 1998 Toyota Camry since Carol had a car of the same make and model. She'd know where all the buttons were without my having to learn them by the manual. I imagined that this car would stand out in any dusty little places we might travel to and hoped that it wouldn't present that "sore thumb" appearance in the towns we would visit. But comfort was going to be key since I knew we'd be putting some real miles on the Camry.

By the time we found the Crowne Plaza Hotel just across the street from the governor's mansion, we had gotten lost on the road into Jackson from the airport for a few miles. We asked at the hotel front desk where we might find a bite to eat. It was just after three in the afternoon and we were disappointed to find that the restaurants in the hotel were closed between lunch and supper. Then we found that the other restaurants in downtown Jackson were also taking a break, so we had to drive to the outskirts of town where we had to settle for a KFC restaurant and some of the usual fried chicken fare—the same stuff we could get at home. The Colonel. The guy my great-great grandpa reportedly looked like. Hmmmmm.

After our meal, in a place where there were almost no diners at that time of day, we set out for a drive around town just to get familiar with the territory. I had decided that trying to get into the Mississippi State Archives Building near the hotel and next to the Old Capitol would be just too much to take on since we had been up and on the move since the crack of dawn. Besides, we learned that the archive facility shut down for the day at 4:30 each afternoon.

After only a few minutes of exploration, the torrential rain we had left behind in St. Louis caught up with us in Jackson. Jackson is hilly and we got caught up in some really threatening flash flooding in the low-lying streets of Mississippi's capital city. At some point, we really felt we were in danger of being swept away or having the engine stall out and decided to call it a day for riding around in the Camry. Just imagine what it might have been like for Rounds ancestors facing one of these thunderous rainstorms in mule-drawn wagons or on horseback! We could buzz back to the hotel in a matter of minutes. Where would they have found shelter from the flash flooding and menacing storm?

I could use some time to rest, make phone calls to the Straughters and the Randles. I had spoken with Mr. Randle before I left St. Louis and he had promised to help even though he'd be out of town on Saturday. That was the day I had decided we would try to find the old Jones Chapel and first see the *Honey Island* site from which our family was spawned.

Later that night, Carol and I met Ruth Land Hatten, the homegrown Mississippi researcher/genealogist I had hired earlier in the year to help sift through the rubble of the Rounds' existence on *Honey Island*. Ruth scored a real victory for the research effort by discovering the handwritten deed that conveyed 216 acres of land formerly owned by Peter James to my great-great-grandfather, Ned Rounds, on March 17, 1886. That was a real spark to find out more. Ruth picked us up at the Crowne Plaza Hotel and took us to what she called a first-class southern diner. Although we could have walked to The Elite from our hotel, we drove. For me, a former unsuccessful restaurateur, The Elite…wasn't. The place was packed, though. While I was apprehensive about not having a jacket and tie on this trip, it turned out my casual shirt and slacks made me among the best-dressed of all the men in the place. Carol, a natty dresser, was, perhaps, over-dressed in her simple flower-print dress. And she didn't have a single tattoo visible on her body as some of the ladies had. I had been suspicious about this being a place that touted both its southern cooking and the fact that the eatery is owned by Greeks.

Carol and I were the only Blacks in the restaurant packed with scores of diners. The young woman at the cash register affirmed a fact that Ruth had told us about in advance. The Elite didn't take reservations. As we stood in the entryway, we quickly figured out that an elderly gentleman, probably one of the Greek owners, seated the hungry at his own pace and at his own will and order. We also soon got the idea that we were being passed over with a nod from the old gent to some folks who had come in after we had. They couldn't have had reservations. No reservations, remember? Were we being accurate in our assessment of how the seating was being done? Or did we have a pre-determined chip on our shoulders? I've learned that can happen.

My sister, as I have intimated, is no shrinking violet. She pushed Ruth and me into snapping up the next table that became available. It had not been cleared yet. The dirty dishes and waitress' tip and the ash tray filled with smoldering cigarette butts still littered the table. Our initiative produced a scowl from the old maitre'd, and Carol and I gave each other that look that assumed that his ire was racially motivated. Perhaps we were reading too much into the situation. I had already decided, before we sat down, just as soon as I saw that all the seating in the diner was booth-seating that I would *not* sit next to our new Caucasian friend in that booth. Sure, it was 1998, but I was not about to pull a modern-day Emmett Till-type act by sitting right next to a white lady in a smoke-filled atmosphere where I, in my own acknowledged bias, determined that there were some rednecks in The Elite that seemed iridescent. Does that make me a racist? I'd wait until *after* our meal to make the assessment.

The menu was quite different than most we were used to up north. Capsulizing the fare offered, it appeared to me that the words "broil" or "steamed" did not appear. I could be wrong, but it seemed that there were choices like fried chicken, chicken-fried steak, fried fish, chicken-fried fish, steak-fried fish and fish-fried chicken steak on that menu. (I admit I've done a bit of exaggerating here to make a point.)

We strategized with Ruth on our plan of action over the next few days. She gave us our crash course in courthouse visits which genealogist Ann Fleming had already given me back in St. Louis. Ruth did a good job of telling us what to look for and preparing us for that which we would find in the courthouses we would visit. She gave us the terminology, the jargon we could spout so that we wouldn't sound like total greenhorns should we encounter any reticent courthouse clerks. After we left the diner, Ruth gave us a quickie night tour of Jackson. All three of us were in agreement that we should forgo the nightcap I had promised so we could turn in.

Turning in is hard to do when one has as much on one's mind as I had that night. Here we were, strangers in a strange land. It shouldn't have felt so terribly strange since it was our homeland; the place in which our roots had begun to bear fruit. I may have gotten three hours sleep that night at best. Carol admits she didn't get much more sleep than that. Would the gentleman, "Red" Baker, show up at the service station on Highway 12 as Mrs. Randle had promised? Mrs. Randle had backed out on meeting us personally. When I had phoned her on Friday evening she reminded me that her husband would be out of town the next day. She had remembered too, she told me, that particular Saturday was the day she collected rent from her tenants. Was this another example of Mississippi shyness? Red was an *Oldtimer*, she assured me, and he *probably* knew where Jones Chapel was—*if* it was. Mattie Straughter would also meet us at Bankhead's Auto Shop, a place owned by a black man. Actually, there were two Bankhead's Auto Shops. The owner of each was the brother of the other one. Each shop was at the opposite end of the stretch of Highway 12 that runs through Belzoni. Mrs. Straughter wanted to make sure we didn't go to the wrong one so she gave us very, very specific instructions.

I also tossed and turned throughout my first night in Mississippi wondering if the ancestral church would be there. I couldn't find a soul by phone from St. Louis who could swear that the chapel would still be standing. I knew how excited and teary my mother and Aunt Willetta would be if their old church were still somehow alive and well. I realized how heartbroken we would all be if what we feared were true: the whole island had been turned into cotton fields and catfish lakes.

Since I am admittedly a near-neurotic economist when it comes to maximizing my time, I was determined not to waste a single minute over the next five days of our brief sojourn. I was so wired that I finally got up and sat at the desk in my hotel room and went over our schedule and jotted down notes on the trip to that point just in case we would find so much information that I would forget some things. I had finally sprung from my bed around 4:45 AM. That is often the time I am just settling in at home. It was the beginning of a complete turn-around of the clock in my brain.

I had originally thought I would wait till at least seven before I would awaken Carol in the adjoining tenth floor suite. When I gently knocked on her door at a time I am generally never awake, I was rather surprised that she was about to hop in the shower to get ready for our Great Adventure. I showered, dressed, and reviewed the Great Game Plan. Forty-five minutes later we went down to breakfast.

Again we found quite a different fare than we generally see anywhere else at breakfast. Sure, the hotel offered all its guests the traditional continental breakfast, but we never saw anyone over the next several days who was satisfied just with just juice, fruit, cold cereal, and a croissant. Most of the breakfast diners, we found, went for the hearty breakfast. Most of the businessmen at a convention going on at the hotel had what I would call a "killer" breakfast: two or three eggs cooked to order in bacon grease, grits, hash brown potatoes, pork sausage patties, bacon strips, fresh-baked biscuits slathered with *redeye gravy*, fruit cup, and coffee!

For the uninitiated, *grits,* are a main staple of every southern meal—breakfast, lunch, and dinner. This coarsely ground *hominy*—corn from which the bran and germ have been removed—came into the southern diet courtesy of the Algonquin Indians of Virginia. When I was a member of the wedding party at Ed and Sherrie Rollins' wedding in Roanoke, Virginia, some years before, I was rather surprised to see that grits were served in elegant silver chafing dishes at two different posh country clubs. The grits were sometimes served in their basic white composition, or sometimes they were served *au gratin*—topped with cheddar cheese. *Redeye gravy,* for the diner from the North, is made by first frying up some ham in a skillet. Take the ham out and pour a little water and/or a little coffee on the brown stuff and grease left in the bottom of the skillet and mix with the stove still on. Then stir the boiling gravy around until big circles (red eyes) appear in the bubbling brown liquids. Grits and redeye gravy were also staples of the *Honey Island* dining experience and a taste for them was carried with the islanders when they later prepared their meals in St. Louis, Chicago, and Detroit. But a warning here. Don't put grits and redeye gravy on your dining table if you are dieting or are trying them for the first time and plan to have a productive day to follow.

On our first morning in Mississippi, I succumbed to the quantity and quality of the food most diners were downing in the hotel restaurant. I justified the heavy breaking of the fast in my mind as part of my research on the Rounds family lifestyle. This is what Ned and West and their kinfolk must have eaten for breakfast in quantity and variety. Just as soon as I finished the hefty first meal of the day, I felt immediately like going back to bed. Carol, who had eaten a much lighter breakfast, was wiser. She was much more alert that day.

We climbed into the trusty Camry and set out on our journey of discovery shortly after 8:30 AM. We were eager to meet our two guides for the day, Red and Mattie. I took the wheel with the mutually-agreed plan that Carol would be the navigator and the Speedometer Monitor on any journeys out from the hotel, and then we would switch roles for any trips back to the hotel in Jackson. I have an acknowledged heavy foot for the gas pedal, and Carol and I chuckled about the projected perils of being pulled over by "Sheriff Bubba" in his Mounty hat and the dark glasses and toothpick clinched in his teeth. Snaring two college-educated Afro-American Yankee investigators traveling over the legal speed limit in a brand new foreign-made car on a quest to discover how their ancestors were screwed out of their land by Bubba's unscrupulous kinfolk would be a real plum for Big Bubba! We also imagined in our chuckles that the two of us would be a real hit for the deputies to taunt down at the county jail. God only knows what we might have to pay in fines to get our drivers licenses and car back in the anticipated kangaroo court. I joked that I had notified my personal banker before leaving St. Louis that she might have to wire me as much as ten thousand dollars to get out on bail if we were arrested and detained in some little dusty town's jailhouse. So, Carol was to watch my speed like a hawk!

At a careful 55 miles an hour for the entire hour and twenty-five minute trip from Jackson to Belzoni, we both felt we were forestalling the thrill we would have if we could, indeed, find the ancestral house of worship called Jones Chapel.

We both marveled again at the lush beauty of the Mississippi countryside. Nothing spectacular, mostly flat as a pancake. But absolutely gorgeous in the green color that springs up from its black and sometimes rich red soil. We two urbanites could hardly get over the uniqueness of the unpolluted Mississippi air. It is not a crisp air as one finds in, say, Cape Cod. It is not the pollen-laden air we breathe in the Midwest. It is far from the smoggy air one can breathe in Los Angeles or Mexico City or Cairo. It's muddy air—humid, but free of industrial impurities that assault the sinuses and nasal passages. There is, for sure, an occasional odoriferous reminder that there are livestock and fertilizer out there in the Delta air, but even that smell is preferable to that which we city-dwellers suck in every day.

The Mississippi Delta countryside is a pool-table green copy of the tropical rainforests I've toured in Yucatan and Guatemala. All that is missing are toucans and parrots and screaming monkeys.

There was the placid pleasantness of those hundreds upon hundreds of acres of man-made catfish ponds. The reflection of the blue sky in the ponds is ringed by the snow-white egrets which ring the ponds looking like so many diners lining up at a cafeteria where fish is the blue-plate special of the day. A gorgeous site until one begins to consider the fact that good farmland—farmland once owned by our kin and others—has been flooded to produce the scaleless delicacies synonymous with good fried eatin' in the South.

We were also taken with the vast stretches of treescapes draped in the kudzu vines which overwhelm shrubs and pines in heavy layers. I had once seen on some TV nature program how this vinelike plant brought originally from China in the 1870s creeps frighteningly, almost while one watches it, to blanket everything in its path while stopping the process of erosion. Since the plant can send roots as deep as ten feet, it's no wonder it takes over an area and that it's sometimes called "the weed that ate the South!" As one drives along the Mississippi countryside, these spells of kudzued trees and bushes start and stop without any logical explanation of why some stretches have no suffocating kudzu vines and some do. One could easily have nightmares about being smothered by kudzu while taking a nap in a Delta park.

Motoring along, one is almost forced to wonder what this land must have been like when the Chickasaw and Choctaw traversed it before the introduction of kudzu, asphalt and gravel, cotton fields, catfish lakes, soy bean crops, fences, and highway signs spoiled the natural green ruggedness of the rolling hills and valleys of pine and tupelo trees. Aunt Willetta had asked us to bring her back some pieces of Spanish moss. We never saw any. Maybe the festoons of moss we had seen so prominently in Gone With the Wind were gone with the kudzu.

We turned off Highway 49 onto Highway 12 going west. There were all the catfish lakes we had heard about, the lakes that probably had flooded over a lot of Rounds land in order to supply the world with its catfish delicacies. This was a large price for Ned Rounds and his heirs to pay to supply restaurants with this taste of the South. Highway 12 was not a much-traveled road in either direction. We found ourselves behind a big green combine and were slowed to considerably below the speed limit. If ever we were going to get accustomed to a slower pace, driving behind heavy farm equipment on a two-lane highway would be good preparation. When the big piece of equipment finally decided to give us a break by turning off the main road, I was pleased to be able to do forty-five again. What an absolutely non-spectacular stretch of road. Green, but nothing to take pictures of for the old scrapbook.

Then—what was this up ahead? It wasn't a highway sign. Those are green with white lettering. This sign was black lettering on white background and it was on the left side of the road. Wait a minute. Wait a minute!

"Carol, did you see that sign?"

"What did it say?

"I'm sure it said 'JONES CHAPEL - 4 MI.' Should we swing around?"

"No," Carol advised. "We'll be late picking up 'Red' and Mattie."

I kept driving west with an accelerated heartbeat that I was sure Carol had too. No doubt she, like I, wanted to savor the fact that it looked like the ancestral church was alive. We were like kids who wanted to save the circular center of the peanut butter and jelly sandwich for last. I drove on several more miles until we saw Bankhead's Service Station right between the Esquire Motel and the KFC on the outskirts of Belzoni.

As I wheeled off the highway, we saw a rather unkempt service station with four or five men sitting on orange crates looking for all the world like an informal panel of blue-collar experts on any subject that would come up amongst the boys on a Saturday morning. A short-honey-colored man with a barrel chest and wearing a "gimme cap" approached our car as Carol rolled down her window. I didn't have a clue as to how old he was. He introduced himself with his handsome, infectious smile as *"Warren Baker But My Friends All Call Me 'Red.'"* I hopped out of the car to greet our new friend/host and to stretch my legs. I nodded to the panel and they nodded back silently. I asked where Mattie was and "Red" told us she wanted to be picked up at her house. Our guide hopped in the back of the car and we were off to Mattie's house, just a stone's throw from the service station, but in a subdivision of lovely brick ranch-style homes with well-manicured lawns.

Mattie came out immediately to greet us, and Carol and I instinctively gave her a hug as if we had known her for years. She took us into her beautiful home and introduced us to her husband, Rufus. Wouldn't Ned have been pleased, I thought: a black man representing all of the county in which the old Rounds family once lived. Rufus excused himself from making the trip with us, saying his wife was the adventurer in the family. Soon Carol, "Red", Mattie, and I set out to find Jones Chapel, with the two St. Louisans a little less apprehensive having seen what we were almost sure was the church direction sign. We were further bolstered by having two charming host-guides to help us find the chapel.

After a ride of less than ten minutes from Belzoni we were back at the church sign. Highway 12 and Boone Deaden Road. **JONES CHAPEL...4 MILES.** I rolled off the highway and onto the shoulder and Carol and I, without saying anything to each other, bounded from the car with our disposable cameras to take pictures of the sign to show back home. I had purchased six of these inexpensive cameras in St. Louis since I am not a photographer and since I have had great luck in the past with these cheap scene-savers for "Kodak Moments." Boone Deaden Road was at first a blacktop road. Then it became a dusty gravel road. We saw another church sign, this one informing us that Jones Chapel was just <u>two</u> miles ahead! I jumped out and took pictures of that sign while Carol took a picture of me taking a picture of the sign. Carol and I began getting nervous and expressing that anxiety. Would it...could it...still be there?

And then, right before our eyes, we saw it! Lump in throat time! Tear in eye time! The little white church that had been such a focal point in the lives of the early Rounds family! Carol and I sprang from the car leaving both our doors wide open. I could tell she had developed about the same amount of tears in her eyes as I tried to deny myself. There it was. Jones Chapel. Somehow I wanted to try to put my arms around the little building. I wanted to hug the church. It was in fairly good shape. If I had to guess, the exterior had probably been painted white in the last couple of years.

We were thrilled to see that our great-grandfather, Westly Rounds, was listed first on the old church cornerstone as a founding deacon in 1894. His name was misspelled, _Ness,_ but we got the idea. There were other names recognizable, too, from the research I had done in St. Louis. There was the name of Tom Simmons, who had married Ned Rounds' daughter, Martha. There was the name of Weldon Jones who gave the land for the church. There was also the name of Emanuel Gray, who took over the _Honey Island_ post office in 1925 after my great-uncle George Byrd gave up the postmaster's post.

There were no buildings around the church. The _Honey Island_ post office once run by our great-uncle George was nowhere to be found. None of the homes of the early islanders was visible for as far as the eye could see. In fact, the eye couldn't see far. Tall cotton fields almost swallowed up the tiny church which stood in the fields as a lone reminder that this was once a bustling community. We walked around the church and took pictures of every aspect that could later be recountable. Carol even found two concrete-encased holes in the ground out back of the church, which just had to be the outhouse _sans_ the wooden shack that once sheltered the two holes from any voyeurs.

What about trying to get a key? Just as we pondered how to get into the chapel, an elderly black man in a blue pickup truck rolled up. "Red" and Mattie knew him. Odell, they called him. He was the area's handyman, retired from whatever regular job he used to hold full-time. He tipped his cap bill to the ladies in a habit acquired perhaps six or seven decades ago when gentlemen did those sorts of things as a matter of courtesy. And in some cases, I would imagine, as a matter of form. He told us that we could probably find a key down at Ol' Herbert Fullilove's place just down the road a piece. Fullilove. There's that name again. Fullilove. I had read about them, written about them, asked my Mississippi researcher to dig up information on them, and had even talked by phone with a couple of them in St. Louis. Fullilove. That romantic-sounding, unusual name. They had been neighbors of the Rounds clan way back in the glory days of _Honey Island._ I had never seen one of them face-to-face. A genuine Fullilove.

Odell led our car with his pickup down the dusty road until we came upon a tidy yellow aluminum-sided house in one of the most godawful littered yards one could ever find anywhere on the face of the Earth. Name a kind of clutter and it could be found in Herbert's front yard—plumbing, railroad, electrical, electronic, automotive, mechanical—it was all there as if Mr. Fullilove would some day find a genuine use for it. An ancient hound dog/guard dog raised a near toothless snout into the air and tried unconvincingly to order us to turn around and scoot, leaving Ol' Herb alone.

Awakened by all the racket, Herbert Fullilove opened his door wearing precious little. Maybe nothing. He squinted from the darkened house in the morning sunlight. And then his well-tanned, round face sprouted the biggest, widest, most infectious, toothy, smile one would ever see in a lifetime. As he started to walk—perhaps stagger would be a better word—out onto his front steps and into the daylight, all the Mississippians, Mattie, "Red" and Odell, began to yell in cacophony for Herb to put on some clothes before he took another step towards us. Any scant raiment Ol' Herb was wearing was about to head south leaving his most private parts public—and pubic! He nodded and disappeared inside his house while the old dog stopped barking and joined a female dog feeding her litter under a pickup truck on blocks.

Herb reappeared wearing bib overalls classically with a strap over only one shoulder. And as he approached us barefoot he seemed to take no note of the piles of dog manure dotting the yard. His unannounced guests were scanning the ground to avoid the stuff, though. As Herbert Fullilove approached us with an outstretched hand I guessed that he would have been about sixty years old. But an extremely young-looking sixty. In fact, as I sized Ol' Herb up and remembered the kind of virtually unwrinkled skin there is in my family, Herb could have been seventy years old. He was built like a man who was no stranger to hard work. Mattie introduced him to Carol and me and he gave us a gracious, but rather shy, howdy-do. Mattie told him that Carol and I were descendants of the Rounds family. Then Herbert asked Carol and me with that big grin that never seemed to go away the question we would hear over and over again in Mississippi from folks who first wanted to establish our legitimacy before uttering another word:

"Now, who did you say your people was?" he asked.

I rattled off a truncated version of the Rounds family tree and then mentioned that I had heard of his family, especially the members who sprang from Taylor and William Fullilove more than a hundred years before. Herbert just nodded and smiled, smiled and nodded. He volunteered nothing except the fact that he had been fishing all night and that's why he was so muddy.

I then violated one of the cardinal principles of talking as a northerner with residents of Mississippi. I blurted out that I understood he had just sold off his land. He was totally non-responsive and changed the subject completely, telling us how much he liked our gold Toyota Camry. Then in the most diplomatic rebuff I had heard in Mississippi, a slap at my insensitivity, Ol' Herbert asked:

"How much would a car like that set me back?"

Touché, Herb. Point well made. If I could ask you within minutes of making your acquaintance something as personal as whether you had just sold your land, you had a perfect right to fire back at me a question you thought was just as personal. I dropped the subject. As I dropped the subject, I picked up on the fact that in the front corner of the littered yard there was a brand new Lincoln Continental.

We asked about a church key to which Herbert asked: *"Y'all try the back door?"*

This response, too, made me feel a little stupid. We had *not* tried the back door. No church in the city of St. Louis would ever leave a back door open. Not even for a minute in an unattended sanctuary. Anybody who wanted to vandalize or break into Jones Chapel would have to know that the church way off the main road had anything to steal. We thanked Ol' Herb and went back to find the back door open.

As Carol and I entered the little church, we were pleasantly surprised to find how well-kept it was way out there smack dab in the middle of a serious cotton field. There was relatively new red carpeting. Surely these weren't the same pews my great-great grandparents, great-grandparents, grandparents, mother, and aunts had sat in. The seating was much too new. There were two huge air-conditioning units in the windows on either side of the sanctuary. There were electric lights overhead. My mother and aunt had mentioned gaslights. And, there were restrooms *inside* to replace the outhouse out back.

I got another big lump in my throat. Here was the place where my ancestors worshiped and went to school. A venerable building that was 104 years old and still in good shape. Walking around in the chapel produced eerie images and mental pictures of how it was in this place a century ago, pictures that were almost like flashbacks. I felt I had been there before. And perhaps I had.

I walked over to the old upright piano which I knew had seen better days even before I actually struck a few chords on it. These well-worn black and white keys were in critical condition and should have been hospitalized for treatment years before. The hot, super-humid temperatures of the Mississippi Delta, I realized, could literally rot the felt hammers on the best of pianos within months of the installation. If ever the invitation to "make a joyful *noise* unto the Lord" could be aptly heeded, this piano was capable of making a noise literally.

Our hearts leaped with joy when we noted in a church bulletin that there would be a church service the next day. We had really lucked out. Or was there more of a Providential hand in this arrangement than Lady Luck?

The church cemetery. Was it still there? Odell, who had come into the church with us, assured us that he knew how to get into the graveyard where *Honey Island* residents had been buried since Weldon Jones gave the land. We once again followed Odell's battered pickup truck—this time with "Red" riding shotgun with Odell. We passed a big patch of cotton field to the left of the church entrance and drove onto what was more of a foot path than a driving road, and into what looked like utter wilderness. And then we got out of our vehicles to walk into what for all the world looked like a jungle.

Carol quickly whipped out the can of *Cutter's* insect repellant Aunt Willetta had advised me to bring and she sprayed both of us down: feet, arms, even the back of our necks, as we closed our eyes and stop breathing during the application. *Cutter's* had gotten me through a vacation in Egypt where menacing tsetse flies flourished. It had to work here, I thought. We thought it was interesting that not one of the three Mississippians accepted my invitation when I punningly offered *"Let us spray."* They wanted no part of the stuff. They had all worked in cotton fields and cane fields with mosquitoes threatening them during every minute of their labors. They didn't seem bothered at all. Perhaps they had built up a certain tolerance or immunity over their many years. Or, perhaps the pesky mosquitoes craved Missouri flesh before they bothered with the same old Mississippi skin they had grown fat on. Carol and I had seen some of the biggest mosquitoes and horse flies imaginable buzzing and dive-bombing us around the church. We would take all the protection we could find. Even so, I was to carry the sting and itch of Mississippi mosquito bites for many weeks after that graveyard visit.

When we got well into the woods, which were a far cry from a pastoral scene, Carol asked Odell if there were any snakes in the graveyard plot.

"Oh, yeah," Odell responded. *"They's snakes and we done seen a 'gator or two in here, too."*

That was it for Carol. She turned and did a full Jackie Joyner Kersee run back to the car. And that is where she sat until our cemetery visit was over some twenty minutes later.

The entanglement of vines, the clusters of broad palmetto fronds, the tall swamp grasses, and even the bramble appeared to both shield the deterioration of the cemetery to the viewer and somehow dress up what was sheer devastation. But they were all signs of gross neglect. Tombstones were crumbling from the humid climate and sinking deeper into the red, marshy clay soil. The sunken earth in the shape of coffins was in some patches the only indication that one was in a cemetery. There were disturbing mounds of earth that indicated the grave diggers in some cases did not dig very deep at all. Some of the caskets seemed to be rising right up out of the earth. That was a spooky sight. I wondered silently why the dearly departed are buried above ground in the state of Louisiana not far from where we stood, but the dead in Mississippi with the same soil conditions are interred.

Strangely enough, there were little piles of artificial palm leaves and flowers scattered throughout the jungle-like burial grounds. I noted one interment that was made in 1992. Incredible, I thought. I asked Odell if folks were still being planted here and, if so, why.

"Well, peoples still want to be buried next to they kinfolk, you know. Next to grandfolk and mamas and poppas and kin. And if they gets buried here, they don't have to pay

nothin' like they would if they gets buried in Belzoni."

Sad. How sad.

We came upon the most interesting tombstone in the cemetery. At the top center of this one was an oval, enamelized photograph of one Elbert Jones, obviously a member of the family of the man who gave the land for the church and cemetery. Elbert Jones is a strikingly handsome young man in suit, dress shirt, and cravat. He appeared to be the epitome of the classy *Honey Island* man, born to a class of farmers and laborers, but able to don a suit and tie and look as aristocratic as any black man in the state. Elbert Jones didn't live long. He was born in 1881 and died in 1904, victim of a yellow fever epidemic that swept through Mississippi and *Honey Island* that year. "Red" studied the face on the gravestone and opined that here was a man who could have passed for white. Seizing the moment at the risk of being too nosey again, I said to "Red" that it looked like he himself had a little mixture of something in his blood. He answered with something I'll never forget. He said with a big twinkle in his eyes and a little smile:

"Oh, yeah. Half my family is colored and half my family is white. Yep. We get together... both sides...for a barbecue at least once or twice a year. And then we go our separate ways until the next family barbecue."

Amazing. Simply amazing.

After Mattie and I took copious notes on who was buried in the Jones Chapel cemetery, we decided to call it a day. The overgrowth and underbrush were so menacing, and the idea of meeting up with a snake or alligator began to register with me as an experience I didn't need while in search of my roots.

I offered to treat our gracious guides to lunch and they accepted. We went to a restaurant on Highway 12 called "Peterbo's." It is owned by the same black family that owns the two Bankhead service stations. After a good and hearty lunch Carol and I thanked our guides profusely and dropped them back off at the place where we had picked them up. We were thrilled when Mattie told us that she and her husband wanted to go to church with us the next day at Jones Chapel.

We drove back to Jackson feeling we had had a really productive day and met some really nice new friends. We were really tired, perhaps more emotionally drained than physically tired, and decided to forgo dinner at a restaurant. We sent for room service food and then crashed for the night. Once again, I didn't sleep well. I awakened around three and got caught up in the anticipation of worshiping at the same church where my kinfolk had praised God more than a century before.

Next morning we had a little less breakfast than the day before since we learned the hard way about heavy southern breakfasts, especially for two people who seldom ate breakfasts at home. Early that Sunday morning we had more adventure than we had anticipated or needed. Somehow we took a wrong turn and found ourselves heading over the Mississippi River into Louisiana. Believe me, it's easy to do. On the cell phone, I called the Straughters and told them we had gotten lost and would be late picking them up. I was too embarrassed to tell them that we were calling from Louisiana. Fortunately, we had set out more than an hour earlier than we really needed to and after taking a circuitous trip back to Belzoni, we were only about twenty minutes late in picking up the Straughters.

I was able to speed to the church after being assured by Representative Straughter that we would not be given a citation for speeding as long as we were with him. God doth provide, I thought. As we rode into the churchyard I was surprised to see about fifteen or sixteen cars, all nice cars, parked in front. We went in to find a lively worship service going on. There were about thirty congregants and a youth choir in white tops and black skirts and slacks singing away up front just behind the minister who was seated in his long black robe with huge red crosses on the sleeves.

Just as we got seated in this historic church that once doubled as the *Panther Burn School* for my ancestors, the first (note that I am specifying the *first*) of the offerings was taken up by the ushers. This was the general offering. When I laid a bill I had retrieved from my wallet on the collection plate, the usher leaned over and whispered: *"Y'all want change?"* I smiled and indicated that change would not be necessary.

After much prayer and singing and shouts of *"Amen!"* the minister took to the pulpit. Rev. M. L. Houston fired up the place to the point that it might have needed twice the air-conditioning capacity it had to cool the sanctuary down. Fire and brimstone are understatement descriptions of Rev. Houston's stentorian Bible-based exposition. He called often for amens from the deacon's bench to his right and from the flock in front of him to give him reassurances that the congregation agreed with his exhortations. He seemed to want to be assured quite often that his flock would wage daily battles with the forces of the Devil and work to achieve the heavenly reward of salvation.

After the half-hour sermon, the young people's choir lit into another toe-tapping selection. I handed an usher a little piece of paper to give to the minister, informing him that some descendants of the Jones Chapel founders were in attendance from St. Louis. When the choir wrapped up its stirring anthem, the minister announced our presence and invited Carol and me to come up and speak. Carol is a deaconess at her church and well-versed in Scripture. With one of the chapel's white Bibles in hand, she gave a sermonette that complemented Rev. Houston's sermon quite nicely. Her presentation was punctuated with loud and enthusiastic amens from a congregation that very seldom heard a woman preach.

When Carol wrapped up her sermonette, a thunderous chorus of amens followed. Then I took the floor down front and apologized for not being the preacher that my sister was. I told them I was more of an historian than a preacher, a bearer of tidings good and bad in my daily television newscasts. But, I told them, I really believed that some divine hand had guided me to them to give them a message. I told them that I was sure that a Supreme Being had led me to them to warn them that they had better begin to work more diligently to preserve their past so that they could have a future. Where were these words coming from?

I told them that the first task was to clean up their cemetery. Clean it up, I admonished, or it will be destroyed by the cotton seed. When the cemetery goes, the church is next. I told them that to prove that I was not an ungracious guest in their midst, I would personally underwrite the cost of a cemetery clean up. I would pay three men to put in full days for a week to get the place spruced up and presentable. Then I volunteered to pay for a sign to designate this sacred ground for many generations to come. What's more, I told them I had been a church organist and choir master starting when I was sixteen. I told them that I still am involved in music and so loved the music I heard that day that I would buy the congregation a new piano on behalf of the Rounds Family of St. Louis. My offers were graciously received with the traditional outpouring of amens.

Rev. Houston thanked both Carol and me for being there and then introduced State Representative Rufus Straughter. He was received with the obvious love that poured readily from this little congregation. Representative Straughter took microphone in hand and reminded the parishioners that this was his third visit to the church. I was impressed with that fact and so was the congregation. When his remarks were over he asked his wife, Mattie, if she had anything to add, to which she smiled, waved a little greeting to the church members, and shook her head in the negative. When she declined, Rev. Houston applauded her decision, quoting the Scriptural advice from the Apostle Paul that women should yield to their husbands and remain silent in the presence of their menfolk. Once again, thunderous amens. Carol gave me an elbow in the ribs that let me know what I had already suspected: she didn't buy the interpretation of the Bible that women should keep their mouths shut in the presence of their men.

Two more offerings were taken up. The "Love Offering" is a euphemism for a cash gift to the pastor. The ministers in these little rural churches do not draw a regular paycheck for their services. Instead, they are supported through "love offerings." In Missionary Baptist churches all across the land—big and small— the participation in this offering is not left to chance. Instead of collection plates being passed, the worshipers march row-by-row up to the front of the church to lay their contribution to the minister in the plate in an act of charity to be witnessed by God, the minister, the deacons, and the entire congregation.

Interestingly enough, Ol' Herbert Fullilove, dressed in slacks, shirt, and tie, appeared out of nowhere; marched up front, laid a piece of green in the collection plate, and ducked into a pew where he appeared to be suggesting to one of the sisters that she come by his house after the service for lunch or something. Mostly something.

Before Communion, the minister arm-carried a little mentally impaired boy with multiple deformities to the front of the church and explained how the boy's mother was having a tough time with his upkeep and his medical bills. Thus, a third offering was taken, causing me to wonder how poor people, as this congregation was, could afford so many tappings.

The Communion of bread and wine was particularly moving for Carol and me. The Eucharist seemed to bond us to the past and bring us closer to our heritage as sonorous, historic melodies, and prayers were offered up.

After the service was over Carol and I, by design, began to solicit and elicit conversations that gave us keys to understanding this community where only two of the parishioners still lived on *Honey Island*. They had all driven in from Belzoni and other surrounding towns to get to the church. I was particularly interested in finding out if, and how, the ancestors of some of these good people had lost their land and were forced to leave the wonders of the island. How did other families find themselves in the same predicament as my ancestors?

From the information culled by Carol and me, here are some of the ways African American landowners were relieved of their *Honey Island* land over the last century by hook or crook. Mostly by crook in the criminal sense of the word.

1. Landowners like my great-great granddad Ned Rounds were too illiterate to read all the fine print in the land deeds. The deed that turned over 216 acres of land to Ned in 1886 is two-and-a-half pages long in handwritten, cursive script. Ned signed some documents we found with an "X" as if to indicate that he understood what he was signing. If he were, indeed, illiterate, as the 1880 census noted, he would have absolutely no way of understanding all the terms. Did he fully understand that if he failed to pay the two five-hundred dollar loans with their ten-percent interest when they were called in, his property could be seized by the sheriff and foreclosure proceedings begun? The fine print on Ned's deeds also stipulated that his property could be sold for the difference in the amount he had in hand to pay off the loan and the amount he was short. He may not have also fully understood that the trustee appointed to administer the foreclosure was entitled to take any farm equipment, along with all the cotton and sugar cane and the produce until the balance of the loan was paid off, no matter how many years it took to satisfy the loan terms. The fine print further read that Ned's heirs would be responsible for his debt for as long as they lived! After the homestead that Ned built came crashing down around 1919, no wonder

every Rounds family member who could flee to points north moved far away to be sure they were not somehow saddled with the old man's debts.

2. We learned at the fellowship hour following Sunday worship that a favorite tactic of unscrupulous white scalpers who lay in wait for the property of Blacks to be seized was this: Blacks would appear at the courthouse to pay their property tax in a timely manner. When they got there, the county clerks, who were obviously in cahoots with the land snatchers, would look in the great book and declare that the property taxes had already somehow been paid. When the black landowner asked how that could be, the clerks would tell them that maybe it was some mistake. But they didn't have anything to worry about, it had been paid already. Maybe by accident, or an erroneous recording. So the poor, black farmer would shrug, scratch his head, and head home thinking that this was strange, but maybe they could just once get something for nothing. Three or four days later the sheriff, who was also in on the deal, would show up at the farmhouse of the black landowner and announce foreclosure. The taxes somehow hadn't really been paid. No matter that the black landowner still had the money to pay the taxes. The payment was declared delinquent and the property applicable for foreclosure. What black man in his right mind in the old days would challenge a white clerk, white sheriff, and white trustee? Carol and I heard this story over and over again from parishioners who told it quite independently of each other.

3. One African American woman who asked specifically that I not use her name if any written account of the plight of black landowners were to be written, told me her grandfather was approached by two white speculators one day and told:

"Yore little ones have to walk a terrible long way to school each day, don't they Billy boy?"

"Yessir, yessir…they do has to walk a fer piece to get over yonder to the church for school."

"Well, how would you like it if they didn't have to walk so far to school, especially in the hot summer and cold winters?"

"Ah guesses ah would like that right smart, yessuh. That would be good for mah young 'uns."

"Well, Billy, my boy, this is yore lucky day."

"How's that, suh? My lucky day?"

"Well, boy, I just happens to have a piece of property right near to Jones Chapel. How 'bout makin' a swap with me?"

"Well, Mr. Ferris. Ah sho would call that a good deal ah guess, suh. If you would be so gen'rous as to swap yo land for mines, ah thinks that could work out for the betterment of the young 'uns. An' ah thanks y'all fuh thinkin' of heppin' out my chirens."

So the deal was struck. Seems beneficent of the white guy to want to make the switch with a black guy so the latter's kids wouldn't have to walk so far to school each day. But here was the rub. The black guy gave up 79.8 acres of land. The white guy only conveyed 47, maybe 48 acres. But who was counting acreage? The black guy, in all likelihood, didn't have the savvy to have the property he received in the deal properly surveyed. And, if he had detected a shortchanging, would he have dared to report it? If he had dared to report it, to whom would he report?

4. Still another way that Black people were screwed out of their land, as Carol and I learned from the Jones Chapel parishioners and others we talked to in Mississippi, happened when whites conspired with members of an African American landowner's family members to have the black property owner declared mentally incompetent. The land-grabbing white snakes, according to the churchgoers, would pay the next-of-kin what appeared to be a lot of money, maybe one or two hundred dollars in cash, to declare the principal landowner either mentally incompetent or an alcoholic. The "mentally incompetent" and "alcoholics," as defined by the co-conspirators, could by law lose their property if they were so certified by a judge whose palm had been greased. Tens of thousands of acres of Mississippi Delta land have been seized by the local sheriff after the landowners were declared to be incompetent to continue to hold the property. Carol and I actually saw with our own eyes more entries than you might want to believe in the courthouse records we perused of landowners who were stripped of their land upon the testimonies and signatures of their own relatives.

5. Some of the Jones Chapel parishioners had stories about their forebears trying to diligently pay their property taxes and being sent on cruel wild goose chases by horseback and wagon between the three courthouses in Lexington, Belzoni, and Yazoo City. Each county, as we have noted, had at one time or another been the seat of government for *Honey Island*.

6. Courthouse fires down through the ages have conveniently lost property deeds.

Armed with all this anecdotal information about alleged scams and subterfuge aimed at my kin and my kin's neighbors, I began to get a clearer picture of how systems in Mississippi operated. These good church people would have absolutely no reason to lie to visitors from St. Louis who seemed to possess no great power to rectify a couple of centuries of wrongdoings. Nor did we purposefully appear to have anything more than a passing interest in setting up a family reunion or satisfying a cursory curiosity about roots.

We were to learn even more. We went after church to talk with a Miss Nettie Green. She lived "down the road a piece" from the church, and she was the last black property owner holdout on *Honey Island* after Herbert Fullilove had sold all but enough land for himself to live on. As we drove off the gravel road onto a little dirt path to her modest screened house, another hound dog/guard dog appeared to announce our arrival more than threaten our presence. Soon a rather large, dark-skinned woman emerged from the screen door. She didn't appear to be overly friendly nor overly anxious to have unannounced guests. But, I thought, that wasn't so strange. I hate unannounced guests, too. The barking dog settled down, we got out of our car and were kind of invited onto the screened porch. As we walked carefully across the grassless front yard to avoid stepping in piles of dog excrement new and old, I couldn't help but notice that Miss Green's yard would take the prize over Herbert Fullilove's for the most clutter in a single front yard. Miss Green must have never thrown anything away. She just threw it in her yard. Among the junk spread arbitrarily over the space were two bedpans. One was turned up as if to catch the rain. The other was turned down as if flung from the front porch like a Frisbee. One can only speculate about whether they were full of what bedpans are supposed to hold when they were hurled into the yard.

Miss Green didn't go out of her way to help her four guests clear a place among the clutter chaos on the porch to find a place to sit, but we were able to each find a space. When Mattie Straughter asked her if she was, indeed, the Jones Chapel church secretary, Miss Green gave a very vague and embroidered answer and rattled something about once having the records but somebody else who was out of town had them now and there was a fire at the church back in maybe the '40s that destroyed some of the oldest records and the records that are left aren't all that thorough and she really couldn't remember about how many pages or notebooks were filed with the church history. For some reason, I didn't believe she didn't have the church records.

Nettie Green is about fifty years old, I would guess. The quick take on her laconic responses to my questions is that she was a bit embarrassed by her this-is-how-everybody-looks-at-home-on-a-Sunday-afternoon attire. None of us expected, I'm sure, that she would be as well-dressed as my sister and Mattie Straughter, both in their Sunday-go-to-meeting dresses. Our uneasy host kept tugging and primping at her house dress attire as if one more tug might magically make her as fashionably dressed as the two other women. The tugging didn't work. She also had a bad case of the "Mississippi Suspicion" we had witnessed from both black and white Mississippians. Just who did we think we were anyway? How dare we ask such personal questions? What were we going to do with any information she slipped and divulged? Were we rich city Negroes looking down our noses at our rural brothers and sisters? Were we really some secret agents of some government agency like the IRS, trying to trick the interviewee into self-incrimination?

Suspicere mississippianus makes the person interviewed watch his/her words very carefully. And the condition makes some interviewees pray as the questions are answered "Oh, Lord, make my words good today for I might have to eat them tomorrow."

The only information Nettie Green released to us after nearly an hour-long chat is that she still owns with her two brothers about four-and-a-half acres of *Honey Island* land. Her family used to own vastly more property on the island, but had lost almost all of it by hook or crook. She also vowed that she would have to be taken kicking and screaming from her property. Or, she swore, she'd have to be taken away in a pine box. I believed her.

We bade a farewell to Miss Green, and just before we reboarded the Camry, she, quite by surprise, granted permission for her picture to be taken with our little coterie. She did not bother to tell me what I found out more than a year later. The Greens and the family of my great-grandfather West's second wife, Mary Lewis, were connected by marriage many, many years ago. That would make Ms. Green indirectly related to the Rounds family. But if the truth were told, all the *Honey Island* families were interconnected. And why wouldn't they be? They all lived so close together and their daily lives for at least four score years and ten were intertwined.

Then it was off to Peterbo's again for a late lunch or early supper. I was famished after a day at church and the futile attempt to reel in Miss Green's responses from Lake Nebulous and sometimes from the Obfuscatory Swamp.

Our Sunday of work was not over. After dropping State Representative Straughter back at home so he could spend some time visiting his ailing mother, we headed out for our next interview with me hoping that Mississippi Suspicion would not engulf us in this interview. After all, Mrs. Mattie Burns Williams had sent for us. She had heard through the grapevine that we were in town and let Mattie Straughter know that we were kinfolk and she wanted to see us. We drove a short distance from the Straughter home to another well-maintained black neighborhood in Belzoni. We were greeted at the door by Mrs. Williams' daughter, Susie Williams Croft. She graciously ushered us in to the den where her mother was sitting comfortably in a rocking chair.

Without saying a word to each other, Carol and I gave each other a silent look that spoke volumes. It is the kind of message transmitted through the eyes only after two people have known each other for more than forty years. What Carol and I were saying to each other through our look to each other was how incredibly much Mrs. Williams looked like our late grandmother, Hattie Rounds Williams Coats. If ever there were a double in the world, this was my grandmother's Doppelganger.

Mrs. Williams seemed warm, but understandably cautious about revealing too much until she was more than sure that we were who we claimed to be. Within a few minutes we discovered that Rounds blood did, indeed, flow through the veins of the interviewee. Mrs. Williams' grandfather was Tom Simmons. He married Ned Rounds' daughter, Martha, who was also called "Mattie." Mattie

Rounds Simmons and Tom Simmons had a daughter named Mary who married Porter Burns. The Burnses produced three children, Theodosia, Mattie, and Milton Burns. Our hostess on that August afternoon in Belzoni was Mattie Burns Williams. She was a great-granddaughter of Ned Rounds, a great-niece of Westly Rounds, and a second cousin to my mother Atlener and my two aunts Gertrude and Willetta. In fact, Mrs. Williams knew the three daughters of my grandmother, Hattie Rounds Williams Coats, better by their nicknames, "Lena," "Lovie," and "Singie." Mrs. Williams was eighty-three years old in September 1998.

Among the images Mrs. Williams painted was that of the old Crescent Theater in Belzoni. She told us how she hated to climb up to the third floor balcony reserved for Blacks in those days of racial segregation. The steps up to the *Colored* section were too dark and steep.

"Colored folks had to climb the stairs way up to a high balcony. They called where we sat the 'Buzzard's Roots.' It was way too high for me to be comfortable up there. We only went to the movies really when we had company in from out of town. None of us even dared think about sitting on the main floor of the Crescent. That would have been big trouble if we tried."

She remembered Goldberg's general store in Belzoni. *"They had nice things, and they were nice people."* Mrs. Williams had recollections of Mr. Goldberg and his sons, Joe and Charlie. She remembered a man named Abe Cohen, who may have owned a share in the store. He often waited on her grandparents, Mattie and Tom Simmons. They were all courteous to all their black patrons, she said.

She knew from stories that her father, Porter Burns, was one of the *Honey Island* men who marched off to menial labor in World War I in 1917. She was one of more than a dozen former *Honey Island* residents who remembered how devastating the Great Flood of 1927 was. She was eleven at the time. She also mentioned some of the same home remedies used by the *Oldtimers* in St. Louis.

Contrary to denials by some Humphreys county courthouse officials that Tchula Lake was never that big, Mrs. Williams seemed pleased to share memories of the steamboats that plied Tchula Lake and docked in front of Jones Chapel. She recollected that candidates for baptism at Jones Chapel would sometimes change into their robes at the home of Mrs. Ollie Joiner because her house was closest to the traditional baptism bank of the lake. Her Christmas memories are full of firecrackers and holly trees with their red berries everywhere and lavish Yuletide suppers of turkey, goose and guinea fowl. Her brother, Milton, taught her how to skin possums and raccoons for "good eatin." Milton sold the 'coon skins.

She fondly recalled the traditional New Year's Day meal of hog's head, black-eyed peas, and collard greens, a variety of kale. She also carried in her golden memories images of my great-grandfather, Westly, who was no practitioner of manual labor. She recalls West napping on the screened porch every day of the week dressed in his "Sunday-go-to meeting" clothes. Perhaps Westly was snoozing to avoid thinking about the fact that his land was slipping through his hands and systematically being sold off to meet the escalating interest rates and taxes.

Mattie Burns Williams also remembered that the work ethic of Mary Lewis Rounds, West's second wife and mother of a passel of youngsters brought into the Rounds family, was quite the opposite of her husband's. Mrs. Williams recalls a snapshot right out of Africa when she thought back to Mary Lewis Rounds:

"She could carry three buckets of water at one time—one in each hand and one on her head. She was a woman who just couldn't sit still. She was always busy doin' somethin.' While her husband just sat around and took naps. They said that Uncle West took after his daddy. He supposedly took a lot of naps, too."

There were many other wonderful memories Mrs. Williams was able to share with us. We loved every minute of her narratives. As we were leaving the house she shared with her daughter, Carol made an unusual request:

"May I just rub your arm? Your skin is just like my grandmother's. I remember rubbing her arm when I was a little girl. Her skin was just so smooth."

Mrs. Williams seemed to love the comparison with our grandmother, and she slowly walked us to the driveway where we boarded our trusty Camry and waved goodbye as we pulled away from the woman who looks uncannily like the woman we called "Mama."

After dropping Mattie Straughter at her house, we headed back to our hotel in Jackson.

What a productive day! What memories! I could not wait to get back to the hotel to transcribe the notes I had taken throughout the day. Although I was exhausted, I knew I could count on an infusion of adrenaline to carry me several more hours towards dawn.

Once again, Carol and I elected to pass on supper at any of Jackson's fine restaurants. We decided to phone room service for a meal. Oddly enough, although it was past time for us to eat our third meal, we weren't very hungry. We were literally filled with excitement and the fulfilment of knowing that not all of the traces of our family's former life had been obliterated.

Our next challenge would be to search for any information we could find about the Rounds family in courthouse records. We suspected those documents would not be handed over freely.

 *Courthouses: The Biggest Challenge*

Next morning, after another night of little sleep for both of us, Carol and I ate what amounted to a progressively diminished breakfast, in the Crowne Plaza dining room. With this being our third breakfast we had learned not to drink too much coffee and juice to make us have to stop one or two times on our journey. We had also learned that we should not eat biscuits and redeye gravy, eggs, bacon, sausage, fruit, grits, hash browns, bagels, and wheat toast so we could avoid the urge to nap immediately after leaving the breakfast table.

Our goal on this Monday, August 10, 1998, was to do a whirlwind tour of courthouses. The schedule I had set for us would involve a trip first to the Holmes County Courthouse in Lexington, then the Humphreys County Courthouse in Belzoni and, if there was any time left, a visit to the Yazoo County Courthouse in Yazoo. I knew that this was an overly ambitious schedule, but I felt we should at least try for it. I thought, for some reason, that Ned and West would have wanted us to try all three.

As we set out for Lexington, I felt a bit guilty about not confiding in Carol all the frightening things I had heard about Lexington. This was the same Lexington that Annie West Rounds had not wanted her son Rufus to visit. And it was the same Lexington that Chalmers Archer called "a separate and unequal place."

No, I didn't think it was necessary to scare the hell out of Carol about this town with such a dubious reputation as far as race relations are concerned. As we drove toward Lexington from Jackson we reviewed our game plan. We would not speed. Carol would talk to all women clerks we encountered. I would talk to the men. We would not give anybody the exact city from which we hailed. I would not pass out any of the business cards I carried in my spiffy black briefcase. If anybody asked why we were digging into our roots, we would tell them that we were simply planning a family reunion and wanted to get a little history to pass out at the gathering. We would approach everything slowly and not give any clerks or officials the idea that we were in a *Northern Hurry*.

After about an hour-and-a-half's drive we arrived in the little town of Lexington. The courthouse in the middle of the town square is the epitome of a Victorian structure. The town's placid appearance gave no hint that it was the site of many horrific crimes against African American Mississippians. We entered the Chancery Clerk's office and found four women clerks in the outer office. Three of them were white; the fourth, a young and attractive black woman. As if she were the ordained person to wait on Blacks, she rose to help us. The three white clerks didn't even move. It was if they had a game plan; just like Carol and I had developed a game plan.

Our clerk was not particularly helpful at first, but we deduced that it was not because she didn't want to help us. Her lack of help was based on the fact that she hadn't been on the job very long. She was a bit baffled by the fact that *Honey Island* had resided in three different counties during its relatively brief history, but she was willing to try to find the documents we sought. Carol and I found it interesting that while she was trying to help us, two white male clerks at two different times came into the records room where we were scouring documents to volunteer to us that they didn't think there would be any record of a *Honey Island* at the Lexington courthouse.

We did manage to find an old map showing the location of *Honey Island*. We knew the island had existed, but we wanted to prove it legally. When we put four map quadrants together, we were able to find the site of the family homestead. We also found a deed that somehow had survived the move from county to county to county and the courthouse fire and the indifference of county clerks down through the years. It was a copy of the deed by which Ned bought 216 acres in exchange for a thousand dollars cash and two promissory notes for five hundred dollars each.

We were also able to find some latitudinal and longitudinal coordinates for *Honey Island* and a survey map drawn up by U. S. Government surveyors Seth McCleary and Schiller Easley in 1827, the second year of the John Quincy Adams administration. We believed this survey would give us invaluable clues to exactly where the property was that Ned had purchased. Our new clerk friend told us the plat map would be very helpful at our next stop, the Humphreys County Courthouse in Belzoni.

I was surprised at a little extra meringue Carol laid on our research effort. She asked the young clerk who had been as helpful as she could have been for her home address so we could invite her to the Rounds family reunion. Since we didn't even have a family reunion planned, I thought Carol's offer was genuine if, at the same time, a bit disingenuous. The clerk complied, giving Carol not only a home address but a telephone number.

Before going on to Belzoni, I decided we needed to buy a couple more disposable cameras, so we went across the Lexington town square to a drugstore where we noticed once again another Mississippi phenomenon. There was the typical black clerk with a white person standing behind them. The black clerk was always, without verbal directions, sent to wait on the black customers. There were two elderly white patrons at the drugstore who had come in right ahead of us and the black clerk had the option of waiting on them first, but the white ladies were automatically referred to the white clerk. And then the rub. As we had seen at a couple of gas stations and in a drugstore in Jackson, the black clerk can wait on a customer, but is not allowed to ring up the sale on the cash register. The black clerk is obviously there just for window dressing. There can't be that many black trainees in the world!

We bade farewell to Lexington, Mississippi, with no appreciable regrets.

We took a scenic back road into Belzoni, and when we arrived, we found quite a surprise on the steps of the courthouse. A well-dressed black woman approached us and asked if we were Carol and Julius Hunter. When we acknowledged that we were who we were, the woman introduced herself as a cousin of ours. She had heard, as apparently everybody else in town had, that we were around looking for our roots. We learned that the courthouse was closed every day from noon to one o'clock, a quaint custom that must have been a layover from the days when the courthouse was not air-conditioned and workers needed an hour break to find a cool place to eat and relax for an hour. There are certainly no courthouses in the St. Louis area that simply shut down for an hour at noon.

We began our conversation with this self-proclaimed cousin with the same kind of reservations and suspicion we had seen many cases before. Who was this woman? Was she a spy sent by some sinister forces to find out what we were trying to find out? You see, we had become quite paranoid. After a brief conversation sitting on the shaded steps of the courthouse, we were able to establish the fact that this stranger was, indeed, a descendant of the Rounds line. The woman was Fannie Scott, a teacher in the Belzoni school system, who was using her lunch period during an in-service session before the school term began to link up with us visitor/relatives from St. Louis.

As it turns out, Fannie Scott, a current resident of Isola, Mississippi, is the daughter of Elvira Rounds Scott who is, at this writing, seventy-five years old. Fannie's mother was the granddaughter of Will Rounds Jr. and Magnolia Ervin. Will Rounds Sr., was Will Lewis at birth, one of the children of West Rounds' second wife Mary, who used his stepfather's surname. He was Fannie Scott's great-grandfather. Willie Sr. was born in Mississippi in 1893. After establishing our kinship and taking up Fannie Scott's whole lunch hour, we exchanged numbers and addresses with Fannie, thanked her for coming to find us, and promised to keep in touch.

Then it was on to heavier lifting. Mattie Straughter had given us the name of every clerk in the Belzoni courthouse and we were instructed by her to use her name to get any help we needed. After the courthouse clock struck one, we went in to present my card to the Chancery Clerk for Holmes County. Since I had learned from Mattie that this official is black, I violated Carol's and my game plan by presenting a receptionist with my business card from the television station. Lawrence Browder presented himself to us as if he were honored to have a television journalist visit his courthouse, but he quickly explained that he was new to the job and probably could be less helpful to us than Jerry Halbrook, the veteran surveyor. Browder asked one of the secretaries to check on the whereabouts of Mr. Halbrook, then quickly retreated to his inner-office. The secretary quickly reported that Halbrook was still out to lunch and probably wouldn't be back until a little before two.

Then, like a ton of bricks, it hit me. Halbrook. Jerry Halbrook. He was the same guy who had promised me three months earlier in a phone call I made that he would try to find and send to me a map of the *Honey Island* property. He hadn't sent the promised map in all that time. Halbrook had also been identified to Carol and me at the Jones Chapel fellowship hour as a person whose family had been buying up a lot of the *Honey Island* property. I could personally find no evidence of that, but it did make me suspicious of why he hadn't wanted to see me get that map in hand. I could not wait to joust with Mr. Halbrook.

At about five minutes to two in the afternoon, Mr. Halbrook approached Carol and me and informed us that he had been told to try to help us. I've been interviewing people for thirty years or more and like to think I've developed some expertise in asking the right question and a good memory for conversations. This is my recollection of how our time with Mr. Halbrook went.

"Yessir, I hope you can help us," I responded. *"Permit me to introduce ourselves. I'm Julius Hunter, and this is my sister, Carol Hunter. We're from St. Louis. In late May I talked with you by phone and you promised me you'd send me a map showing Honey Island. Since this is August and I haven't gotten the map, I thought I'd come down to Mississippi to personally pick it up."*

The face on this short white man with the big shock of white hair turned a beet red. My attempt to embarrass him was working just fine. But I was having some second thoughts—as I imagined Carol was—that I have violated an important part of the game plan by correctly identifying our names and place of origin. For some reason, I didn't think the information would be indelibly etched on this little guy's brain. He looked for all the world like a white-topped pot-bellied stove in a blue shirt. After meeting him, I deduced that he would not have become my best friend if I were to move to Belzoni.

"*What kind of map did you say I promised to send you?*" Halbrook asked as he rubbed the nape of his neck and squinted up at two people who are taller and darker than he is.

"*You promised to send me a map of* Honey Island. Honey Island. *You don't remember our phone conversation?*"

"*No, I'm afraid I don't. But I reckon if I didn't send you the map you say I promised you, there must not be such a map of that place…that Honey whatever you say it is.*"

"*Well, we're sure there is such a place.*"

"*Well, I don't know anything about it and I've been here for many a year.*"

I suppose investigators with less grit than the dynamic duo of Carol and Julius Hunter would have accepted this denial, thanked the clerk, and turned to walk away. We both got the feeling that Mr. Halbrook was totally unaccustomed to hearing any black folks acting so uppity in such a short time.

"*On the way in here, out in the corridor, Mr. Halbrook, there's this giant map of Humphreys County.*" (I was careful to pronounce the name of the county 'UM-phrah' County as all the natives called it.)

"*Yeah? What map is that?*"

"*The huge map that was drawn up in 1948. The map we passed on the way into this office.*"

"*Show me. I don't think I know which one y'all mean.*"

How in hell, I asked myself, could the senior surveyor in this office pass a mammoth map every single day to get into his office without paying any attention to it? The map had to be at least four feet by four feet. We walked around the corner from the main office and there it was. I pointed to it like the next statement should be Halbrook's.

"*Well. What's your point? I don't think this map has any—what did you say the name of that place was? That Honey whatever…?*"

"*It's called* Honey Island *and here it is right here.*" I pointed to the spot on the big map as adroitly as a good TV weathercaster points to an approaching cold front or high pressure area. "*Here it is.*"

"*Hmmmmm. Guess I never noticed this place before. Yep, there it is alright. Honey Island.*"

I thought to myself, *Jerry Halbrook, if just one of those people back at Jones Chapel Church is right, your family has been buying up property on the island for years. And maybe even you have some silent interest in the real estate deals.*

"*Well, from the size of it,*" Jerry continued, "*looks like it was probably never more than a little colored <u>neighborhood</u>…never incorporated or anything.*"

"*I beg to differ with you, sir. Honey Island was, at one time, much more than a little colored neighborhood. In fact, sir, Honey Island once had its own U. S. post office.*"

"That would be hard to believe. Where'd you come up with that notion?"

"It's more than a notion, sir."

I reached into my surprisingly neat and orderly new black briefcase and quickly held up before Halbrook's squinting eyes a document from the historian of the U. S. postal service in Washington. I didn't let Halbrook touch the document. I thought I'd just dangle the exhibit in front of him to titillate him a little.

"This is from Meg Ausman, the historian of the U. S. Postal Service in Washington. She confirms that there was, in fact, a post office on Honey Island."

"Y'all sure 'bout that?"

"Extremely sure, sir. Our great-uncle, George Byrd Jr. was the first postmaster, sworn into office in 1907. November 7, 1907, to be exact."

Halbrook paused. He rubbed his chin. He scratched the back of his head a few strokes. Then he smiled a smile that was not a real smile.

"Well, I guess y'all know more than I do."

I then felt that I needed to pull him back a bit with regard to his pride so he would not look as wily and ignorant of his job as he had appeared to be up till now. Carol seemed like she was chomping at the bit to hop in, but she held firm to our game plan.

"No, Mr. Halbrook. This is your county and your courthouse. We're just visitors here and strangers in a strange land just trying to get a little bit of information so we can set up our family reunion. All we need to do is find out a little deed information about some land our great-great-granddaddy bought down here in 1886."

He flinched. "1886! Boy that's a long time ago. Don't think we got anything in here that goes back quite that far. Did you check with the folks over in Holmes County? I 'spect that's where you people will find what y'all want. I reckon that's where you should check."

"Well, sir, we've been there, done that, and they told us to check over here with you. But first things first. Is there any way my sister here could help you find a copy of that big map? She works for our city's redevelopment agency and she's good with searching records."

"Well, I could look, but I know I'm not going to find what y'all want."

"Can Carol go with you while you try to find a map?"

Halbrook shrugged and gave Carol a half-beckoning sign to follow him into another record room. The second they left, I began the quickest scouring and perusal I have ever done in my life. I scurried to try to locate relevant books among the hundreds in the room from floor to ceiling that might be of some help. Bingo, a second book from the ceiling in one stack looked like a good prospect. Its binding read: *DEEDS / HUMPHREYS COUNTY, MISSISSIPPI / 1880 - 1890.*

There was another set of the giant maroon leather-bound record books. That set read *HOLMES COUNTY PROPERTY TRANSACTIONS.* They were neatly shelved by decades. Fantastic!

When Carol and the reluctant Mr. Halbrook returned to the main record room, I was fully armed with my directions for this senior official. Carol, in triumph, waved a legal size map he had found and copied. It was a map showing the names of some of the first black property owners on *Honey Island*. The names of Emanuel Gray, Henry Cade, George Byrd, and Weldon Jones were on this old map. But no Ned Rounds. We had to be getting closer, though. My dialogue, such as it was, with Mr. Halbrook continued.

"Now, Mr. Halbrook, sir, we know you're anxious to get us out of your hair so you can get back to work, but could we trouble you for just one more lil ole favor?"

I was surprised, as Carol must have been, at how much of a Mississippi accent I had adopted to make this "lil ole" request of Halbrook.

"Yeah, I do need to get back to work. Guess I spent a lil more time with you people than I had planned. Whatdya need now?" Halbrook sighed as if we had required him to run outside, pick up the Camry, and bring it back inside on his shoulders.

"We'd like to look just a while in some of these old book you got here."

"Which books? Don't think you'll find anything in these books."

"Well, if you don't mind, we'd like to check out that book way up yonder."

As I pointed out the second book from the ceiling in one shelved vertical row I couldn't believe I had conjured up the term "up yonder" to point out which book I wanted. There must have been some guidance from the spirits of Ned and Westly Rounds on the use of that phrase. I've never used it before and probably won't ever again.

"Y'all want me to climb all the way up there up there to get that there book way up there?

Halbrook appeared to be really getting his dander up now. He put his hands on his hips and I could swear his ears were getting redder. We couldn't see his neck, but...he was really getting pissed!

"I don't mind climbing up there," Carol volunteered.

I realized the psychology she was using on the old guy. If a lady could climb up the library ladder to get a distant record book, certainly no self-respecting gentleman would let a woman do a man's job. Her offer worked.

"Well, I guess. I guess I can go on up there. Y'all are gonna really be disappointed, though. No Honey Island up there."

Halbrook made the effort look like he was climbing Mount Everest. He puffed and huffed and gave us the impression that he hadn't done that much exercise in his entire life, certainly not in his long tenure as a county surveyor. He came down the library ladder like a Mississippi Moses carrying a stone tablet down the mountain. He handled the book awkwardly. I don't think he was faking that. The decade of handwritten documents on heavy pages that were at least two feet by two feet must have weighed a ton. Gasping for breath from this short exercise, Halbrook laboriously toted the book to a library table and let it slam down causing a puff of dust to escape and my dust allergy to activate.

Even though we could sense he wanted to get rid of us, Ole Jerry seemed a bit fascinated by the sophistication of our search and the homework we had obviously done. In very short order we turned to the page that constituted the deed in which Ned bought lots five and six in township 27 from Peter James Jr. Then, under Halbrook's wary eye, I swung around and nodded as if given his tacit approval to the removal of three other massive record books I had pinpointed while Carol and Halbrook were map-making in another room. These were some of the Holmes County Property Transactions, the ones for *1890-1900, 1900-1910*, and *1910-1920*.

Halbrook looked completely flummoxed; fleeced. His furrowed brow gave clear indication that he was not a happy camper. As he leaned on a file cabinet, he might have quickly decided that to show more anger would only give us clearer indication that he had tried to hide information from us and had failed miserably. I piped up with:

"I can't believe how much of your valuable time you've given us today, Mr. Halbrook. And I can't tell you how much we appreciate your patience in dealing with such rank amateurs as my sister and me. Now if we could look at just one more of your books."

"Y'all mean you want more books? Why, y'all already have more books off the shelf than anybody ever took down before at one time. Whadya have already, four or five books?"

Jerry Halbrook was coming unglued. He was acting like we had torn up his entire record library; like we had asked for the moon and were now begging for the stars, too. I sensed that my sister had some choice things to say to Halbrook, but I silently commended her for holding her tongue and holding her fire.

"We need just one more book. One more lil ol' book. We're trying to find out how much one of the last 'Honey Island' residents sold his property for. I believe it was just last year."

"Well, sir. This is Mississippi and if this fella sold his property just last year, we may not have even got a chance to record it down here yet. Could be another year before we get around to recording that recent a transaction. So I don't think you'll find anything here on that one yet.

"And y'all gotta understand where y'all are," he continued. *"Here in Mississippi neither the buyer or the seller has to put down a particular price on the county books. They can just put down somethin' like 'for ten dollars and other considerations.'*

"The 'other considerations' part helps block folks out from knowing just how much was paid. And here in Mississippi a seller don't even have to put down the exact dimensions of the property that changes hands. A fella could put down that he was sellin' to so-and-so two hundred acres of land 'more or less.' Hell, that could damn near be three hundred acres of land. But the 'more or less' part covers the rest of the territory.

"Just so the buyer and seller have winked at each other, if you know what I mean. And if you're sellin' a piece of land to a good friend or relative, you can put down the term 'for love and affection' to stand up for the value of the property. And it's all perfectly legal in Mississippi. So that's why, even if you find the transaction y'all are talkin' 'bout, the

paperwork ain't liable to tell y'all all that much."

"Mind if we look?" I asked more coolly than I wanted to.

"Where y'all gonna look?"

"How about that book right under your arm? The one you're leaning on."

Halbrook raised his arm as if a prized monarch butterfly might escape the sanctuary of his armpit. When I nodded that was, indeed, the very book I wanted, he couldn't help hide the fact that he had had enough. With the shortest leave-taking announcement ever uttered, Jerry Halbrook was gone. He had spent the better part (or worst part, to him) of an hour with us, and we knew he'd be kicking himself as soon as he got back to his office.

We applauded ourselves for prevailing. Except Carol expressed a claustrophobic shudder at being closed up in a dark, musty room with no windows and just one way out.

With our new treasure trove of reference books, we looked first at what we figured would be the easiest task—checking out how much Herbert Fullilove had gotten for his *Honey Island* property. We found it quickly. And guess what? The little speech Halbrook had given us about all the loopholes the state of Mississippi allowed to obfuscate the specifics of a land deal matched the sale of Ole Herbert's property to a "t." Right down to the "for ten dollars and other considerations" bit and the "more or less" recorded for the acreage. Did Halbrook have prior knowledge of the Herbert Fullilove deal? Or were deals like that so common that he was simply reciting a boilerplate? We may never know for sure.

What Carol and I found in the record books was shocking and heartbreaking. Like a very clear road map, we were able to track the systematic sell-off of the Rounds *Honey Island* homestead, first by Ned himself, and then by Westly. In addition to the distressing news about the sell-off of the family land, we also discovered that Ned owned more property than we had first thought. Four hundred and twenty-six acres—more or less.

The jettisoning of the Rounds *Honey Island* property began in earnest in 1899 and continued for a painful twenty years.

Sadly, there are few physical traces of *Honey Island* today. It has become an undistinguished part of the Humphreys County land mass and in its reincarnation the verdant farmland appears as many hundreds of acres of cotton fields and miles and miles of lakes dedicated to the spawning of catfish. In fact, Mississippi— and Humphreys County in particular— calls itself "The Catfish Capital of the World."

It is ironic that such a big commercial enterprise as the farmed fish trade would erase *Honey Island*. Next to farming, fishing was a fairly big business when the Rounds Family and their neighbors were comfortably ensconced in their rather isolated heyday. Fish caught in Eagle Lake, Tchula Lake, Horseshoe Lake, Bee Lake, and the Yazoo River was as likely as pork, beef, or fowl to end up as part of one of the Rounds' feasts. In fact, fish from *Honey Island* and its environs was packed down in ice and shipped by train as far north as St. Louis. The most prosperous *Honey Island* farmer of fish was Mark Clark who sold thousands of pounds of fish each year to the Meletio Fish Market in St. Louis. Clark, an enterprising black man, owned a section of Eagle Lake and from his personal body of water he shipped fish by the wagon loads to the big Meletio market and other points north. The wagons made the slow runs to Belzoni in Clark's wagons which were drawn by two-horse or two-mule teams. They traveled the four- to five-hour trek to Belzoni to meet the trains headed north. The dirt road to Belzoni was dusty and on hot summer days and unnavigable during heavy rains and infrequent snow. Clark might have wished that the mules and horses could have traveled faster to keep the ice melt at a minimum and thus keep his bream, catfish, bass, and perch fresher.

After about an hour of finding, copying, and photographing some documents, we left all the reference books in neat stacks and made our exit. Weirdest thing, though. It was only about three-thirty in the afternoon and the clerks who worked in the outer office had disappeared. There was neither hide nor hair of the chancery clerk or Mr. Halbrook, either. Their offices appeared be locked tight. Spooky. It was very early to have closed the chancery office. Carol and I looked at each other as we let the worst of our imaginations take over.

"*Let's get the hell outta here!*" I suggested.

"*Let's,*" Carol agreed.

And we did. Hastily!

My sister and I had finally come to the homeland and we had conquered some formidable obstacles in finding out from whence we had come. Odds were that we would find nothing. But we had discovered far more than we had expected.

We had suspected that the story of Ned Rounds and his *Honey Island* family, friends and neighbors was an extraordinary story. And what we found out exceeded our expectations.

Ned Rounds and His Honey Island Family, Friends and Neighbors

Those of us who are descended from Rounds ancestry can rest assured that we spring from very good stock. By every account—oral tradition or official records—the Rounds Clan has, for more than 175 years on American soil, been a proud, industrious, God-fearing, law-abiding, enterprising, independent, resourceful, tenacious, and family-oriented unit. There may have been a scalawag here or there, a scoundrel or two there or here, and a skeleton or two which managed to slip through a keyhole or under a closet door. But we don't have to own up to either if we don't want to, because *selective memory* is also a very strong Rounds trait. When all else is denied us, *selective memory* becomes a treasure worth its weight in gold.

The earliest Rounds forefather about whom we can find any detailed documented information is Ned Rounds. Through the years he told some inquiring minds that he was born in 1825 and others that his birth year was 1833. Census enumerator Henry Christmas reported for the 1880 census that Ned was born in Kentucky in 1825. In 1900, though, Holmes County census-taker F. A. Howell said Ned was born in Kentucky in January 1833. In 1900 then, Ned was either 75 or 67. Did Ned himself supply the information, or did the census-takers talk only to a neighbor? We will never know, but subsequent discoveries confirm for us that Old Ned did try to trim some years off his actual age.

It is an interesting fact that there is a lot of obfuscation in the Rounds family about birth dates. We can only offer conjecture about whether the muddying of the waters about when one was born was intentional or strictly a lapse of memory.

Remember here that *selective memory* has been one of the strong suits of the Rounds family members for more than a century.

Ned is listed on the 1870 Holmes County census, but it took some good detective work to ferret out the identity of my great-great granddad on that document. As we found with many records and documents, the spelling of names is so very often a highly inaccurate exercise. Enumerators, scribes, and county clerks often used their imaginations on how the names recited to them were spelled—especially if the subject before them was, like Ned, unable to spell his or her name. Couple this fact with the poor or flourished penmanship found on courthouse records, and one can understand quite easily how Ned is listed as *"Ed Rouwn"* on that 1870 census record.

The black man listed as Ed Rouwn was married to a woman named Ellen. That was the name of Ned's wife. Both are listed as unable to read or write. Both are listed as having been born in Kentucky. They are the only African American marrieds recorded in that 1870 Holmes County registry. A child Martha is listed as part of the household. Ed and Ellen also have a child registered as *Weston*. Too much of a coincidence with the Rounds' daughter Martha and the son who began spelling his name *Westly*. The ages of all four are either exactly or close enough to those birth dates listed in subsequent documents. Ned gave his age to the 1870 enumerator as forty-five. That concurs with the 1880 census birth year for him of 1825.

Add to this the fact that my Grandmother Hattie would always mention that her grandfather was from Stonewall. That's where he shows up in the 1870 census. She never added the "plantation" part in her storytelling, but I have learned through scores of anecdotal interviews with Blacks and Whites that deletion of the word *plantation* is a conscious or unconscious attempt to *unremember* the despicable nature of human bondage.

How did Kentucky-born slaves Ned and Ellen Rounds end up in the Mississippi Delta as the property of Peter James Sr., on the Stonewall plantation? James' next door neighbor according to the 1850 and 1860 censuses was a *"Negro trader"* named James Anderson. The "Negro" part of Anderson's professional title did not refer to Anderson's own race. It identified the African American people he traded like cattle. When Peter James arrived in Mississippi to try to make a fortune in the cotton business he would have had to go no farther than the doorstep of the slave trader right next to the property he bought to stock the plantation. Anderson may have had a direct connection to the slave trade in Kentucky.

With the help of archivist Jane Julian of the Kentucky Department of Libraries and Archives in Frankfort, we were able to get a good lead on Ned's past before he was sold into Mississippi slavery. In 1850, a white farmer named John Rounds resided in the town of Maysville, Kentucky. Could it be sheer coincidence that one of Ned's sons was named John Rounds? Maysville is in Mason County up near Cincinnati. The same census for Kentucky also lists a white farmer named Lewis Rounds who lived in Boone County and some Caucasian Rounds living in Knox County in 1850. In chasing down leads, we cannot discount some white Kentuckians listed in the 1850 census who spelled their surnames "Rouns."

Some other clues about just who Ned Rounds was can be found in the yellowed pages of the 1860 Holmes County slave schedule. A male of Ned's age is listed first on James' slate of slaves. Slaves weren't listed by name—age and sex was all the identification considered necessary. This male appears to be the oldest of the nineteen males and twenty-one females listed as the property of Peter James Sr.

Since no white overseer is listed on the Stonewall plantation manifest, perhaps Ned held that responsibility. Some of the white planters who moved to Mississippi to seek their fortunes could not tolerate the harshness and brutality of white overseers hired from the local stock. In his book, *The Hairstons,* Henry Wiencek recounts that Lowndes County Mississippi planter John Hairston "became so disgusted by the cruelty of the (white) overseers (imported from Virginia) that he met secretly with the slaves and urged them to resist and run away" when they were severely punished. Ned's owner, Peter James Sr., came from Pennsylvania before settling in the Mississippi Delta and may have felt more comfortable with a black slave "supervisor" of slaves.

There can be little doubt that Ned held some special status on the Stonewall plantation. In the scores of conversations she had with me over the years, Grandma Hattie always insisted her granddaddy was *never* a slave. She often chuckled about her grandfather's hands: "They were big, but smooth as a baby's bottom." Her description obviously did not fit the hands of a man who had picked cotton or done other hard, menial work.

Very likely Ned was one of the *"slaves virtually free,"* a term coined by noted historian John Hope Franklin in the late 1940s after an extensive study of the status of those held in bondage on southern plantations. Franklin found that some slaves were "owned" by their masters only on paper. Franklin also refers to this echelon of slaves as *"quasi-free Negroes"* and an *"American anomaly."* These slaves were given virtual free rein to move about freely, set their own work schedules, hire themselves out for odd jobs, and ply their skilled and semi-skilled trades quite independently especially on Sunday, the traditional day off for slaves. They were often required to carry some identification and learned not to venture too far away from the home-base plantation lest they be captured and claimed as the property of the catcher. To attest to the prevalence of free Blacks in the area around Stonewall, the 1843 Yazoo County tax rolls tell us that Ned's owner, Peter James Sr., lived on property adjacent to two *"free Negroes"* with the surname of Jackson. Ironically, an 1831 Mississippi state law forbade free Blacks to remain in the state and that law was still on the books when the Jacksons lived on the next property to Peter James and eventually to Ned Rounds.

A clear fact is that just seven years after government-ordered manumission, Ned is listed in the 1870 census as an independent farmer, not a sharecropper as some of the Rounds clan became after emancipation. Ned declared fewer personal assets than the adjoining black farmers: Alfred Johnson declared his net worth at $200; James Jackson told the enumerator he was worth $250; black farmer Ed Shaw declared his net worth in 1870 to be $300. And Ned? Just $157. Not even rounded up or down to $150 or $160. Why would a shrewd, secretive, and successful money-handler like Ned Rounds come clean with a census enumerator about how much money he had in his private cookie jar? Remember this is the same man who sixteen years after this estimate of his worth had that thousand dollars in cash to purchase a big parcel of land.

Ned had, indeed, become a wealthy man by the late 1880s. His name was known from Belzoni to Yazoo City as a canny capitalist who controlled a vast amount of cold cash. According to family legend and courthouse records, this extraordinary man who had probably once supervised slave labor, parlayed his managerial skills and eye for building on a buck into the position of laying out a small fortune in cash in 1886 for his biggest land purchase.

According to my grandma, Ned Rounds became a respected "banker" operating from the farmhouse he built on *Honey Island*. Stories abound in the Rounds family that even before the slaves on the Stonewall plantation were officially freed in 1863, they trusted Ned to "hold" their money for them. After emancipation, his reputation as a fair and honest banker earned him many more customers. Part of his success was that he employed an interesting twist on modern banking. Instead of paying his customers a nominal interest on the money he kept safe for them, Ned charged the depositors a small fee to guarantee the security of their nest eggs. What's more, from his asset total, Ned made loans at a respectable rate of interest. He was even said to have some Caucasian customers. In an additional fee-based service, Ned served as a head-hunter, an agent supplying and managing labor outside the Stonewall plantation grounds. He eventually hired field hands from a labor stock he trusted to work the hundreds of acres of cotton fields he purchased on *Honey Island*.

There was yet another service provided by the president of *"The First Bank of Honey Island."* Stories were handed down that when someone whose money he was keeping came to Ned to make a withdrawal—to buy something like a mule or a wagon or a piece of land—Ned wouldn't release the money at the drop of a hat. He'd have to first see the proposed purchase for himself and give it his stamp of approval before turning over the money he was keeping. He became notorious for denying a customer his money when he thought the money was being spent on a bad deal. Ned was even reported at times to be a tight-fisted judge of human behavior. It was said that if a customer came to Ned and asked for five dollars of his own money to go into town, buy a couple of big cigars, do some gambling, maybe pick up a loose woman, and get drunk on a Saturday night, Ned would give him a caution and only three dollars. The customer was, according to the stories, eternally grateful to Ned after he survived the Sunday morning hangover that Ned's stinginess had saved the poor guy two bucks which otherwise would have been blown.

Whenever Ned received a deposit or needed money for a withdrawal or an investment or a loan, he would head out to the dense pine woods beyond the Rounds family farm compound. Word spread far and wide that this was his *modus operandi*. According to family legend sparked by Grandma Hattie, one day when Ned slipped into the woods he was waylaid by two robbers. When they yelled *"Stick 'em up!"* or *"Your money or your life!"* or whatever robbers yelled in the late nineteenth century, the would-be bandits were flabbergasted and outright disappointed to discover that *Honey Island's* banker didn't have one penny on him!

He swore he didn't know a thing about buried money, explaining that he was simply taking a little walk to check on his farm which ran all the way down to the river. What money? The embarrassed bandits let the well-respected and well-connected banker go. He did not know them, which suggests that they must have come from outside *Honey Island*. Ned's big secret, according to my grandmother, was that he never kept any money in those pine woods. He had constructed an in-ground safe covered up with straw and a couple of chicken coops in the hen house out back of his house. He took the trip out to the woods as sheer subterfuge to draw attention away from the location of the real stash of cash.

Need a ride into town? Belzoni or Yazoo City? Ned Rounds was the man to see. He would never drive you himself, though. That would have been too much like work for him. For a nominal fee, though, he would gladly lease you a horse- or mule-drawn wagon for the day. The choice of beast depended on how fast one wanted to get to town and back to *Honey Island*. He'd let you know that a horse cost more that a mule to rent. He'd only lease to relatives or those whose money he held. That way he'd be sure of your return. Ever the fair capitalist, the transportation fee was based on one's ability to pay.

There were a couple of other services Ned provided for his *Honey Island* friends, family, and neighbors while at the same time pumping up his own personal fortune. He provided loans with affordable interest, based sometimes on the interest he thought a customer could pay. And while he never hung a shingle outside his house, there was the "Ned Rounds Pawn Shop." He would "hold" a ring, pocket watch, shotgun, or saddle for a certain sum with the idea that the item could be sold if not reclaimed in a certain time. Grandma Hattie remembered that her grandfather always had nice jewelry and "doodads" that he wore and used.

With his cleverness and all the fiduciary irons he had in the fire, we can now figure out how this genius Ned—a man who could neither read nor write— produced nearly two thousand dollars for property purchases over the decade beginning with 1886.

Ned's physical being was as impressive as his banking skills. He was reported to be more than six-feet tall; a big-boned man who eventually through his lack of physical exertion and his love for good, rich, fatty foods put about three hundred pounds on those bones. His size, no doubt, contributed to his aura as a powerful man.

Grandma Hattie also remembered that her grandfather, Ned Rounds, was the spitting image of Colonel Harlan Sanders. Yes, the Colonel Sanders she thought looked so much like her grandfather was the same guy who is associated with the popular finger-licking Kentucky Fried Chicken. She remembered that his hair was silky white and worn long at shoulder length. He sported a white moustache and goatee that were fashionable among Kentucky gentlemen—facial hair kept neat and trim among those who lived and hailed from the land of Ned's birth.

His skin, according to his granddaughter, was a light olive hue. In a characteristic that remains in the family today among the men and women of the Rounds clan, there were no wrinkles on Ned's face even when he was a very old man. There were intimations that Ned was the illegitimate son of a white Kentucky planter. The light color of his skin may have been responsible for these rumors and for his higher status and his assignment as an overseer. Throughout the nation's period of slavery and beyond, lighter-skinned blacks became the house servants while those with darker skin were relegated to the cotton fields.

Ned, and later his son Westly, took every opportunity to dress in a suit and necktie or cravat. He is said to have topped off his banker's attire with a fedora, the hat that became popular among sophisticated gentlemen after 1831.

What of Ned's beloved wife, Ellen? Her birthplace on several census reports was also Kentucky, and we can assume that she, too, was sold to Peter James Sr., and traveled to Mississippi with her husband. She was with Ned for the 1870 and 1880 censuses. By the 1900 census she had passed from her family's life. Ned is listed as a widower living alone by the turn of the twentieth century. Had Ellen lived, and had she given consistent information about her birthday, she would have been sixty-five in 1900.

According to the 1880 census, Ned's mother and father were also born in Kentucky. Genealogists speculate that Ned's parents most likely came to Kentucky from Virginia, since most early nineteenth century residents of the Blue Grass state migrated from the Old Dominion. The genealogies of African

Americans in the New World are often sketchy because we were very often, upon being plucked from the soil of Mother Africa, listed as chattel...property... goods...merchandise. As such, the slave master exercised the right to name or rename his property, placing a brand or tag on the chattel to keep it subservient to the white population. In most cases, the black slave was given no surname. Not until after the Civil War were last names generally used.

For first names, slaves were sometime allowed to keep their African name or a name that told from whence they had come in Africa, such as in the Ball Family of South Carolina's Binah, Pino, Angola Amy, or Ibo Clarinda. Sometimes male slaves in particular were given absurd or anachronistically grand names like Jupiter, Plato, Caesar, Adonis, Goliath, Cupid, or Pompey. Female slaves who were not given the same kind of superordinate names like Cleopatra, Queen Esther, or Sabina could be given diminutive monikers like Big Mammy, Little Sally, Nanny, or Pinkie.

Author/scholar Edward Ball found in his research of the family who owned more slaves than any other single family in the nation's history that mulattoes were often fathered by the so-called young masters, the unmarried heirs to a plantation. In his bestseller, *Slaves in the Family,* Ball noted that:

"Mulatto children were often given names that distinguished them from the larger slave population, and Frederick was such a name. Checking other slave lists, I found this was the only Frederick on any of the Ball (plantations) for some twenty-five years."

Ned certainly bears one of those British names that would suggest a closer relationship to a master than most other slaves would have had. Ned is, of course, the diminutive of *Edward.* Ned is identified as Ed in the 1870 census of the Stonewall plantation. Veddy British.

HONEY ISLAND

By 1880, Ned is identified as a gentleman farmer in the area of Holmes County, Mississippi called *Honey Island.* Ned was actually one of the pioneers and co-founders of this community that was once-racially-integrated, then eventually became an all-black community. Its land mass of rich, black soil was once surrounded by a lovely necklace of lakes and swamps and brakes and forests including Eagle Lake, Tchula Lake, Bee Lake, Dead Man Lake, Town Lake, Grassy Lake, the Yazoo River, Matthew Brake, Morgan Brake, and that virtually impenetrable marsh land to the southwest, the *Panther Burn Swamp.* By some oral accounts, the little island was hidden to a great degree by the lakes, swamps, brakes, and river.

Few pioneers coming in from either direction could find "Ned's Paradise" easily. According to one *Oldtimer, "You definitely had to know where you were going to find it."* Many would-be homesteaders may have turned away at the swamp or the brakes or the river not knowing that just on the other side of them was rich, fertile, farmland with rich, deep, black alluvial soil—sometimes subject to devastating flooding—but with a wonderfully long growing season when it wasn't raining more than the area's average fifty inches of precipitation each year. *Honey Island's* geographic obscurity contributed to the relative peace its inhabitants enjoyed. Except during the Civil War.

Honey Island was, during its farming heyday (and hay day), snugly nestled between two "big" cities. Well, they were never really all that big. Belzoni was to the north, Yazoo City just to the south. When a *Honey Island* resident during Ned Rounds' day and up through the 1930s told anybody he or she was *"going into town,"* they no doubt meant going into Belzoni. That was the *Honey Islanders'* first choice of the two cities. Yazoo City also got a lot of business from Ned Rounds, his family and neighbors. The transportation to either town involved hitching up a mule or two to the family wagon.

Holmes County, the seat of government in which Ned Rounds signed the papers on his first land deals, is named after Mississippi Governor David Holmes. The fourth territorial governor, Holmes was named the state's first governor when Mississippi became the twentieth state of the Union in 1817. He later served in the U.S. Senate. The area was, of course, Indian territory before Holmes or any other settlers set foot in the region. The Choctaw and Chickasaw let the territory in the west central section of what was to become the "Magnolia State" slip through their hands. They first officially lost the land, which they never fenced or surveyed or intended to own, on October 18, 1820, through the terribly lopsided *Treaty of Doak's Stand*. Ten years later, these unfortunate Native Americans were further swindled out of their Mississippi home grounds in a document called the *Treaty of Dancing Rabbit Creek*. It was just two years later, in 1832, the Choctaw and Chickasaw were forced to give up the remaining land rights they held in Mississippi through the ultimate bamboozle history will forever call the *Pontotoc Cession*.

The population of Mississippi exploded in the decade between 1820 and 1830. Just those ten years alone saw an estimated 30,000 settlers staking out property the Native Americans had been tricked into giving up. That decade saw a 175% increase in the pioneer population when compared with the number of whites who had staked claims recognized in the 1810 U. S. census. What is more amazing is that seven million acres of land were sold in that decade of boom between '20 and '30. Almost all the purchases were made on credit—no cash down and shaky payment terms were the order of the day. My great-great-grandfather, Ned Rounds, was given no such deal by the buyers who later sold land to him. President Andy Jackson was so angered by the sloppy handling of Mississippi land deeds that, by executive order, he slammed the door on easy credit in 1837. Most likely Ned would not have been given any "deals" anyway because of his race. Federal land offices were required under Jackson's new decree to accept only cash on the barrel head. No more E-Z Credit! That action caused land prices to drop like sow bellies after feed time. President Jackson's executive ruling caused speculators to look for land west of Mississippi. Texas became the next big target of those who had more land-grabbing dreams than cash.

Some of the oldest settlements in the area near the future Rounds homestead on *Honey Island* dried up and blew away. Towns like Georgeville, Montgomery, Rankin, and Vernon were erased from maps just as quickly as they had sprung up. The town of Rankin, nearest Old Ned's eventually-owned property, was one that just vanished after President Jackson's order. Mileston, remembered by all the *Honey Island Oldtimers*, was a casualty of westward expansion. The little towns met their demise just a few years after the mass exodus began from *Honey Island* following the devastating Great Flood of 1927. There's not much more than a gas station today in what was Milestone, a town where the *Honey Island* postal rider used to go shortly after 1900 to pick up the mail that had arrived by train for the Rounds family and their neighbors from points north.

The big, foreboding swamp the *Oldtimers* remember was the *Panther Burn Swamp*. This large bayou still appears on today's maps while *Honey Island* has virtually disappeared from the face of Mississippi maps and road signs and memories. The *Honey Island* schoolhouse—which doubled as the Jones Chapel Missionary Baptist Church and was the one-room schoolhouse attended by many members of the Rounds family and their neighbors—was listed as the *Panther Burn School* in early state records. It was the *Panther Burn School* that provided my mother, her two sisters, and their contemporaries, with their basic education.

How did the swamp and the school and the area get a name associated with the elusive panther? Apparently there actually were panthers roaming the woods and hillsides around *Honey Island* when the Choctaw, Chickasaw, and earliest white settlers first crossed paths. Charles Hoessle, director of the St. Louis Zoo, believes the wild cats seen by the early residents of the Mississippi Delta were actually mountain lions. Hoessle also tells us that down through history these big cats have enjoyed the most far-flung range of habitat of all wild felines in the United States. Hoessle also notes that these animals the Choctaw and Chickasaw respected and the first white interlopers sometimes hunted to protect their lives and livestock, have had more names than any other big cat. They are variously called panthers, wild cats, cougars, pumas, catamounts, concolours, leopards, jaguars, and painters. Although their coloration varies greatly from the basic tawny hue, the basic animal by whatever name is anatomically the same. Hoessle has no doubts that "panthers" actually roamed the Mississippi Delta and were revered by the Indians and feared by the settlers. They were known for their stealth, their speed, and the fact that they had no fear in attacking prey three or four times their size.

"Burn" is an old Scottish word for a brook, a little river, or a well fed by a brook. *Honey Island* was just about twenty five miles northeast of the marshy *Panther Burn*. The first inhabitants of the area around *Panther Burn*, the Chickasaw and Choctaw Indians gave us many of the terms we still use today for the land and water configurations around *Honey Island*. The Choctaw provided our vocabularies with the descriptive words to describe a marshy area: *bog* and *bayou*. Just before the Native Americans were pushed out and eventually forced onto a reservation seventy miles east of *Honey Island* as the crow flies, the first white settlers of the land were of Scottish and Irish birth. Tiny towns within a few miles of where *Honey Island* flourished as a prosperous farming community bear Scottish names like **Baird** and **Glen Allen** and **Inverness.**

There appear to be more lakes within a hundred-mile radius of *Honey Island* than in almost any other part of the United States. The cornucopia of lakes is really something unique and beautiful. The lakes in the *Honey Island* environs are big, curvaceous, and meandering. If one were coloring them blue on a map, one would have to avoid staying inside any lines to give the bodies of water their due. Each has a peculiar formation which is intriguing and enchanting. The *Honey Island Oldtimers* fondly remember fishing in, boating on, and being baptized in Tchula Lake, Bee Lake, Eagle Lake, Bear Lake, Ole Lake, Gar Lake, Deadman's Lake, Wasp Lake, Silver Lake, Townson Lake, Lake Discovery, Fullilove Lake, Long Lake, Grassy Lake, Horseshoe Lake, Hard Cash Lake, Fish Lake, and Big Kilby Lake. None of these lakes during their best seasons was a sniveling little spit of water. Each had and has its own personality and has never been too hesitant to overflow its banks to join its flooding cousins during the rainiest of seasons. Together they could make the Delta farmer and wayfarer come to full knowledge of what the term *nightmare* means.

The two lakes that impacted most on the lives of the *Honey Island* inhabitants were Eagle Lake and Tchula Lake. Lake Tchula, right across the road from the Jones Chapel Church, was a dependable fishing site, but it was Eagle Lake that provided most of the fish the islanders ate. *Honey Island* resident Mark Clark had quite a large section of Eagle Lake on his property. In fact, many of his neighbors thought and still think Eagle Lake *belonged* exclusively to Mr. Clark. His lake was the source of many tons of fish packed in ice and shipped by Illinois Central train in the earliest days of the island to such northern markets as St. Louis.

Because Tchula Lake was right across the road from the little whitewashed church at which many of the *Honey Island* residents worshiped, it was also the body of water in which members of the Missionary Baptist parishioners washed away their sins during the moving and colorful baptisms. The earliest Jones Chapel congregations could look right across the road and see in that once beautiful lake a site of commerce, recreation, and spiritual renewal. The children who attended the *Panther Burn School* could skip stones, skinny dip, and fish in Tchula

Lake when nobody else was using it for grownup-type purposes. The youngsters knew better than to try to swim in the water just across the dirt road from their church/school. The sinkholes there were treacherously dangerous. Nobody could remember how everybody knew that fact, but sanctified baptisms and recreational swimming were done in a more shallow spot a quarter mile from the church/school.

Some of the *Oldtimers* remember that Tchula Lake, during its golden era, was big enough to provide docking for steamboats bringing supplies and sometimes the mail to the islanders. Lake Tchula seemed to be a good area for the steamboats to turn around and head back to the spacious Yazoo. The steamboats, which delighted young and old with their deep-throated steam whistles, mesmerizing paddle wheels, and fantasmagoric general appearances, made most of their visits across from Jones Chapel when the lake and the Yazoo River which fed it were high. That was mostly in the spring, fall, and winter. Sometimes the lake was too low in the summer for the steamboats to ply its waters and chug and churn through their turnaround exercises.

When *Honey Islanders* were baptized in Lake Tchula or took a dip to cool off in the sweltering Delta summer heat, they had to watch out for the snakes and alligators that also enjoyed Tchula Lake's charms. Mattie Williams remembers that the alligators would sometimes lie floating camouflaged on logs in Tchula Lake.

"You couldn't tell the gators from the logs," she recollects, *"so you had to really keep your eyes open if you were fishing or swimming in the lake or if you were having a picnic down on the banks of the lake."*

Some of the *Honey Island* men would show off their macho images by sneaking up on and catching a gator. First thing to do was lasso Brother Gator's powerful snout and tie it shut. Then the gator cowboys would throw a burlap bag over the alligator's head so he couldn't see what was going on. During the whole process of capture they had to keep watching out for the ferocious power of the gator's tail. One sound smack from that tail could slam a full-grown man into the next county!

"They're good eatin', course you could only eat the tail," Mrs. Williams remembers. *"The rest of it was real tough. But if you took off the hide, cut the tail meat in chunks, dunked it in an egg batter, rolled it in seasoned cornmeal, and deep-fried it, you had a real treat."*

In addition to its plethora of lakes, the Mississippi Delta which created *Honey Island* has its unique *brakes*. A *brake* is a product of a tropical rain forest. It's a thicket overgrown with brambles, cane, bushes, and shrubs. Generally, you won't find *brakes* in the United States outside the South. Near and around *Honey Island*, travel is still impeded by the enchanting Snake Creek Brake, the Mathena Brake, Morgan Brake, Toney Brake, Horseshoe Brake, and the Tipton Brake.

Then there are the creeks—pronounced *"crick"* in Mississippi. Tesheva Creek, Snake Creek, Fannegusha Creek, and Black Creek are among the scores of other watercourses.

As we paint the picture of the *Honey Island* environs, we cannot leave out the several bayous blossoming from some of the aforementioned lakes and the Yazoo River. The Yazoo is a devilishly meandering snake of a river which seems to be totally unsure of where it wants to go, how it wants to get there, and what it wants to be when it grows up from time to time.

The Yazoo is prolific. It loves to produce bogs and bayous. There's the Gunn Bayou, French Bayou, Atchafalaya (pronounced by the natives *Sha-fa-LAH-ya*) Bayou, Tipton Bayou, and the Parker Bayou. All are near *Honey Island* and all are well-known to the *Oldtimers.*

What incredible geography lessons the kids must have had at the *Panther Burn School* if a teacher had asked the youngsters to name and write down all the rivers, brakes, lakes, creeks, bogs, and bayous that surrounded them and influenced their daily lives!

It is, indeed, a favorite prank of all these Mississippi Delta bodies of water to join hands—or at least join fingers—in certain spring and winter seasons designated by the Almighty to challenge Mississippi farmers in the same spirit in which the Biblical Job is challenged. Some Delta farmers have been able to ride out the flooding, regroup, and go on to face other challenges. Other farmers like those in the Rounds line couldn't stand up to the on-again, off-again caprices and onslaughts of the hell of high water.

One Andrew Haynes appears from the government's General Land Office documents to be the earliest owner of a *Honey Island* homestead. He made his first land purchase of record in Mississippi in 1835—some ten years after Ned was born in Kentucky. On September 25, 1835, a plot of 78.48 acres of *Honey Island* land was registered to Haynes. Over the next five years or so Haynes snapped up homestead parcels totaling nearly 1,103 acres of rich soil ideal for farming cotton, sugar cane, corn, and some tobacco. Haynes' acquisitions stopped for some reason on December 10, 1840.

Andrew Haynes probably did not see the black clouds that were forming over the property that the Rounds family would eventually own. There were disputes over slavery and over states' rights issues brewing when Haynes began buying up his Mississippi properties. Surely those disputes weren't of sufficient fury to warn him that the land he purchased encompassing *Honey Island* would, within a quarter-century of his getting the deed in hand, become a real hotbed of military battles, skirmishes, encampments, hideouts, and retreats. *Honey Island* and the land and waterways in its vicinity were not the least bit cooperative with the Civil War efforts of either side of this monumental and devastating conflict. The island often showed its inhospitable nature to outsiders by bogging down their transport during its rainy seasons, stopping short forward advances in its reedy marshlands, thwarting passage by its lack of passageways, and generally hiding itself from the outside world when it wanted to take the stand of pacifist.

CIVIL WAR YEARS

During the War Between the States, *Honey Island* got its first national attention as a strategic military point as early as November 12, 1862. That's when Union General William T. Sherman, camped at Memphis, wrote to Admiral David D. Porter, commanding officer of the United States Naval Forces at Cairo, Illinois:

"Now my information is that eleven large, fine (rebel) steamboats are on the Yazoo (River) below Honey Island; *nine in one group and two on farther down."*

On March 26, 1863, Union General C. A. Dana penned a communique to Secretary of War E. M. Stanton in Washington that he had learned from a planter who lived on the Yazoo River:

"That river is fortified (by Confederate troops) at Shell Bend and at Honey Island *much more powerfully than at Greenwood."*

Scouts for the southern army reported back to their superiors in a January 6, 1864, letter from Major W. H. Cameron to Lieutenant Colonel Thomas M. Jack encamped at Meridian, Mississippi:

"In the southern counties of the state bordering on the lake shore our operations are chiefly confined to collecting cattle and hogs. Upon Honey Island…*there are upward of 2,000 head of beeves which are obtainable when the rise of water in the swamps forces them to the mainland."*

Since we believe that Ned Rounds and his family were in the *Honey Island* area by 1860, we can only imagine that some of the cattle and livestock that Ned herded and fed were among the "beeves" Major Cameron espied and craved to feed his hungry troops.

We confirmed information that my great-great granddad and his family witnessed a stream of troops—Confederate and Union—who went AWOL and hid out in the murky swamps and piney woods in and around *Honey Island*. General H. Maury reported to the Confederate high command on March 12, 1864:

"…some few scattered outlaws are still lurking about in the swamps and still have to be hunted out with dogs. They have scattered in every direction; some west, but most for Honey Island *and the coast. They brag that they will get Yankee aid and return."*

The Confederate Army communiques also indicate that southern soldiers were hiding out in and around *Honey Island*. In an order dated April 25, 1864, Confederate Lieutenant Colonel Thomas M. Jack directed troops to:

"… move upon Honey Island *and clear it out, driving such men as may have sought refuge there over into Louisiana."*

Ned Rounds and his family may then have seen something truly incredible to them: African American soldiers in Union uniforms arriving on the *Honey Island* homesteads to ferret out the deserters. Major Martin M. Pulver of the North's Twentieth Infantry, Corps d'Afrique Expeditionary Forces, wrote to his superiors:

"On the morning of the 4ᵗʰ (of April 1864) I landed three companies on Honey Island *and crossed over to the East Pearl River, coming out just below the mouth of McCall's River."*

To further indicate the terror, confusion, and involuntary involvement Ned Rounds, his family, and neighbors surely experienced as the war raged on—and to tell us how soldiers on both sides of the conflict hid out on *Honey Island* after giving up the will to fight—we find this communication written by Confederate Brigadier W. L. Brandon to his high command in Alabama and Mississippi on August 14, 1864:

"A number of Yankees, in concert with deserters, both from Honey Island *and vicinity, have been committing serious depredations in the region of country bordering upon Jones and Jasper Counties, driving off large numbers of negroes and a great deal of stock."*

There are more than a dozen other communiques written by both southern and northern field commanders that specifically cite *Honey Island*. Interestingly enough, the last mention of *Honey Island* we can find in the wartime annals of either army is a letter written by the commander of an all-Black unit. On September 13, 1864, Lieutenant Colonel Alfred Hall, leader of the Seventy-fourth U. S. Colored Troops, wrote to his command at Fort Pike, Louisiana, that his troops were conducting a frantic house-to-house search for rebel soldiers on *Honey Island*. The black soldiers first searched a deserted house once owned by one John Porter. No luck. Then they barged in on a house owned by *"the Widow Joyner."* She told them she had seen three rebels armed with shotguns and pistols riding like bats out of hell earlier that morning. Apparently, the isolated Confederate soldiers had seen the black smoke bellowing from the stacks of the *J. D. Swain*, a crippled old steamer the Union detail had commandeered. When the boat chugged into Lake Tchula, Mrs. Joyner told them the Confederates had fled. A frustrated and empty-handed Colonel Hall wrote to his command center:

"There are probably a number of rebel calvary at Honey Island*, but with our steamer it was useless to attempt their capture, our approach being known to them hours before, and unless they choose to fight us they could easily avoid us. Although unsuccessful in overtaking any rebel force, <u>the inhabitants expressed the desire that our troops come often</u>."*

When the water was high, it was actually possible to see thick, black smoke belching from smokestacks of the steamboats that plied the Yazoo River. That fact alone may have prevented any Civil War blood from being shed on *Honey Island*.

Many of the *Honey Island Oldtimers*—including my mother, aunts, and Mississippi cousins—remember the Joyner family members who are descendants of the Widow Joyner. The Joyner's little house right on the banks of Tchula Lake was an important place for the Jones Chapel Missionary Baptist flock and for those who chose to wash away their sins in the lake. The Joyner house was where the newly-converted changed into and out of their baptismal robes for at least six decades after Union army troops quizzed Mrs. Joiner in their effort to chase down the enemy.

Ned Rounds left no hand-me-down stories about what he saw, heard, and experienced while Union and Confederate troops stormed through and around *Honey Island* during the Civil War spying, pillaging, and plundering at will. He would certainly have been old enough to have been conscripted into the army— he was in his late thirties while the war raged.

Nor did he leave any official records of service in the military during the war. There were approximately 180,000 African Americans in 163 units who served during the War Between the States. The father of the man who married Ned's granddaughter, Ninnie, fought with distinction. George Byrd Sr., served with the Tenth Regiment of the U. S. Colored Infantry. The fact that he had children before 1860 and after 1865, but not during the war years, does hint at an absence from home, maybe the result of some wartime activity.

A Mississippi soldier who bore the Rounds family name was a casualty of the war. Charles Rounds served in Company G of the Fiftieth U. S. Colored Infantry. He died on August 12, 1863, in Vicksburg, a casualty of disease contracted in the line of duty.

There were only two dirt roads into and out of *Honey Island* during the Civil War. *Boone Deaden Road,* which the author recently found, is still located on the island's southern boundary. My sister Carol and I traveled from its southernmost point north until it intersects just east of *Honey Island* with what the *Oldtimers* remember as *Full Love Road.* The Jones Chapel Church is located just off Boone Deaden Road. Many *Oldtimers* now in their eighties and nineties remember the road as *Boone's Deadenin.'* So many of them call it that one has to wonder if the current name on the road signs is wrong. In fact, some of the *Honey Islanders* who live in the region today swear that the road is called *"Boose Deadenin' Road."*

Full Love Road was named after the prominent *Honey Island* family, the Fulliloves. When one speaks of the Fulliloves today to any of the *Oldtimers*, the question invariably comes up *"Do you mean the white Fulliloves or the colored Fulliloves?"* We can't be sure which branch of that particular family gave the road its name. Regardless, the early roads traversed by the *Honey Island* residents in their mule-drawn wagons were always soggy in spring, dusty in summer, and sometimes snow-covered and impassable in winter. Fall was just about the best time to use these unpaved roads for a trip to a neighbor's spread or into Belzoni or Yazoo City.

Full Love Road and *Fullilove Cemetery* and *Fullilove Lake* are also named for the prolific and illustrious *Honey Island* family with the romantic surname. The family is still so much intact that many of its members held a family reunion in Chicago in 1998. There is little doubt that the name is a southern elision of the words *full of love*. The racial listings for the entire large Fullilove clan spans the possibilities. Some of the Fulliloves to this day live as Whites; some live as Blacks and some of Ned Rounds' Fullilove neighbors were listed in various courthouse documents as "Mu" for mulatto, a person of mixed black and white blood. The word comes from the Spanish for *young mule*—a not-too-flattering etymological genesis of the term used primarily throughout the South for these light-skinned people.

The head of one branch of the Fullilove Family of *Honey Island,* Mississippi, and there were several, was Taylor Fullilove, or Fulilove as it was sometimes spelled. Taylor Fullilove was born in Alabama in 1852, so he was three years older than Ned's son, Westly. Mr. Fullilove's wife is not listed in the thirteenth census of the United States, recorded in 1910. We might, therefore, assume that she had died by that year. Divorces were rare, indeed, in the Victorian Age in general and the turn-of-the-century South in particular. Death appears to have prevented the frustrations that lead to a couple formally splitting up and getting official papers of dissolution of a marriage.

Census information tells us that there were at one time or another twelve Fullilove children in the Taylor Fullilove branch. Six of them still lived with their father on *Honey Island* by 1910. They were 25-year-old Mary, 26-year-old Margaret, 21-year-old Henry, 18-year-old Minor (a daughter), 16-year-old Geneva, and George Fullilove, age 13. The children's paternal grandparents also lived on the Fullilove farm. Robert Fullilove is interestingly enough listed as "B" for Black on the 1910 census, while his wife, Adeline is listed "Mu." Grandpa Fullilove's age is listed as 88; Grandma Fullilove was ten years younger than her husband.

So far as education in the Fullilove home was concerned, Taylor Fullilove and all his children but one were recorded as being able to read and write. The census-taker did note that George could read but not write. The children's grandparents are both recorded as being illiterate.

The Fulliloves were probably among the lightest-skinned residents of *Honey Island* before 1900 rolled around. In fact, some of the Fulliloves passed for white after they grew up and left the secret of their black blood firmly behind them in *Honey Island*. Of the 7.5 million Blacks registered by the 1890 U. S. census (11.9 percent of the total population) 15.2 percent were recorded as mulattoes. Compare that number to the 12 percent of the African American population tagged by the census-takers as being of mixed race just ten years earlier. Interestingly enough, government statistics tell us that the mulatto population was actually lower in the South than in any other part of the nation. Mulattoes like the Fulliloves, Roundses, Pattersons, Hansons, and Fieldses of *Honey Island* constituted 159 out of every 1,000 Blacks in the South, 390 per 1,000 in the

West, and 644 per 1,000 in the North.

A rather curious practice began showing up in many of *Honey Island's* black families from the earliest days of this unique community. In the households of the islanders of pure African descent there appeared mulatto babies. So as not to come face-to-face with the fact that these children of mixed race were the offspring of the black woman of the house and a white man outside the household, these children were often listed by census enumerators as *"niece" or "nephew."*

Such was the case of a member of the Westly Rounds family. The 1880 census finds a ten-year-old girl living with Westly and Hager Rounds. Her name was Josephine McDaniel. While every other soul in the house is listed as "black," this "niece" is listed as a mulatto. Could young Josephine have really been a discarded niece of West or Hager? Even though Hager would have had to have given birth to this child at age thirteen, might Josephine actually have been a stepdaughter to West sired by a white man named McDaniel? None of the *Oldtimers* remembers a Josephine McDaniel. There are no family stories about her. After the 1880 census, she seems to have just slipped from the pages of history. If her skin had been light enough, perhaps Josephine "slipped over" and passed for White as so many thousands of other Blacks did in the South and the North.

A black couple, Sallie and Riley Kelley, who worked on the Peter James plantation near the Rounds homestead on *Honey Island,* had a child of mixed race living under their roof. Another Black *Honey Island* couple, Ruffin and Ernestine Maize, had two daughters listed as Black while their third and youngest daughter was reported by the enumerator in 1910 to be "mulatto." Recessive genes? Or was it what was called in the Old South, *miscegenation?* Or perhaps one's color or race was simply a subjective judgment call made by the census-taker.

Ironically, the parents of these interracial children would have found it socially uncomfortable to get married should they have chosen to do so. Some of the *Oldtimers* remember that sexual liaisons with white men—especially the plantation master or town brutes—was not usually the idea of the black women who bore their children out of wedlock. Nobody can remember an incident in which a white woman became pregnant by a black man. It is the consensus among former *Honey Island* residents that the black man would not have lived long after the impregnation. Although racial intermingling in Mississippi was strictly forbidden and harshly punished, another state got the jump on Mississippi in formalizing punishment for the taboo. Indiana began levying fines in 1840 to punish any white person who married a person with more than one-eighth African blood. Offenders could pay fines of up to $5,000 and serve prison terms of up to twenty years! The Indiana clerks who issued the marriage licenses and the ministers who married interracial couples could also be slapped with a fine— the clergymen up to $10,000.

It took the Mississippi state legislature four decades to catch up to Indiana in this matter of race-mixing. That body passed a law in 1880 making interracial marriages in the Magnolia State illegal.

Some of the mixing of races in and around *Honey Island* was between Blacks and Native Americans. Chalmers Archer Jr. notes in his book, *Growing Up Black in Rural Mississippi*:

"Seeing Indians, I found as I became a little older, was not at all an uncommon phenomenon. There were a lot of them in the area and a great deal of intermarriage between Negroes and Indians. Just look around and see how many Indian-looking Negro people are living around here (Holmes County) today."

The complexion, high cheekbones, and naturally straight hair of Ned and Westly and their descendants would suggest some mixing of Black and Indian blood if those traits are not from some Caucasian planter or overseer.

Back to the Fullloves. Along with the Rounds, Weldon Jones, Patterson, and Clark families, they were thought of as well-to-do. They owned a considerable chunk of *Honey Island* property. Some of the *Oldtimers* remember that some of the Fullloves kept to themselves, seeming to prefer isolation. Islanders remember seeing some of them only when they came to pick up the mail at the *Honey Island* post office or a Fulllove or two could be spotted in Belzoni picking up staples. Some thought the family members had their "high yeller" noses turned so heavenward because of their fair skin. They appeared to some to be shunning any notions that would associate them with the African blood that coursed through their veins. Others thought the Fullloves remained remote because of a sad family embarrassment they had difficulty hiding.

The young, fair, tall, and beautiful Minor Fulllove was mentally ill. Apparently, from the time of her birth in 1892 she was "never quite right in the head." "Tetched in the head," as some of the old-time islanders put it.

Poor Minor would sometimes roam *Honey Island*—in her neat dresses and pink ribbons tied to the tips of her long, black silky tresses—from dawn till dusk. To the tsk-tsking of some of the Fulllove neighbors, Minor could be heard alternately howling, moaning, gurgling, screaming, growling, baying, sobbing, laughing, chirping, and shouting—all while making grotesque facial expressions and "slobbering like a dog with the mange," as one *Oldtimer* remembers. Although she was given free range of the island, it seemed to suit her sad fancy most of all to walk 'round and 'round and 'round a lake on the Fulllove property. Nobody seemed to be afraid that she might fall into the lake and drown. Though she never did, the pitiable child would get almost totally and hopelessly tangled sometimes in the grey Spanish moss that dripped from the ancient trees that ringed the Fulllove's lake. She was a veritable apparition; an eerie, swamp creature after a few turns around the lake.

In the stillness of a *Honey Island* night, the *Oldtimers* remember that Minor's piercing, oxyphonic screams could be heard for miles. Some of the *Oldtimers* who remember Minor well recollect that she always had a big, bloody, ulcerated sore on her arm. It never healed because she kept biting the sore and screaming as if she were being torn into by a pit bull. She would leave the house most of the time with the sore cleanly bandaged. Then within minutes of her wild appearances around the island she would rip and tear at the bandage with her teeth until it was completely chewed off.

Some islanders wondered why her father, grandparents, and siblings would allow her to wander away from their farmhouse so often. Other islanders reasoned:

"Honey, if you had a chile that was makin' all them crazy noises, wouldn't you let her get out away from you pretty much all the time?"

The pitiful child unwittingly and half-wittedly terrorized the island's pets and livestock and frightened the living hell out of some of the little children, at least the ones who were not mean-spirited enough to laugh, mock, and poke fun at her. She baffled the *Oldtimers* who clucked and whispered their opinions about why the otherwise lovely girl had lost her mind. More than a few times one of them was heard to mutter the *"there but for the grace of God"* line that made them give their healthy and quite normal offspring an extra hug. Some gossipy pronouncements were that Minor cracked up on the death of her mother. Others were certain she was possessed by the devil himself. Still others swore she was living punishment for some sin that her father, Taylor, had committed. There were even more sinister stories floating around the island about how Minor's mother had died and the hand the father might have played in her death. The promoters of this dark tale, it should be pointed out, could produce absolutely no proof of their theory.

To compound the tragedy of Minor's sad life, she became pregnant and bore a child when she was just a child herself. Nobody knew for sure who the father of the child's child was. Nobody on the island every saw Minor's offspring and nobody could ever say for sure what ever happened to the child of this child. Who was the father? There were more suspects—inside and outside the family— than there were lakes in the Mississippi Delta. A brother of the wretched young creature was the prime suspect.

Poor Minor's tragic mental condition would get the least sympathy from white southern segregationists and their kin in the North. Pro-slavery activists like John Calhoun had, for half a century before Minor's birth, used the 1840 federal census to support their theory that the combination of race-mixing and freedom spelled certain mental insanity for a significant number of Blacks. For the first time in the nation's history, the U. S. census of 1840 enumerated the number of "insane and idiots" in the general population. It concluded that the incidence of mental illness was eleven times higher among freedmen than among slaves. Four years after the census reported these statistics of questionable authenticity, a Massachusetts physician and specialist in mental disorders, Dr. Edward Jarvis, found the census finding preposterous. Dr. Jarvis, the father of the American Statistical Association, reported that many towns in the North had listed more insane Blacks than their total Black populations. Jarvis found something even more ridiculous about the 1840 census. He discovered that some towns that had listed insane Blacks among their populations had no black residents at all! A loud protest by professional statisticians around the country and by a group of New York Blacks got absolutely no reaction from Congress and no change in the ludicrous census report.

Minor's mental distress surely had nothing to do with her mixed blood or the fact that her family was free during the awful period of slavery. If there were incest involved in the conception of her own baby, that child might have some mental problem.

Another *Honey Island* family bore what would have been to others an embarrassment. Caesar Cummings, the son of a respectable island family, was what the residents called a "water head." We would more respectfully and intelligently refer to him today as hydrocephalic. *Oldtimers* remember that his head was "three times bigger than a normal person's" and was, in fact, so large that the poor boy—when he finally learned to walk—had to toddle along with his head leaning to one side or another. Jonas and Della Cummings loved their son, even with his highly visible birth defect. They, along with Caesar's older brothers, Cleo and Thomas, took good care of the boy and didn't mind the stares he drew from even the most understanding soul. Little Caesar would never be abandoned in an environment as loving as *Honey Island*.

HONEY ISLAND: A LAND OF MILK AND HONEY

Since the Rounds family and many of their neighbors lived so well and were so self-sufficient, they needed far fewer trips into town than those in surrounding areas who were not blessed enough to reap the *Honey Island* bounty.

Ned's sizeable house was on a higher elevation than his cotton fields below. He hired the newly-freed, the down-and-out, and those who needed jobs to support families to work the Rounds' cotton and sugar cane fields. According to his granddaughter Hattie, he would stick his big hat on a broom and prop it in one of the six windows on the front of the house almost every one of the week's six work days. That was so the workers in the fields below him would look up occasionally and see a shadowy figure that appeared to be watching and supervising them. But, as the story goes, while the hat on the broom was framed in a window, Ned would spend a good part of the day napping. The subterfuge apparently worked. The field hands toiling in the distant shadow of Ned's house would swear that he was the most vigilant overseer they had ever known.

Ned's wife Ellen was, according to the old stories, considered by a small cadre of local women to be so well-off that they hatched a scheme to poison her tea. The plot failed. The tenacious Ellen drank, but survived, the tainted tea. This remarkable woman was listed in the 1880 census report as a laborer. Other wives on that government enumeration are posted as "keeping house" while dear Ellen is listed as doing more for the Rounds household than housekeeping. Perhaps it was necessary for her to do most of the back-breaking hard work on the farm so that her husband could take meticulous care of the business side of the farm dealings, concentrate on his job as "banker," and mediate and moderate the concerns of his vast family. And, of course, an essential part of his day was the business of taking little siestas.

The womenfolk who were fortunate enough to be born into or marry into the Rounds family had specific chores which no self-respecting married man would ever be expected to perform. The ladyfolk were kept busy minding the young 'uns, feeding the chickens and livestock, gathering the eggs, milking the cows, cooking three meals a day, and washing and ironing and mending the laundry. During any free time they had, the Rounds women—as with all the other *Honey Island* ladies—were expected to take a turn in the fields picking cotton, shucking corn, hacking cane, or tending the produce gardens. The exceptional industry of the kind the Rounds women exhibited began to fade outside of the Rounds compound and was rapidly becoming old-fashioned in the South of the 1870s. According to the authors of *Freedom: A Documentary History of Emancipation, 1861-1867*:

"(Black) women whose households included wage-earning men or older children were especially likely to spurn labor in the field gangs. Freed women on one estate refused to cultivate any crops except those in their (own) gardens. Rejecting to join other workers in the fields, women on another plantation served notice that they were 'ladies and as good as any white trash.'"

The Rounds women were all diligent and dedicated to the proposition that hard work on a family-owned compound was a far better lot than working as slaves or as sharecroppers.

Mondays were the traditional days to do the wash and hang the clothes on long lines held by tall posts out back of the house. Tuesday was the day for ironing those fresh-smelling clothes. In the late summer and fall, while the Rounds men—with the noticeable exception of Ned and his son Westly—labored in the fields, the Rounds wives and daughters canned many hundreds of fruits and vegetables for the winter. The items were "put up" in Mason jars. When the paraffin was poured on the top of each food item in the jars to seal out air, the jars were capped and stored in a dark, cool closet in the kitchen or in the smokehouse that doubled as an icehouse for the entire long summer.

In the winter, a kiln—as *Honey Island Oldtimers* called it that—was constructed to preserve Irish potatoes, sweet potatoes, turnips, and onions. A flooring of straw bales was laid out, and then around that base, cornstalk stacks would be stood to form thick walls, and a roofing of stalks would be put on top. The produce would be put inside the well-insulated kiln and a tarp put over the construction to keep the produce warm enough to keep it from freezing. With the canned goods and the kiln-protected produce, the dining room table fare didn't look much different in January than it did in June.

The men plowed and tilled, hoed and planted, and hacked and harvested the crops. The *Honey Island* farmers and laborers also butchered the hogs and pigs, plucked the chickens and other fowl, and together kept the houses and outbuildings on the Rounds properties patched up against the perennial attacks of time and climate.

The farm which Ned Rounds established became a prosperous property. There were, according to the *Honey Island Oldtimers*, at least four or five mules, half a dozen horses or more, hogs, cows, pigs, chickens, ducks, turkeys, and geese on the big Rounds homestead. In addition to the cotton, Ned's farm produced corn, sugar cane, and a veritable cornucopia of vegetables including greens, cabbages, turnips, cucumbers, tomatoes, potatoes, yams, and okra. The Rounds farmers also grew pumpkins and watermelons and cantaloupes. All the peaches, pears, and plums that could not be eaten by the large Rounds family or bartered in exchange for a neighbor's goods or sold in nearby Mileston or Belzoni were canned. Ned and Ellen also grew flowers which were sold, shared with neighbors, or used to adorn the long dining room table that was always covered with a tablecloth at supper time.

Ned, and later his son West, demanded a clean tablecloth for every meal. Both father and son always got fully dressed for supper, including a string tie or a bow tie neatly tied onto a starched white shirt. These country gentlemen even insisted on a linen napkin for themselves at mealtime. The rest of the family members might have a nice, clean piece of cloth to serve as a napkin, but Ned and West always had to have a finished linen napkin. Some of their descendants also remember that neither Ned nor West would ever eat any foods with his fingers, not even the common finger foods like corn on the cob or fried chicken. Never. West, no doubt, inherited the edict from his father that proper etiquette in a civilized household required that all victuals be consumed with a knife, fork, or spoon. Barbarians and those ancestors from another continent ate with their hands. Little children were allowed to attack their food with their fingers—as long as they weren't too messy.

There are many stories handed down about the Rounds' generosity. Whenever neighbor Louise Fields ran out of milk for her family—and that was often two or three times a week—she'd pop over to the Roundses with her bucket. She was the plump little mulatto wife of James Fields and the mother of four children, all listed on the census as "Mu" except the father. Even though the Fields family was not a poor family, they were never turned away from the Rounds' door. Mrs. Fields would always make a joke of her milk-mooching. She'd always sing out with a smile as she swung open the Rounds family back door without knocking: "I'm here for the news!" Many dozens of times the member of the Rounds family who began filling the neighbor's pail would ask: "So what news do you want?" To which Mrs. Fields would say with a laugh that never lost its rosiness: *"Don't need to tell me now, honey. I already got it."* "News" was her euphemism for "milk." Neither Mrs. Fields nor anybody else who dropped by to "borrow a cup of sugar" in any of its forms of neighborly hospitality was ever charged one red cent or even expected to reciprocate for the Rounds' bountiful gifts.

The house that Ned built was, of course, one of the biggest on *Honey Island*. It was a one-story, rambling, eight-room structure built of wood. The four bedrooms were large and comfortable and held a maximum capacity of sleepers on any given night. The large living room was cozy and inviting and featured something that none of the other Rounds neighbors could boast—an organ. A pump organ. Although we cannot be absolutely sure about the brand name of the organ in the Rounds house, it was probably an Estey harmonium. Deveaux and Kenney observe in their book about ragtime piano artist James Scott that these organs "were popular among poor but upwardly mobile blacks" around the turn of the century. They note that Booker T. Washington was a critic of the instruments in the homes of Blacks who would put "fifty cents down and (pay) fifty cents a week for the rest of their lives to own an Estey pump organ." Washington wrote in his book, *Up From Slavery*:

"In these cabin homes (of poor blacks) I often found (extravagant and irrational purchases). I remember on one occasion when I went into one of these cabins for dinner, when I sat down to the table for a meal with four members of the family, I noticed that, while there were five us at the table, there was but one fork for the five of us to use. Naturally there was an awkward pause on my part. In the opposite corner of that same cabin was an organ for which the people told me they were paying sixty dollars in monthly instalments. One fork, and a sixty-dollar organ! The organ, of course, was rarely used for want of a person who could play upon it."

The Rounds teenagers and their chums would gather around that organ on many Saturday nights. The organ was the focal point of some real partying. The little kids in the family and in the neighborhood were barred from even being in the living room when the teens like my mother and aunts convened. The youngest of the young would always sneak a peek or a listen from another room in the house or from outside on the front porch. Any brats caught in the act of spying would be chewed out, chastised soundly, and chased away. The adolescents didn't even bother to play or sing any church music with organ accompaniment. The teens probably got enough of religious music in their two hours of Sunday school, three hours of church service on Sunday mornings, and four or five hours spent with the Baptist youth group on Sunday nights. Nope. The teeny-bopper get-togethers around the organ in the Rounds parlor were strictly for honky-tonk, blues, and ragtime. None of the young people ever played the organ well, but even a one-finger rendition or two-finger duet emulation of some of the popular songs they heard on their family Victrolas was enough for some real fun. The only time hymns emanated from that organ in Ned's parlor was when Miss Ollie Joe dropped by. She was the church organist at Jones Chapel. Miss Ollie also taught piano, voice and organ lessons.

The kitchen in the Rounds home was always a gathering place, especially in winter when the big wood-burning stove furnished extra heat for hearty conversation. Here, too, as with all the things with which Ned surrounded himself, the kitchen stove was bigger than those of many of his neighbors. Whereas most of them had ranges with two burners, Ned's kitchen stove had six. Only a few well-to-do families like the Joneses, Clarks, and Fulliloves had kitchen ranges of comparable size. The huge iron stove had a big water tank attached to the back of it that was always kept filled. That steaming hot water was used for a multitude of purposes, like washing the dishes, laundering clothes, and taking baths. Sometimes the hot water on the stove, when placed in a tub with some Epsom salts added, furnished a soothing foot soak for tired tootsies.

It was known for miles around that the Rounds family never considered a person with an appetite to be a stranger. Many feet that parked under Ned Rounds' dining room table—especially for the lavish suppers—did not belong to relatives by blood or marriage. All who entered the Rounds home were welcome to dine on the family's prosperity. While Ned was master of the house and after Westly inherited the homestead, there would have to be two seatings for each of the day's meals around the big culinary communion table. The table sat ten comfortably at one time. Generally, the women who cooked would be among those who ate during the second seating. No pity needed to be expended about their having to wait to eat. This custom led to a family saying that is still heard today: *"Never worry about the cook!"* The cook always got a chance to nibble and sample the food she served long before the diners ever saw and consumed it. Notice that I say *"she"* served. That's because men seldom, if ever, cooked except in rare circumstances.

With all its amenities, the Rounds homestead—like those of their neighbors—originally had no indoor plumbing. To answer the call of nature required a sprint of about five hundred yards out back to the outhouse. As you might expect, Ned's outhouse was bigger than those of most other folks. His was a two-holer. One of the holes cut into the outhouse bench was for children, the other for adults. A trip to the outhouse was a dreaded venture, especially in the dead of night or the dead of winter or when it was raining buckets, and especially if one were scared of snakes, wasps, bees, spiders, or the Unknown. Then one had to resort to the chamber pot, or "slop jar" as this necessity was commonly called on *Honey Island*. Remember, there was no electricity on *Honey Island* when most of the *Oldtimers* lived there, and a night trip to the outhouse was, as Black poet James Weldon Johnson wrote of Hell, "blacker than a hundred midnights down in a cypress swamp." It can't get much darker at night than that. A trip to Ned Rounds' outhouse was avoided at all cost by children who were afraid of the dark. Perhaps that was why there were two seats. An adult could sit and keep a scared child company in the middle of the night.

Bath time on the Rounds homestead—almost always on Saturday nights—took somewhat of an effort. A big tin tub hung on a hook out back of the house. One took the tub into a bedroom, or sometimes kids were given a bath right in the kitchen. Once set, the tub could be filled with enough hot water for a good bath from the water tank connected to the kitchen stove. Sometimes the patient bather would fill and heat a teapot several times and then add cold water until the bath water was just right. Soap was made right in the house from lye and animal fat. A paste of baking soda and water mixed in the palm of the hand made an effective deodorant and teeth-cleaner.

There was also a larger-than-everybody-else's smokehouse out back of Ned and Ellen's house. Hogs and cows were butchered as needed. The hams and beef were often salted, dried a bit, and then hung until cured in the big smokehouse. A country ham from the smokehouse was a treat not only at Thanksgiving and Christmas, in the Rounds household, one would never know when a big country ham would be brought out with all the bounty of the Rounds homestead. It was here at *Honey Island* that the tradition of the lavish non-holiday breakfast, lunch, and supper was established. These feasts were—and are—devoured only after the head of the household, or a special guest is invited to pray. This simple prayer, sometimes embellished a bit, has been offered up around the Rounds' tables for at least a hundred and fifty years that we know of.

"We thank you, O Lord, for the food we are about to receive to nourish and comfort our bodies for Christ's sake. Bless the hands that have prepared it. And bless those who hunger and thirst for food and drink and for knowledge of thy word. In Jesus' name. Amen."

When Ned, West, or any of the Rounds men drove into town they purchased enough supplies to last them for a very long time, especially just before the long winter season. For all the mouths that had to be fed at any of the Rounds' dining tables, it was not at all unusual for a general store purchase to include a hundred-pound sack of sugar and a barrel or two of flour. As much as two hundred pounds of ice from the old tin-roofed Belzoni icehouse would be lugged back to the island for the Rounds' iceboxes. A thick layer of sawdust and a canvas tarp were put over the big ice blocks to slow their melting on the long road home. Kids, including my mother and aunts, who got to go to the icehouse would always gleefully beg a big sliver of ice wrapped in a newspaper cone to lick on the long way back home. They could stay cooled by their precious ice shards as they rode in the back of the wagon under a hot sun.

So self-sufficient were Ned and his sons that they set up their own cotton gin. Not only did they gin the cotton they grew on *Honey Island*, they also took in the cotton of their neighbors from miles around for processing. For a fee, of course. Ned was a generous man but he believed in free enterprise and entrepreneurship. The Rounds farms also produced tons of sugar cane. Did they have to take it into a big town to sell in its raw form? That would not have been the Rounds way of doing things. They had the equipment and the mule-power to process the cane right on Ned's and eventually West's farm. An old mule, whose days were generally numbered, laboriously and reluctantly treaded a circumference that created a circular trench around the huge vat in which the cane was ground to a pulpy syrup. Round and round and round and round the old mule trudged, prodded by a whack or two or three occasionally from a Rounds kinsman assigned to keep the mule on its toes. Was this not a better job for the animal than the journeys it used to make all the way into Belzoni and back? The trench that circumscribed the vat had to be filled in with cinders and dirt occasionally to keep the mule from slipping down into a perilous position in which a leg could be broken and a hitch snapped.

The same Rounds children, like my mother and two aunts, who begged for ice in Belzoni would beg a big piece of the unprocessed sugar cane to chew on. That's whenever their mothers would allow them to have a treat that wouldn't spoil their supper. The sweet pith from the cane fields was boiled in another enormous, scorched iron vat and the Rounds had a rich, thick, almost black molasses product to eat, sell to, or barter with neighbors. Or they could take the homemade molasses into one of the larger towns to market when there were any other reasons for making the long journey.

There were dozens of *Honey Island* residents listed by the enumerators in the decades just before and after the turn of the twentieth century as "Mu." Notably they were members of the James Fields family, the William Fulliloves, the Taylor Fullilove family, some of the James Hansons, the Willie Wilsons, the Huffmans, the McCoys, the John Kerns brood, the Pattersons and the McCains. Unmarried residents like John Griffin, the brothers Emmet and James Huffman are listed in the *Honey Island* stats as mulattoes. Anderson Patterson, the head of his household, is listed as a black resident while his wife and three children bear the "Mu" stamp. Same sort of listing for James Hanson and his wife and four children. As for Anthony Wallace and his family, Wallace is listed as "Mu," but his wife and six children are listed as Black. Same for Westly Rounds, Ned's son. Although Ned and Ellen Rounds are listed as Black, the 1910 census lists the then fifty-six-year-old Westly as "Mu."

It is highly likely that the early census-takers made a cursory sight judgment with regard to race. Many Blacks were not particularly proud of their white ancestry, just as many whites were not particularly pleased to have even a drop of black blood in their veins. Whether mulatto, quadroon, or octoroon, sometimes the race-related social status could go either way in determining how one lived the rest of his or her life.

There were actually some Caucasian families living on *Honey Island* farms in the post-Choctaw era when the Rounds family set up a homestead. The Shipp family farmed on the island in the 1880s. A white man named George Brown lived by himself on *Honey Island*, according to the 1880 census and worked as a mechanic on the island helping to keep farm gear working. There was the Peter and Mary Ella James family. The Jameses maintained a sizeable plantation where they hired a retinue of white employees. There was the young Lula McCarr who mostly taught the white children, but would teach a black child if the parents of the child promised to keep quiet about the book learning. She may have helped teach my great-grandfather Westly Rounds to read since the Rounds family compound was on land Peter James sold to Westly's father, Ned. Also working on the James plantation was a white woman named Ruth Irby who was just a couple of years younger than Miss McCarr. Irby is listed in the census report of 1880 as a boarder on the Peter James plantation and could have supported herself by doing the laundry, cooking, or serving as a nurse. The two women employees shared a small, crude little house on the plantation. W. D. Lawson was a white man who worked as a bookkeeper on the James plantation. In fact, Lawson helped any of the black farmers who were not getting their financial records kept by my great-great-grandfather, Ned Rounds.

The Whites all began to drift away from *Honey Island* just before the turn of the twentieth century in a pattern that would be repeated many thousands, perhaps millions, of times in towns, cities, and suburbs all across America. There was very often white flight when a community became and becomes too heavily Black. Tom McMurtry, his wife, mother, and four sons were about the last Whites to leave the island farm community. They were still around *Honey Island* for the 1910 U. S. census as the last white family around. The McMurtry family was gone by the 1920 government tally. Just into the century, *Honey Island* was an all-black farm community of more than eighty families, including those listed as mulattoes. It was apparent that there was a Victorian-era feeling on the island that birds of a feather should flock together. The few whites who remained may have felt a bit intimidated and pushed out by the surging influx of Blacks during the '80s and '90s.

While *Honey Island* maintained its black homogeneity from about 1890 until the 1940s, there were always thriving white-owned plantations encircling and sometimes encroaching on the property owned by Blacks. The editor of the

Lexington Advertiser, James T. Buck, took a 1935 tour of the *Honey Island* environs by bicycle to write a series of articles on the plantations in the region. Buck unabashedly made the trip to boost subscription sales. In the first of his articles, Buck refers to *Honey Island* as *"the garden spot of the delta."* The newspaperman visited and evaluated the Montgomery, Oak Grove, Hyde Park, Good Hope, Warfield, Graves, and Albino plantations. Most of these are listed as being actually <u>on</u> *Honey Island,* which leads us to believe that the physical boundaries of *Honey Island* were so fluid and so undefined that there were varying interpretations of just what constituted this historic site.

Many once-proud and independent families like the Roundses fell victim to what I call the "Four F's:" *foreclosure, floods, farming changes,* and *flight* to the urban North. The beaten-down black farmers on *Honey Island*, like my great-great and great-grandfather, were often more than willing to sell out to the white farmers who were anxious to snap up the rich Delta farmland after losing it for decades to the black farmers.

NED'S GROWING FAMILY

Ned and Ellen's oldest child, Lucy, was born in 1855 and was a year older than her brother, Westly. Lucy married a *Honey Island* laborer of mixed race five years her senior named John Bonner in 1875. The Bonners had two children, a boy they named Bob, born in 1876, and a little girl named Ellen after her grandmother, born in 1879. It is believed by some of the *Honey Island Oldtimers* that Bob succumbed to illness and did not live to adulthood. Ellen grew into a lovely young woman and married one John McGee in 1902 when she was twenty-two.

George, who followed West in the family, married a woman named Frances. They had eight children. Daughter, Martha, who was called "Mattie" by family and friends, grew up to marry the industrious young laborer, Tom C. Simmons, in 1887 when she reached the age of twenty-one. Tom was six years older than his wife. He left the little bachelor house he shared with his pal, Joe White, to take on a new wife and a new life. Martha and Tom were wed in the same year in which seventy African Americans were reported lynched in the United States, Florida enacted a railroad car segregation law fashioned after the 1881 Tennessee law, and the first "Negro League" baseball team, the *Union Giants*, was founded in Chicago by named Frank Peters. But *Honey Island*, Mississippi, was so isolated from the world that neither of the newlyweds, Tom or Mattie, would know about these newsworthy items. Neither would any of their relatives, friends, or neighbors have known. There were no newspapers flowing into *Honey Island* and the community's first post office was still twenty years away.

Ned and Ellen Rounds also had a son named John who was seventeen years younger than his brother Westly. John was born on *Honey Island* in 1873. Another son, Eddie, was born in 1875. Ellen Rounds was forty-two years old at the time, quite an advanced age for a woman in rural Mississippi to give birth.

Ned's sons would work the family land as laborers, with Westly as overseer. Each eventually married and brought his wife and then the couples' children into the quite large Rounds clan. John married a fine young woman named Cornelia Sparles on December 5, 1895, when he was twenty-two years old. John's kid brother, Eddie, took Miss Clarissa Crutes as his wife on New Year's Eve, 1897. He must have concurred with his older brother John that age twenty-two is a good time to get married.

Ned was considered by all his neighbors to be a prosperous gentleman farmer, if for no other reason than that he stood at the helm of a large nuclear and extended family spread out over the hundreds of acres he was bold enough—or foolish enough—to purchase. As the men and women who bore the Rounds name married and had children, that meant more hands to till the soil and plant, chop and pick the primary crop, cotton. Through his own enterprising resources Ned was, with the help of some of the other black families who lived on the *Honey Island* farmland, able to purchase a cotton gin and crude sugar cane refinery. That made Ned and his neighbors quite independent of the yoke borne by all the black sharecroppers all around their *Honey Island* paradise.

There are still remnants to this very day of the plantation on which Ned Rounds served as a "slave virtually free" more than 140 years ago. The original Stonewall plantation from which he moved from virtual enslavement to financial freedom and from beyond whose gates he set up a little independent kingdom, is known today as the Stonewall Planting Company. It is a 105-acre soybean and cotton farm outside Thornton with an official address on Bee Lake in Holmes County. A new entrance sign with landscaping went up just a short time ago. With the technological advancements that replaced arduous, forced manual labor, the Stonewall Planting Company, a limited partnership, today employs just twelve workers to do the work that was once done by more than three dozen slaves.

Were he alive today, I wonder if he would recognize the place. It's sad, isn't it, that nobody there would recognize him?

I've often thought about the particular eras of history in which I might like to live and in which I would have hated to live. While I obviously would not choose a period in history in which I would have naturally been a slave... I do think I might have enjoyed living on *Honey Island* during its post-slavery era in which my ancestors enjoyed lives of prosperity and fun.

 # The Deed Is Done

The first white settlers of the *Honey Island* territory appear to be pioneers from South Carolina. They set up temporary stakes just across the Yazoo River east of the eventual Rounds homestead. They organized a town and named it Franklin. Although it was incorporated and a small Presbyterian church was set up there just ten miles northwest of Pickens in 1836, Franklin has dried up and blown away. Pickens remains.

We've already established that the first owner of the land that eventually became *Honey Island* was one Andrew Haines who began snapping up lots on the island in 1835. He eventually owned, strictly for re-sale, more than a thousand acres of *Honey Island* riverfront property. Dr. Benjamin W. Sanders appears to be the next big *Honey Island* land tycoon of record. Five years after Haines, sometimes spelled Haynes, had jumped into the Mississippi Delta marketplace, Sanders followed with the purchase of the traditional 78.48 acre lot. Sanders had official papers documenting his ownership of Lots 1, 4, 5, and 6 in 1840 shortly after the land was put up for sale by the State of Mississippi. Ned Rounds evidently purchased Lots 4, 5 and 6, approximately 426 acres, about four decades later. Even though his land was slip-sliding away just before the turn of the century, Ned purchased another 160 acres on December 8, 1897. Was he mad? Or was he just tenacious?

Dr. Sanders, the second *Honey Island* land baron of record, was a Mississippi state legislator and president of the board of the Franklin Female Seminary. He accepted the seminary leadership on January 5, 1839, but it was a term shortened by his death. He died at home on August 31 of that year. Shortly after his death, his wife experienced more grief. The Sanders' one-year-old son, John Barbour Sanders, died on May 20, 1840. According to his will probated in February, 1842, Dr. Sanders left his property to his "affectionate wife and family of small children."

We fast forward now in our look at the *Honey Island* story to the period immediately following the end of the Civil War. This period gives us many clues on the later disposition of the land that became Ned Rounds' homestead. Reconstruction era Republicans in Congress wanted to punish the rebel landowners as harshly as possible for their secession and for the bloody, costly war they had promulgated. Although land grants and deed transactions regarding Mississippi land and properties throughout the Old South had come to a virtual halt during the war, the U. S. government began to exercise its muscle and authority once again after 1865. Part of the punishment meted out to the secessionists was the issuance of free government land to poor Whites and Blacks who could afford to "prove" up the land. In the year the Civil War ended, the General Land Office found itself with almost five million acres of Mississippi land at its disposal.

The government anxiously reaffirmed the Homestead Act of 1862. Under that law anybody, Black or White, who was head of a household or a single person, at least twenty-one years old, a citizen of the United States or declaring intentions of wanting to be one, and who had never "borne arms against the United States or given aid and comfort to its enemies" had the right to claim as much as 160 acres. All a would-be landowner had to do was construct some kind of house, no matter how crude, and improve the state of the land. If that individual could prove he had fulfilled these requirements for five years, he could get an official deed to the land. Provisions could be made to cut the five-year term short by buying the land at the government's minimum fee per acre.

The Southern Homestead Act of 1866 affirmed that "no distinction or discrimination shall be made in the construction or execution of this act on account of race or color." The 1867 Act limited the maximum acreage of the land one could acquire to 80 acres. That is why four of the five lots Ned would buy twenty years after the restrictive act was passed were 79.68 acres each. Confederate war veterans and Confederate sympathizers were prohibited from land deals with the government until 1887.

There was, however, a catch to the Homestead Acts of '66 and '67. Whereas thousands of newly-enfranchised Blacks in the Deep South could build a shack on a patch of land and clean it up for crops, many could not afford the initial $9 filing fee. With many of these African Americans having worked so recently as slaves, they didn't have the money to buy the farm equipment, tools, seed, and supplies to make the required improvements. Then there were some unscrupulous land office clerks who boosted the fee to whatever amount they thought the black applicant *didn't* have. That was the same basic scheme used to set up the "poll tax" that Blacks were required to fork over in Mississippi and throughout the Deep South to prevent them from voting decades later.

Even with these barriers thrown at them by racist white clerks, historian Michael Lanza found that under the Southern Homestead Act more Blacks than Whites were successful in proving up their land. Lanza found that of the 8,797 entries under the Southern Homestead Act, 6,415 applicants in Mississippi failed to satisfactorily prove up the land and stay on the property for a full five years. However, 35 percent of the black homesteaders proved up while only 25 percent of the whites who tried for the free land qualified. To further attest to the tenacity and resourcefulness of the black homesteaders in particular, all of the best farmland in Mississippi had generally been snapped up before the Civil War. That is, no doubt, why the more than four hundred acres Ned Rounds was able to purchase so relatively easily were available to this black farmer in a time and place in which African Americans were held in less than high esteem. Somebody, somewhere, for some time had known long before Ned arrived with cash in hand that while the soil beyond the banks of the Yazoo is rich, the farmer who plants beside the temperamental river is destined to be poor. Poor soil and thick timberlands greeted many of the black farmers outside of *Honey Island* who tried to clear what was left. Those land applicants who attempted the monumental task of taking down the big trees on land they tried to eventually own were often failures at logging. Those who were better farmers than lumberjacks were often bought out by big money interests who wanted the properties for their timber.

Ned Rounds would have been forty-one years old when the Southern Homestead Act was passed by Congress in 1866, but there is no evidence that he was among the determined black homesteaders who made the grade and took claim of land in Mississippi. Ned, a one-time slave on Peter James' plantation, paid his own way when the chains of bondage were formally cut.

From all accounts we could find, Ned had some special kind of status that kept him from feeling too harshly the bonds of slavery. Author Henry Wiencek who did extensive research on the multiracial Hairston family for his book, *The Hairstons,* reports that in the Mississippi of the 1830s and thereafter:

"Robert [Hairston] allowed his slaves a degree of autonomy and freedom of movement and had trouble with the more rigid control over slaves that was expected in Mississippi, where masters never gave slaves any autonomy."

Wiencek also found that Hairston, the laid-back Scotsman who owned seven plantations, became perturbed by the harsh treatment given his slaves by the overseers he hired to run his Lowndes County plantation a little more than a hundred miles northeast of *Honey Island* as the Jim Crow flies.

"John [Robert Hairston's brother] became so disgusted by the cruelty of the overseers

that he met secretly with the slaves and urged them to resist and run away."

This unorthodox sympathy for slaves was, without a doubt, the exception to the Mississippi rule of keeping slaves in line. The Peter James family, with their northern roots, may have recognized their slave, Ned Rounds, for the exceptionally bright man that he was and, thus, may have given him freer rein than many other African Americans in that region of Mississippi.

We do not know for sure how Ned came to occupy the first property on which he is recorded as a full-fledged farmer on August 9, 1870, by the census-taker. That's when he and his family are listed simply as living in the 354th dwelling visited by the enumerator. It is in this listing that a black man who was once a slave is listed in equal title with the white farmers around him. And the Roundses—with their surname badly misspelled as Rouwn—are listed simply as the 383rd family visited that year. Perhaps Ned and Ellen couldn't help with the spelling. Perhaps the enumerator was just plain tired in the brutal Mississippi heat and humidity after visiting 382 families before he got to Ned and Ellen's farm.

We can assume, though, that this is not the same piece of land Ned bought in 1886. In 1870 the Rounds neighbors on either side were the Austin and Lucy Ramsey family and the Thomas Jones family. In 1880, the neighbor farms flanking the Ned Rounds farm were the Peter and Mary Ellen James family on one side, and Ned's son West and his household on the other side. Since no record could be found after a thorough search, we may deduce that this 1870 farm is a parcel completely separate from Ned's 1886 purchase.

We know for sure that Ned actually purchased 216 acres from his white neighbor and plantation owner, Peter James, in 1886 for one thousand dollars cash and two promissory notes for five hundred dollars each. Later land records in the Humphreys and Holmes County courthouses indicate he had purchased a little more than two hundred acres before this 1886 purchase. Those earliest of transactions have unfortunately been obscured through a series of courthouse changes, a devastating Holmes County courthouse fire in 1893, and sloppy bookkeeping by courthouse officials in the three different courthouses, including the one at Yazoo City. Deeds of purchase seem to be missing, but Ned later sold this land so he must have owned it.

Since we were able to dig up some records which show that Ned started selling off parcels of Lots 3 and 4 of the 239-acre package on January 19, 1899, we can make a more accurate assessment of the total amount of land he owned. A land purchase deed recorded at 10 AM at the Holmes County courthouse by Clerk James Woods and dated July 30, 1886, reads:

"Know all men by these presents that for and in consideration of the sum of one thousand dollars to me in hand paid this day the 17th March, 1886, and the further consideration of two promissory notes of even date with this one Maturing first of January 1887 for Five

hundred dollars with 10% per annum interest from date until paid as vendors lien for this payment of some being retained on the within described land, I have this day signed and delivered unto Ned Rands [sic] his heirs and assigns forever and further solemnly agree to warrant and defend title to the same the following described land situated and lying in Holmes County Mississippi to wit: Lots 5 & 6 sec 27 Township 15 Range 2 West and all appurtenances thereto belonging containing two hundred and sixteen acres more or less

Witness my hand & seal   Peter James

    Witnesses: T.W. James

          James E. Lee

The deed was then notarized by Justice of the Peace H. P. Hosmer on July 24, 1886:

State of Mississippi

Holmes County

Personally appeared before me a Justice of the Peace in and for said County and state the above named T.W. James one of the subscribing Witnesses to the foregoing deed who being first duly sworn deposeth and sayeth that he saw the above named Peter James whose name is subscribed thereto sign, seal and deliver the same to the above named Ned Rands that the said deponent subscribed his name as a Witness thereto in the presence of the said Ned Rands and that he saw the other suscribing [sic] Witness James E. Lee sign the same in the presence of each other and on the day and year therein named In testimony whereof Witness my hand and seal this the 24 day of July AD 1886.

                  H. P. Hosmer JP

Ned Rounds' signature—or in the case of this man who could not read or write—his "X," was never affixed to either of the two documents. Only the seller of the property has to sign the deed.

The 216 acres of land were not enough for my land-hungry great-great grandpa. Even though there is every indication that he had difficulty paying off this first loan that required ten percent interest on two promissory notes of $500 each—financial obligations that became due very quickly after the agreement—he is on record as having purchased 160 additional acres an unlucky thirteen years after this first purchase. On December 8, 1897, Ned, in the late winter of his life stepped up and purchased, from an F. D. Watson land that was described as Lots 2 and 3 in Section 27, township 15, range 3 west in Holmes County. Ned put down $750 dollars on New Year's Day, 1898, and had to come to the table with $750 plus eight percent interest the following New Year's Day, 1899. This put his land holdings at 376 acres in Holmes County, Mississippi. He was obviously over his head.

March 17, 1886 Land Purchases / Ned Rounds:

  $1,000 Cash

  $500 Promissory Note @10% / annum / Due 1 / 1 / ' [87?]

  $500 Promissory Note @10% / annum / Due 1 / 1 / '88

December 8, 1897 Land Purchases / Ned Rounds:
   $750 Cash
   $750 Promissory Note @ 8% / annum / Due 1 / 1 / '98

In sharp contrast to the land transactions for which Ned shelled out his hard earned cash are documents which clearly tell us how the white family who sold Ned land acquired their parcels for virtual peanuts. Peter James Sr., born about 1788 in Pennsylvania and the father of Ned's neighbor, Peter James Jr., purchased at least three parcels of land under the Cash Entry Act of Congress passed on April 24, 1820. His acquisitions, interestingly enough, were purchased during the administrations of three different U. S. presidents: 87 acres of Mississippi land on October 1, 1825, under the signature of John Quincy Adams; 79 acres under the document signature of Andrew Jackson on October 20, 1835 and 80 acres of land on August 10, 1859 in a grant under the signature of James Buchanan. Although the price of all of James' land purchases may have varied by a penny or two, all those properties cost him on average about $1.25 an acre. That's $1.25 per acre! Two hundred and forty-six acres for $307.50. Contrast that with the 216 acres Peter James Jr., sold to Ned Rounds for more than $9.25 an acre.

Neither the United States of America nor the early land speculators ever gave Ned Rounds such a deal on a single square foot of land. Ned and his heirs worked and died trying to pay off his inflated land debts; obligations they could never meet. They lost everything in honest efforts to satisfy the deeds when the cards in the deck were stacked against them.

The fact that Ned Rounds is listed as an independent farmer in the 1870 and 1880 censuses indicates to us that his branch of the family did not work as sharecroppers after the Civil War. If they had, he and his nuclear family would have worked under some harsh work rules. The verbal contract between sharecropper and plantation owner was strictly a one-sided proposition, with the latter-day-master given the upper hand in every detail. To further cloud Ned's socioeconomic status in the two decades following the Civil War and the emancipation is the fact that he had somehow come into so much cash by 1886. Former sharecroppers who are among the *Honey Island Oldtimers* remember their single, end-of-the-year payment for their back-breaking work was often only a few dollars. All the *Oldtimers* who had worked "on the place" never got anything approaching the thousand dollars that Old Ned had in hand twenty years after Reconstruction began.

Ned Rounds' purchase of his *Honey Island* farm was paid for half in cash in 1886 on March 17; notarized on July 24, and filed on July 30. The slow pace of the filing over five months was not at all unusual in nineteenth century Mississippi—or anywhere else for that matter. The two neighbors, buyer and seller, one black, one white, must have trusted each other. Or it just may have taken that long for the witnesses and the two principal partners to all get together with the officials needed to record the transaction legal.

Peter James was, without doubt, a shrewd speculator in Mississippi Delta land. A document filed at the Holmes County Courthouse in Belzoni on November 23, 1885, shows that James purchased a piece of land at a cut-rate price under an act of the Mississippi State Legislature passed on February 1, 1877. That measure was made possible by a land grant to the state of Mississippi by an act of Congress dated September 28, 1850. In this transaction, James purchased 39 and 98/00 acres for $39.98. Just one dollar paid per acre. This is land James turned around and charged buyers like Ned Rounds, who were less cognizant of the state's bargain basement deals, at least ten dollars an acre. It was all legal and fair. We shall see later that the way in which Ned and his son, Westly, lost the land is steeped in questionable ethics.

A bigger question than who the white man was who would sell a black man a sizeable chunk of real estate in 1886 Mississippi is the question of where in the world would a 61-year-old black farmer who reportedly could not read or write get one thousand dollars in cash to cinch the deal with Peter James. Who was this black man who had the temerity to promise to make two more payments of five hundred dollars each at 10 percent per annum interest? Old Ned's purchase was just twenty-six years after a rebellious Mississippi had seceded from the Union and just sixteen years after the bloodied but unbowed Magnolia State had gained Congressional approval to re-enter the Union it had left.

Did Old Ned sell enough molasses, corn, and cotton at market to save up that amount from the time we know he was already an established agribusinessman in 1880? How much money did he rake in from selling his produce? How much did he earn as the "First National Bank" of *Honey Island*, the human and humane banking institution for Blacks who didn't know how to handle their money? Did he earn any considerable sum from leasing out the cotton gin he owned to his neighbors? Some of the *Oldtimers* remember that he also owned a modest cane refinery. Was he able to profit from that installation? Was Ned able to borrow the thousand bucks from his considerable large family and/or his host of friends and neighbors? Did Ned combine forces—and assets— with his children for the purchase even though his is the only name on the deed? Or did Ned simply apply the time-honored and still-revered Rounds Family Credo: *"MAKE A DIME; SAVE A NICKEL!"*?

We can get an idea of how much money a thousand dollars amounted to in 1886 by looking at some numbers supplied us by financial analysts at St. Louis-based Huntleigh Securities. Had that $1,000 been invested at the time of Ned's purchase and let lie for 112 years at 3.75% interest it would yield $61,754.39 today. If a government bond earning a compounded interest of 6 percent per year had been purchased, allowing for $61,754.39 to be eaten away by inflation (an average over the 112 years), the bearer of the bond could claim $682,742.46

today. Or, looking at it still another way, if the down payment Ned made had earned the same amount of interest he took on for the two promissory notes— 10 percent—that money would be worth approximately $43,000,000 today!·

Those lots were, by the way, extremely imprecise packages. Lots 2, 3, 5 and 6 of Section 27, Township 15 in Holmes County, owned by the Rounds family for awhile are identified in this quaint way on the original document as: *"...from whence a sweetgum tree South 24 degrees East fifty four links, thence South 16 and 2/ 100 chains from a hackberry tree South 28 degrees..."*

Imagine purchasing a piece of property based on two trees as markers! Whatever would happen to one's land claim if the tree marker were chopped down or blown over in a storm? I've been told that deeds are like this for twenty states, mostly east of the Mississippi. How strange!

A "chain," by the way, is a civil engineering term for a chain of 100 links of equal length having a total length of either 66 feet (Gunter's chain or surveyor's chain) or of 100 feet (engineer's chain). A "chain" can be further identified as four rods, poles, or perches; 0.10 furlongs; 1/80th of a mile; 22 yards; or 66 feet. A mile is 80 chains. The land bought and sold by the Rounds family was— when there were no distinctive trees about—measured just like officials determine a team's right to a first down at a modern-day football game.

Henry Christmas, the physician who also served as the U. S. government's enumerator for Holmes County where *Honey Island* used to be, was clearly confused by Ned's status and relationship to Peter James. Original copies of the 1880 census form clearly show that Christmas originally thought that Ned Rounds owned his own house. Peter James's homestead, with his wife, three sons, and retinue of servants, is listed as "Dwelling 19, Family 19." Ned Rounds and his family flow from Christmas' ink pen as "Dwelling 20, Family 20." But then, Christmas strikes and blocks out the inked entry to indicate that Ned was living in the same house as the James family in 1880. The original Rounds house where Ned resided with his wife Ellen and children: the then fourteen-year-old Martha, seven-year-old John, and five-year-old Eddy may have originally been slave quarters—an appurtenance to the big house. Ned had, by the turn of the twentieth century, added onto the house until it had six to eight rooms, by the account of some of the *Oldtimers* who had either lived there or visited there. It was six years after that confusing census entry that Ned was purchasing 216 acres from Peter James.

Recently uncovered records in the Humphreys County Courthouse in Belzoni show that Old Ned, the wheeler-dealer, bought another parcel of land on December 8, 1897. This transaction was for *"160 acres more or less."* Here's how the official deed reads:

F. D. Watson
To Deed

Ned Rounds

In consideration of the sum of Fifteen Hundred Dollars to be paid as follows: $750.00 on the 1ˢᵗ day of January 1898 and the sum of $750.00 on the first day of January 1899 which last mentioned amount bears interest from January 1ˢᵗ 1898 at the rate of 8% per annum both of which amounts are evidenced by the two promissory notes of the grantee herein of even date herewith & for the payment of which a lein [sic] is hereby redeemed on the land herein after conveyed. I do hereby sell & convey unto Ned Rounds the following lands in Holmes County, Mississippi to wit Lots 3 & 2; Section 27, Township 15 Range 3 West containing 160 acres more or less.

Witness my signature this 8ᵗʰ day of Dec. A.D. 1897.

F. D. Watson

After the deed was drawn up, the transaction was quickly notarized by the county clerk. Very quickly. Same day. That is totally uncharacteristic of land dealing in Mississippi, I was told. Many other transactions we found in Magnolia State courthouses took days, months, and sometimes even years to consummate in a "slow-as-molasses-in-January" pace. One can conjure up several reasons for the same-day service Ned got in the acquisition of the additional 160 acres. Was he given a high pressure sales pitch by F. D. Watson? *"Have I got a deal for you, Ned. Buy this land now or somebody else will get it. You need to get these lots 'cause they're right next to your other property and you can end up owning that whole area some day."* Watson may have coerced my great-great grandpa.

Reading through courthouse documents, Ned was not required to sign his "X" to the deeds. That most certainly must have worked to the advantage of those who stood like vultures in line to snap up the foreclosed Rounds properties. Imagine buying 216 acres of land and then another 160 acres today without ever signing one's name. Only the seller signs the deed. Ned may have signed the notes. Those don't have to appear in courthouse records. Did he understand all the terms? That's another question.

A good lawyer today might have had Ned's debts completely absolved when the Humphreys County sheriff rode out to notify my great-great-grandfather that he had defaulted on the two mortgages. *"Mr. Sheriff, may I see my client's signature on those notes?" "Mr. Sheriff, can you prove my client understood those papers?"* But coming back down to earth from Planet Dream-On, that would never have happened for a black man in the Mississippi of Ned's era. While Ned's "X" wasn't needed to buy his property, it appears on courthouse documents when he began to jettison his property just before 1900.

In spite of the sadness one might have with today's perspective about those land deals a hundred years after the fact, I'd like to think that Ned was *cool and confident,* not *ignorant and incompetent.* I'd like to imagine, too, that when asked by F. D. Watson if he could come up with the $750 in less than a month to make a land buy, Ned, dressed nattily in suit and tie, might have responded:

"Elementary, my dear Watson."

There is little evidence that Ned had enough of an entrepreneurial streak to buy the property with the forethought of turning it over quickly and making a profit as many of the white land dealers did so often. There just must have been a gleam in my great-great-grandfather's eye about being a land baron. We can only hope that he was thinking of the future of his large family's security and prosperity. At any rate, Ned, with his titular purchase of hundreds of acres of land, had far exceeded the expectations for a black man of his day and time. He was a landlord! By the turn of the century, he had avoided the yoke worn by sharecroppers after the shackles of slavery had been thrown off by many hundreds of thousands of Blacks.

Anecdotal and courthouse accounts indicate that Ned most certainly did not personally do the arduous work the other members of his family would have done in the blistering hot, muggy cotton, corn, and cane fields. Ned was, according to all legends, not a worker. He was, as we have said before, more of a manager of people, an entrepreneur, a banker-of-sorts, a foreman, a supervisor. But he was not personally into manual labor. Exactly how he would have escaped the rigors of the sharecropper's life is not clear to us. His weight may have played a part in the leisurely lifestyle he is purported to have enjoyed all his life. This "no love loss for labor" philosophy was passed down from father to son, from Ned to Westly. Westly was never known by the *Oldtimers* to break a sweat either.

****

Mississippi did not react well to the defeat of the Confederate cause in the war. Nor did she react well to the harsh punishments she received during Reconstruction. The Civil War bloodbath might have led to an epiphany for the Magnolia State, an opportunity to rectify some social sins and ills. But the postwar era put Mississippi in a stubborn mood, and onto a bitter and vindictive road.

Mississippi historian and history professor John Ray Skates puts it this way:

"...out of the destruction of war, Mississippians faced an opportunity to develop a new order to replace the old, to recognize that their old institutions had led them to divergence and disaster, and to start anew. Or they could reaffirm the old order, perpetuate and defend in the face of defeat as many of the antebellum institutions as possible.

"...Mississippi would reaffirm and re-embrace the old institutions under different names. Sharecropping and the Jim Crow system provided the same economic and social controls over the freedmen that slavery furnished before the war."

sharecropper, n. a tenant farmer who pays as rent a share of the crop.

One might expect that the 1863 Emancipation Proclamation would have signaled a thunderous mass exodus from the plantations that had kept African American slaves and their descendants in bondage for three hundred years.

Incredibly, that was not the case. After their shackles were unceremoniously cut away, hundreds of thousands of now former slaves elected to stay on the plantations to take on a new and almost equally degrading occupation as *sharecroppers*. To dress up their new titles, they were sometimes referred to as *tenant farmers*.

By all the accounts of the *Oldtimers*, a sharecropper was about a quarter step up from being a slave, if that much. While no member of the Rounds family can—or cares to—remember anything about slavery in the immediate family, a Rounds in-law was the closest former slave with whom we can identify. Annie West Rounds remembers the sad stories her grandfather told her about the cruel and peculiar institution of slavery. Rufus West Sr. was born a slave on a Mississippi plantation in 1843. He told his children and grandchildren that he never knew what his real last name was. As a young boy wearing only a burlap overshirt he was sold to some white people named West. He adopted their surname.

To illustrate one of the cruelest practices of slavery, Rufus West's brother was a very young boy when he was sold away from his family to slaveholders named Green. The brother took the surname Green. They were separated for decades while working as slaves on separate but nearby plantations. Then one day an astute train conductor at a railroad station who knew Rufus and his story noticed the physical similarities of Rufus and a black man who was working as a laborer in the Greenwood railroad station. He told Rufus: *"You say you lost your brother when both of you were sold to separate families? Well, I'll bet you a nickel that man over there is your long, lost brother."* And it was! The two men nervously recited the names of their mother and father and incredibly there was a match! There followed a tearful, but joyful, reunion on the rail station platform. The reunited brothers would never again lose touch with each other.

Rufus West would not talk to his children and grandchildren about the specifics of the hard life he and his family lived as slaves. Nor would he share stories about the harsh punishments meted out to independent-minded slaves or slaves who were not working at the capacity the masters or their overseers divined. It was all too painful to talk about it. He'd give brief answers to questions about the slave pain…if the questioner knew the proper question to ring a bell. Rufus West Sr. did recollect that his mother and the other slaves had to pray and hold worship services quietly and in secret to avoid harsh beatings. The former slave lived until 1928 when he died at the age of eighty-five. He had survived the awful institution of slavery and had endured the despicable quasi-slavery experienced by the sharecropper.

Under the sharecropper system, the whip that drove slaves in their backbreaking work disappeared, but in some cases, the plantation bell was just as feared as the whip. It rang out on most post-Civil War plantations at the crack of dawn to drive the sharecrop workers into the fields; pealed again on many plantations to give the field hands a short midday lunch break; sounded still again to announce that lunch was over. Interestingly enough, the plantation bell never sounded to ring out the end of the work day. It was only the descending darkness blanketing the cotton fields that signaled to the 'croppers that their grueling day in the field was finally over. It was not at all unusual for sharecrop workers to put in a fourteen-hour day—just as much time as the slaves had worked. The only difference was the couple of lunch breaks. And it was not at all unusual for a single slave or a single sharecropper – including those in the Rounds family – to pick three or four hundred pounds(!) of cotton in a single day.

History Professor John Ray Skates notes in his book, *Mississippi: A History*:

"Mississippi's dependence on cotton was perhaps greater after the CivilWar than before. The state became neither more industrialized nor more urban, neither more cosmopolitan nor less suspicious and insular."

The family of Chalmers Archer Jr., worked near the Rounds family homestead as Holmes County, Mississippi, sharecroppers and he remembers:

"On the plantation everybody was supposed to work except the very old and very young. Even the women were expected to do field work. Many times the older women had to work in the field, then leave and prepare a noon meal, take the meal back to the field for the other workers, then continue field work in the afternoon till dusk. Life on this plantation was as harsh in the 1930s as it had been a century before."

Mississippi plantation life appeared to be just a little easier for John Rounds, West's younger brother. John and his rather large family worked as sharecroppers after almost all the Rounds land was lost on *Honey Island*. Ned's sons Westly and George are listed as laborers on the Rounds family farm in the 1880 census. But John Rounds, who was seventeen years younger than his brother Westly, found no Rounds land left to work or inherit when he was ready to support his wife, Lutisha Syfax Rounds, and their eventual eight children—Eddie, Thelma, Josephus (called "Joe"), Lola Belle, Joanna, Almedia, twins Jessie and Essie, and Thaddeus. John and Lutisha and their brood worked as sharecroppers on the Glennburr plantation. The place, near Greenwood, was also called the Lucas plantation after old Thomas Lucas who had owned it under the oppressive rules of slavery and now was plantation master under slightly different suppressive rules (which were almost as unbearable for the laborers as the life they led in formal bondage). Glennburr plantation was nine miles north of Greenwood, right next to Money, Mississippi.

A living witness to the grueling life of a sharecropper is Annie West Rounds, now a St. Louis resident. She has vivid memories of toiling in the cotton and corn fields of the Glennburr plantation with her husband and father-in-law. All the Rounds children and grandchildren who were old enough to blister their fingers for life while plucking the cotton from the bolls and shucking corn by the hundreds of bushels worked for Old Mr. Lucas, too. Mrs. Rounds recently told me:

"*Jesse and a couple of our boys would go down to Ole Man Lucas' mule barn at the crack of dawn and get our two mules. We didn't own them, of course, but we could use them. The menfolk had to catch them every morning and harness them up. Them mules was ornery cusses, didn't want to work. And flat-out wouldn't work for somebody different every day. They had to know you before they'd work for you. And if you didn't be rough with them, they would just sit down or stand still and wouldn't budge. We needed them, though, to pull the wagon when we were chopping cotton and thinnin' out the fields. And we needed those big ole mean mules when we had to haul anything into or out of Greenwood. Quite honestly, I was always scared to death of them mules. I don't think you city folks has a single idea about how big and how mean of spirit a mule can be.*"

"How long was your typical work day during harvest and how many days a week did you have to work?" I asked her.

"*We headed out to the fields around six in the morning on a summer day. We worked our tails off until around eleven o'clock. That's when the field hands could go to lunch. We had a two-hour lunch—which is a lot more than workers on some other plantations had. We heard that some of them only got a half-hour or forty-five minute break. Guess we were lucky the plantation owner, Mr. Lucas, let us have two hours for a lunch break. Even when Ole Man Lucas got too old to run the plantation, his son-in-law, Mr. Hal Quackenbos, let us continue to have that two-hour break. We were worried for a time that the younger man, Mr. Quackenbos, would cut us back, but, thank God he didn't.*"

Mrs. Rounds told me that the designated cook in the family was permitted to leave the fields as early as ten-thirty each morning to start getting lunch ready. It was a coveted position that not everybody could fill. The cook not only got to leave the sweltering fields early, she/he got to nibble on the fare that was being served. Then of course the dishes had to be washed and cookware cleaned up and put away, so the cook might have gotten back to the cotton and corn as much as an hour after the field hands reported back to their stations. Annie Rounds was the cook for her large and hard-working family. She would generally wash and lay all the produce out the night before heading to the fields the next morning. That would make her work easier when she came in from the morning field work. Lunches were hearty affairs with such offerings as sliced tomatoes, cooked greens, hash browns, fried corn, fried fish, smoked sausage, cornbread, cheese, fried pies, or cobbler. A worker who gulped down lunch in fifteen or twenty minutes could have the rest of the lunch time to snooze.

Mrs. Rounds remembers that everybody in her large family would find a cool place on a hot day to pause from their labors and eat some lunch. Some took a nap. Some took a bath to cool off. Mothers of infants used the two hours to breast-feed their little babies. Youngsters who were too young to pick cotton— and they started working sometimes by the age of seven or eight if they were not sent to a school—might be left unattended to play while their parents labored in the field. Sometimes the young children of field workers were left in the care of a child who was barely two or three years older than the infants. The children of Mississippi sharecroppers had to grow up fast.

When the Glennburr plantation lunch break was over, the sharecroppers on the place would be expected to work until about seven o'clock or until sunset—whichever came first—or sometimes on plantations with the harshest overseers, whichever came second.

A plantation that was whispered by the Lucas field hands to be much harsher on the sharecroppers was the Racetrack plantation right next to Glennburr. There were reports of whippings and other cruel punishments for the least little infraction. Annie West Rounds remembers:

"That Racetrack plantation was a awful place! We would hear about some of the 'croppers getting beat up by the overseers and all sort of stuff. Ole Mr. Lucas was strict, but he wasn't near 'bout mean as them white people that ran Racetrack. At least Mr. Lucas didn't 'ride over us.' Racetrack had them white overseers who would ride through the cotton rows on big ole horses. And they would cuss and yell at the workers they thought were slackin' off and not workin' hard enough. The overseers over there would also carry sugar cane sticks and give colored folks in the field a whack across their backs to make them work faster."

"Why would the sharecroppers," I asked, "put up with this kind of harsh living conditions when they were technically, legally free? Why wouldn't they just pull up stakes and move on to someplace where they wouldn't have to put up with that kind of treatment?"

"Where would they go?" Mrs. Rounds asked, turning the question back to me and my naivete. *"Where would they go? Moving your entire family would be more than a notion. Times were hard back then in Mississippi. Lot of folks was scared to leave a plantation. That ole Klan was still operatin' and scarin' colored folks in the 1940s, '50s, and '60s. You leave a plantation and nobody might ever see you again. Chances are the overseers that rode over you by day was the Klan that rode over you by night."*

The daily life of typical Mississippi sharecroppers like the John Rounds family and the Jesse Rounds family was capsulized in a poignant poem written by author/ poet Anthony Walton, a descendant of African American slaves in Mississippi and now a resident of Brunswick, Maine.

Reconstruction

Free to plant
Free to hoe
Free to chop
Every row
Free to harvest
Free to pay
Free to borrow

Free to stay.

In fact, a law passed by the Mississippi State Legislature in November, 1865, strictly forbade newly-freed Blacks from roaming the state without supervision by a white person. African Americans who didn't establish a labor contract with a white landowner by the second Monday of January 1866, could be arrested and charged as vagrants. This was because, as Governor Ben Humphreys stated after the war:

"Several hundred thousand of the negro race, unfitted for political equality with the white race, have been turned loose upon society; and in the guardianship she (Mississippi) may assume over this race, she must deal justly with them, and protect them in all their rights of person and property."

Governor Humphreys added, lest any literate slave or abolitionist got too carried away by excitement:

"... it should never be forgotten... that ours is and shall ever be a government of white men. The purity and progress of both races require that caste must be maintained."

Moreover, the state of Mississippi in that 1865 legislation made it against the law for Blacks to own weapons and prohibited the engagement of Blacks in "riots, routes, affrays, trespasses, malicious mischief, cruel treatment to animals, seditious speeches, insulting gestures, language or acts, or assaults." Many decades later, Blacks like the Rounds family felt the Reconstruction-era Black Code hanging around their necks like millstones.

"Were Mr. Lucas and his son-in-law, Mr. Quackenbos, excessively cruel or downright mean to the sharecroppers at Glennburr plantation?" I had another question for Annie West Rounds.

"Naw, the 'croppers at Racetrack used to say we was spoiled over at Mr. Lucas' place. They used to say we had it too easy. They'd call us 'Mr. Lucas' Pets.' We heard they didn't get but a half-hour lunch sometime. As I told you, we got a couple hours rest around noon. And we didn't have to work on Saturdays. Naw, Mr. Lucas and them wasn't so much mean to us except not payin' you at the end of the year. That's when 'croppers got paid, just once a year. Mr. Lucas and Mr. Quackenbos were known for shakin' their heads when you went to get your money at the end of the year. They would tell you that you didn't have any money coming, you didn't make quota on your cotton or corn. But they never told us what quota was. How could you make quota if you didn't know what you was shootin' for? What 'quota' there was was in their heads. They never bothered to make it plain for us to understand.

"I know my family worked hard and shoulda always got some money at the end of the year. One year, my husband, Jesse, and my kids and me picked thirty-one bales in six weeks! Thirty-one bales in six weeks! And there's fourteen-hundred pounds to the bale. You do the arithmetic. How many pounds is that? And we didn't get any money from Ole Man Lucas that year. But he did give Jesse a car that year. Not a new car, a used car, but it was in pretty good condition. Mr. Lucas was known for givin' the 'cropper men old cars instead of

pay."

"Well, how did you make ends meet getting paid only once a year, and then sometimes not even getting paid then?" I asked. "I remember when I first started teaching in 1965, teachers were paid once a month, and that was hard. I made a healthy $5,250 a year as a first-year St. Louis teacher and that was a lot of money then. But all of my colleagues and I were generally trying to borrow money by the last few days of the month before the next paycheck."

Annie paused and then answered:*"Well, of course, you could always borrow some cash from Ole Man Lucas. He would charge you interest on the money you borrowed. But we never knew how much interest we was payin', and the way we was brought up, you never asked a white man stuff like that. And on Saturdays my husband, Jesse, and our boys could go over to a plantation in Itta Bena and do what we called 'work by the hundred.' That meant you could work about five or six hours and pull in a hundred pounds. They'd pay you sometimes five dollars per hundred. And that was considered pretty good side money."*

"So," I said. "If Mr. Lucas had paid your family for the thirty-one bales you brought in, with fourteen-hundred pounds to the bale, and at five dollars a hundred. Let's see, that would have been $2,170? If you gave Mr. Lucas his half, he would have made $1,085 and you would have made $1,085."

"You do the arithmetic, Honey. But it didn't work that away. Shoulda worked that away. Didn't, though. See, the deal with sharecropping is that the white man is supposed to get half the crop for letting you work on his land and the 'croppers are supposed to get half. But that half thing was only for the truck crops we brought in, not for the cotton and corn. The white man got all the cotton, all the corn. Mr. Lucas was supposed to allow us something for the cotton and corn but we never knew how much we got for it 'cause he'd open up that big ole book that him and Mr. Quackenbos kept and he would say like 'I paid a doctor bill for y'all back in March. And you borrowed $75 from me on June 22. And your store bill was such-and-such. And I had the screens replaced on your house and so-forth and so-on. And it looks like you done used up all the profit you coulda got from the cotton and the corn.'"

"It doesn't seem fair does it? What you were involved in seemed to be unfaircropping," I suggested as I coined a word that seemed to be very appropriate.

"When it come to dealin' with the white man, fair don't have nothin' to do with it."

"I guess this is a stupid question, but nobody every questioned, ever challenged the bookkeeping of Mr. Lucas and Mr. Quackenbos?"

*"That **is** a stupid question, Honey."*

"Were there any times when you thought you'd have to go hungry on the plantation?"

"Not really. We had our own hogs and chickens and cows and things. We'd butcher a hog in the fall, around October, salt the meat down and then hang it in the smokehouse where it would get smoked for about an hour a day until it was cured. We smoked hog with dried china berries and hickory chips sending out smoke from a two-gallon bucket. We'd buy

sausage casings at a store in Greenwood and make a lot of sausage that would get hung up in the smokehouse. One big hog could almost feed a whole family for almost a year. We didn't throw anything on the hog away.

"And we had our own vegetable and fruit and stuff we grew in a little garden out back of the house. That's one thing about Ole Man Lucas. He had a big garden patch next to the big house. We was always welcome to take anything out of his garden we needed: tomatoes, pumpkins, squash, cabbage, and greens. And we could always get cool, fresh milk for our children if we were outta milk. He used to say he didn't ever want any of his babies to go hungry. He loved little colored babies. And he made sure that every house on the place had screens up at the windows, 'cause he would say that he didn't want any of his babies to get bit by no mosquitoes. Guess he looked on our children as future field hands."

"Did you have to go into Greenwood to buy staples like flour and meal and sugar?" I asked.

"No, we could get just about everything we could get in Greenwood at the commissary right on the place. It was a big ole long building with shelf after shelf of some pretty nice things. It was divided in two parts. One was the dry goods side where you could buy clothes and material to make clothes…real nice material. The other side of the commissary was for groceries and things. We could buy cornmeal and flour and sugar and canned goods over there on that side. We could buy as much as we wanted and didn't need any cash to buy. There was an old colored fella that used to wait on us. Name of Willie Taylor. Guess the bosses could trust him. He had got pretty crippled up and couldn't work in the fields no more. And he could read and write and figure, so he had a nice job. He wouldn't give us no deals or breaks or anything, though. He was straight up workin' for 'The Man.' Willie or Mr. Quackenbos would just write it down on our bill what we got and it would be taken out of what we was supposed to be paid in December. Guess that's how come we sometimes didn't have anything coming at the end of the year—we had used it all up on money we borrowed from Mr. Lucas and stuff we bought in the commissary. And any medical expenses we owed. And we never had even a clue on whether they was cheatin' us or not."

"Did Mr. Lucas look after the health of the sharecroppers on his place?"

"Oh, yeah, he was real good about that. If anybody got real sick or anything and needed a doctor or a midwife. We didn't have any medical insurance or anything so Mr. Lucas would pay for the doctor. And if you really needed surgery or anything and had to go to the big hospital in Greenwood, Ole Man Lucas would take care of the bill.

"But most folks never got all that sick. I knew of one girl on the Lucas place that got TB. But most of the little sicknesses me and my family got we could handle with just some home remedy stuff, or just wait for it to pass. Then we knew, if we did have to have a doctor, it would be coming off what we coulda got paid in December. It wasn't like Ole Man Lucas was gonna just pay for your doctor out of his pocket and outta the goodness of his heart or anything."

Chalmers Archer Jr., also remembers life in Holmes County for sharecropper families:

"...many illnesses and deaths of blacks remained a mystery. Unless people exhibited classic symptoms, nobody knew for sure what disease they really had. This fact makes statistics on black deaths suspect for that era. Also, Mississippi elects its local county coroners through popular elections, and this means every death certificate for people who die outside of hospital care is suspect. (Mississippi) county coroners can be elected even if they have only a high school diploma.

"Whenever anyone 'had the doctor,' you could be sure that person was desperately ill. Blacks were reluctant to seek medical help for two reasons. First they lacked the money— even though, as my father recalled, 'a visit to the doctor cost fifty cents to one dollar.' Second, white physicians frequently did not want to treat black patients and showed it through their demeanor. This caused many blacks to avoid doctors until their conditions were medically hopeless."

Considering this account of Holmes County medical treatment for Blacks, the Glennburr plantation workers—including the Rounds family sharecroppers and farmers—were fortunate enough to have doctors in Belzoni and Yazoo City who would see black folk. Yazoo City was where Dr. Fullilove and Dr. Miller had offices. There were only a couple of doctors who would make house calls to *Honey Island.*

Honey Island native Thaddeus Rounds, a grandson of Old Ned Rounds and nephew of West, now lives in Chicago. He celebrated his seventy-eighth birthday in February 1999. This outspoken Rounds descendant does not want anyone to paint a picture of Mr. Lucas as a kindly, benevolent Santa Claus. To the contrary, Ted Rounds remembers:

"Old Man Lucas could have a mean streak that stretched a mile. Back in 1939 when I was about eighteen, I went to Mr. Lucas to borrow twenty-five dollars. I needed it to buy some things the family really needed. It was the spring of the year and Old Man Lucas had pulled off one of his usual tricks at the end of the year before. He told my family once again that we didn't have any money comin'. Even though I was so young, the baby in the family, I was kinda the head of the house because—I don't know how to say it—but I was the only one in the family that wasn't afraid to speak up to white folks. That's just my nature. Been that way all my life. Still that way. I figure I'm a man just like any white man is. But all the other black folks, the old people, was scared to death to even look a white man in the eye when they was talkin' to us. We were to look down and grin and shuffle and just say 'Yahzuh, Mr. Lucas. You sho is right, Mr. Lucas.'

"But not me! I never did catch on to Mississippi ways. They called me a 'uppity nigger' all the time. And you know, I took that as a compliment. Bein' called that would have scared the old folks to death. And even in 1939 a black man who mouthed off could get a whuppin,' get strung up, and lynched—or just disappear, never to be seen again. We had heard about a old boy on a plantation over yonder who they say had raped a white girl. They came in the middle of the night and took him off in the middle of a field and cut his private parts off. All the black folks could hear him out there screamin' and cryin' like a baby. But, you know everybody was scared to go out and get him 'cause the same thing could happen to them. In a minute! So the old boy died. He just bled to death. When he stopped cryin' and hollerin' they went out and got him and, of course, he was dead. No trial. No judge. No jury. No nothin'. That was Mississippi justice. Even in the '30s and '40s and '50s. Anyway, I goes to Mr. Lucas to try to borrow this money. He twitched up that ugly old red and white face of his and yelled that he figured that my family was already in the hole to him by $200 from last year.

"'Why you niggers always need more money?' he screamed at me with that hoot owl face of his gettin' more red than white. 'Get outta here you black son of a bitch! And don't come in here askin' for more money no more!'

"'Guess you know there are some **white** son of a bitches, too?' I yelled back at him. He seemed to be shocked that I would dare talk to him—a white man—like that. He seemed to be huffin' and puffin' and almost foamin' at the mouth and he just bawled up his fists and turned and ran, as best an old man his age could, from the commissary into his house. You woulda thought he was gonna have a stroke or somethin'.

"'Guess we gonna have to teach you a lesson, you black-ass bastard,' he turned and yelled at me. He snatched open the door and disappeared in the house.

"One of the old colored guys who worked on the place, I believe his name was Jim Garner, says to me 'Boy, you sho in a heapa trouble now. I reckon he done gone in the house to call the sheriff! You betta get outta here, boy. They gonna be comin' after you in a minute!'

"Well, callin' the sheriff did mean bad stuff back in them days. The sheriff might coulda been the same fella who was the head of the Klan in your town. And there was cases where the sheriff would gun down some colored man, shoot him in the back and claim it was self-defense. Sometimes the sheriff and his boys would shoot a colored fella and then put a pistol in the dead man's hand to prove that self-defense stuff. The white man could be real hard on colored folks they say got outta line. 'Course they could be hard on us even when we didn't get outta line. Some time to us it looked like they would get liquored up and decide to beat up on or string up a colored man just for the fun of it. They seemed every now and then to lynch a black man for sport. Like they were goin' out to shoot rabbits or 'coons or some animal.

"Before we went to the Lucas place, when I was about nine or ten years old, I remember we worked on the Bobbitt plantation just north of Greenwood. One evening just before dark we saw four white men come and pick up one of the colored 'croppers and take him away. This wasn't too strange to us 'cause white folks always took a colored guy along with 'em when they went fishin' or huntin'. The colored guy would do everything from paddle the boat to baitin' the hooks to whatever when they took one fishin'. And when they went huntin', the colored man they took with them would scare up the game and tote whatever they shot. He was kinda like a porter.

"Well, anyway they took this man off the Bobbitt plantation and we didn't think any more about it until that same colored man that they took away started beatin' on our door just before the sun came up. We looked out the window and there he was. Completely covered in blood from his head to his toe. I can still see him in my mind to this very day, just like it was yesterday. And that was almost seventy years ago! Poor fella looked like he had all his front teeth busted out. Blood was just a' gushin' outta his mouth. Probably had some real bad internal injuries. He had tried to stuff cotton right off the stalk into some big gashes on his face and body. And he was beggin' for us to open the door. But my daddy didn't want to be the next one on their list, so he just threw the poor man a blanket out on the porch. That guy rolled up in that blanket and cried like a new baby for the rest of the night. I had never in my life heard a grown man cry like that. I tried to pull a pillow over my head so's I couldn't hear him any more. But if you heard him for even a minute, you would be hearin' that sound in your mind for the rest of your life.

"I gotta tell you, I asked myself more than a few times when I was a little kid why The White Man hated The Colored Man so much. I mean, what in the world did we ever do to them? We didn't asked to be brought over here to be treated the way they treated that man that ended up on our porch. It's a damn shame, isn't it? What did we ever do to them? We mostly just stayed amongst ourselves, mindin' our own business.

"When first light came, my daddy and mama took some rags they soaked in turpentine and tried to clean up the blood on the man. Every time that coal oil hit raw flesh, the man would scream so loud they had to hear him in the next county. Then my daddy went down to the mule barn and hitched up two mules to a wagon and drove the man into Greenwood to see a doctor. That fella was beholdin' to my parents for the rest of our time on the Bobbitt plantation. Claimed they had saved his life. And they had. Even though he had lost a bucket of blood just on our porch.

"Needless to say, I didn't sleep worth a damn for many months after that. I would have nightmares for a long, long time after that. Kept wondering if that could happen to father. Or my mother. And I knew it could. Imagine a kid having to see and hear stuff like that.

"Back to what happened on the Lucas place when I talked back to the bossman. When Old Man Lucas ran in the house and Jim warned me that trouble was brewin', I ran home and told my daddy and mama what had happened. They got that worried look on their faces. 'Specially my mama. With my smart mouth and my uppity attitude I guess mama always thought they'd be cuttin' me down from a tree some day before I was even twenty-one.

"Anyway, they told me I had better get outta there. So I quickly packed up a few clothes and a family friend drove me to Greenwood. It was hardly an hour after I had that run-in with Lucas that my sister-in law, Annie, her father Rufus West and me hopped into Willie Foreman's '33 Chevy and with him at the wheel we raced off. I sat low in the back seat…low enough to not be seen too easily, but not low enough to be called hidin' out in case we got caught. My nerves were really jangled.

"You better believe we kept lookin' back to see if we was bein' followed. I slumped way down in the back seat. Grandpa West kept warnin' Willie not to drive too fast so's not to call any attention to ourselves. It seemed kinda strange that we needed to get the hell outta *there fast, but we couldn't go too fast.*

"We headed to Greenwood to my Aunt Ninnie Syfax's house about four miles away. She was a spinster who lived by herself.We got there about eight o'clock that night and after we had all hugged and Annie had cried a bit they all left right away to get back to the Lucas place so all of them wouldn't be missed if anybody came around lookin' for me that night. That's why my mother and father didn't make the trip with us. Everybody thought it be the smart thing to do for them to be at home all night.

"WhenWillie drove off, I was really more angry than scared. My life had been turned upside down. Not for something I did, but for something I thought I just had to say. Aunt Ninnie was scared to death and turned out all the lights early. I was just hopin' that they wouldn't do anything to hurt my kinfolk to get them to tell them where I was. But my mama and daddy could just say I ran off and they didn't have a clue where I had run off to. My folks made a point not to tell my brothers and sisters a thing about where I was so they wouldn't know anything to tell if they got pressured.

"Needless to say, I didn't sleep too good that night. Neither did my Aunt Ninnie. First thing in the mornin' she got a friend of hers everybody called 'Kind Friend' to drive me in his old cab to Grenada about thirty-two miles away. Never did know what that fella's real name was, but the name 'Kind Friend' sure did fit this time.

"See, we knew that they'd probably be lookin' for me to board a bus at the Greenwood station so we tried to outfox 'em by my gettin' on the bus at Grenada.Then I took a bus from there and went on to Belzoni where I thought I would be safe—for at least a while. It's all kinda scary, isn't it? The idea that a young boy wasn't safe and could be actually killed for speakin' up to a white man who had called him names. Guess that's part of the reason my whole family ended up North. It was just too dangerous for black folk in Mississippi. I, for one, am glad I got outta there...alive.

"I went to work for the Turner Brothers in a cotton compress. They owned everything in Belzoni that had anything to do with cotton. I worked at their cotton compress. See, a bale of cotton is about four feet tall. The machines I worked on would pack the bail down to about two feet tall. I sometimes think back on that experience of getting off the Lucas plantation alive. Lord knows they coulda lynched me...strung me up...beat me to death just like they did with so many colored folk back in those days. But if I had it to do all over again, I know I would've done it the same way. Old Man Lucas was no better than I was and he had no business talkin' to me like he did."

Thaddeus Rounds, as odd as it seems since he didn't take well to authority on the plantation, went on to serve with distinction in the U.S. Army's 741st Gunner Battalion in the South Pacific. He was stationed in New Guinea and saw actual combat three times. He told me he has often thought about how he went off to war and how he served his country to guarantee some of the freedom and liberty he and his family never had in Mississippi when he was growing up.

Before they took the chance to pick up and move to the relative leniency, but traditional year-end swindle by Messrs. Lucas and Quackenbos, John and Lutisha

Rounds, Ned's son and daughter-in-law, had worked for awhile on the Quafaloma plantation right next to *Honey Island.*

Members of the Rounds family and its extensions were also known to have worked as sharecroppers on the adjoining plantations with the romantic sounding names of Sweet Home and Wildwood. Annie West Rounds' parents, Rufus West Jr., and Ella Purdy West worked on the Sweet Home plantation just north of Greenwood, Mississippi. The John Rounds and Jesse Rounds families attended worship services at the Sweet Home Baptist Church in the early decades of the twentieth century. The neat little church with its adjoining cemetery still stands today as a lone remnant of the Sweet Home plantation. All the sharecropper homes and the big house are gone today. The West and Rounds families used the confusion and devastation caused by the Great Flood of 1927 to slip away from Sweet Home to go to the Lucas plantation, Glennburr. Annie West Rounds, who was seven years old at the time of the deluge, remembers the flood waters were so high her family went by boat from one plantation to the other.

Although *Honey Island* has all but disappeared from Mississippi maps like a dozen other little towns, there is more proof that it not only existed but was an actual town. *Honey Island,* in accordance with that November 1865, Black Code had to be an incorporated town in order for Blacks to own any property on it. There is plenty of courthouse and census data to document the fact that the Rounds family and scores of their African American neighbors actually owned the farms they tilled.

While we may never know anything more than the fact that Ned did, indeed, have sufficient cash money to pull off the deal on March 17, 1886, we can be sure that year was not a wonderful year for people of color in the United States in general and Mississippi in particular. In 1886 there were recordings of seventy-four Blacks being lynched across "the land of the free and the home of the brave." That was exactly the same number of reported cases of Blacks strung up by mobs the year before. And how many lynchings went unreported? The next year, according to government reports, seventy Blacks were hanged by mob action. Just two years after Ned's biggest land purchase, the state of Mississippi beat the U. S. Supreme Court to the punch in its thinking on Plessy v. Ferguson by declaring eight years before that landmark ruling that any railroad that ran through Mississippi had to designate separate waiting rooms for blacks and whites. We don't know how many of the reported sixty-nine lynchings that year might have been provoked by a black person taking the daring stand that Homer Plessy was to take later in 1896 or Rosa Parks was to take in Montgomery, Alabama in 1955.

There is more strong evidence that life was hard for the Blacks who tried to advance themselves in post-Civil War Mississippi. During the period of Reconstruction and for years thereafter, it appeared that recalcitrant Whites in

Mississippi tried to punish Blacks just as harshly as the Republican-controlled Congress in Washington had tried to punish the rebellious rebel states. For example, just four years after my great-great granddad made his biggest farmland purchase, the Mississippi Constitutional Convention—without even bothering to submit its decrees to Mississippi voters—imposed a two-dollar poll tax on voters. That then-exorbitant fee would deny tens of thousands of black Mississippians a chance to cast ballots. The 1890 Mississippi convention also barred anyone who " could not read, understand, or interpret any section of the State Constitution" from voting. While Ned Rounds would have certainly considered the two dollar fee no more than peanuts, he would have flunked the poll test when it came around to the question of whether or not he could read or write. The 1880 census clearly declared that Old Ned could neither read nor write. Did the census enumerator want to keep Ned Rounds from voting by recording an illiteracy? How could a man with absolutely no education amass a thousand dollars cash six years after that 1880 census? We can only wonder if Ned's former master, neighbor, and person who sold him the land, Peter James Jr., could have interpreted any section of the Mississippi State Constitution? An even bigger question on this issue is whether, if Peter James and his neighbor Ned Rounds would have taken a wagon together into Belzoni to vote after 1890, would James have been charged a two-dollar poll tax and would he have been quizzed on the text of the State Constitution? Would Ned have had to overcome both obstacles in order to vote with the literacy measure thrown in for extra measure?

Blacks owning their own property in the Old South after the Civil War had its precedence more than a decade before Ned's land purchase. For example, in 1874 Georgia, Blacks owned 350,000 acres of land. In 1891 Virginia, Blacks owned $3,207,069 worth of land, more than a third of the total land.

There were, in all probability, more lynchings than were actually reported, especially in the Deep South where law officers were often a part of the mob action to hang Blacks. Were Blacks who just disappeared from their farms, homes and off roads and fields reported as lynched? We will probably never know for sure.

****

Some of the now elderly former residents of *Honey Island* remember that the largest of the original farms of its residents were referred to as *"places,"* as in the neighboring Henry Cade place, and Bob Anna place and George Byrd place. The latter *place*, by the way, was named after George H. Byrd Sr., whose son by the same name was *Honey Island's* first postmaster. The 1900 census lists a section of Holmes County farmland as the "Ned Rounds place." In other parts of Mississippi and throughout the south, a "place" would otherwise be called a plantation or estate. The major parcels of land were later subdivided into smaller farm homesteads. Eventually, *Honey Island* was made up of about a dozen places and there were 82 families living on the island by the late 1800s. "Place"evolved into popular use after the word plantation was scrapped because of its connotation of slave labor. It was not uncommon for the places to take the name of the property owner who first settled it or who held the biggest land mass on it. Domestic servants from the South who eventually came to work in the North were said to be "staying on the place" if they lived in servant quarters in the house or on the property of the employer. The expression was used well into the 1960s.

One of Ned's neighbors for whom a "place" is named was a mulatto named Bob Cade. Only Cade, his wife, Julia, and their three children, Alex, Fanny, and Henry lived on the place. Their field hands—not slaves—helped farm the place. Unfortunately, for family pride and heritage bragging rights, the *Honey Island* enclave of which Ned was a founding father and a major landowner is usually listed in early Holmes County courthouse records as *Panther Burn Place* and only on a few very obscure documents can one find a handwritten inscription: *Ned Rounds Place.*

When Ned started purchasing land on *Honey Island* he just might have had a vision. He might have looked ahead and hoped his contribution might increase the chances of a bright future for all the children he saw in profusion all around him. Children were a valuable commodity on *Honey Island.* And they *did* represent for Ned and his family and neighbors *hope* for a better, brighter day.

 *Family Mergers, Birthin'*
Babies, and School Days

There was one particular Biblical directive the *Honey Island* residents practiced religiously: "Go forth and multiply!" We cannot be sure how deeply, truly, religious the Roundses and their neighbors were. The *Golden Rule* was certainly followed in principle by the Rounds clan and the other island residents. None of the *Honey Island Oldtimers* we talked with could come up with any flagrant violators of *most* of the Ten Commandments. There are a couple of the tenets of the Tablets that may have been ignored just a few times by the *Honey Island* guys and gals according to the memories of the *Oldtimers*—but that *selective memory* seems to get tapped once again when asked concrete examples of what the sins and who the sinners were. One *Oldtimer* did chuckle when the subject of sin came up in a fireside chat: "*Seems like that part of the Lord's Prayer that says 'Forgive us our trespasses' got some pretty strong emphasis from some of the brothers and sisters some Sunday mornings.*"

No matter how often the Rounds family and their neighbors went to Jones Chapel Missionary Baptist Church, we must remember that the evangelist Billy Sunday once said, "*Going to church every Sunday no more makes a person a Christian than going into a garage every day makes a person an automobile.*" The *Oldtimers* remember that some of the *Honey Island* farmers, who worked ten to twelve hours a day for six or seven days a week, were inclined to remain reclined on the Seventh Day rather than taking the time to get all gussied up to sit in church for the traditional three or four hours of Baptist worship on the Sabbath.

We can tell, though, that *Honey Island* residents did, yea verily, "go forth and multiply." Ned and Ellen Rounds had Lucy in 1855 in Mississippi. That's the first record we can trace back to find the Rounds family in the Magnolia State. Of course they might have arrived earlier. Westly was born the following year. George was born to Ned and Ellen in 1860 and Martha in 1866. She was the first Rounds baby born after the Emancipation Proclamation; the first Rounds family member who was not a slave although her father was never, according to his descendants, treated like a slave. He was, as we have been able to determine, the overseer on Stonewall plantation.

John Rounds was born to Ned and Ellen in 1873, and Eddy entered this world and the Rounds clan in 1875. The then fourteen-year-old Martha, like her mother, was later listed in the 1880 census as a laborer. Seven-year-old John was listed as a student.

Ned and Ellen's son, Westly or "West" (pronounced, "Wess" and misspelled on a church cornerstone and courthouse documents as "Ness") Rounds, and his first wife, Hager (an obvious misspelling of the Biblical name Hagar) who was born in 1857, had only one child before the 1880 census was taken. Ninnie, who was so loved by all, was born in 1878. My grandmother, Rhoda Hattie—who chose to be called Hattie—was born in 1881 and was the oldest child of West and Hager still living at home after her mother died. Before her death, Hager and West also had Ambrose, born in 1883; Carrie, who entered the *Honey Island* world in 1886; Henry, born in 1890; and Lillie B. in 1892. Then Hager passed. (Remember, black people in the South never "die." They "pass." More on this philosophy/theology later.)

The birth of Carrie in 1886 must have been a signal to Ned that he needed to move his extended family off the Stonewall plantation where Peter James Jr. had allowed him to farm and get his own legal property. Please note that no census data ever lists Ned as a sharecropper. He moves from slave/overseer to farmer...his own man. No obligation to share his crops with James Jr. This special treatment was not unusual. Before and after the emancipation, white slave owners often gave land on the fringes of their plantations to trusted slaves as a reward for their hard work in bondage or—as in Ned's case—for service as an overseer or tradesman.

On December 9, 1895, West Rounds married the widow Mary Hughes Lewis who lived nearby. She brought into the Rounds household four children from her marriage to Robert Lewis. Minnie was born in 1890; John, in 1892; Willie, the following year; and a child with a uniquely-applied and very interesting name, Robert Lee Lewis, was born in 1895. Although the census-taker, one King B. Benjamin, lists Robert Lee as a boy, *he* was actually a *she*. Robert Lee was a girl! There is some speculation that she was named after the Confederate war hero Robert E. Lee who died nearly three decades before her birth... but she was named exactly after her father, Robert Lee Lewis...who was probably named after General Lee. The gender slip-up highlights the inaccuracy of some census data and should have been a lesson to Mr. Benjamin and other government scribes that they must assume nothing. Although we have no evidence that West took formal steps to adopt his second wife's children, some of the Lewis children eventually used the name Rounds.

After West and Mary were wed, *his* children and *her* children had to make room for *their* children. Inez was born to West and Mary in 1897. Annette, born in 1898, did not survive infancy. Mary gave birth to twins Eva and Elmer in 1901, Perry two years later, and Benjamin in 1905.

It was not at all unusual in this endogamous community for families to merge upon the death—make that *passing*—of one spouse. *Honey Island* children must have wondered in their little slice of Mississippi paradise which of their school chums might one day become a sister or brother. It happened often.

Education was important to the Rounds family. Ned and Ellen didn't have any formal "book-larnin'." The School of Hard Knocks was enough of a teacher. Ned used his "mother wit" to succeed and prosper. Life in Kentucky, where Ned and Ellen were born, and throughout the south for those held in bondage, was still brutal during Ned and Ellen's lifetime. In 1856, just a couple of years after Ned and Ellen moved to Mississippi, a Kentucky slave named Margaret Garner tried to kill her children to keep them from being recaptured in Ohio and dragged back by bounty hunters to a slaver in Kentucky. She succeeded in killing one child before she was caught. On her way back to Kentucky she unsuccessfully tried to drown herself and another child in a river. Ned had once told his granddaughter, my grandmother Hattie, that he had known a slave woman who intentionally threw her young baby girl off a porch to break a limb or worse— so that her child would not have to labor in the fields as a slave.

The frequent confusion in the early-to-mid nineteenth century over which Blacks were slaves and which weren't was a big problem throughout the South, before and after the Roundses migrated from Kentucky. There was, no doubt, real and legitimate fear that whenever the *Honey Island* residents took a wagon or buggy ride into Belzoni or Yazoo City before 1863, the journey might be their last as an almost-free Black enjoying the beneficence of a master who did not put Ned and Ellen and their children under the brutal boot. Before the Emancipation Proclamation and even a few years beyond, Ned and Ellen and the other Blacks who were the property of Peter James Jr. and other planters had to carry their identification papers with them whenever they left the confines of the plantation. If they didn't have proper papers they could have been kidnaped by highwaymen who made a living snatching undocumented slaves and some freedmen, too. Even after formal freedom was given, some of the *Honey Island Oldtimers* remember that Blacks traveling off their farms had to carefully conceal the shotguns and pistols they took with them for protection lest a local law enforcement officer or a vigilante posse turn the weapons on the carriers or strip them of their weapons.

In 1860, when my great-grandfather, West, was five years old and living with his mother, father, and sister as rather privileged slaves on the little piece of property Peter James Jr. had given Ned to farm, there were 10,684 free Blacks in the state of Kentucky where Ned and Ellen Rounds were born, but only 773 freedmen in all of Mississippi.

Since he could not read, Ned Rounds would almost certainly have never have been told by his master or any other Whites about a convention of southern states that met in nearby Vicksburg in 1859, just three years after Ned and Ellen's first child was born in Mississippi, possibly on the Stonewall plantation. The convention adopted a resolution demanding the re-institution of the slave trade. The Vicksburg Southern Commercial Convention organized the *African Supply Association* in an attempt to bolster the dwindling slave trade. Mississippi would secede from the Union only a few years after Ned and Ellen arrived in their new state. Insurrection would certainly follow if white planters had told their slaves about that meeting. It was all so very frustrating and confusing—and dangerous— for slaves who weren't sure of their status around the time of the convention. There was only one thing the Roundses and their neighbors could do to protect themselves: keep quiet and mind their own business. They continued to work hard and push their children to get better educated than the oldsters were.

There are no stories or records to indicate that any of the slaves and freedmen on and around the Stonewall plantation ever made or heard any demonstrations or speeches to abolish slavery. Nor are there any indications that the Rounds family members in Mississippi ever took part in any plots to overthrow the system of manumission. There was a slave named Jefferson Rounds who on April 5, 1863, rose up in rebellion on a plantation in Terre Bonne County, Louisiana, with nine other slaves after John Calvin Potts, the plantation owner, fled in bankruptcy and went back East. Jefferson Rounds and the sixty or more other abandoned slaves refused to work for a government-appointed overseer and hired a white lawyer to petition Provost Marshal General T. J. Bowen on their behalf. Quite surprisingly, the slaves were allowed to work and harvest crops on the old Potts plantation without white supervision for about a year.

When Union Colonel Charles C. Nott inspected the unsupervised Potts plantation he reported some things that seemed to surprise him and would most assuredly surprise his superiors:

"At the request of some of the contrabands on the plantation of Major Potts I have visited the plantation & certify to the following facts:

1. They (the slaves) appear to be of unusual respectability & bear a good character, giving all the evidence of neat, thrifty, and industrious laborers.

2. They have broken up and partially planted with corn as nearly as I can compute about sixty arpents of land and have acquired some corn & cotton seed sufficient I should judge for planting this ground.

3. *From what I have learned they have thus far received no cut from the government but have supported themselves creditably by their own exertions and labor although a very large proportion are aged men, women and children."*

Even though the bold and unprecedented experiment of allowing the slaves—with Jefferson Rounds as a leader—to control their own destinies was a success, the plantation was taken over by Union troops just before emancipation and an overseer, a Mr. Wright, was placed in charge of the plantation. Can you imagine the turmoil should word have spread throughout the southland that African American slaves were successfully working a plantation without white supervision? Once they were freed, many of the slaves stayed on and worked as sharecroppers. Jefferson Rounds and the other one-time Potts slaves had proven what Ned Rounds would later show the Mississippi Delta community: Blacks neither required the shackles of slavery nor the invisible bondage of sharecropping to ensure hard work and resourcefulness.

West Rounds was certainly prodded by his illiterate parents to get a good, and at least basic, education. West set a good example for all his children and grandchildren and for Rounds generations to come. He taught himself to read using a Bible as a textbook. West, no doubt, also took reading lessons from a young white teacher named Lula McEwen who lived on the Stonewall plantation and tutored the James' three sons. The 1900 and 1910 census reports confirm that, unlike his father and mother, West Rounds could read and write and speak English. So that all he met would know for sure that here was a literate man, West always carried a rolled-up sheaf of paper or a newspaper with him.

Of the ten Rounds-Lewis children living at home in 1900, the census lists eight of them— Hattie, Ambrose, Carrie, Henry, Lillie B., Ninnie, John, and Willie—as students. All were educated in the little Jones Chapel co-founded by West Rounds. Annette Rounds was just two years old in 1900 and daughter Robert Lee was just four, too young for school.

BIRTHIN' BABIES ON HONEY ISLAND

"... two-thirds of what I know about deliverin', carin' for mother and baby, what to expect, what was happenin' and was goin' on, I didn't get from the class. God gave it to me. So many things I got from my own plain motherwit."
                        -*Mississippi Midwife Onnie Lee Logan*
                        To the Mississippi Board of Health, 1938

With all due deference to the bumper harvests of corn, tobacco, cotton, and sugar cane grown on *Honey Island*, and despite the fecundity of the livestock, the most prolific and nurtured crop on *Honey Island* was its children. The islanders were major producers of children. In an overwhelming majority of the cases examined, *Honey Island* parents loved and gave great care to their offspring in very strong nuclear family and extended family concentric circles.

There were some whispered cases of questioned paternity, but in our study of *Honey Island* records we found not one case of abject abandonment of a child. We did find some children who were actually raised between the households of two or more relatives and even the house of neighbors. And we found absolutely no cases of elective abortions. At least none that the *Oldtimers* were willing to talk about. No child we could find in our perusal of records going back to 1880 was ever purposely abandoned on *Honey Island*. Children who were orphaned or abandoned by a derelict parent were quickly taken under the roofs of relatives, neighbors, and, in some cases, of perfect strangers.

In the early 1900s, *Honey Island* babies were generally delivered by one of two local midwives. The *Oldtimers* remember one of them only by the fact that she was an elderly woman named *"Mizz* Jones." The other island practitioner of the obstetrical arts was Mary Lewis Rounds, my great-grandfather's second wife. These two women were actually called *granny midwives,* a term used generally by African Americans in the southern states to convey the fact that many of these itinerant health care nurses were often of an age to be a grandmother. They were also called *cotton dollies, mammies,* and *mammy nurses* when they delivered the babies of plantation slaves and their white mistresses. After emancipation, many of them stayed on the plantation to do the same kind of work. Two independent studies—one by B. B. Mongeau in 1974 and one by D. A. Susie in 1984—found that Mississippi midwives were viewed by their rural communities as "charismatic leaders." They practiced their trade based on techniques brought from Africa and the Caribbean. Some early and isolated midwife practices like putting an ax under an expectant mother's bed to relieve labor pains were rooted in the primitive.

The two *Honey Island* midwives, according to the *Oldtimers,* were known—as their colleagues all over the south were—as favoring absolute privacy and some degree of secrecy about their personal techniques when they were birthin' babies. Aunt Willetta, before she reached the teen-age years, was given the exceptional privilege of "assisting" at several births on *Honey Island* officiated over by her step-grandmother, Mary Rounds. My aunt, now approaching the age of ninety, can still remember the forcefulness with which a midwife could take over a house when she arrived to deliver a baby.

"My step-grandmother and 'Mizz Jones' were known to kick everybody out of the house when a baby was coming. Especially the daddies. They weren't allowed to hang around. Mama Rounds would always say that the husbands got in the way and were no count as a helper.

"All the children would be sent away to a friends or a auntie's house or some place because they would be frightened by all the hollerin' and screamin' that went on. And boy,

there was a lot of that with most women. See, they didn't have pain killers and drugs and stuff in the old days to make it easier for the woman who was birthin'."

"Why did Granny Midwife Rounds pick you, Aunt Willetta, as an occasional assistant?" I asked my aunt recently.

"Well, I guess she recognized that I was the only young girl in our whole big family who never panicked. Wouldn't faint when I saw blood. And loved to help people out of their pain and suffering. So she let me put ice packs on the foreheads of some of the neighbor-ladies who were giving birth and let them squeeze my hand as hard as they could. I really think she wanted to teach me how to deliver babies so I would one day be a granny midwife even before I got old enough to be a grandma."

Even as she stands on the threshold of nonagenarian status, Aunt Willetta still remembers that her step-grandmother kept a large black bag near the front door, ready to answer the call day or night at a minute's notice. Some of the *Oldtimers* remember that *"Mizz* Jones" kept her delivery tools in a big burlap bag. That kind of bag became an absolute no-no when the state of Mississippi imposed some tough rules of sanitation on midwives.

"We youngsters knew never to touch that black bag. We learned early that it was not a toy. And messin' with it was serious business!"

Since she was the only person in the house who knew the contents of that black bag, what was in it? What did her step-grandmother carry as tools of the trade?

"As best I can remember, she had a white cap kinda like today's nurse's caps—except it was round. And she had a gown. I think both the cap and the gown were made from a white sheet. She always kept both—spotless clean—in the bag. She had scissors that didn't have sharp points on them. That was to cut the baby's cord. She had a bottle of rubbing alcohol and some cotton balls she used to sterilize her hands after she had scrubbed them down with soap and water. And, let's see, she had camphor oil and smelling salts, a ball of string to tie off the cord, a roll of adhesive tape, some of that silver (nitrate) stuff to put in the baby's eyes and one of those—I think you call it an aspirator or something—to clear out the baby's nose and mouth. And, oh yes, she had a little scale to weigh the baby on. She would write down the weight of it in a little black book."

"That seems like an awful lot to get into one bag," I commented.

"Well, it wasn't a little bag. She kept it packed so neat and tight, everything fit just so. Really, everything she'd take on a call didn't go into the bag. She'd keep a stack of newspapers at the door. And she'd take an extra clean sheet with her. Sometimes a blanket in winter."

"How did she get to the house where the mother was expecting?"

"Seems to me that the husband usually came for her. Sometimes in a car, but most often in a wagon or on horseback. She'd have to ride double if the husband came for her on a horse."

My questions continued. "What was the actually delivery like? Was it done with the mother in bed?"

"No, no. They'd take a high back chair and turn it upside down and backwards from the way you'd sit in it. The woman would sit on the floor on some newspapers that were covered with a sheet so her head and back were lying on the slant of the chair. Never in bed. There was always a lot of blood. That's why a lot of newspapers were spread out on the floor. And, honey, that woman she would usually scream and holler and push and push and yell until that baby was squeezed out."

"How long did your step-grandmother stay with the new mother after the baby was born?"

"All depended on how easy the birth was and whether the mother bled more than usual after delivering. Most of the time she'd stay one night. But sometimes she was away from our house for two or three days if the mother or the baby wasn't doing good. When she stayed that long it was usually waiting for a doctor to get there. There was a lot of cleaning up to do after the birth. All that blood. In all the cases, it was the general rule that a new mother stayed flat on her back for two full weeks. I just can't believe that some of the women today are bouncing out of the hospital and going home with the new baby the day after they deliver!"

"And, pray tell," I concluded, "what was the going fee for a granny midwife on *Honey Island*?"

"Well, it usually depended on how much the family could pay. Mama Rounds would sometimes get as much as five dollars. But most often she got less than that. Sometimes she got some cash and then got to take any produce the farm family was growing. She didn't need much of that, though. We had so much stuff growing on our farm. Sometimes she would take a keg of honey or sorghum, or maybe even a couple of dressed chickens."

Granny midwives like "*Mizz* Jones" and Mary Lewis Rounds began to disappear from active duty after the Mississippi Board of Health voted on April 21, 1921, to begin training and licensing midwives in an effort to standardize techniques and reduce the number of infant and maternal fatalities. In addition to the basic training courses midwives were given at a monthly meeting conducted by a licensed nurse, the granny midwives of Mississippi were given Wasserman tests for syphilis and inoculations against smallpox and typhoid fever. Granny midwives on *Honey Island* and around the state of Mississippi were even forced to stop having women deliver while sitting on the floor. The bed had to be used by the latter-day state requirements—even though Willetta remembers that the floor was used for delivery to keep the mother's bed clean.

There were an estimated five thousand granny midwives in Mississippi in 1921. By 1985, there was just one Mississippi midwife with a license. We're not sure how many babies were delivered on *Honey Island* or in Mississippi before the State Health Board intervened, but we do know from statistics that from 1927 until the last midwife retired in 1985, there were 109,458 live births recorded in the state. Deaths from delivery for mother and child were incredibly high in Mississippi before the 1921 law, especially among the African American population. These mortalities were drastically reduced after licensing was required. Aunt Willetta remembers that her step-grandmother got certification because she could read and write. But "*Mizz* Jones" quit delivering babies after the law required a lot of paperwork from licensed midwives. "*Mizz* Jones" could not read or write.

The case can be made that parents tilling the soil had less than altruistic motives for taking good care of their children. Newborns represented future field hands. But love seemed to flow everywhere inside *Honey Island* homes between parents and their children and between siblings. Ironically, from the earliest days of the institution of slavery, white masters made no bones about it: they were consistently interested in the health, growth, and development of the children their adult chattel produced. For obvious reasons.

In a non-scientific survey of forty-one *Honey Island* farms selected at random—approximately half the farms on the island—the 1910 census shows the presence of 131 children under the age of eighteen. That's approximately three children per household who had not reached the age of eighteen yet. This statistic does not cover the children who still lived at home who were over the age of majority.

Our random, unscientific survey gleaned from the 1910 U. S. census report found in the forty-one homes examined there were six sets of twins under the age of twenty-one: Marcia Green's twins, Mary and Martha, born in 1895; Julia and Ella Collier, both twenty years old; Amos and Hattie Cook's fraternal twin boy and girl, Katie and Willie, then seven years old; Jake and Anna Jones' newborn nieces whose mother died delivering twins Julia and Katie; Ed and Martha Jones' newborn duo of Elisha and Elijah; and West and Mary Rounds' twins, Eva and Elmer, who were born in 1901.

Another unscientific observation about the *Honey Island* families is that in almost all cases, children appeared to be spaced exactly two years apart, give or take a couple months. My grandmother Hattie's daughters were born exactly two years apart. George and Frances Rounds' children are listed in the 1900 U. S. census as ages 17, 15, 13, 10, 5, and 3. Willie and Alabama Wilson's son and daughter are listed as 20 and 18 in the 1910 census. In that same year, General and Sallie Turner's children are posted as 23, 21, 19, 17, 15, and 12. James and Annie King's offspring in 1910 were 20, 17, 15, 13, 10, 8, and 1 years old. In 1910, the Taylor Fullilove children were 25, 23, 21, 18, 16, and 13. The Henry and Julia Cade children fit the pattern perfectly, too, with their ages in 1910 of 13, 11, and 9. Anderson and Susie Patterson's youngsters were 17, 15, and 13 in 1910. There are many, many more examples of this near-perfect two-year spacing between kids born into *Honey Island* families.

These were surely the days before any widespread use of birth control medications, devices, or techniques. But, these were also the days before widespread use of baby bottles, formulas, and *Enfamil*. *Honey Island* mothers breast-fed their children for up to a year after their births. During the period of nursing, it is a medically accepted fact that women are less fertile. Nature's own way of controlling the birth rate.

Definitive medical studies have much to say about the cause of this phenomenon of the two-year spacing between births as in *Honey Island* families. A 1994 study by Benefo, Tsui, and Johnson of Brown University titled *Ethnic Differential in Child-Spacing Ideals and Practices in Ghana*, reports:

"Postpartum sexual abstinence may be a major determinant of fertility and of maternal and child health in sub-Saharan Africa. Respondents in most ethnic groups believe their abstinence to be adequate. A key motivation for abstinence is the unwillingness to have sexual intercourse with nursing mothers."

In a 1982 article in the *American Journal of Clinical Nutrition*, R. E. Brown reports that:

"...the prolongation of postpartum anovulatory cycles in breast-feeding women, coupled with sexual mores that postpone sexual relations while a woman is breast-feeding in certain groups, will serve to prolong the interbirth intervals. Populations where breast-feeding is customary have been shown to have fewer births than populations where the women do not breast-feed and where infants are artificially fed."

In the medical community, the period of breast-feeding in which the woman is less fertile is called *lactational amenorrhea*. The phenomenon which accounts for the two-year spacing between *Honey Island* family births is also confirmed by researcher Peter W. Howie, M.D., of Dundee, Scotland, who writes:

"Lactational amenorrhea is an important role in child spacing. Recent research has led to a consensus regarding the status of lactational amenorrhea as a method of family planning.

"Although it has been known for a long time that breast-feeding causes a variable period of amenorrhea, it is only during the past 10 years that scientific research has been focused on its role in fertility regulation."

WHAT'S IN A HONEY ISLAND NAME?

With all the heavy work that both parents had to do to keep their families and farms together, naming babies did not appear to be a top priority among the *Honey Island* residents. There were far too many other things on their minds. Hence, among the earliest islanders there was a William Williams, a Patterson Patterson, a Jefferson Jefferson, and an Anderson Anderson.

The names some of the children were given at birth on *Honey Island* were sometimes puzzling, if not colorful. Of course, Biblical names like Isaiah and Ezekiel, Moses, Hagar (sometimes spelled Hager), Ruth, and Sarah were very common. Islanders Ed and Martha Jones had twin sons born in 1910 they named after the ninth century Hebrew prophets **Elisha** and **Elijah**.

Some *Honey Island* parents could be very creative when the time was taken to name a new baby. What was the origin of **Lavossa**, as in Lavossa Byrd, George and Ninnie Byrd's son? The curiosity and origin of the name was perhaps the reason early on in his life Lavossa was simply called "**Lee**" Byrd. There is no clue as to the origin of the first name worn by Ollie Jones' little granddaughter. **Examena** Jones was certainly a name that no one else on the island could claim. A *Honey Island* baby girl was given a name very much like the preceding moniker. There was actually an **Exerminue** Fullilove born on the island in 1906. She passed in 1992.

John and Millie Griffin named their son after the texture of his hair. He was named **Curly** at birth. King Benjamin (an interesting name in itself), the enumerator of the 1910 *Honey Island* census, no doubt heard Curly's mother and/or father pronounce the name of the then one-year-old child in their thick southern drawl and recorded his name as "**Cully**"—as in "*cully hay-yuh*,"or as it would be pronounced in the North, "curly hair."

The *Honey Island* child with the most descriptive moniker, without a doubt, was the girl baby born to Rans and Lula Betten on the island in 1898. They named her simply enough, **Little Bit**. For the rest of her life and no matter how old she got and what size dress she eventually wore, she would be called Little Bit Betten.

Christian names on *Honey Island* were also taken from military leaders, presidents, and statesmen. There were **George Washington** Johnson, **Thomas Jefferson** Jackson, and a **Booker T.** Jones. There was a guy who lived the next farm over from George and Ninnie Byrd whose name was simply **George Washington**. This George was born in 1855. **Monroe** Horton was born in 1902. His parents, Johnie and Mary Horton, apparently began to run out of names after they named Monroe. Their second child, born in 1906, was named **Burbon** (as it was spelled). He was followed two years later by a boy they tagged **Extra**. **Extra** Horton. Perhaps his birth came as a surprise to his parents or perhaps they had to find extra room for their newborn. The Hortons had another child after Extra. Short of names, they named the newborn after his father, **Johnie** (with one "n" and an "e" on the end of it).

Speaking of being strapped for names, **J. B.** Allen's parents simply gave him initials as a Christian name. In fact, Peter and his wife, **M. E.** (Could that be a variant of *Emmy*? It is more likely from other records that her name was Mary Ellen.) listed all three of their children with the 1880 census enumerator as simply **W. T.**, **S. L.**, and **D. A.** Allen. Or that just might have been the work— or lack of work—of a lazy census-taker who, tired of writing the multiple copies he had to make, took to using initials only.

James and Annie King named their daughter born in 1893 **Lady Gay**. She went through her childhood and into adulthood as **Lady Gay King**. There were other *Honey Island* kids and adults with impressive titles for their Christian names.

There was **King** Byrd and **Commodore** Williams and **Caesar** Calloway, **General** Turner, **Caesar** Cummings, **Prince** Wood, **Marshall** Hughes, and **Colonel** Moore. There was one name that appeared to be a reversal of standard placement of Christian name and surname as in **Anderson Peter**.

One young man who lived on the island and eventually became head of his own household had what must be recognized as the most calming and pacifying name one could find and utter: **London Greene**. Say the name softly and aloud several times in succession and one can conjure up one verdant pastoral scene in England after another.

There was a **Pearlie** in the Watkins and Fullilove families, a **Pearl** in one branch of the Jones clan and a great-granddaughter of West Rounds, my cousin, **Pearline**. There was an **Ivory** in the Betten family on *Honey Island*. The name of the island just may have inspired Horace and Irma McDaniel to name their second child, born to them in 1897, **Honey**.

When my grandmother's first husband, Anderson Williams passed, she remarried and became **Hattie Coats**. The Byrd family of *Honey Island*, related to my family by marriage, actually named a girl baby **Canary. Canary Byrd**.

There were *Honey Island* names with syllables obviously lopped off them with the southern brogue. There was **Wash** Rounds, **Lonzo** Griffin, **Cretia** Miller. And there was **Narcis** Reid.

Honey Island kids were named after states as in **Montana** Hart, **Nebraska** McCoy, and **Alabama** Wilson.

Sometimes it seems that *Honey Island* parents took their own sweet time in naming their newborns. When the census-taker came around to the McDaniel farm in 1900, the couple had not gotten around yet to naming their five-month-old daughter. Neither did the Bonner family, also related to my family by marriage, have a first name to give the 1900 census enumerator for their daughter who was born to them in August of 1899. Or at least the census enumerator didn't record any name.

By far, the *Honey Island* name which characterizes those "to the manor born" while at the same time recognizing those who work in the manor was the name of the island resident who was 80 years old when listed on the 1880 census. His name was **Butler Noble.**

Almost every *Honey Island* child was given a nickname, virtually at birth. My mother Atlener's nickname was "**Lena**." To this day she is known only as Lena. That wasn't quite as exotic as the sobriquets for my Aunts Gertrude and Willetta. They were known affectionately, even after they turned eighty, respectively as "**Lovie**" and "**Singie**" although their given names are used too. I've recently talked with dozens of their contemporaries in Belzoni, Memphis, St. Louis, Chicago, and Detroit who couldn't remember the real first names of the "Williams' Girls."

A close *Honey Island* friend of my mother and two aunts had perfectly good three names. Joe Nathan Turner was, for some reason, called "**Gene**" by everybody.

Inell Rounds was known to all her *Honey Island* kinfolks and friendfolks as "**Baby**" long after she became a senior citizen. As Joe Nathan "**Gene**"Turner's sister, Sallie, approaches her ninetieth year she still answers to the cute name "**Sug**," pronounced like the first syllable in **sug**ar. Her sweet disposition helped Elmer Round's wife, Gertrude, earn the name "**Honey**" for life. Sallie and Joe Nathan Turner's sister, Willie, was known until she passed in 1997 as "**Titty**."

My three sisters and I knew my Grandmother Hattie's distinguished-looking brother, Ambrose, as **Uncle A**. His contemporaries called him **Bud**. And go figure this. My mother and aunts' half-brother Commodore Williams answered to the name of **Jeb**. It is no small wonder that Ninnie and George Byrd's son with the moniker that sounded more like a mouthwash than a first name, **Lavossa**, who was called **Lee**, preferred his nickname, **Kid**.

Standard nicknames for African American men are almost non-existent. Sure, the forefather of the Mississippi Rounds Clan had an informal nickname for a legitimate name. Ned is, of course, the standard diminutive of Edward. We can almost be certain the name "Ned" was given to great-great-grandfather by someone white, probably someone from England, where "Ned" is a popular nickname. My mother and aunts were given their nicknames by the children of a white family for whom my Grandmother Hattie did laundry. One of the *Oldtimers* told me: *"White folks just loved to give colored babies names. It was like they was namin' their little dolls or dogs or kitty cats or somethin.'"*

Once given a formal Christian name, African American males to this day do not generally respond to shortened first names. A William is a William. A James is a James. An Edward is an Edward. A black Charles is a Charles. Among the general African American population today you will seldom find a "Bill," "Jim," "Ted," or "Chuck" unless they were given the nickname in college somewhere. In fact, I've known dozens of black men named Charles in my lifetime. I have, to this day, yet to meet a black Chuck. I walked to high school every day with a James Trimble. He remained James throughout high school and didn't become a Jim until his college years. My childhood buddy, Arthur Kinnel, became Art only after we were adults.

I carried the weighty, Roman imperial name Julius all through grade school, all through college, all through my teaching and advertising career, and did not take on the nickname "Jules" until I became a television newsman in 1970. I was besieged until that year with the question: "So, what do people call you for short." Or "What do your friends call you?" I dared not tell anyone until this writing that my family called me "June Bug" until I became an adult. And, I would frown on, and not respond to anyone—family, friend, or foe—referring to me by that name today.

The reluctance—or the downright refusal—of black males to take on a shortened name, no doubt, can be traced back to the days when an African American male grew from "boy" to "uncle" with no "manhood" between the two. As in "Uncle Ben." It is the reason Sidney Poitier tells the sheriff in the movie *In the Heat of the Night* "They call me **MR.** Tibbs." Don't call me Jack or Pete or Ned. Call me by my formal name to give me status as a man.

Since I have known many African American women who have not generally objected to being called Betty and Liz and Judy and Katie, the preference among black women does not appear to be as persnickety. On plantations, though, both during and after slavery, black women grew from "girl" to "Aunt"—as in Aunt Jemima—without ever being recognized as a woman with a formal name.

Perhaps the *Honey Island* child with the name most filled with cruel irony was that pitiful mentally ill girl named **Minor Fullilove**. Would that the cruel beast on the island who got her pregnant when she was just a child had thought of the significance of her name. She was literally an innocent minor who was at an inappropriate time full of love.

SCHOOL DAYS ON HONEY ISLAND

School for the *Honey Island* children consisted of a one-room classroom experience for all ages at one time. Youngsters were expected to be in school daily in one of two schools held in church chapels in the area: the narrow sanctuary of Jones Chapel or the equally simple facility in the sanctuary of Quafaloma Chapel. The latter, right near the Holmes County/Humphreys County line on Tchula Lake, was the outgrowth of a school for black children on the old Quafaloma plantation. It was thought of by the boys and girls on *Honey Island* as the more exclusive school of the two.

School began each weekday morning at eight and ended at three in the afternoon. The hours were loosely kept depending on the mood of the teacher, or in some rare cases, the debilitating heat of the day. The absentee rate was extremely high during the height of the harvest season when every hand in the family was a field hand—unless the hand was that of a toddler, of course.

Recess was not always a certainty if the teacher was miffed by the poor behavior or the poor recitation responses of her wards. There were sometimes as many as thirty youngsters in the one-room Jones Chapel Panther Burn School and sometimes as few as fifteen depending on absenteeism, vagaries caused by such uncontrollable elements as epidemics, short-term illnesses, inclement weather, flooding, peak crop harvest time, pressing home responsibilities, or truancy. There was no segregation by grade nor gender in the little school. The youngsters could sit anywhere they wanted and had no assigned seats.

Of course, the students who were approaching puberty and who had successfully passed through this hormonal milestone didn't want to be caught dead sitting near the first through sixth graders. St. Louisan Susan Blow's idea for kindergarten had not reached the *Panther Burn School* at Jones Chapel by the 1930s, even though Blow started the idea in the United States in a program first sanctioned by the St. Louis School Board in 1878.

The children on *Honey Island*— both before and after the turn of the twentieth century—started school at the tender age of five. The Susan Blow concept was based on a school start of six years of age. Many of the *Oldtimers* remember that children generally started school when they were potty-trained and weaned from home life.

Some of the *Oldtimers* also remember their teachers as fairly humorless, but totally dedicated to their profession and the education of their young wards. Perhaps the reason the teachers who taught at the Jones Chapel school were so strict with their students is that these educators realized that their time with their students was, often out of necessity, a relatively short span. It was perfectly acceptable in the earliest days of the *Honey Island* settlement for girls to leave school for good to help raise the family when their mothers became ill or when they passed. It was perfectly natural for a male pupil to abandon school forever to help parents who would rather have an extra field hand with a basic education than an egghead who was cooped up in a schoolhouse when the chickens needed feeding in the henhouse. Each time the youngsters left school for the weeks of peak harvest, the teachers never knew for sure who would be returning after the crops were brought in. For that matter, the *Honey Island* teacher could not ever be sure who was going to show up from day to day.

A half-hour was generally the amount of time allowed for lunch at the Jones Chapel Panther Burn School. But sometimes, depending on the teacher's mood or the teacher's other obligations— like a parental visit, a problem with errant students, prep time for the afternoon lessons, or the need for a personal break— the lunch period could become the lunch hour.

The students all brought their lunch pails, unless they lived close enough to sprint home where they would chow down and await the ringing of a big handbell to summon them back for the afternoon session. Lunch—in those pre-bologna sandwich days—consisted of whatever the family had left over from breakfast or from supper the night before, or from supper the night before the night before. Mothers generally fixed the lunch pails for the tots. It was an important badge of having grown up when a youngster was allowed to fix his or her own lunch. Having an older child with that badge was particularly helpful to the mothers when there were five, six, seven, or more kids in one family. Dads on *Honey Island* never even thought of getting involved in the preparation of food. That was work clearly assigned to the womenfolk.

All manner of victuals were carried in those school lunch pails. A common lunch item, which would make today's cardiologists and nutritionists faint in horror, was the big hunk of fatback that was so often slapped between two hunks of homemade bread. For the uninitiated, fatback is the fatty part of upper hog , quarters resembling bacon. Fatback is often cured by smoking, salting, and/or drying. Yep, *Honey Island* kids would chomp this cholesterolic nightmare at noontime! *Honey Island* school children would also dine on homegrown produce, hard-boiled eggs, a hunk of cheese, fried chicken, a big pork chop, and a slug of cake or pie. Fried pies were especially favored since the fruit-filled treats were easy to eat without a utensil.

To wash it all down, kids would line up at the nearby water pump, right next to the post office which was right next to the school/church. Boys would sometimes show their manly muscle and chivalry by pumping water for the girls. The *Oldtimers* remember how murky the pump water could be, especially the first water that gushed out of the mouth of the pump. Sometimes the water reeked of sulphur. Some *Honey Island Oldtimers* were not too sure the local water was bad for their children and grandchildren and themselves. After all, they thought, well water from the pump has a lot of good stuff in it to enhance good health. Heck, you could see all the minerals and stuff real plain in the unfiltered, unpurified water! The youngsters who could afford it would buy a soda pop from my great-uncle George Byrd or my great-aunt Ninnie at the post office confectionary right next door to the church/school. There were other sweet treats to purchase at the post office. Many of these purchases would be called junk food by today's parents and nutritionists.

In addition to the natural segregation the students themselves set up in the little one-room school according to age, boys and girls also segregated themselves outside at recess. During the free play period, at lunchtime and after school and chores, the boys would shoot marbles in smoothed out patches of ground while the girls would jump rope or play *jacks*. Jacks—or *jackstones*—are little six-pointed objects that are scooped up from the ground in a number of different sequences before a little ball that has been tossed into the air hits the ground. The girls would also fashion dolls out of the abundant supply of corn husks. Some of the *Oldtimers* remember a hazard for the girls making dolls and workers harvesting in those cornfields. Sting worms—corpulent, wriggly, green, corrugated critters—loved corn as much as humans did. The bare hand or arm that came into contact with the pesky pests came away with a puffy, itching welt wherever the worm's tiny hairs touched.

When love hit the air and young boys started noticing young girls and vice versa, it was sometimes difficult on *Honey Island* for the two youthful lovers to get together to steal a little smooch or two. No respectable girl, no matter how much in love, would ever walk home alone with a boyfriend. There were always a bunch of younger kids who made it a point to tag along with the pubescent pair while giggling and finger-pointing. Once kids got back to the family farms, chaperoning by watchful parents was the order of the day—and night. Remarkably few kids had kids on *Honey Island*.

Joe Nathan "Gene"Turner, born in 1915 as one of the nine children of Charity and Archie Turner, had a tougher time than most of his chums getting together with his first true love. When he was fifteen, he fell in love with the beautiful Annie Mae Scruggs. The real trouble for Joe, when Cupid first struck, was that Annie Mae lived more than an hour's walk from his family's farm. To make matters worse, she went to the Quafaloma School in the little chapel just outside *Honey Island*. Joe was first smitten by her charms while attending Sunday School at the church. The first love of Joe's life was actually the daughter of the white master of the Quafaloma plantation and a black servant woman named Mary. When Mary was pregnant with Annie Mae, a humble and sympathetic black man named Buss Scruggs stepped in to marry Mary and make her respectable. There was never any doubt about who the girl's real father was. Such was the lifestyle on *Honey Island* and throughout the Deep South. Among black *Honey Island* families, a child listed by census enumerators as "mulatto" often sprang up out of nowhere. Actually out of somewhere: a sexual liaison between a black slave or servant or sharecropper woman and a white master or overseer.

Such unfettered but hushed race-mixing could be seen in the family of *Honey Island's* Sallie and Riley Kelsey. They worked as a maid and cook on the plantation of Peter James, the man who sold Ned Rounds a big chunk of property. The 1880 census enumerator lists the Kelseys as black. One of their two children, the then fifteen-year-old Joe is clearly listed under the race column as "Mu." Joe's then five-year-old brother Eddy is listed as Black. There was some obvious confusion about who was a "Mu" and who was not. *Honey Island* resident Ruffin Maize is listed on the 1910 census as mulatto, his wife, Ernestine is listed as a black woman, two of the daughters, Ida and Martha are listed as black, but their baby daughter, Leola is recorded by the enumerator as being a mulatto. The mysterious appearance of a child of mixed race showed up in and all around *Honey Island*. Somehow, no records we viewed ever showed the appearance of a black baby in a white household.

Some genealogists dismiss the miscegenation statistic by citing recessive gene pools and such. And some others write off the appearance of a mixed race baby in an all-black family as just a judgment call on the fairness or darkness of the skin by the enumerator. *Honey Island* residents and their neighbors in the South whisper theory horses of another color.

Gene Turner remembered his first love, the pretty young "high yeller" girl as if it were yesterday:

"Boy, when that old love bug hit me, it hit me hard! All I could think of every day and night was my sweet Annie Mae. The boys I ran with used to really kid me about how love-

silly I got to be. My family attended Quafaloma Chapel where the Scruggs family went to church. That was the only time I could see her except when I could walk the hour or so to see her at her home. Her parents were always nice to me, but they were always within earshot when Annie Mae would entertain me in the parlor. I don't think her real father, the white plantation owner, liked me or any other dark-skinned boys from hanging around her. I never saw much of him, but I heard her real daddy kept a close watch on her comings and goings. While her parents were courteous to me, funniest thing, they never served me anything but a cool glass of water when I made it over there, though. I guess they didn't want me to get too comfortable and stay too long."*

Gene remembers that he was sometimes hot and parched of tongue when he got to the Scruggs' house. He was also dusty or muddy depending on the weather and the season. After getting to the section of *Honey Island* known as *The Quarter*, the young suitor would have to walk across the nearly dried-up Tchula Lake when it was at its lowest point in the summer. In the winter when the lake was at its high point of the year, Gene would have to borrow a boat from anybody in *The Quarter* who would be kind enough to loan him one. He'd then paddle across the lake to visit Annie Mae.

"Some evenings when I got to Quafaloma—usually on a Saturday evening—it seems that I couldn't stay long once I got there because it would start to get dark and I would have to start out on the long road home across Tchula Lake. That's because everybody had to get up early to go to church the next morning. But as the saying goes, I was willing to climb a mountain and swim an ocean to get to my true love."

Did the winsome Annie Mae feel the same way about Gene as he obviously felt about her?

"I really think she loved me, too. But she was about a year or two older than I was and I think she had a hotter body than I did. She was attracted to me because I played the piano as a kid. I sometimes played in church and I once told her I would secretly dedicate anything I played to her. And she knew that; felt that. My heart was broken a couple of times in this crazy love affair. First of all, Annie Mae's real father, Mr. Peaster, sent her off for a while to a boarding school in Louise (Mississippi)."

Annie Mae's stay at the out-of-town school was short-lived. Reportedly she was caught in a scandalous sexual liaison. Some said it was with a male teacher. Nobody was talking in Annie Mae's family, so nobody knew for sure. She was expelled and returned home in shame. Gene remembers that there could have been a lot more shame if anybody had known the salacious details of the scandal.

After a few years at home after the school scandal, Gene's precious Annie Mae became pregnant. Not by him, Gene is quick to proclaim.

"That was the second time my heart was broken…when she got pregnant. I knew the baby couldn't be mine. We never had sex. Never even had the chance to. She told me when she got back after that year away that she wanted to get married. As much as I loved her, I wasn't quite ready yet. Remember now what I said about her having a hot body, hot blood.

When I told her I wanted to finish my education so I could be a teacher, that's when Annie Mae got in a family way and went off and married a guy name of James Baity. He was a mulatto, too. He didn't have much schooling, but was going to inherit his daddy's farm some day. So she married Baity. Even after that, I carried a torch for Annie Mae until I was a grown man. I never talked to her after she married James. I lost her, I guess."

Turner did go on to get a good education. He went off to Greenwood High School in Greenwood. He then taught English and music at the Jasper County Training School outside Jackson in Newton, Mississippi, where he also coached basketball. He later attended Jackson State University where he upgraded his teaching credentials. Perhaps Annie Mae's decision was her loss.

Sadly, Joe Nathan Turner died within months of his sharing the poignant story of his unrequited love affair with the elusive and frisky Annie Mae when he was a youthful *Honey Island* neighbor of the Rounds family. His passing brings to mind the bittersweet days of our youth, how fragile life is and how important it is to record the stories of our loved ones who are in their golden years.

Back at Jones Chapel where almost all the Rounds offspring went to school, Turner was in class with my mother and aunts. As soon as some of the older children learned to read, write, and cipher at Jones Chapel, they helped the teacher, *Mizz* Coats, teach the younger children. Turner loved to help teach the younger children what he had learned.

Since there was no forced segregation of the sexes, boys and girls could sit right next to each other in the one-room school if they wanted to. This open-seating pattern often led to the usual pranks kids play on the opposite sex. Those who got caught usually got a rap on the knuckles with a ruler and were made to sit in a corner in the front of the schoolroom facing the wall. Errant girls usually received lighter sentences than bad boys, but not in all cases. For major offenses, the punished were even paddled. Sometimes the guilty youngster would be ordered to go out back of the church/school and bring back a "switch," a sapling size branch from a tree for a "switching" applied to the derriere right in front of all the other kids. The tree yielding the switch might be the rattan, a kind of palm. The youthful witnesses to crime and punishment would often snicker as the penitent inmate howled, begged for forgiveness, and prayed for absolution. There was a psychological thing going on here with the switch punishment. Usually the first two or three switches were rejected by Mizz Coats. She never, never accepted the first one broken off a tree out back.

This highly effective exercise of having a child go out back to eventually get the appropriate-sized switch must have been some southern custom. Or some particularly Mississippi custom because Grandma Hattie often made my three sisters and me go through the exact same process.

Mizz Coats' stern style, depending on whom one asked, provoked either terror too heightened for learning, a good educational foundation, or the recurring urge to play hooky. There was no truant officer back in the days the *Oldtimers* remember. Parents got a little white card report card at the end of each school year on which the students were rated with regard to their classroom comportment and mastery of the "Three R's." If the card candidly reported unacceptable behavior, non-acquisition of basic skills, and/or rampant truancy, a youngster might just be ordered by his father or mother to go out back of the schoolhouse/church and get a you-know-what from a tree. Then, in front of the whole class—with Mizz Coats looking on with an *"I told you this could happen"* smile—the juvenile offender would get a father-administered switching aimed at switching him into a pupil more academically proficient and attendance oriented.

At the end of the school year, around the first of June, there was always a proof-of-performance production given by the Panther Burn School students for their parents at Jones Chapel. The showing off of what had been learned was in the form of a little theatrical play and songs. The older kids recited great works like the Preamble to the U. S. Constitution, Lincoln's *Gettysburg Address*, part of William Ernest Henley's *Invictus*, the one that ends with *"I am the captain of my soul,"* or Tennyson's *Charge of the Light Brigade* with its driving *"Half a league, half a league onward"* cadence. The *Honey Island* parents would applaud wildly at the end of a recitation of prose or poetry even if the limited education of those parents didn't allow them to fully understand what they called "pretty words." They took exceeding pride and hoped that a good education—something very few of the adults in the audience had—would guarantee their children better, easier lives than they, the parents, had.

"Mizz Coats" was actually Mrs. Elizabeth Coats. She was married to the same John Coats who, after Mizz Coats passed, married my grandmother, giving her that rather curious name of Hattie Coats. He apparently gave her little more. The first Mrs. Coats, the dour school teacher at Jones Chapel, was not at all liked by many of her wards. She was tough, short-tempered, and, according to some of the *Oldtimers* she taught, she looked for all the world like a witch. She was an inveterate sourpuss, they said. Some of the *Oldtimers* may have made this judgment call based more on the harsh punishment she meted out daily than on her physical appearance. She was tall and willowy and wore only long black dresses down to her black comfortable shoes.

She passed in 1919 after a long and illustrious career. It was pneumonia, or maybe it was pleurisy that took her away from her job of teaching the young islanders. The cause of one's passing was not too specific in the olden days on *Honey Island*. In fact, one usually passed from a *"short illness"* or a *"long illness."* Short illnesses were the result of things like heart attacks and their subsequent periods of no recovery. Long illnesses were often the results of cancers, a word seldom used way back then. *Pneumonia* was often a good catch-all term for the malady that took so many islanders away to the burial plot just beyond Jones Chapel or to the little plot out back of the family farmhouse.

Few of the children, except the best students—her "pets" as the bad or average kids called them—shed real tears when they learned that Mizz Coats wouldn't be back because of her death. The conservationists among them might have reasoned that no more trees out back would be stripped of their branches. Mizz Alberta Howard was the next teacher at the Panther Burn School.

Mrs. Coats' husband, John, remained a widower for only a short time, then he went on almost immediately to make some lives in his next domestic situation miserable. When he married my grandmother, he brought his four children into the union to share space with Grandmother Hattie's three young daughters. He was later accused of making improper advances on her middle daughter and the then fourteen-year-old Willetta, out of fear and quite reluctantly, bolted the island and became the youngest member in her branch of the family to move up north to St. Louis. Ole Man Coats treated his new wife with either cruelty or neglect depending on what day or hour it was. The new Mrs. Coats threw the scoundrel out when she learned that he had another wife and family living in Lexington, Mississippi.

After Grandma and her oldest and youngest daughters had moved to St. Louis to join the middle daughter, Willetta, the persistent but not believably penitent John Coats had the audacity to write to his ex-wife to feel out the possibility that he might move to St. Louis to join her and her three daughters. "Mama," as we all called her, was the most kind and Christian woman anybody on *Honey Island* or later at West Side Baptist Church in St. Louis would ever meet. We are told the letter she sent him in response to his plea to reconcile should have been penned on asbestos paper and not proofread by any of her daughters or her minister or, perhaps, even by God Himself.

Willetta made the most out of being so quickly and scandalously uprooted from her idyllic home on *Honey Island*. After several domestic jobs taken just to make ends meet she picked up good training as a beautician at Poro College founded by Annie Turnbo Pope Malone. Malone borrowed the term *Poro* from the name of the men's secret society found throughout West Africa, especially in Sierra Leone among the Mende people. This school, which in reality offered no baccalaureate degree to barbers and beauticians, not only taught hair stying, it taught grooming skills and secretarial and bookkeeping classes. Here Willetta mastered the beautician's art quickly and went on to become a popular beautician.

Mrs. Malone was reaping the benefits of her prolific line of cosmetic products for black women and men. Her products and styling style became very popular on *Honey Island* too. Born in 1869, she began experimenting with a product specifically for the hair of African Americans while she was a high school student in Peoria, Illinois. After high school she continued her experiments with chemicals and developed her first marketable products in a humble frame shack just across the river from St. Louis in Lovejoy, Illinois. In 1918 Mrs. Malone opened the Poro Beauty College in St. Louis. In 1922 Mrs. Malone donated $10,000 for a children's home in North St. Louis which still bears her name today.

By her eighteenth birthday, Willetta was a stylist of good repute. In the tradition of the Rounds family, when life served her lemons, she made lemonade. She admits now that she is in her late eighties that she never ever really liked being a student at the *Panther Burns School*. She acknowledges that although it was really risky business, she is not all that sorry she dropped out of school at such a young age.

Some *Honey Island* fathers, in particular, were lenient with their sons and allowed them to leave school for good—or for bad—by age fifteen to help out on the family farm. In some rare cases for the Rounds family, the boys were needed to try to meet the elusive quotas set for sharecroppers on the latter-day plantations. Since Ambrose Rounds, a younger son of Westly Rounds, was sixteen and still in school in 1900, we can assume that his father thought that school was more important than becoming a full-time farmhand. In 1900, George and Frances Rounds' sons, Wes (named after his uncle, Westly) and William were in school at ages seventeen and fifteen, another example of the importance of education in the Rounds family—at least for the boys.

The 1910 census lists the then thirteen-year-old Inez Rounds as a "laborer." But how could that be? All her sisters and the other girls of that age were at school.

The *Oldtimers* knew well the job at which young Inez labored, especially the womenfolk. While her peers and siblings were laboring at learning the A, B, C's and minding their p's and q's, Inez was having a ball traveling around Mississippi working with her mother, Mary Lewis Rounds, as a beautician. Inez and her mother "did hair." It was hardly hard labor—more a labor of love—and profit. Mary and Inez would pack up their bag of cosmetology tools and head out for Tchula, Belzoni, Silver City, Brozville, and Thornton. The tools of their trade included combs, brushes, straightening irons, curling irons, pomades, hair oils, talcum powder, aprons, wash cloths, towels, rubbing alcohol, oil of camphor, shaving cups, soap, and brushes.

They could buy their tools in Belzoni but they often sent off to Chicago and St. Louis for their patent hair and skin products and beauty items like lipsticks, eye shadow, eye liner, rouge, and face powders. The products they received by mail order from Chicago were those of the famous and fabulously rich Madame C. J. Walker. Sarah Breedlove McWilliams, Madame Walker's real name, was born in Louisiana, the daughter of former slaves, in 1867. Her parents died when she was just five years old. Just as a young woman from the Rounds clan had to seek her fortune at age fourteen, Sarah Breedlove was shoved into an early venture into adulthood. She married Moses McWilliams at age fourteen. She and her daughter were left without a husband and father just six years later. She worked as a laundress in St. Louis beginning in 1887, one year after Ned Rounds purchased his *Honey Island* farm.

This former St. Louis washerwoman developed a commercial product that straightened hair and was even purported to grow hair. She created the product to treat her own alopecia. Declaring it a success, she opened labs in St. Louis, Chicago, and, in 1905, in Denver. She married a gentleman named Charles Walker and in 1908 when things were beginning to go sour on the Rounds homestead on *Honey Island,* the woman who was to become America's first black millionairess opened a business in Pittsburgh. Two years later "the Walker Method" was introduced to beauticians and barbers in Indianapolis. Madame Walker spotted the fact that before her day there were no cosmetic products aimed specifically at African American consumers. In 1919, after Madame Walker had moved to New York, she hosted the first meeting of the International League of Darker People at her plush estate. Among the founders of this organization was Adam Clayton Powell Sr., the renowned pastor of New York's mammoth Abyssinian Baptist Church. To attest to Walker's popularity, in 1924 she was honored by the American Federation of Negro Students as one of that year's most respected and influential Negroes. She was the only woman named among a list of great African American men including George Washington Carver, W.E.B. DuBois and Booker T. Washington.

Willetta Williams Perkins, a great-granddaughter of Ned Rounds, attended Poro College after she left *Honey Island*. She learned some skills there that led to her becoming a popular beautician. The hair products created by Walker and Malone, used as needed to curl or straighten the hair of black customers all across the country, sure beat the lard, the Vaseline, and sometimes the lye mixed with hair grease on *Honey Island* and in every other town and city in America where African Americans wanted to spruce up their appearance. News of the products developed by these two exemplary entrepreneurs reached *Honey Island* and the ears of Mary Lewis Rounds. Black women and their daughters in all the little Mississippi towns visited by the mother-daughter team of circuit beauticians looked with anticipation to the return visit of the two and eagerly prepared a place in their kitchens to get a "do." West and Mary didn't mind at all that Inez was not in school in her early teen years. After all, she had acquired a trade that she could use for the rest of her life.

Honey Island: The Cauldron for Cooking, Curing and Conjuring

The idyllic island that Ned Rounds helped establish with family and friends was surrounded by little Mississippi towns with colorful names, like **Darlove** and **Midnight, Eden, NittaYuma, Itta Bena, NittaYuma, Money, Egypt, Hard Cash, Silver City**, and the perfect name for a sleepy, tiny town—**Nod**. In the old days, a trip into one of the bigger towns like Belzoni, Yazoo City, or Isola would take the better part of a day. When my great-great-grandfather, Ned Rounds, rode into Belzoni right after the Civil War, the town was nothing more than a hole in the wall. In fact, Old Ned would have first known Belzoni as "Greasy Row." That's what everybody called the place in the 1880s when Old Ned began buying Delta property. Belzoni got its first name because of the little town's row of raucous saloons. They were, at the time, just about Greasy Row's only real estate. Though the nearest town to the Rounds homestead never became a boom town, it achieved a better-sounding name when it was incorporated in 1895 and named after Giovanni Battista Belzoni. He was a noted Italian explorer and Egyptologist who had died more than seven decades before this Mississippi town was named after him. Belzoni's current mayor, Tom Turner, an affable and enthusiastic chap told me:

"So far as I know, Giovanni Belzoni never set foot in this area. But there was this guy from Massachusetts, Alverus Fisk, who moved to Natchez and bought a very large plot of land he turned into a thriving plantation. It stretched all the way from Natchez going north from theYazoo River all the way over to this area. He named his place 'Belzoni Plantation' after the explorer he greatly admired. In fact, Fisk founded the first public library in what is now Belzoni. When our town got its charter back in 1895, it seemed a

natural to name it after the large plantation it set on."

Belzoni certainly sounds a lot more prosperous and sophisticated than "Greasy Row."

In those relatively carefree but arduous days of yesteryear, the Rounds family members and their *Honey Island* neighbors and friends could hitch up a horse or a mule or two to make the long trip into Belzoni to shop at the general store or Goldberg's dry goods store. They might take the grueling seven-mile wagon, buggy, or horseback ride into town on a narrow, rutted dirt road to bank with an establishment other than the savings and loan Ned Rounds operated without an official charter.

According to all the *Oldtimers,* none of the Belzoni merchants cared one whit what color a customer's skin was. In fact, there was only one color the shopkeepers and bankers in Belzoni and Yazoo City cared about. That was green. As in money green. Easy credit was guaranteed to any *Honey Island* resident who appeared to be "set down for a spell."

Belzoni was always the first choice of the *Honey Island* residents when they hitched up their horses or mules or cranked up their horseless carriages for a trip into town. Yazoo City to the south was the second choice. It was farther away from *Honey Island* than Belzoni and required more time away from home. Yazoo City was settled by white pioneers from Alabama, Georgia, Kentucky, North and South Carolina, and Tennessee as early as 1824. It was first called *Hannan's Bluff.* In 1839 the little town was named *Manchester* after the city in England. Then just a decade later, the name was changed to *Yazoo City.* Yazoo is an Indian word for "death." When Ned Rounds, his family, and *Honey Island* neighbors rode into town before 1900, Yazoo City had fewer than three hundred full-time residents. It has a little more than twelve thousand citizens today.

Honey Island's second town has been a virtual *Phoenix*—as in the bird of Greek mythology which rose from its own ashes to new life. In fact, Yazoo City has had to emulate that fabled fowl twice in its history. The town was burned down as a casualty of the Civil War in 1864. It was rebuilt, only to burn down again in 1904 in what is considered the worst fire in Mississippi history. The entire business district and dozens of homes were wiped out by this inferno.

Just about the time Ned Rounds first surfaces in the area about 1855, Yazoo City was in the deadly aftermath of a devastating epidemic of yellow fever. Had Ned, his loved ones, or neighbors ventured into Yazoo City two years before 1855, they would have likely perished from the jaundice, violent vomiting, and hemorrhaging that the victim experienced. The ubiquitous Mississippi mosquitoes visited a second yellow fever epidemic on Yazoo City in 1882, a time when Ned Rounds and all those around him were definitely susceptible.

What might be almost as remarkable as the longevity and relative good health of the *Honey Island* residents in the decades before the turn of the twentieth century, is the number of young married couples who were the same relative age as Ned Rounds' son, Westly, and Westly's wife, Hager. West was twenty-four and Hager was twenty-three in 1880. There were, in that year, thirty-one married couples with both partners under the age of thirty. Some worked on their family homesteads; some of the young couples worked as servants on large *Honey Island* plantations; some of the young marrieds worked their own little farms. When the children are factored into this equation, my great-great-grandfather Ned Rounds, at age fifty-five in 1880, was an old man, more than twenty years older than he was expected to live in that era.

Such a youthful populace in 1880 would appear to have assured *Honey Island* the same degree of longevity as some of its elderly residents. The fact that there are only two descendants of these original islanders living in the last two houses still standing on the place in 1999 attests to the ravages of those *Four F's*: foreclosure, flooding, farming changes, and flight to the North.

The general longevity of the *Honey Island* residents might send many an actuary to his grave trying to figure out the source of long life among the islanders. In fact, there is one lifestyle factor among the residents of the agrarian island that members of today's medical society might not be able to explain: their daily diet. In this current age of *cholesterophobia*, what the *Honey Island* farm families ate is exactly what we are told today to avoid because these foods cause heart attacks, strokes, and hardening of the arteries.

****

lard, *n.* 1. the rendered fat of hogs, esp. the internal fat of the abdomen...

Breakfast on *Honey Island* in the good old days the *Oldtimers* remember was always a sumptuously large salute to cholesterol: eggs fried in butter or lard, hash browns sizzled crisp in butter or lard, abundant bacon, link sausage or sausage patties, maybe a big slug of fatback if no bacon or sausage was available, jellied and buttered buttermilk biscuits with lard used as the shortening, a hunk of cheddar cheese, and a big glass of right-from-the-source whole milk or buttermilk to wash all those arteriosclerotic treats down. All the recipes for biscuits called for at least a half cup of lard.

Lunch in any of the Rounds households on *Honey Island* or in any of the neighboring homes might consist of whatever was left over from breakfast added to what might be today's medically-disapproved treat of crackling bread dunked in a bowl of buttermilk. Crackling bread, if consumed with reckless abandon, should guarantee work for heart specialists. To make this little treat for six (and *Honey Island* residents would make more than six helpings, for sure) requires two cups of cracklings. Cracklings are made of salt pork—blocks of preserved hog fat diced and fried and rendered down to crisp crunchlings. Then half a teaspoon of baking soda is added to a cup of buttermilk; two cups of cornmeal are then blended into the mix.

Finally, as if there isn't enough presence of polyunsaturated pig parts in the batter, the cook should splash in two tablespoons of bacon drippings from the coffee can always found on a shelf or sink next to the kitchen stove. The tradition of saving bacon grease in a coffee can survived the trip up North for all good expatriate southern cooks. After the mushy mix is formed into *pones*, the crackling concoction is baked in a 350-degree oven for about twenty minutes. If one wanted, one could spread a little butter (more cholesterol) onto the crackling bread right as it comes out of the oven. That was one popular *Honey Island* lunch— crackling break mixed up with buttermilk.

Supper (never called "dinner" in the South) on *Honey Island* might center around crispy fried chicken. For all the mouths that were generally fed around the Rounds table, it would be nothing for the cooks to fry up three or four chickens. After all, there were chickens aplenty busybodying around just outside the kitchen door. The children were always mesmerized and sometimes terrified to see an adult go out to the chicken coop, grab an unsuspecting bird, get a good grip on the cackling, flapping fowl's neck and with a quick snapping semi-circular motion pop the chicken's neck from its body causing a gush of blood. The incredible phenomenon of this event is that the headless body of the chicken would run around the barnyard for twenty or thirty seconds after the decapitation. But we digress. Back to supper:

With the fried chicken as the center of the meal, the accessory dishes were always *at least* a couple of starches: grits, hominy, corn, rice and/or potatoes; candied yams; collard, mustard, or turnip greens; pickled beets; fried green tomatoes; dinner rolls (make that **supper** rolls), and redeye gravy.

If fried chicken was not the main meat of choice, *Honey Island* residents had a plethora of hog parts from which to choose. Beef was available to the *Honey Island* diner, but pork was the favorite meat. Hams—often smoked, pork chops, pigs' feet, ribs, smoked jowls, snoots, pig ears, pig tails, tenderloin, neck bones, sweetbreads, ham hocks, shanks, maws and chitlins all came from the hog. The latter two delicacies are respectively the hog's stomach and intestines. They are listed together here because they were always cooked together.

To cook hog maws and chitlins is a laborious chore. The maws must be parboiled to facilitate the removal of the fatty membrane. The cleaning of the chitlins—the intestines—is a particularly messy and smelly job in that some of the hog excrement clings to the things. There's a membranous skin which must first be removed before cooking. To help clean chitlins, it was not at all unusual for *Honey Island* cooks to add a little bleach to the tub in which the intestines were being washed. Bleach!!!

After the cook is satisfied that the maws and the chitlins are clean enough, there are two ways to cook the innards. One way is to cut the stuff into strips, dip in a flour-based batter and deep-fry. But that recipe was seldom the first choice of *Honey Island* cooks. They preferred to put the maws and chitlins in a huge pot, add about a fourth of a pot of water, add salt to taste, throw in a couple big hot peppers, a couple big onions cut in half, about four big stalks of celery, about six cloves of garlic cut in half, and about four bay leaves broken up. Then they put the lid on and lined the top of the lid with bread slices or thick slices of white potato. This step cut down—but did not fully eliminate—the awful smell of entrails cooking. Then the cook turned the heat under the pot to a medium temperature.

They planned to boil the contents of the pot for six or seven hours—or even longer! In fact, there is a tongue-in-cheek saying among the Rounds family members that one should also put a nail in the pot of maws and chitlins before cooking them. According to the laughable family legend, when the nail is soft, the chitlins are done!

As kids, my sisters and I exaggerated our disdain whenever chitlins were cooked in whichever household we were in at the time. It is a pretty bad smell. It is the same basic smell that one can experience in England when kidney stew is being made. One gets the same effect of the maws and chitlins in Scotland when *haggis* is the meal of the day. But I must admit I have, on many occasions, eaten maws and chitlins or "wrinkle steaks," as they are affectionately called. These innards are always eaten with cornbread, coleslaw, potato salad, and spaghetti in the homes of *Honey Island* descendants and soul food-eating southerners throughout Dixie. Lots of Louisiana hot sauce must be splashed on the boiled chitlins and maws.

I don't know and have never been able to find out how this particular entree came to be such a harmonious combination. You can still find this combo on northern tables of former southerners. Legend has it that after the slave master and his family ate all the best parts of the hog, the throwaways that were left became the basis of African American soul food. Makes sense.

There is another rule to observe. One never, never eats chitlins in the summer time. They must be eaten only in the colder months. That's because the coagulation of the liquid surrounding the innards is pretty thick and artery clogging. Field hands back in the old days could not stand up to the sluggishness that a big meal of chitlins could cause in the hot summer months. Better to eat the stuff in winter when there were no crops to bring in and a good nap could be had after eating "wrinkle steak."

It is a curious fact that some of the finer supermarkets now sell chitlins in frozen packs with a guarantee that they have been thoroughly cleaned and are all ready to drop into the pot frozen as they come or thawed. Some of the original *Honey Island* residents would, no doubt, roll over in the very graves that eating chitlins helped put them into, were they to see pre-cleaned frozen chitlins in vacuum packs in high-class supermarkets! And sold as a delicacy! Hah!

Honey Island butchers didn't even throw away the hog's hooves. They could be ground and boiled to make the precursor of *Jello,* or the gelatinous stuff that held together hog scraps after butchering. That stuff was called "hog head cheese," a dish cooled after boiling and sliced for serving like any cold cut. Head cheese, the dish made on *Honey Island*, is the same dish that the Germans call *souse.*

When chicken or pork or beef were not served up as the main meat at supper, the *Honey Island* hungry could belly up to fish which were abundant in Tchula Lake, the Yazoo River, Eagle Lake, and even the Mississippi River. There was carp and trout and perch and bass and lots of other fishes for the Delta tables, but the all-time favorite was buffalo fish. Buffalo fish was not only a strong-tasting fare, it was dangerous to eat because of the tiny spiny bones on the "small side." The "big side" of buffalo fish was safer. But all the *Honey Island* residents knew that when a buffalo fish bone got stuck in the throat, only a huge wad of bread followed by a big gulp of liquid could dislodge the bone into the stomach where it might still be a problem. One thing for certain about any fish that appeared on the table of the Rounds family or their neighbors—that fish would be fried. Deep-fried in a cornmeal batter in lard or bacon grease.

Ice-cold lemonade made with a couple dozen fresh lemons and sweetened until syrupy was a favorite wash-down libation after a heavy fried chicken or pork-part meal. For dessert there were pies—more often *cobblers*—of a number of varieties offered with fruits freshly-plucked from the family orchards out back of the house. Peach, apple, currant, blackberry, rhubarb, strawberry, or cranberry pies and cobblers were favorites. A cobbler is a deep-dish fruit pie with a rich biscuit crust and flour dumplings with lots of sugar and sometimes raisins and nuts added. Cobblers generally have no top crust.

Then there were pies made of some things that aren't used much any more. There was a navy bean pie from beans that were often called *Yankee beans.* Green tomato pie was a southern treat. While sweet potato pies were a traditional product of the golden yams dug up on the farms, there are actually some recipes for *Irish potato* pies made from white potatoes. There were, of course, pecan pies, egg custard pies, and lemon meringue pies—although the latter two pies didn't last long because of the hot weather. But then, generally, they weren't expected to stay around uneaten for long. Three or four pies were sometimes stacked one on top of the other so that when sliced, the diner had a selection of each on the plate. If there was any heavy cream to whip up, the pie slices got a good unhealthy dollop of whipped cream to crown them.

Every good southern cook knows that you just can't make a good pie crust without the omnipresent lard. One *Honey Island* pie crust, I learned from watching my grandmother cook, took at least one-and-a-half cups of lard. In more recent times, three sticks of *oleo margarine*, a butter substitute, were a must for a good crust.

A large variety of cakes was also produced in *Honey Island* kitchens. There was carrot cake, butter cake, coconut layer cake, lemon cake, pineapple upside-down cake, gingerbread, and the most popular of all—the pound cake. The latter got its name because the cake had approximately a pound each of butter, sugar and flour. The products of nut groves—hickory, walnut, and pecan—could be added to almost any pie, cobbler or cake for an extra added attraction. Icings were rare since they would melt and get icky in the torrid Mississippi heat. Gingerbread did have to have the obligatory lemon sauce, rum sauce, or whiskey sauce as a topping.

Ice creams were a popular delight after Sunday lunch or after Sunday supper. As with all things the Rounds did or owned, this prosperous *Honey Island* family served and consumed the biggest proportions. Ice cream churns in the Rounds kitchens were of the five-pound variety. Ice cream was made in the old-fashioned hand-churned makers, mostly with the kids given turns at churning the concoction for up to an hour. A rich custard of eggs, milk, butter, sugar, vanilla extract, nutmeg, and cornstarch with a pinch of salt would be whipped up. The imaginative ice cream creator could let the imagination run wild with add-ins of fruit and nuts. The custard would then be poured into the bucket in the center of the bigger bucket. Next, ice from the ice shack (the smokehouse when meats weren't hanging from the rafters) would be packed around the center bucket, salt poured on top of the ice, the top with its churn handle put on the custard bucket and round and round the Roundses would crank the handle until the custard was frozen. At the Sunday ice cream socials at Jones Chapel, there was unofficial competition to see who could bring the most inventive frozen custards. Never mind a declared winner, though. It was all good.

The *Honey Island* sweet tooth was further satisfied with three kinds of popular homemade candies. There were taffies, peanut brittle, and molasses whips. All of them were the bi-product of the sugar cane fields and the molasses they produced. Oddly enough, the taffy and the molasses whips needed vinegar to complete the recipe, as much as a half-cup of vinegar for five pounds of taffy and a tablespoon of vinegar for the molasses whips. Taffy had to be pulled and pulled and pulled (with clean hands heavily greased with warm butter) to get it to its confectionery perfection. Sometimes, a girl and a boy who were "sweet on each other" would pull taffy on a Sunday afternoon. That's where the expression "I'm stuck on you" emanates.

I loved to watch my grandmother, my mother, and aunts—all *Honey Island* natives—making peanut brittle when I was a young boy. They'd put a couple of cups of granulated sugar in a huge black, time-tested skillet, turn up the heat, and, stirring often, let the sugar melt until it was golden brown and syrupy. A teaspoon of Watkins Vanilla Extract and a pinch of salt would be added. Then a couple of cups of peanuts (called *goober peas* on *Honey Island* and throughout the

South) would be thrown into the hot molasses. (*Goober* actually comes from a Kimbundu African word for peanut used by the Bantus of Northern Angola, *nguba*.) When the hot concoction was still bubbling, the candy-makers in my family would pour the hot mix onto waxed paper or onto a buttered dish until it cooled and hardened.

No wonder great-great-grandpa Ned eventually weighed three hundred pounds! It is a wonder that *Honey Island* residents, given their lard-rich, fat-laden diets, flew so defiantly into the face of actuarial charts. When we lose touch with Ned Rounds on paper, the year was 1900. Ned was probably sixty-seven years old and living alone. He probably lived at least a few years longer, despite his fatty diet. West Rounds lived to be seventy-two, and he was far from alone in the septuagenarian crowd. The ages of eighty, ninety, and even a hundred were also not rare among the *Honey Island* residents and their descendants, including my kinfolk.

There were at least two factors that helped to keep the Stork more active on *Honey Island* than the Grim Reaper. One important element is that the islanders, with perhaps the exception of Old Ned and his son Westly, were physically active all day. The Reaper generally backs off from those who are reaping and sowing and plowing and chopping and washing and ironing and walking from sunrise to sunset every day. The more tempting targets for Dr. Death are those who eat big meals like the islanders did and then napped and lounged and stayed plopped in their rocking chairs.

The other factor that might have helped the Islanders live long lives is the virtually pollution-free air they were breathing down on the farm. Sure, there was the thick, black smoke that billowed from the smokestacks of the hundreds and hundreds of steamboats that plied the Yazoo River. Filtered by the natural baffle of pine trees and magnolias in their shawls of Spanish moss, the pollutant would have had plenty of time to dissipate in the thirty miles or so from the river to the island farms. The steamboats the *Honey Island* residents saw turn around right across the road from their little Baptist church in Tchula Lake would chug their way back into the Yazoo River and didn't need much power for this maneuver. So, there was not so much black smoke billowing from the stacks to foul the *Honey Island* air. Many of the former islanders soon came to miss their clean Island air they grew up breathing after they moved to the smoky northern meccas of St. Louis, Chicago, and Detroit. The only respiratory problems the *Honey Island* residents would have experienced would have been from the hand-rolled cigarettes, cigars, and pipes the men and women, and sometimes children, smoked.

****

With these hearty senior citizens as a shining example of just how long a person could live, the folks on *Honey Island* didn't put much faith in physicians.

Or dentists, for that matter. They'd put more faith in a good "horse doctor"—a veterinarian—than they would in medicine men. If a member of the Rounds family or any of their neighbors rode into Belzoni and Yazoo City, it was generally not to see a doctor. The islanders relied heavily on home remedies passed on from generation to generation with fairly good but not guaranteed results.

HONEY ISLAND HOME REMEDIES

"100 years ago people afflicted with affections and infirmities entrusted themselves to faith, and to themselves to catch-as-catch-can cures, dredged folklore wisdom and remedies found in home pantries and medicine chests.

"In those horse-and-buggy days, village Apothecaries offered drugs and chemicals for 'cures' which our forefathers concocted in their own kitchens and administered to the ailing with tablespoon and prayer.

"Today, it is hard to tell whether ancestral potence or potions actually invigorated growth of the family tree. Today you, like your forebears, take these nostrums solely at your own risk."

-Jean Cross
`from *In Grandmother's Day*

Sometimes—if ever so rarely—the islanders journeyed into Belzoni or Yazoo City to see a doctor or dentist. Some of the Rounds family who lived closer to Greenwood would go into town to see either Dr. Bates or Dr. Nelson. They were the only two doctors who would treat "colored." These two doctors would actually travel to the neighboring plantations to treat sharecroppers. But trips into town to see a doctor in the old days were uncommon, indeed. The *Honey Island* residents who lived around the Rounds family in 1880 enjoyed relatively good health, except during the epidemics like the yellow fever plague that killed off many of the islanders in 1904. One casualty was the handsome Elbert Jones whose father donated the land for Jones Chapel. Elbert is buried in the cemetery right next to the little chapel where my sister and I saw his tombstone with the picture.

Many of the early *Honey Island* residents—including the sturdy Rounds Clan—flew boldly into the face of the statistics on life expectancy for their eras. For example, a Rounds neighbor, Old Butler Noble, was in "right smart" good health at age eighty when the enumerator came around in 1880. The census-taker found and noted no outstanding maladies in this hearty octogenarian. The census enumerators did make some notes in a column set aside to list illnesses. For example, forty-year-old *Honey Island* wife, Jane Johnson, was battling colic in 1880. With the exception of two islanders suffering from "ophthalmia," an eye inflammation, all the other *Honey Island* residents were in fine fettle except for eighty-year-old Moses Telford. Poor fellow had a broken leg.

Ned Rounds' seventy-nine-year-old *Honey Island* neighbor, William Wright, was still working his farm in 1880. Wright's twenty-year-old son, Hercules, was performing herculean tasks in the field. It is true that John Nixon was eighty-six years old in 1880, but he still vigorously worked his farm every day. And Nixon and his thirty-three-year-old wife had children aged eleven and three! Alfred Braddock, age seventy-five, was still planting and harvesting the crops on his *Honey Island* farm in 1880. What's more, Braddock and his fifty-year-old wife, Patsy, had five young children including the then four-year-old Nancy. That year, 1880, was a year in which the average life expectancy for the nation's black males was thirty-four; black females, thirty-eight. It's a good thing that *Honey Island* dwellers didn't read statistics. That may have been just one of the reasons they lived beyond statistical expectations.

The other elements that contributed to *Honey Island* longevity—in spite of the cholesterolic diet—were the hard work, the gene pool, the fresh, unpolluted air, and the relative isolation from the towns and cities which spawned epidemics.

Each day on *Honey Island* brought the medical challenges to a community without its own doctor and with the nearest physician as far away as a ride into Belzoni or Yazoo City. The Islanders rose to the task of curing themselves, their loved ones, and work associates by necessity. Some of the so-called "cures" weren't cures at all. Some of the nostrums, according to some of the *Oldtimers*, worked wondrously. Some of the home remedies passed on to us by some of the *Oldtimers* seemed to mask, as much as to relieve, the conditions for which they were used. Others seemed to supply a psychological preoccupation with feeling better, which may have correlation to psychosomatic illnesses and the "mind over matter" theories used by shamans.

Every year at springtime, *Honey Islanders* felt the uncontrollable urge to purge. They tried to clean out their systems with all manner of elixirs, tonics, laxatives, purgatives, teas, and foul-tasting concoctions learned about from grandmothers, Indians, missionaries, shamans, voodoo practitioners, and witch doctors. According to some of the *Oldtimers*, the nastier the taste of the medicine—and the more violent the reaction to it—the more effective the "cure" was thought to be!

Becerra and Iglehart, in their thesis *Folk Medicine Use: Diverse Populations in a Metropolitan Area,* opine that folk medicine in Western societies is "derived from the ancient Greek theory of the four bodily fluids—blood, phlegm, yellow bile, and black bile" and is "characterized by the qualities associated with fire, earth, water, and air, respectively. Those qualities are heat, cold, moistness, and dryness." One can almost bet the farm that for all the residents of *Honey Island,* any ancient medical theories were Greek to them. Surely not a single Islander had read anything about the Greek theory of the four fluids. Yet surprisingly, many of the home remedies conjured up in the Mississippi Delta did take into account blood, phlegm, yellow bile, and black bile—fire, earth, water, and air.

Sometimes a resident of the island would take a swig of "moonshine" to try to cure what ailed him or her. That would definitely be an association with both fire and water. The hootch, often taken in a hot toddy, certainly created a euphoria that caused the drinker to forget what it was that ailed him/her and then sink into a deep sleep. Besides, some may have thought it was a pretty stupid idea to raise all the corn on the island if some of it couldn't be used for medicinal purposes.

Even turpentine was used unwisely as a medication by some islanders. A drop or two on a teaspoon of sugar, in a cup of hot water, or directly applied to an aching tooth with an eyedropper was a popular treatment among many *Honey Island* residents. By today's standards, turpentine should have had dubious effectiveness on parasites or worms, but it was used widely to get rid of internal critters. Perhaps the patient felt so much better after recovering from the ill effects of ingesting the turpentine that he or she forgot how bad the reason for taking it felt. Turpentine was also poured directly onto certain types of blisters, boils, cuts, and skin abrasions. Ouch!

A particularly vile patent "remedy" for getting rid of winter accumulations of bad stuff in the body was a product called *black draught*. Even though the standard pronunciation of the word "draught" is "draft," the *Honey Island* residents pronounced it "drawt." The black powder, which some said tasted like "black powder that had gone bad," came in a square box that could be purchased at the drugstore in Belzoni. It was, by all accounts, the most awful stuff anybody had ever tasted. But that was good! The disgusting purgative powder was teaspooned into a cup; boiling hot water was poured over it; the "tea" was allowed to sit until the sediment settled to the bottom of the cup. Then while holding one's nose, the broth was downed in one long gulp. The dire consequences of ingesting black draught should not be discussed in polite company, and certainly never around the dinner table. Suffice it to say the black draught consumer was wise to stay near the outhouse.

Castor oil was the other popular laxative. One could take two teaspoonsful shoved right into a gagging mouth or mix a tablespoon of oil from the castor bean with citrus juice. My Uncle Walter brought a couple of unusual ways of taking castor oil with him when he came up to St. Louis from *Honey Island*. He'd spread a tablespoonful or two on a slice of bread or pour the bad-tasting oil on a tablespoon of baking soda. The results were guaranteed either way. And I don't want to talk about it anymore.

Powdered sulfur was another popular element of home cures on *Honey Island*. Mattie Burns Williams remembers sulfur was mixed in water or molasses to help treat measles. A sulfur poultice was good for cuts and burns, too. Mrs. Williams remembers that her parents depended on the foul-smelling jimson weed to bring down fever. The word *jimson* is a corruption of the word *Jamestown*,

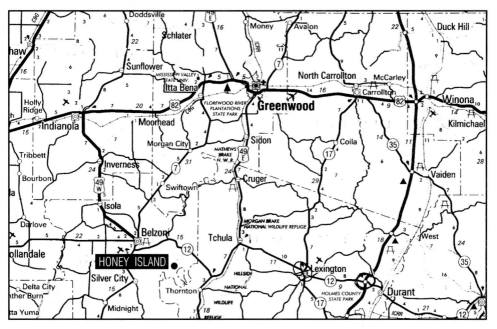

Honey Island is located just southeast of Belzoni, Mississippi.

Westly Rounds and second wife, Mary Lewis Rounds. My great-grandfather always carried a rolled up newspaper to show that he could read.

My dear Grandmother Hattie (1881-1978) as a young woman. She was a major guiding force in my life.

Ben Rounds and his mother, Mary Lewis Rounds, with an ox who became Ben's pride and joy until the family moved to Chicago. Ben destroyed all copies of the photo so Chicagoans would not consider him a rube.

An ox-drawn cart was used for work and occasional play on *Honey Island.*

Minnie and J. C. Cummings' house was near the Rounds *Honey Island* compound. It burned to the ground in 1978.

The Jones Chapel Missionary Baptist Church was co-founded by my great-grandfather, Westly Rounds, in 1894. The church is alive and well today!

This highway sign announces that the church where my relatives worshiped and were schooled is alive and well.

Jesse Rounds, his wife Annie, and their large family eked out a meager living as sharecroppers after the Rounds family land was lost.

My Great-aunt Ninnie helped her husband, George Byrd Jr., run the *Honey Island* post office. She died of a vitamin deficiency in a family that ate well.

My very dapper Great-uncle Henry Rounds suffered from a mental affliction that caused him to be institutionalized for most of his life.

Annie Rounds' grandfather, Rufus West (1843-1928), took his new master's surname when he was sold as a young boy. His brother took the last name Green from the slave master to whom he was sold causing the brothers to lose touch for many decades.

My Aunt Willetta; Aunt Gertrude; and my mother, Atlener; were all born on *Honey Island*—the daughters of my Grandmother Hattie and Anderson Williams.

My Great-uncle Ambrose left *Honey Island* to take a job, which was prestigious for an African American of his era, with the Chicago post office.

Willie Lewis Rounds also had a coveted job. He was a dining car chef on the Wabash Railroad.

Joe Nathan Turner had a youthful love affair on *Honey Island* with a girl who did not return his love.

My Grandma Hattie took this antiseptic with a Civil War era formula well into her nineties for almost anything that ailed her.

My aunts, Gertrude and Willetta, in 1915. Aunt Willetta turned 90 in 1999.

My Grandma Hattie, or "Mama" as everybody called her, celebrates one of her last birthdays with her loving family.

My cousin, Eva (Aunt Gertrude's daughter and Pearl's sister), in 1946.

Thaddeus "Ted" Rounds served in World War II. He once smarted off to a plantation owner and had to flee for his life.

Ted says he is as feisty in his golden years as he was back on the plantation.

My Aunt Willetta and a dashing WWII serviceman head out for a night on the town in 1941.

My late Aunt Gertrude and my mother, Atlener, in 1929 in their Sunday-go-to-meeting clothes for a worship service at Jones Chapel.

King Byrd was the son of my great-uncle and aunt, George and Ninnie Rounds Byrd. He became a prominent private investigator after he moved from *Honey Island* to Chicago.

The author (at right) in 1957 is shown with his best friend Gerald Broyles and his first girlfriend, Juanita Divers. Note the hats.

Humphreys County Courthouse.

The author (top right) and his sister, Carol Hunter (bottom right), dig through documents in Humphreys County Courthouse in Belzoni, Mississippi.

The Fourth Rounds Family Reunion was held over the 1999 Labor Day weekend in Memphis. A total of 117 family members from 11 states shared fun and family history.

as in Jamestown, Virginia, where the plant's medicinal values were purportedly first discovered. The white or lavender flowers from this *Datura Stramonium* plant can be poisonous if taken in massive quantities, but the *Honey Island* home medicine practitioners knew the right amount of the plant to boil for a curative tea to bring relief to the patient with a high fever.

Coal oil, commonly known as kerosene, was not just burned in lamps. It must have also burned the lining of more than a few *Honey Island* bellies when taken internally to get rid of worms. *Oldtimers* put a few drops of this oil distilled from bituminous coal on a teaspoonful of sugar to kill any of the parasitic worms that could set up housekeeping in intestinal passages. Kerosene mixed with sugar was also applied to burns. Coal oil drops on sugar was also a popular *Honey Island* remedy used to fend off bad colds.

Also employed to bring relief from colds or flu, lemons and onions seemed to be the most prevalent core cure ingredients. The *Oldtimers* put lemon and honey in tea for a cough cure. Lemon was combined with whiskey, olive oil, castor oil, mint, other citrus fruits, and onion in various teas and toddies. Onions were often called on to cure coughs, colds, sore throats, and respiratory ailments. One popular cure I saw my grandmother and Uncle Walter, in particular, use for coughs and colds involved the *Alleum cepa*—common onion by its botanical name. Grandma Hattie and Uncle Walter would get a large onion and cut it up over a small pot. A cup or so of black molasses was poured over the onion and about a tablespoon of vinegar was added. The "stew" was then simmered very slowly and for a long time until the onion was boiled down. The thick cure could then be ladled into a cup or bowl and eaten for something less delicious than any dessert treat they could have cooked up.

One of the least offensive cold remedies that made it to St. Louis from *Honey Island* involved a concoction of rock candy, honey, and pine tar. Grandma Hattie could buy rock candy and a bottle of pine tar at the exotic-smelling drugstore on the northeast corner of Finney and Vandeventer. I'd love to go into that store with her when she needed to buy pharmaceuticals, send a money order, or cash her Social Security check. I can still smell the place. If I had to try to reconstruct its odoriferous ambiance I would need camphor or oil of wintergreen, rubbing alcohol, sulphur, cigarettes, and vanillin. I think that would do it. And that rock candy! What wonderful stuff that was. Bet you can't even find it anymore— especially in drugstores.

Camphor in wax form or in its oil form was applied externally and a little bit taken internally to relieve chest colds. The solid forms of camphor could be rubbed onto any skin eruptions. The wax balls of camphor I saw my grandmother put to use I later found out to be mixed with white beeswax and a vegetable oil. She called that *camphor ice*. The *camphorated oil* I saw Mama use was one part oil of camphor added to four parts cottonseed oil. Although the *Oldtimers* swore by the powers of camphor, those of us who have not depended on the medicinal value of the odoriferous stuff may have serious questions about any medicine one can take both internally and externally!

Sometimes when an Islander had severe arthritis pain in an arm or hand or leg, a couple of pennies would be tied over the painful part. Not too different from the copper bracelets worn today to conduct electrical impulses to the pained area. There was and is something about copper that is thought to bring a cure.

We could never calculate how many cases of severe diaper rash were curbed by a home remedy that would never be sanctioned by today's pediatricians. The *Honey Island* infant's mama or grandmama would put some flour in a big black skillet and heat it until it was a nice brown chocolate color. When it cooled it was applied to the baby's bottom, and it apparently did its job. The leftover browned flour was put in wax paper till its next application. In a pinch, the flour tanned for the baby butt could be used to make a nice brown gravy when a little chicken fat, beef broth, or turkey drippings were added along with some hot water or milk.

Honey Island children surely prayed they wouldn't ever get chicken pox, mumps, or measles. The parents—or maybe a grandmother—procured the jawbone of a hog, cracked the bone, and scooped out the membranous marrow. This soft, bloody, terrible-smelling pork tissue was then packed around the patient's face and neck and the affected areas were then covered with flannel or disposable clean rags. The *Oldtimers* swore by this home remedy. The patient swore *at* it. Its effective quotient may have been boosted by the fervent effort made by the patient to get well so the awful stuff would not have to be re-applied. Hog bone marrow was effective in another way. It spelled prevention, since the young patient's chums avoided getting the highly contagious childhood disease. They couldn't be paid enough lollipops or licorice whips to come within ten feet of the stinky shut-in. My sisters and I remember Grandma Hattie glopping this *Honey Island* goop on our swollen cheeks when we were kids.

If a *Honey Island* resident of the Old School would get a fever blister on his/her lip, a common cure was found right above that blister on either side of the head. With a paper clip or a hairpin, the islander scooped around in the ear and got out a little dab of ear wax. That was said to help the fever blister shrink and hurt less. I personally am glad that they now make something called Blistex.

A home remedy that would seem particularly unsanitary by today's standards was the way in which bee stings on *Honey Island* would be treated. Field workers often carried a coffee can with them into which they would spit their plug tobacco juice and snuff expectoration. When stung by a bee or wasp or by ants, the worker would simply apply a bit of the tobacco spit to the sting. The itching was relieved almost immediately and the worker could continue without feeling the effects.

Chigger bites—a major problem in the field and in the woods—were relieved by moistening the affected area with a little kerosene or turpentine and then, using a lighted match, setting a quick fire to the area. The pesky, blood-sucking chigger would get its little butt end burned and could be expected to back out of the skin. If tweezers were available, they could be used to pull the burrowing parasite out. More turpentine, kerosene, or tobacco spit could be applied. *Honey Islanders* referred to chiggers as *jiggers.* Jigger bites were not taken lightly, as the six-legged skin invader is a carrier of typhus.

Sometimes when a child on *Honey Island* had what was believed to be asthma or any inexplicable wheezing or paroxysms, goose grease was rubbed on the patient's neck and chest. There is no documentable evidence that the fat from a goose had any medicinal value, but this same folk approach that was used in the Deep South apparently had its origins in Western Europe.

There were patent medicines that could be purchased at the Belzoni druggist's shop. For those whose hard labors caused them aching backs and pained bones there was *Sloan's Liniment.* It was so powerful that the user was cautioned not to rub it in. If one did so, one would find the top level of skin peeling away in blisters.

Another popular Rounds family purchase at the pharmacy was *Dr. Tichenor's Antiseptic.* This concentrate was intended to be rubbed on cuts, scratches, minor scrapes, bruises, and insect bites. The manufacturer also encouraged its patrons to use the concentrate as an effective gargle against sore throats and colds. The user always seemed to be in a happier frame of mind if a bit of the stuff were swallowed in the gargling process.

The scene on the bottle label, as I remember it as a boy, was an heroic Civil War battle tableau in which Confederate troops were apparently prevailing. Why would Union forces appear victorious on a medication founded so deep in Confederate territory? This patent medicine remedy that my Grandma Hattie swore by—and this born-again Christian woman was never known to really swear, at least publicly—was created by Dr. George H. Tichenor. He was born in Kentucky just twelve years after my great-great-granddaddy was born in the same place.

Tichenor, listed in records as an "acting assistant surgeon," was wounded at a battle near Memphis in 1863. When amputation was offered as the only treatment option, Tichenor convinced the army sawbones not to unceremoniously whack off his leg as was the custom with most severe wounds of war. He insisted on treating himself with his own formula. Somehow he managed to save his damaged leg and in the process introduce the first use of antiseptic surgery to the Confederate Army. Dr. Tichenor, encouraged by patients and friends, saw the formation of a commercial company that manufactured the elixir.

Hattie Coats believed this tonic to be the next best thing to a panacea. This incredibly healthy specimen of a woman lived to a ripe old age—from 1881 to 1978—with virtually no patent or prescribed medications in her medicine cabinet. With *Dr. Tichenor's* making its mass marketing debut in 1905, she could credit the cure of her infrequent headaches, back aches, toothaches, nausea, sore throats, and colds for more than seven decades to her penchant for pouring a few drops of *Dr. Tichenor's* on a teaspoon of sugar and swallowing it in one gulp. Or yodeling with the stuff in the back of her throat.

Funniest thing about Grandma Hattie's unsolicited money-back-guaranteed endorsement of *Dr. Tichenor's Antiseptic*. She was the staunchest of teetotalers! If Baptists were allowed to name saints, Hattie Rounds Williams Coats would have been at the top of the list of those to be beatified. She was always extremely proud of having signed a Women's Christian Temperance Union pledge in Belzoni, Mississippi, back in the 1890s to eschew that demon rum. Yet she was an avid consumer of an antiseptic concentrate that boasted being **70 percent alcohol**! From the smell of the stuff, a good portion of the rest of the "miracle medicine" was oil of wintergreen or something of that odoriferous ilk. Granny was not one to read the fine print labels of home products. You can be sure those of us who loved her never bothered to let her know she was taking in a solution that was stronger than some bar booze!

Grandma Hattie would be pleased to know that the makers of *Dr. Tichenor's Antiseptic* now boast of having sold nearly a half-million bottles of the stuff. And I can't begin to imagine what she would think about the fact that *Dr. Tichenor's* now makes a toothpaste!

If one cut oneself while cooking in the kitchen or working in the tool shed, *Honey Island* residents often made a poultice of moldy bread packed into the wound. Isn't that basically what penicillin is? Another treatment for cuts was to pack some chimney soot into the wound. Doesn't seem very sanitary, but it did stop the bleeding.

For a severe headache or persistent migraine, a curious and perhaps unique *Honey Island* treatment was sometimes recommended. As much as a half-cup of salt was packed in a mound on top of the chronic sufferer's head. Then the salt dome was tightly bandaged in place with a scarf tied into a turban. Nobody remembered it ever working, but perhaps there were some psychological benefits and diversion of the malady even if no medicinal relief was produced.

Mattie Williams swears the wet salt mound placed on top of the head did indeed help her get rid of a headache or two when she was a young girl on *Honey Island*. The salt was held in place with a piece of cloth fashioned into a turban. My Aunt Willetta had mentioned this same remedy. When asked why headache sufferers don't use this strange remedy today, Mrs. Williams laughed and said: "'Cause they got aspirin today, honey. They got aspirin."

The formula for aspirin, *acetylsalicylic acid,* was not created until 1899. The painkiller did not find its way onto the shelves at Turner's Drugstore in Belzoni until the era in which most of the Rounds family had either fled Mississippi or passed from this veil of tears into a painless Heaven or a Hell in which a headache would be of minimal concern.

Acid indigestion or severe *griping* or cramping could be helped along by the ingestion of a common kitchen and medicine cabinet item. In addition to its usefulness as a deodorant and tooth cleaner, baking soda was used to cure gas, indigestion, heartburn, or cramps. A teaspoonful stirred in a class of warm water often produced an uproarious belch and subsequent relief from the heavy or spicy meal. In these days before TUMS, the islanders would sometimes swallow a half teaspoonful of nutmeg or cinnamon or both to try to relieve a tummy ache.

Dentistry was not a polished profession either before or after 1900. Said one former *Honey Island* resident who saw both sides of 1900: *"Heck, nobody much went to any darn dentist 'cause nobody thought they knew anything more about pulling teeth than the rest of us who weren't dentists!"* Tooth-pulling was brutal on the island. The puller approached the pullee with a pair of pliers after the workbench tool had been sterilized with boiling water. The para-dentist then sat straddling the patient with the aching or loose tooth. Following a count of *one...two...three,* the offending tooth and part of its roots were crudely yanked from the patient's head. The clever would-be dentist often fooled the patient by yanking the tooth out on the count of one or two. It was nothing at all for a *Honey Island* resident to pull his/her own tooth. A traditional game was sometimes played to get a loose tooth out of a child's mouth. A string was gently tied around the youngster's loose tooth. The other end was then tied to the doorknob of an open door. Then the door was slammed shut. BANG! The sound of the door slam was more startling than the loss of the tooth. The bloody gums would then be rinsed with the gargling of warm salt water to close the wound.

If neither the home remedies nor prayer and fasting cured the residents of *Honey Island,* the stricken, smitten, and afflicted would be carted off to Yazoo City to see one of the two doctors who would see black patients, Dr. Fullilove of the *Honey Island* family or "Doc" Miller. Both of them were Black, although Dr. Fullilove could have passed for a Caucasian.

My grandmother, just after she married her second husband, John Coats, in 1923, went into Yazoo City to see the physician she trusted most, Dr. James Miller. She was having some severe lower abdominal pain that *Dr. Tichenor's* could not tame. Her husband and his son Dan drove my grandma in the old family jalopy. After waiting her turn in his office, the good doctor examined her and diagnosed an appendix problem. He told Grandma Hattie:

"You've got two ways to go with this thing. We can operate on you and take your

appendixes out. Or we can send you back home while you try out something you can get without a prescription. What'll it be, Mrs. Coats?"

My grandma was never much for doctors or hospitals or medicine or surgery or being pampered too much. Her answer was quick. She'd try any alternative to keep from being cut on.

Dr. Miller gave her a prescription that wouldn't require any prescription, at least not of the written kind. He instructed my grandmother to go down the street to the general store and buy herself eight bottles of olive oil. Yes, olive oil! Yes, eight bottles! He advised her to drink one of the bottles each day for a week and a day. Then she was to send word to him by the next islander to come into town on how she was doing. Grandma Hattie obediently followed the doctors orders. She might have even felt better than she did when she went into the doctor's office now that she knew for certain she wouldn't have to go under the knife.

To make a long story short, she walked out of Dr. Miller's office and down to the drugstore, bought the eight bottles of olive oil, and her new husband drove her back home. She reportedly took a good swig of the olive oil in the car on the road home. Guess what? The olive oil remedy worked! After polishing off the eighth bottle of olive oil, Hattie Rounds Williams Coats had no more lower stomach cramps. She had few other illnesses for the rest of her long life, and never spent any time in a hospital until she was well into her nineties.

Dr. James Haggin Miller of Yazoo City was no quack. He was a graduate of New Orleans Medical College and the I. W. Simmons School of Medicine. He gained his medical certification from the Mississippi State Board of Health on November 16, 1899, after four years of professional studies, "four courses of lectures," four years of hospital residency, and four years of practice. (I'll make nothing of the sidebar fact that the secretary of the Mississippi State Medical Board which certified Dr. Miller was Dr. J. Hunter, who, so far as I can determine, is not even remotely related to the author of this book.) When my grandmother saw her favorite physician in his Yazoo City office about 1923 for the appendicitis problem, she was about forty-two years old; Dr. Miller was fifty-seven.

After Dr. Miller's younger brother graduated from Meharry Medical College in Nashville, Tennessee, and was certified by the Mississippi State Medical Board on June 1, 1901, he took over the Yazoo City practice. L. F. Miller was eleven years his brother's junior. Meharry Medical College was formally opened in 1876 as a department of the Central Tennessee College, with a grant from Samuel Meharry, his four brothers, and the Methodist Church to address the disproportionate rates of disease and death among the nation's black population. Today, Meharry is the largest private, historically black institution exclusively dedicated to educating health care professionals and biomedical scientists in the United States.

When there were no consultations with physicians like the Brothers Miller, some of the *Honey Island* home remedies were the direct products of New Orleans and the voodoo priests and priestesses who mixed superstition with medicine. Admittedly, Dr. James Miller, who had his medical training in New Orleans, would have been quite familiar with these concoctions. One can only wonder if his olive oil application for appendicitis distress was something he learned in medical college or picked up from New Orleanian folk medicine.

One way *Honey Island* residents warded off common diseases and ailments was the infamous *asafetida bag*. It would also ward off anybody who came within three feet of the wearer. One *Oldtimer* said it smelled like a combination of "*rotten garlic and dead rat.*" One wouldn't think the stuff would have such a putrid smell since the root that gave the islanders the purported cure is in the same family as carrots, celery, parsnips, and parsley. Here's how it was employed: the little homemade bag was tied with a string and worn around the neck. Its contents were the most obnoxious, god-awful smelling concoction you've ever whiffed. You could buy the stuff at the drugstore in town. The gum was taken from the roots of any umbelliferous plants of the genus *Ferula*. Its effectiveness was doubtful, but some of the *Oldtimers* swore by it. A few islanders would wear the bag for a few days at the beginning of each month to guarantee themselves good health until the bag was put around the neck at the beginning of the next month. If they ended up with a bad cold or worse, the *Oldtimers* would blame it on a weak batch of the root, throw that bag away, and get a new, fresh bag.

Not quite as nasty-smelling as the asafetida bag was the awful mustard plaster. The compound, made up of ground mustard seed and ground black rubber, was made into a paste (or later bought at the drugstore) ready for the liberal application to the back or chest. The stuff was then covered with scraps of flannel. For a chest cold or skin condition or even as a purported cure for clearing lungs of mucus and phlegm, the smelly mustard pack was just the remedy on *Honey Island* and in northern homes spun off from the Mississippi Delta. Don't let the mustard pack stay on your chest overnight. The concoction has been known to leave a burn.

Lest we overlook how fatal the art of trying to cure serious illnesses at home can be, we can be reminded of the tragedy that hit the *Honey Island* home of Arch and Charity Turner about 1911. Their daughter, Sally, who celebrated her ninety-first birthday on July 4, 1999, was one of nine children in the Turner household. She remembers:

"*My daddy and mama didn't believe in running us kids into Belzoni or Yazoo City every time one of us had a cold or the hiccups. And even if they were believers in doctors, they couldn't have afforded to take us to one. After all, there were nine of us children, and counting my mother and father, that would have been eleven folks that could have seen a doctor at one time or another. We always had lots of food and a good warm house and nice* clothes, but my parents never had a lot of cash that could go to paying a doctor's fees. But somewhere around the time I was two or three years old, all nine of us young ones got a bad case of the measles. I mean we were broke out all over! There were red spots all over our bodies and I can remember our lips being broke out and it even felt like we couldn't swallow or anything 'cause our throats were swollen up.

"In hindsight, I'll bet my mother and daddy wished they had packed up all us kids in the wagon and took us into town to see a doctor. Instead, my parents boiled the hulls from ears of corn and made a tea out of that. They called that 'shuck tea.' That stuff didn't do a bit of good. Two of my older sisters died right there at the house. With measles. Claudia was thirteen; Nancy was eleven. I guess I made it through the grief because I was so young and really didn't realize everything that was going on. But it seemed to me that my parents were never quite the same. There always seemed to be a sadness in their eyes after my sisters passed away from measles. But they still never took the seven of us who survived to a doctor."

HONEY ISLAND SUPERSTITIONS

The asafetida bag was emblematic of the superstitions of the *Honey Island* residents. They shared some of the common superstitions harbored by all those who looked to sinister forces to punish them for certain infractions they eschewed like the plague. Broken mirrors, black cats, and leaning ladders were shunned. Stepping on a crack on the sidewalks of Belzoni or Yazoo City was avoided at all costs. Stepping on a crack would, for sure, break the offender's mother's back. Since there were no epidemics of mothers with severe sacroiliac problems on the island, we can assume that their kids did a pretty good job of not stepping on the cracks in town. The superstitious islanders would also avoid "splitting a post." That's when two people walked toward a post, a telephone pole, or any other vertically posted stave and one went on the left side of the post and the other person on the right side. That could cause all manner of bad luck, *Honey Island* residents believed. In many island homes, a guest had to leave the house through the same door though which he/she entered. You just couldn't go into some islander's front door and leave by the back door. Bad luck. Who needed it? Long after she came to St. Louis, Grandmother Hattie was a courteous but vigilant sentry about which door one used to enter and leave her house.

Pregnant women on *Honey Island* would be carefully instructed by their mothers and grandmothers to *never—never!*—look directly at any reptiles. If they did, their baby would certainly be "marked." Babies born with grotesque birth defects or with permanent blotches on their skin were said to have been "marked," and their mother must have surely gazed directly at a snake or frog while she was carrying her child.

One common superstition on the island spelled bad news for any merchant or peddler or lender or landlord. Some of my Mississippi ancestors, current relatives, and their *Honey Island* neighbors absolutely, under no circumstances, by any means would ever, ever *"break a bill on Monday morning"*—as in dollar bill or five-dollar bill. That would, according to superstition, bring the spender some bad, bad luck. Doing business on a Monday was perfectly okay if one had coins. No business deals would ever be consummated on a Friday, no matter how small the transaction. Those who relied on the exchange of money for *their* daily bread could pray that they didn't find any customers or debtors who observed this cardinal rule about breaking bills on Mondays *and* the practice of doing absolutely no business on Fridays.

A couple of curious *Honey Island* holiday practices that were more tradition than superstition were observed on New Year's Day. On the first day of each year, it was bad luck for a woman to enter one's house before a man entered it. The man who arrived at the crack of dawn would bring the household good luck for that entire year. The early morning guest was rewarded handsomely for being the early bird. This early bird caught some things a whole helluva lot more tasty and tantalizing than a worm! He would be treated to a lavish breakfast washed down with eggnog heavily-laced with "hootch" at any and all houses at which he presented himself as the first visitor. Many island men saw themselves as special envoys in this custom. They'd make it around to three or four houses on New Year's morn. They all could be found snoring away somewhere by noon. Uncle Walter Johnson carried this early-bird custom from Mississippi to Missouri and could be counted on to visit our house and those of most of our St. Louis relatives every New Year's Day. He, too, could be counted on to be snoring at home by noon. o

On New Year's Day there was little variance in what was served for the big supper on *Honey* Island, and later in St. Louis. Hog's head and black-eyed peas, of course. The hog was supposed to represent prosperity; the peas, fertility. From the number of times the stork visited *Honey Island* during any given year, heaven knows there was no need of a legume for fecundity. And heaven knows… Heaven was very important to the *Honey Island* residents.

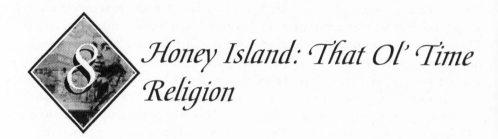# Honey Island: That Ol' Time Religion

Back in 1893, when the *Honey Island* community was approaching a population of some eighty black families, it was decided that it was high time to build a church for the community. Residents of the island had been holding prayer meetings and Sunday School classes in each other's homes. Weldon Jones, a prosperous black farmer, volunteered to give a portion of his land for the construction of the church. We are not sure if he insisted in the terms of the gift that the church be named after him, but his was the name the new house of worship was given when it was completed in 1894. Jones' name is listed first on the church cornerstone laid by the *King Hiram Grand A. E. & A. M. Masonic Lodge*. Of course, the inner-sanctum workings of the Masons are secret, but I did learn from a search of a biblical encyclopedia that King Hiram was the king of Tyre in the tenth century, B. C. Masons everywhere must have admired this particular king because, as outlined in the chapter five of the Bible's First Kings, Hiram floated a big shipment of cedar and pine and an army of carpenters down the Sea of Galilee upon the request of King Solomon to help the Hebrew leader build a spectacular temple. The wood and workers weren't exactly a gift and without strings. The timber and carpenters by mutual agreement would cost Solomon twenty thousand bushels of wheat and two hundred gallons of olive oil every year of the Phoenician king's reign! The wise Hiram wanted to keep the peace with the newly-anointed King Solomon. Shrewd man, that King Hiram.

The prosperous Rounds' neighbor Weldon Jones gave the *Honey Island* community its first church and, like King Hiram, got something in return. The church was named after him. **WELDON JONES...HE GAVE THE LAND**, the

Jones Chapel cornerstone text begins.

Although one finds Jones Chapel today with snow-white siding, the cornerstone the Masons laid more than a hundred years ago stands propped against the front of the church framed in slate with the grey slate framed by sandy-yellow bricks. The *Oldtimers* remember that the original sanctuary was a wood frame structure. Some members of the congregation told me that they remember the church being a lot bigger before a big storm huffed and puffed and blew the church down in the 1930s, leading to the eventual rehabbing of the building.

When the church was dedicated, Weldon Jones and his wife Celia were the parents of Adam, age four; Weldon, III, age two; and Burwell who was an infant when the church held its first worship service. Their sons Ralph and Booker T. were born later. The generous Joneses also took in three grandchildren, Albert, Louisa, and Fay. The 1910 U. S. census lists twenty-eight members of the Jones family living in five households right next to each other. Weldon Senior was forty-six years old at the time he donated the land for the church; his wife, Celia, was thirty-one.

The Jones Chapel Missionary Baptist Church called the Rev. W. P. Watts as its first pastor. On the cornerstone, the first deacon listed is my great-grandfather, Westly Rounds. How is it that his name is misspelled on the cornerstone as it often is on deeds and documents? He is listed as *NESS ROUNDS*, a clear error by the stonemason who either misheard his directions or took the *W* for an *N* on the sheet of paper the church secretary handed him to chisel in stone. Alas, Westly Rounds' name is thus listed in a couple of Humphreys County Courthouse documents with the same misspelling. Westly's nickname was West—pronounced "Wess" by everybody. When one closely examines the penmanship of clerks and census enumerators, one can see how the flourished penmanship of the day could lead to the misreading of a *"W"* for an *"N."* There can be little doubt that it's Ned's son, Westly who is the first deacon listed on the new church's cornerstone. He was rather young to be a head deacon. He was only thirty-nine when the church opened its doors for the first time. Perhaps I should try to get a stonemason to correct the error—for family pride and for posterity.

The other deacons listed are Ned and Westly's neighbors and good friends: **NICK BATTLE , CHARLIE BYRD, JAKE GREEN, TOM SIMMONS.**

Tom Simmons married into the Rounds family. Of course, the endogamous relationships on *Honey Island* might have led me to say that Martha Rounds married into the prosperous and upstanding Simmons family. But, Tom married into an equally upstanding and prosperous family, as well. Tom married Ned Rounds' daughter, Martha, also known as Mattie, in 1887—seven years before the church cornerstone was laid. The 1880 census lists Tom as twenty years old. That means he was also a young deacon in 1894—just thirty-four—four years younger that his brother-in-law, Westly.

Jacob Green, known to the Rounds family and all his family and neighbors as "Jake," was thirty-nine when the Jones Chapel cornerstone was laid. His wife, Mariah, was the same age. They had three children when the church was founded. Daughter Nancy Ann was twenty when she first entered the new church, Caroline was seventeen, and Jacob Jr., was nearly fifteen.

The Rounds family became cinched with the family of Deacon Charlie Byrd at Jones Chapel when my great-aunt Ninnie married George Byrd at the church, four years after it opened.

Shortly after it opened, the church sanctuary began to double as the one-room Panther Burn School.

The updated cornerstone tells us that a remodeling project was begun at Jones Chapel Church in 1958. The rehab job was completed in 1961 under the leadership of the Rev. M. C. Valentine and Head Deacon J. C. Cummings.

Later in the church's history, the Rounds family and their religious neighbors secured the services of a circuit preacher, the Rev. Rutger. He was able to get to Jones Chapel only once a month. Still, there was Sunday School conducted by the deacons and Sunday School teachers. There were activities for the young folk every Sunday evening at four o'clock for three or four hours. These loosely organized evening programs featured Bible study, testimonials, hymn-singing, praying, and sometimes a fire-and-brimstone sermon to the *Honey Island* kids about the wages of sin they could earn through promiscuity. The youngsters were duly warned about the one suspected resident of the island with whom they should never associate under any circumstances—Satan. While the preachers and deacons would have to acknowledge that they had never personally *seen* Beelzebub, they might have confessed during the segment of the worship services set aside for oral testimony that they had certainly been tempted by him more than a time or two during their lifetimes. They had certainly seen the Devil's handiwork around the island.

Once a year—usually at the end of a torrid August—there is a religious "revival" at Jones Chapel. For two full weeks! Those nighttime spiritual renewal services, I learned when I visited Mississippi in August 1998, are, after more than a century, still very much alive and well-attended. The goal of the revival is threefold: to enlist new soldiers in the Christian Army, to stop the backslide of those who had forgotten their initial pledge to walk the straight and narrow path through *Honey Island*, and to reassure the faithful that they were on the right track for eternal life. Revivals are noisy events...as in the psalmist's exhortation to *"make a joyful noise unto the Lord."* No matter how tired the congregant is, it is absolutely impossible to doze during the services. There is yelling and screaming and howling and singing and loud music and prayers. Percussion instruments, even those of the most primitive nature, are employed to drum up converts and make that joyful noise. In fact, there are attempts to make a joyful noise unto the Lord with one's voice and with almost all the instruments mentioned in Psalm 150. On a clear night, much more noticeable than the monotonous raspy song of the crickets, one can hear the ecclesiastical rantings and ravings of the visiting preachers and deacons.

The poet James Weldon Johnson likened the voices of the African American preacher men to trombones as they ranged several octaves in the ecclesiastical effort to get their messages of salvation across to the perfect, the prurient, and the penitent. The preacher bellows, bleats, brays, blasts, blares, blurts, booms, blows, and bounds and bounces up and down the altar area until he literally scares the hell out of the congregation. He is always soaking wet after his exhortations. At some revivals there is the "tag-team" sermon in which visiting preachers and deacons take turns in rapid succession denouncing sin and Satan. They jump and jerk and jabber and jig and point to Judgment Day as the ultimate date of jubilation for the faithful and damnation for the unrepentant sinner. Here's how Johnson characterized the sermon at a typical revival camp meeting:

"And God will divide the sheep from the goats...the one on the right; the other on the left! And those who have washed their robes in the blood of the Lamb...they will enter into the pearly gates of Heaven where they will be given harps of gold. And in golden slippers they will walk up and down the golden streets and sing in glorious chorus with the angels and heavenly hosts.

"But to those on the left, God will say: 'To Hell, sinner! To Hell! And their cries like howling, yelping dogs will go up with the fire and smoke from Hell. And they will descend down...down...down into the bowels of Hell belching out fire and brimstone. But God will stop His ears! Too late, sinner! Too late. To Hell, sinner. To Hell! Sinner, oh sinner:Where will you stand on that Great Day when God's a gonna rain down fire???!!!"

The revivals at Jones Chapel were held under the stars for as many as *five* hours each night at a time that didn't interfere with the work day or supper. The proceedings were illuminated by the learned in Scripture, as well as by torchlights ringing the congregation. The smoke from the torches helped keep some of the curious mosquitoes away from the parishioners who fanned themselves with reed fans. A few weathered hand fans were supplied by an undertaker in Belzoni who was more likely to see the fans with his name and picture on them get pitched than he was to see the fan-holder on a slab in his mortuary in town.

On the first Sunday following the full fortnight of spiritual renewal on *Honey Island*, the Jones Chapel flock looked forward to the holy sacrament of baptism. On the appointed day, the candidates for baptism and the congregation gathered at Jones Chapel early in the morning to beat the Delta heat. When all were assembled, the old Negro spirituals *Take Me to the Water* and *I'm Going Down by the River of Jordan* were belted out with fervor and animation as the congregation filed down to Tchula Lake in snakelike fashion—but certainly not in a serpentine fashion that could conjure up any images of that infamous snake in the Garden of Eden. When the profusely perspiring procession reached the lake, the homes of Matt Fields or Missy Cannon or Ollie Joyner were used for the candidates to leave their shoes and change into their glory garb. The women candidates for baptism would use one house, the men another. The women shed their Sunday-go-to-meeting clothes for the white robes and white shower caps usually made by the Ladies Aid Society. The men who swore they would forsake sin for the first time in their lives neatly folded their trousers and shirts to don their black robes.

Then the official baptism service got underway. After a mix of mournful and toe-tapping spirituals and hymns peppered with deacon-led prayers, the righteous preacher man would loudly invoke the power of the Holy Spirit in a prayer that took on sermonic proportions and epic length. The choir and congregation, with heads bowed and eyes closed, softly moaned their harmonic accompaniment to the preacher's prayers, intoning the melodies of *Old Rugged Cross* and *Softly and Tenderly Jesus is Calling*. Their sonorous humming provided soulful foundation for the clergyman's obligato of petitions, admonitions, prohibitions, and premonitions about what Heaven will be like for those who had their sins washed away in Lake Tchula.

Two deacons with long bamboo poles kicked off their shoes and cautiously waded deep, deep, then even deeper, into the lake using their poles as crosiers and as depth indicators for those disciples who would follow them into the chilly, murky water. As they stood in their sentry-like pose with poles in absolute perpendicular alignment with the surface of the placid lake, they looked like gatekeepers at the portals of Heaven. The pastor would then place one hand firmly on the arm of each sinner and one hand atop the head. In the name of the Father, Son, and Holy Ghost, he totally immersed each new believer in Christ until he or she disappeared beneath Tchula's sun-glistened surface. Gasping for air as they bobbed up from the lake in a spray of water, the trembling converts would often scream, shout, or babble hysterically, knowing now that he or she was truly *saved* and need not fear the change of venue from *Honey Island* to the hereafter. Heaven would now most assuredly be their next home when they left *Honey Island*—unless they moved to St. Louis or Chicago or Detroit before they passed away. Or, as they would have said on *Honey Island:* "*before they passed.*" The *away* part of that phrase was never used in conversation. It was as if there were sometimes a question about whether *away* was a euphemism for Hell instead of Heaven.

After the baptism ceremonies, the soaked but redeemed neophytes to Christianity would slip back into the Fields, Joyner, or Cannon house, slip out of their wet robes, dry out with towels provided by the Ladies Aid Society, and slip back into their church-going best togs. The recessional back to Jones Chapel was as high-spirited as the return from a New Orleans funeral. There were hugs and kisses and congratulations all around in this typically friendly church family.

****

"Greetings for your safe return after having accompanied the dead to his final resting place. Greetings for the sad loss of a beloved one. May his soul rest in perfect peace."
—Traditional Yoruba greeting to bereaved family members

Next to the sacrament of baptism, the rituals for the dead were the most dramatic at Jones Chapel.

The *Honey Island* community's attitude toward the dead and those who survive the deceased seem to have come straight from West Africa. That's where most of the U. S. slave population was kidnaped and shipped to the New World. Funeral services in the Deep South and in northern cities where slave descendants migrated are carbon copies of West African services to honor the dearly departed. An elder of the Yoruba tribe of Nigeria, for example, expresses the transiency of life this way:

"The whole life span of a man or a woman is a journey. That is our belief. When you are going to start your life, you go through a journey. Even when you are coming to the life, you go through a journey. And if you want to develop on the life, it is a journey. So it is just journey, journey all the while."

There are many spirituals sung by the descendants of *Honey Island* residents and their neighbors to this day that mention the word "journey." Often the word journey is prefaced by the word *"pilgrim,"* as in the soulful spiritual *I Want Jesus to Walk With Me.*

Death for many African tribesmen was and is today just another of the many journeys in life as one goes to sit nearer to God. Death stands between the world of human beings and the world of the spirits, between the visible and the invisible. In simpler terms, black preachers in *Honey Island,* St. Louis, Chicago, Detroit, Memphis, and in scores of other cities large and small express these same themes in their funeral services today.

Funerals at Jones Chapel Missionary Baptist Church—even as late as the 1969 obsequies for the late, ninety-year-old Brother J. C. Cummings—reflected the theme of one journey ended and another just beginning from *Honey Island.* Brother Cummings, whose father was a co-founder of Jones Chapel with my great-grandfather, West Rounds, and who was fifteen years old when my family's beloved church was founded, was eulogized at Jones Chapel on Sunday, November 9, 1969, when his earthly journey ended. It could have, according to its form and rituals, been held a hundred years earlier. Since the period of slavery, African American funerals were traditionally held on a Sunday because that is the only time during the week those held in bondage were given a day off, or in some cases, a half-day off. That custom still exists today. In olden days, if a dearly beloved party died on a Monday, the body would be held in the home or the funeral parlor until the following Sunday, unless the body was in an extremely deteriorated state like Ninnie Rounds Byrd's was after her death from pellagra. To this day, black corpses are held from burial as long as possible, particularly to get the funeral held on a Sunday when most people don't have to work.

Attendance for a funeral would always be better on a Sunday. Now, as then, one did not have to know the deceased well to attend the funeral service. Perfect strangers were and are likely to consider the occasion of a funeral as a social event.

Then, as now, the Sunday funeral service is held right after the morning worship service. The funeral director needed only about an hour to get the casket, floral arrangements, and relatives in place for the procession. Many members used...and use...the break between worship service and funeral to grab a sandwich at the church or dash home for heavier fare. The funeral for Brother Cummings was held at two on a Sunday afternoon. The *wake* had been held at the Johnson Funeral Home the night before. In the years before the Johnsons set up their mortuary, wakes on *Honey Island* were held in the home of the deceased—in the parlor preferably, but also in the living room, bedroom, dining room, or, in some rare cases, outdoors.

A wake, then as now, was held generally on the night before the funeral. With the coffin left open, relatives, friends, friends of relatives, and friends of friends gather at the home of the dearly departed or at the funeral parlor for visitation. The custom of the wake can be found in most cultures. In the Christian tradition, wakes were originally a vigil and may have been started by Jesus' remonstration to his apostles in the Garden of Gethsemane when he asked the dozing, perhaps snoring, disciples: *"Can you not watch with me one hour?"*

Even in the presence of the embalmed, often cosmetically overdone corpse, the mood and atmosphere at the wake was and is seldom somber. There is, at best, seemingly little respect for the dead at a wake. Interestingly enough, the Irish are also known for their traditional turning of what could be a grave occasion (pardon the tasteless pun) into a party, with the deceased the only one who is not having a good time. Booze, more often than not, flows at many Irish wakes. Out of respect for the dearly departed, the tippling is never supposed to go on in the same room in which the corpse lies in repose.

Novelist Leon Uris has perhaps the simplest and most descriptive definition of what a wake is to the Irish. He describes it this way:

"The wake is the period of time from death until the body is conveyed to the care of the church which is generally the evening before the day of burial."

There are colorful written accounts of wakes going back centuries, which also fit the wakes held on *Honey Island*, the South, and by Blacks whose families hail from south of the Mason-Dixon line. Edward MacLysaght of Kildare, Ireland, wrote in 1683:

"Their wakes are also over dead corpses, where they have a table spread and served with the best that can be had at such a time, and after a while attending (in expectation the departed soul will partake) they fall to eating and drinking, after to reveling as if one of the feasts of Backus."

Maria Edgeworth penned these words in 1810 describing an Irish wake after pipes, tobacco, cakes, beer, and whiskey were served:

"Deal on, deal on, my merry men all,
Deal on your cakes and your wine;
For whatever is dealt at her funeral today
Shall be dealt tomorrow at mine."

There are other key similarities between the Irish wake and that of black Baptists, including those on *Honey Island*. For one thing, once the deceased had breathed a last breath, the immediate neighbors were informed and rushed over to comfort the bereaved and helped prepare the room for the wake on *Honey Island*. That would mean setting up a board between two chairs on which the corpse would lie, changing the bedclothes, or going down to the carpenter's shop or the blacksmith's shop to get a ready-made coffin. The neighbors, whether in Dublin or in *Honey Island,* might also help wash and dress the body in clothes presentable for viewing. If the neighborly duties involved washing, starching, and ironing a dress or pressing a man's suit, it was done lovingly. Some of the *Honey Island Oldtimers* remember that a seldom-worn men's suit or a woman's dress that had been in mothballs had to sometimes be ironed out before it became a shroud.

Uris writes that "Candles are lighted in candlesticks near the remains" at an Irish wake. That was also done in the parlors of *Honey Island* homes when there was a death in the household. The Irish practice called *"keening and crying"* was an expected part of the wake and funeral. African American mourners were and are also expected to loudly weep, wail, and gnash their teeth. Uris writes further of Irish tradition:

"The vocalizations over the dead are very important. The mourning family (once the body is laid out) produces either muffled sobs or loud wailing related to the depth of sorrow. In the event that the death was considered a 'great loss' (a parent leaving a large family or tragic or early death) keening is more intense and heartfelt."

There was certainly a lot of keening at Jones Chapel on *Honey Island*. As the custom of the wake and funeral continues today, there is keening at the wake and funeral of nearly all African American Baptists, Methodists, Pentecostals, and Episcopalians. The keening at these solemn times among Blacks is generally reserved, however, for the funeral service proper.

Uris continues his description of the Irish wake and funeral:

"Supplies are brought in—bread, meat, food of all kinds, whiskey, stout, wine, pipes, tobacco, snuff. (Tobacco and snuff are extremely important as is alcohol.)"

Black Baptists and Fundamentalists break with the Irish over the issue of tobacco products being an important part of the wake and funeral gathering. Black mourners, however, have been known to have a drink of alcohol at a wake or after the funeral—so long as the drinking does not go on in the presence of the corpse or the revered elderly.

Food is abundant at the wake and funeral in the Black culture. When my dear cousin Pearl *passed* in July of 1998, following a family tradition I had seen since childhood and which had it origins on *Honey Island,* I went to the supermarket early on the day after her death and purchased a twenty-two pound turkey, a twelve pound ham, tubs of potato salad and coleslaw, bakery rolls, cases of soda pop, beer, a 1.75 liter bottle of whiskey, paper plates, napkins, and plastic forks and spoons. All of this was hauled into my Aunt Willetta's house since she had inherited the position of family matriarch from my grandmother, Hattie Coats. I was not at all surprised that over the next several days until the wake for Pearline, friends, neighbors, associates, and members of her church brought over a ton of food to duplicate or augment the food and drink I had brought. In fact, one close friend of the family brought a fully cooked turkey to Willetta's house before I could even bake the one I had held to be cooked the day of the wake. In a custom that may have been started more than a hundred years ago— or back in Africa, there is a lot of food stuffed down mourning faces before the wake, after the wake, before and after the funeral.

According to Uris, in Irish tradition women who are carrying a child are not advised to stare upon a corpse for fear that it will cause freakish deformity to the unborn child. That superstition was also prevalent on *Honey Island.* The Rounds family and their neighbors believed that a pregnant woman gazing upon a dead body might "mark" the baby with a deformity or mental illness.

Baptist and Methodist teachings forbid the consumption of alcohol, so one would not find the wake of an African American on *Honey Island* to be saturated with alcohol. That did not mean, however, that a band of friends and relatives might not repair to the home of a mourner for a little alcoholic toast to the dead.

Wakes in the traditional African American culture feature what practitioners of reserved, conservative, and less demonstrative religions might consider as bizarre and as pagan and as quaint as the Irish wake. There is, with an open casket the focal point of the gathering for Blacks with southern roots, a macabre tendency for the mourners to talk to and touch the corpse at the wake. It is very common for friends and relatives to pat the hands of the deceased. Gently rubbing the forehead of the departed is also a common custom. One can expect at least one close relative or loved one at the wake to plant a kiss on the lips of the corpse. All this goes on while there is generally raucous laughter, loud talking, and weeping, wailing, and gnashing of teeth adding a seemingly incongruent descant to the air.

One is guaranteed to hear, at least every five minutes at a wake, some mourner observe after leaning over the face of the motionless subject of all the attention, *"He looks just like himself." "She looks just like herself."* Morticians and funeral directors always like to hear this compliment. That means they did a good job with the hair and makeup on the dead body. Sometimes, if the deceased had become disfigured by disease or an accident, or if the hair stylist had come up with a hairdo that the dead person would never have allowed in life, there is the converse rating given by the mourner/inspectors: *"Boy, she really doesn't look like herself, does she?" "He just don't look the same, does he?"*

The 1969 Jones Chapel funeral for Brother J. C. Cummings, who married into my family, followed a boilerplate that has withstood the test of at least a century. The July 1998 funeral of my cousin Pearline Johnson Scales was just like that of Brother Cummings. First, with the mourners already seated in the church of the funeral parlor, there is the processional of the choir into their designated section of the sanctuary—usually at the front/center of the church. Often the choristers sing something or hum something mournful as they march into the church. The song always has a non-Gregorian toe-tapping beat. The organ and/or piano takes a strong lead. When the choir is in place, the funeral director leads the family into the church with the minister at the head of the procession. Music continues, subtly but audibly, under the reading of Scripture. The minister most often will intone the words of the Twenty-third Psalm as he leads the grieving family into the church right behind the casket, which is moved along by the pallbearers. Parishioners now rise to their feet out of expected respect when the family enters the church.

Family members always take the first few pews in the front and center of the church, a reserved area often marked off by white ribbons and bows. The nearest of kin to the deceased are generally seated right in the front pew, just a couple of feet away from the corpse in the open casket. A deacon or assistant pastor then offers a rhythmically-intoned prayer for the dearly departed. That entreaty is followed by a choir selection that has more of a bump, more of a beat than the processional hymn. *Take My Hand, Precious Lord* is good here. Then there are remarks by one of the deacons welcoming the congregation to this occasion and inviting them back for Sunday service. It is an unabashed commercial for the dearly departed's church.

A solo almost always follows. It is considered most moving if the solo song builds to a crescendo as the organist or pianist pulls out all the stops. Nothing then can keep the congregation from pulling out all its stops with loud *"amens!"* and shouts of *"Yes, Jesus!"* Various and sundry remarks by various and sundry church officers come next. At Brother Cummings' funeral there were six different sets of remarks. At some black Baptist funerals there may be more than a dozen speakers. At the funeral of my stepfather, Buck Cannon Outlaw, in March of 1999, there were fully eleven speakers. Some of them hadn't seen nor spoken with Old Buck in many a year since he had come to dislike the minister at the church he had served as member and usher for more than fifty years. Many speakers at his funeral, I surmised, were taking the opportunity just to be seen and heard.

Buck's mourners heard his pastor from whom he was estranged, my mother's pastor, the assistant pastor at my mother's church, the head of the usher board at the church he had not attended for many years, his next door neighbor with whom I never perceived him having a close relationship, my sister Laura who had been warned not to express any feelings on my behalf if she just had to speak, her son Jerry, the funeral director, his church's secretary who didn't probably remember him from the very large congregation, and two other speakers whose comments and identities didn't make enough of an impression on me to remember them. But I distinctly remember the speaker count as an overwhelming and yawn-provoking eleven. From my mother's whispers between her teeth *"That's enough. Sit down now,"* I gathered that even she deemed that number of speakers excessive. The speakers had tested her patience even though their fawning praises were made about a man to whom she had been married for forty-one years, a man who could count his closest friends on less than one hand. And every remark of a speaker at these occasions was and is—whether a complete sentence or not—liberally doused by the congregation with *"Amen!"* *"Amen!"*

****

 The funeral of my cousin Pearl was particularly sad for those she left behind to mourn her death. From what I had heard about them, it could just as well have been a Jones Chapel observance of death. I was impressed that the church was packed. I could have had no idea that Pearl had so many friends outside her family. But why wouldn't she? I was also impressed that there was not one, but three ministers, who offered eulogistic remarks: Pearl's current pastor, and two of her former ministers. Let us take a personal assessment here of how many of us could have one current and two past pastors speak at our funerals.

Each of the ministers spoke of how silently Pearl had worked her magic inside his congregations. She was never a big speech-maker. She had never issued ultimatums on compliance with her thoughts or her leaving the church, they said. She had, instead, always offered a small reasonable voice that stated the case and left the judgment and the merit of her ideas to others. Whether her platform won or not, she could always be counted on to work diligently to carry out the will of the majority.

****

At the obsequies for *Honey Island's* Brother Cummings, there were "remarks" by Brother E. D. Howard, Sister Zenetha Johnson, Brother Charlie Grayer, Brother King Roscoe, Brother Alex Green, and Sister Gertrude Howard. Vocal solos were thrown in to separate the comments of deacons and elders and organization chairpersons and church officers. It is traditional that each vocal soloist tries to outdo the other and get a louder response quotient than the previous singers. Sometimes, the funeral planners hold back the most powerful and inspirational singer for last. In the cases in which there is only one soloist, that crooner may choose to hold back the most heart-rending selection for the high point of the funeral. That's just before the closest relatives and other mourners march up to gaze down upon the dearly departed for the last time before seeing them again in Heaven.

Brother Cummings' funeral employed four different soloists trying to tear up the congregation and rip the souls out of the next-of-kin. Yea, verily, it is thought in the black funeral experience that if relatives don't break up, shout out, scream, or faint dead away they must not have loved the deceased person very much. The more emotional the reaction of the closest relative, the closer they appeared to be in life. After all the solos and remarks, the printed program for Brother Cummings' funeral offered this invitation:

"3 Min. Expression, those that desire."

Some of Brother Cummings' friends and fellow churchgoers gave their brief reflections on the life and times of Brother Cummings. "Acknowledgments" then followed another solo. Those acknowledgments were read by Sister E. Fullilove. This part of the traditional African American funeral service can be tedious. It is usually handled by the church secretary and often includes mention and word-for-word reading of every sympathy card, telegram, note, letter, or card attached to a floral piece the family of the deceased received. I have heard a couple dozen acknowledgments or more read verbatim by a church secretary. Particularly excruciating can be the reading of some of the syrupy, poorly-rhymed "poetry" in some of the greeting cards.

And there is still more reading! At the last rites for Brother Cummings, Sister Olivia McCollin stepped to the lectern to read his obituary—word for word! The late Jonas Cummings had amassed a full page of credits. Black congregations today have generally shortcut this portion of the program by having the organist or pianist turn up their soulful selection switch a notch while the congregation members are asked to read the obituary silently to themselves. When a reader like Sister McCollin reads the obituary aloud, there is an implied open invitation to the congregation—those who are still awake—to shout out their congratulations to Brother Cummings for each step along the straight and narrow path of righteousness with their loud *"amens"* and *"alrights."*

One's obituary—as printed and read aloud—is one's life-time batting average. It is one's odometer reading. It is one's self-portrait shared with all who read it.

An obituary is one's resume; one's curriculum vitae which will never need to be shown again after the funeral. If we could get all the information about our lifetime achievements and association with God and man onto our tombstones, obituaries would be less important. But, if we or our survivors want the world to know what we have given to life, what we have accomplished, how close to God and the church and the community we have been—better get a good writer. And in some cases, better get a good creative writer.

Obituary-writing must be poetic to be interesting. It doesn't fly if it is too prosaic. For example, Brother Jonas Cummings didn't just die. *"The angel of death came in the home of Brother Cummings and put the seal on our esteemed brother and friend."* The angel didn't smite him or take his life or kill him. The angel *put the seal* on Brother Cummings. How poetic.

Another essential feature of the obituary in black culture is that the time of death must be affixed to the statement. That time of departure is generally rounded off to the nearest hour. The angel doesn't put the seal on anybody at 11:43 AM or 6:57 PM. It is always an exact rounded-off hour. The angel's seal was put on Brother Cummings at *"9 AM, Nov. 2, 1969."*

The date of birth—in this case, December 28, 1878—was and is always followed immediately by a statement of when the dearly departed *"confessed his/her hope in Christ."* There are various interpretations of just what that means, but it generally means the point at which the decedent decided to become a Christian and renounce all the evil stuff associated with the Devil. The opportunity is given in all Baptist and in some other Protestant denominations either on the First Sunday of the month or at every service. That opportunity is called "The Invitation," and is a call to all sinners to come down to the front of the church, make their confession in the form of some testimony, and be subjected to a "laying on of hands" by the preacher and/or the deacons and elders of the church. Following that little ceremony, the penitent is soon after baptized and is expected to live a life without sin. The earlier in his/her life the deceased confessed that hope in Jesus, the more impressive it is in personal testimony and on the eventual printed obituary. A congregation reading an obituary can also be impressed if the deceased recognized sinful ways and confessed that hope on a deathbed. Hallelujah!

Brother Cummings, a pillar of the Jones Chapel flock, was, as we have mentioned, ninety years old when the angel with the seal touched him. According to his obituary, Cummings became born-again in 1903 when he was twenty-five. The then pastor of Jones Chapel, Rev. H. H. Harris, baptized the new recruit. We don't know exactly what kind of person he was before his religious conversion, but we do know that Jonas Cummings was married for a year before he became a Christian. He wed Miss Della Hogan in 1902 and had four children with her. His wife and two of his children were touched by the angel with that seal of death before the angel found Brother Cummings. After Della's death, Cummings married one of Westly Rounds' stepchildren, Minnie Lewis Rounds. Their union produced one child they named Mabel.

Jonas Cummings left behind his second wife, daughter, and two sons, Caesar and Cleo, to mourn his death. Caesar was sixty one years old at the time of his father's death and still lived on *Honey Island* with his dad and stepmother; Cleo was sixty three and had moved to Memphis. Mabel was, at the time of her father's death, living in Chicago. Jonas had four grandchildren and eighteen great-grandchildren.

What more can we say about the life of Jonas Cummings—that longtime friend and relative of the Rounds family? He was certainly the epitome of the *Honey Island* native. Well, there was apparently quite a bit more to say at Cummings' funeral. After all the aforementioned remarks and solos and prayers, obituary reading, and acknowledgments we've mentioned, his funeral was still not over. The pastor of Jones Chapel hadn't even delivered the official *Eulogy* by this point. While we do not know the exact length of Rev. M. C. Valentine's oration at Jonas Cummings' obsequies, verily, verily I ask of you, breathes there a Baptist preacher in all of God's Kingdom who will be outshone by any array of speakers and vocalists who precede him? Even though the mourners had heard from eight different speakers, four different soloists, an unknown number of friends and associates who had taken the opportunity to use the three-minute opportunity, and three selections from the choir, the highlight of the funeral is always the minister's eulogy.

The Missionary Baptist preacher gets a chance to opine without penalty whether the deceased is, at the time of the funeral service, angling with the angels or continuing to deviate with the Devil. After often flat-out lying about the current whereabouts of the dead, the minister's next job is to comfort the grieving family. Here the clergyman may be hard-pressed to exhume meritorious qualities of the corpse which anybody living can recall. Next, the preacher gets a chance to scare the hell out of the living with his references to Judgment Day and the angel that will inevitably find them with that seal. Finally, the minister gets to seize the opportunity at the funeral to issue a not-at-all subtle invitation to any visitors present to come back and hear him preach again on an occasion that is not so sad. If he does a better than average job of eulogizing, everybody within earshot—even the unchurched—will want the good reverend to speak at their funeral or at the funeral of a loved one. The good reverend could even be asked thereafter to officiate at a wedding or baptism.

Soaking wet by the end of his sermon, Rev. Valentine had received a sufficient number of *"amens"* and *"preach, brother"* and *"alrights"* to rate high praise for his praise of the late Brother Cummings' commitments to Jesus and church and family. The eloquent warning to those who refused to straighten up and fly right had whipped the congregation up into such a froth heated by fire and brimstone that the Rev. Valentine felt sufficiently comfortable in yielding the floor after only twenty minutes.

But the funeral service was still not over. There had to be the last viewing of the body in its open coffin. The ushers (pronounced *urshers* in many Baptist churches then and now, North and South) began directing the mourners row by row from the back of the church and in a very orderly fashion to the front of the church, so they could gaze down appropriately at the corpse. And yes, there was more touching, more patting, and words whispered to the body.

The choir at this point began a slow, lilting, swaying version of something soft like *Come, Ye Disconsolate* as the mourners filed by. Even the closest members of the family of the deceased who are heaven-bent on showing resolve and cool begin to crack under the vision of seeing so many grief-stricken faces in the parade past the open coffin. Little terrified children are sometimes literally dragged up to the coffin to gaze upon a grandpa or a grandma or an uncle or cousin or perfect stranger. It was and is the conventional belief that such an experience made a child grow up to realize the horror and pain of death. There is often fear and dread and terror on their little faces as they come face-to-face with the work of that Angel of Death with that "seal." The choir moans and sways:

"Come, ye disconsolate, where'er ye languish;
Come to the Mercy-seat, fervently kneel.
Here bring your wounded hearts, here tell your anguish;
Earth has no sorrow that Heav'n cannot heal."

By now, tears are flowing freely throughout the little church. There are a few wails; then piercing screams. The *Oldtimers* think this is becoming a good funeral. So many people are falling apart. The choir continues the low harmony with mesmerizing lilting and swaying:

"Joy of the desolate, Light of the straying,
Hope of the penitent, fadeless and pure;
Here speaks the Comforter, tenderly saying,
Earth has no sorrow that Heav'n cannot cure."

Many of those who pass the open bier turn to kiss the immediate family members of the dearly departed. Family members now seem more broken; chests heave; trembling racks the bodies of the front row mourners. Some mourners—family, friends, and associates—faint.

"Here see the Bread of Life; see waters flowing
Forth from the throne of God, pure from above.
Come to the feast of love; come ever knowing
Earth has no sorrow but Heav'n can remove."

Now the only ones who have not passed by the open coffin are the immediate family members. Two attendants from the funeral home—one on each arm of the mourner—take each family member up individually for the peer down. Cousins are taken first, then aunts and uncles.

Then each offspring of the deceased. The spouse is taken up by ushers last.

By now, the choir's repertoire has built up to some real toe-tapping and much louder selections. If the choir is small, a soloist with a soul-piercing voice may take over here. This is as we begin to approach the climax of the closest next of kin being taken up to the coffin. The pace and volume of the music comes now to an all-time crescendo.

> *"There's a high-way to Heaven;*
> *None can walk up there*
> *But the pure in heart.*
> *There's a high-way to Heaven,*
> *Walking up the King's highway."*

Very often the *"nurse unit"* accompanies the funeral home attendants to help with the spouse because it is not at all unusual for the wife or husband's knees to buckle as they would, but for the support of the attendants' support, faint into a heap. As the spouse is dragged weak-kneed from the coffin, the nurse unit members in their crisp white uniforms and nurse's caps and white gloves step in to administer the only comforting medications they are legally allowed to dispense: a whiff of smelling salts and perhaps a sip of water. This unit is really a para-medical team at many Baptist churches, given basic first-aid training. They, along with the church *urshers,* are often the church units under most assault as the bereaved, sometimes with arms flailing and feet kicking, demonstrate violent emotion. Mourners sometimes try to climb in the coffin with their loved one, and have to be restrained forcefully. Sometimes even during a regular Sunday morning worship service, the dramatic parishioner will be *"overcome by the Holy Ghost"* and will begin jumping up and down, running up and down the aisles, even leaping over pews, in a supposed trance-like state. Some *Oldtimers* refer to the fits the faithful sometimes throw as simply *"getting happy."* When filled with the Holy Spirit, church members may make the sound of rushing winds through their pursed lips or the *chug-a-chug-chug-chug-a* sound of a train picking up speed. They are sometimes heard speaking some form of glossolalia; speaking in mysterious and incomprehensible tongues inspired by the Biblical story of the Tower of Babel.

The behavior of the truly born-again is strange. It would be totally out of place in most Catholic, Episcopalian, Lutheran, Methodist, or other sedate mainline churches. But *"shouting,"* as the activity described here is generically called, is a frequent phenomenon at Baptist and Pentecostal venues. In fact, while the Christians of the world who are far less demonstrative in their expressions of faith would call this "shouting" a bizarre act, you ought to hear what the "spirit-filled" have to say about the "soul-dead." In some fundamentalist congregations as Jones Chapel was and is, one is not considered a true believer unless he/she has had one of these episodes which look to the uninitiated like a seizure.

Among the biggest skeptics in the world about this phenomenon—if they would be honest—are the ushers and nurses in the congregation. They, for example, know exactly who is most likely to get *"sanctified"* during a worship service or funeral. They really have the demonstrative brothers and sisters pegged. You can note how they position themselves to contain certain spirit-filled folk. The ushers and nurses begin to learn the techniques, theatrics, and violent expressions of certain members. They have learned that certain people are more likely to demonstrate on certain occasions. There are even some undercurrent theories floating around some congregations that the determination of what a spirit-filled member might do is sometimes reflective of what kind of togs they are wearing. If the person has a new hat or new dress, tie or suit—look out!

If a brother or sister is abundantly corpulent or muscular, the ushers may have to send in more than three or four of their best catchers to tussle with the spirit-filled soul in order to restore calm in the church, protect themselves from bumps, bruises, scratches, and contusions, and sometimes keep the true-believer from harming himself/herself.

If these wild and violent demonstrations of a filling with an invigorating spirit are genuine, watch the faces of the ushers who successfully catch, ensnare, subdue, and calm those who get happy. Why are they smiling during the whole episode? Why, at the end of the episode, do they wipe their brows with their crispy white hankies and wait for a chorus of amens to rise from the congregation to substitute for applause? If some ushers wore hats, they'd surely tip them to the audience after wrestling down a particularly aggressive, spirit-filled congregant.

As Brother Jonas Cummings' funeral service began to wind down in Jones Chapel on *Honey Island,* the funeral director from the Johnson Funeral Home Chapel was next on the program to thank folks for coming out and, as is the mortician's standard duty, he informed the congregation about the order of the burial service to follow. Brother Cummings was interred right in back of the church in the Jones Chapel Cemetery. Then the undertaker issued the call for all those who would like to assist in another ritual to come forward. These were the mourners who filed to the front of the church to accept—one each—the floral arrangements that had been packed around the coffin. The ushers and newly-deputized ushers took the flowers and plants outside to put on top of the grave once the casket was lowered into the ground and the sod shoveled on top. Any members of the family or anybody in attendance is invited to take flowers home with them as mementos. There are some reports and some suspicions in the African American community that florists would sometimes sneak back into cemeteries and recycle the flowers they had sold.

While Jonas Cummings' funeral might appear to be long and drawn out, it was pretty much a standard length for a Baptist funeral, an hour and a half to two hours. Some Baptist funerals are much longer. Perhaps a record was set by the July 1998, funeral for the renowned Rev. Cleophas Robinson of St. Louis. The preacher and pioneer gospel recording artist was given a final sendoff in a five-hour service!

The funeral director at the Jonas Cummings' funeral the called for the six "active" pallbearers and four "honoraries" to come to the front of Jones Chapel to carry the casket to the cemetery out back of the church. The band of pallbearers was made up of *Honey Island* natives. It might be said that there were no youngsters among them. They included the sixty-five-year-old William Hanson; Charlie Grayer and Spencer Fields, both seventy-one years old; and Alex Green, who was a spry eighty-year-old at the funeral.

Among some African cultures and among some African American funeral traditions to this day there are different levels of mourning and outward expressions of grief depending on the life status of the deceased. Historian Gbenga Sonuga writes of Nigeria's Yoruba tribe:

"Not all deaths are regarded as sorrowful in Yoruba culture, as the belief is that anyone who has lived long enough to see his children and grandchildren happily settled in life has achieved plenty. His children should therefore thank God for having been so lucky as to have enjoyed their parents for so long. The children are deemed lucky people who should be congratulated. On the other hand, if a young person should die, this is regarded as most unfortunate and pathetic for a child is expected to outlive his parents. That the parents should see him die and buried is considered a great tragedy. There is much weeping and sorrowing."

The weeping and sorrowing at Jones Chapel Missionary Baptist Church funerals on *Honey Island*, Mississippi, have been intense for more than a century. When the post office right next door to the church opened in 1907 with great ceremony and with great personal pride for the Rounds family, few could have known that the passing of a beloved person who worked in that little building would cause such heart-rending grief at another *Honey Island* funeral.

# Honey Island: Delivering the Mail

Honey Island residents were mighty proud to have their very own post office. It was located right next door to Jones Chapel. The wood frame "shotgun" building was run by George Byrd Jr., and his wife, Ninnie. She would have been a great-aunt, my grandmother's older sister. George and Ninnie, the granddaughter of Ned and Ellen Rounds, were married at Jones Chapel in May of 1898.

George was thought to have married well, even though the Byrds, too, were respectable residents of the *Honey Island* enclave. George's father, also named George, had fought with distinction as a soldier with the Union Army in the Tenth Regiment Infantry of the United States Colored Troops. Perhaps the older George was able to buy his *Honey Island* acreage from the pension he claimed and got after the Civil War. His unit saw heroic action in the capture of Fort Powhatan on May 5, 1863, and later that year, the unit was at Petersburg and Richmond. George and Ninnie had their own farm when they were wed and then later inherited the property of George's father.

Until the *Honey Island* office opened, residents got their mail from the Tchula Post Office which opened on May 23, 1834. George Byrd Jr. received his commission as the first postmaster of *Honey Island*, Mississippi, on November 7, 1907, almost seventy-five years later. He got his appointment from Postmaster General George von L. Meyer. Had Byrd's post office been a first, second, or third class facility, his appointment would have had to get the blessing of President Theodore Roosevelt. The size of the little *Honey Island* post office made it a *fourth*-class facility, even though George Byrd, by all accounts, ran it with the efficiency of a first-class post office.

Standing before a Holmes County Justice of the Peace on that November day in 1907, former full-time farmer, George Byrd Jr. raised his right hand and repeated these words to launch a new career:

"I, George H. Byrd, do solemnly swear that I will faithfully perform all the duties required of me and abstain from everything forbidden by the laws in relation to the establishment of post-offices and post-roads within the United States; and that I will honestly and truly account for and pay over any money belonging to the said United States which may come into my possession or control; and I also swear that I will support the Constitution of the United States. So help me God."

Postmasters take an oath longer and more detailed than the one taken by the President of the United States.

Byrd earned far less as postmaster in a year than his wife's grandfather, Ned Rounds, carried around in his pocket. Records show that *Honey Island's* dutiful dispenser of stamps and pigeon-hole filer of letters earned only $130 in 1909 and $100 in 1911. No postmaster in the entire nation in charge of a fourth-class facility earned more than $1,000 a year in the year George Byrd Jr. took his oath of office. That was a respectable amount of money in 1907, but it's without a doubt the reason Great-Uncle George held on to his farm. Postmasters of fourth-class facilities were compensated on the box rents collected and they received a commission on postage and canceled postage-due stamps. To increase his income, George became a salesman bound by certain professional restrictions. His charter required him to treat all patrons with courtesy and consideration. Although he would have been the last person in the world to use foul language, his commission "strictly prohibited" him and all other postmasters from "the use of abusive or uncivil language." He was, however, known to approach a postal customer in his dry, polite monotone:

"Can't remember the last time you wrote your mother in Jackson, Billie."

Or he'd drone in a not-too-scolding manner:

"How's that new grandbaby in Chicago, Sarah? Written to your daughter lately?"

Or George would advise ever so subtly:

"Mornin', Miss Cora. Say, didn't your son Benny just turn eighteen? 'Bout time for him to have his own P. O. box, isn't it?"

George would have to push a lot of stamps and box rentals to get any kind of decent commission. This had to be a job he loved. It certainly would never make him a rich man. All the *Oldtimers* who knew him think George Byrd Jr. took the job because it allowed him to wear a tie every day. The position at the post office made him look so official. Here's why George and Ninnie needed to hold onto the farm: the year that George took the oath a postcard cost just one-cent—truly a *penny postcard*. A first-class stamp cost only two cents in 1907. (Note that the words "only" and "just" are not used here to suggest that these stamps were cheap for 1907 purchasers but to compare them to current prices.)

The price of a first-class stamp was bumped up to three cents on November 3, 1917, while Byrd was still postmaster. The *Oldtimers* remember that George was less than excited about the price hike since it became quite clear to him that *Honey Island* folks began to cut down on their letter-writing when the price went up. The extra penny, George had to explain to many of his customers, was tacked on to help defray the cost of the United States' foray into World War I. Byrd breathed a sigh of relief when a nation-wide uproar and a major decline in letter-sending persuaded Uncle Sam to lower the cost of a stamp to two cents once again. That took place at war's end on July 1, 1919. It appeared to George that letter-writing on *Honey Island* increased with the drop-back.

Some monumental events happened during Byrd's postmastership. Parcel Post was launched by the U. S. Post Office in 1913. The Post Office started using motor vehicles to collect and distribute mail in 1914. The last known mail robbery of a stagecoach was solved in 1916. Though there was little benefit to George's customers, airmail took off for the first time in 1918.

Postal regulations required George to keep his *Honey Island* facility open during regular business hours Monday through Saturday. If any mail was scheduled to come in on the Sabbath Day, Byrd was required to open the post office for at least an hour on Sundays.

Postmaster Byrd had yet another official responsibility. He was required by the postal authorities to administer the oath to pensioners that allowed them to get their pension checks.

There was one perk in particular that pleased George's wife, Ninnie. She knew her beloved husband would never be drafted to go off to war as long as he served as postmaster. The office exempted Byrd and all other postmasters in the nation from military service. But, his job description noted that he was required to serve on jury duty.

George Jr. was a loner—well suited for the mostly solitary job of sorting and stamping mail. He had inherited his father's farm and frame. He was tall and slender and always impeccably dressed. He didn't mix well with his neighbors. He was quiet, laconic and thought by some to be stand-offish. The only time George Byrd showed any flair was when he became one of the first *Honey Island* residents to own a horseless carriage—a Model-T Ford. On some of his friendlier days, George could be convinced to don his motor car goggles and driving gloves and give a spin along *Honey Island's* dusty wagon-wheel-rutted dirt roads to screaming kids, like my mother and my two aunts, who waited for a turn. Occasionally, an *Oldtimer* or two would take a chance on his or her life by mounting the newfangled contraption which some of the *Honey Island* naysayers were sure would be a short-lived city folks' invention. The horse would never be replaced, they asserted.

Steering was hard because of those wagon ruts, but apparently George took a delight he seldom expressed openly in chauffeuring the curious around town. The Byrd boys, King and Lee, were obviously proud of the black horseless carriage that gave them lofty status among their young chums.

In sharp contrast to George's dour, withdrawn personality, Ninnie was considered by one and all to be—as a family member who knew her well opined—"sweet as a lamb." She was pretty with her long dark, straight hair parted in the middle and topping her slender frame. She had light and smooth sepia skin, laughing eyes, and a great sense of humor. She had no difficulty in engaging anybody of any age in lively conversation. Just the opposite of her withdrawn husband, George. Ninnie always had a busy day. When she wasn't sorting and stamping mail at the post office, she was a housewife and mother of two active boys: King (called "Sonny" by everybody) and his younger brother, Lavossa, who was always called either Lee or "Kid" Byrd, even when he became a senior citizen.

Honey Island's post office was also a confectionary—a canteen where one could buy candies, cookies, smoked link sausages, and cheeses. A favorite treat for the kids was a flat six-inch by seven-inch rectangular pink or white icing-coated gingerbread cookie called a "stage plank." Visitors to the post office could wash all that down with a NeHi soda pop or a three-cent bottle of "big orange" soda.

The *Honey Island* post office also featured a comfort that no modern-day postal facility can claim openly. There was a corner in the back of the place that was shielded by a curtain. Behind that curtain was a cot for George or Ninnie to use if either had worked into the night and didn't want to take the long walk or drive to get to their farm home in the pitch black nights with nary a street light. When business was slow on a hot summer's day, a little afternoon nap for the postmaster or his wife was possible. Ninnie's boys and her favorite niece, Little Willetta, would occasionally take a little nap in the corner of the post office when school was out. Today, Aunt Willetta remembers those naps from more than eighty years ago.

The mail for the Rounds family and their neighbors was picked up at either Belzoni or at a little train station at Mileston, Mississippi. Mileston was little more than a train depot with a little store. *Honey Island's* letters, cards, and parcels were picked up and delivered to George Byrd's U. S. post office each day by the ever-faithful Mack Hart, a farmer who doubled as *Honey Island's* mailman. Mack was born in 1869 in Alabama. He and his wife Annie, two years younger than he, had eight children ranging in age in 1910 from eighteen to one: Mack, Lou, Susie, Katie, Walter, Ida, Willie, and Montana, the infant. Every morning, Monday through Friday at the crack of dawn, Mack, a tar-black round man with thick lips that always looked rosy red, would pack his round tin lunch-pail, saddle up his trusty steed and ride into Belzoni or Mileston to meet the train. He was one dedicated son-of-a-gun! Neither scorching sun nor rain nor sleet nor hail could keep him from his appointed round-trip into one or the other of the bigger towns.

As the sun came up each week day, Mack knew he wouldn't get back home to his wife and children and farm each day until early afternoon. Mack probably felt comfortable leaving his farm since his sons Mack Jr., and Lou were old enough and capable enough, with the help of their mother and sisters, to take care of the farm. Although the trail was long and lonely, Mack seemed to love his work. He was always whistling some song with trills in it like bird calls, and perhaps he alone knew the names of any of these tunes. Mack took pride in the fact his rides into town and back were at least an hour or two faster than the average islander could make the trip. When he'd saddle up, he would really move out! He couldn't possibly have kept up the pace all the way to the train. But he sure looked impressive leaving his house and galloping off into the sunrise!

The lunch Mack Hart packed—or maybe his wife Annie helped him pile high— was a culinary masterpiece in its vertical construction. It was typical of the lunches packed by all islanders who weren't sedentary. Shut-ins would have died from the heaviness of a *Honey Island* lunch. It was meant for hard workers who could burn off the sheer weight and calories of the repast.

After gulping a quick breakfast of cornbread soaked in buttermilk, or grits and redeye gravy, or rice and bacon and eggs, or anything that was left over from supper the night before, Mack would pour directly into the tin bucket about an inch of the thick, black molasses manufactured from the sugar cane on the island. Then he would scoop about a quarter of a pound of rich yellow butter from the butter tub. He'd then mash and stir the butter into the gooey syrup. Next, on top of this mixture he'd throw about four big biscuits, a hunk of cornbread or recently-baked supper rolls. On top of the bread—in whatever its form—Mack would toss three or four pieces of fried chicken, a big hunk of roast beef or a couple of fat pork chops. This whole caloric, heavy, solid lunch, consumed on the trail or in the field, would be washed down with a quart jar of whole milk, buttermilk, lemonade, or water. And that was lunch. Supper would be much bigger than that!

One day, Mack Hart tied his trusty, sweaty steed up to the hitching rail in front of his post office after a trip back from the big city and got some news that was more devastating than any of the news he carried back and forth in his saddlebag for the islanders each day. It was news that Mack and everybody else around had expected for a long time. Tragedy had struck the Byrd and Rounds families and anyone else who loved or knew Ninnie. She had *passed*. It was a slow and painful demise. She died of something that was called at the time *pellagra*. We know a lot more about this horrible disease now than George and Ninnie and the doctors knew back then. Pellagra is a disease that is caused by a deficiency of niacin in the diet, by an absence of green, leafy vegetables.

Author/historian John M. Barry writes of the horror of pellagra:

"The disease, caused by poor diet, begins by draining the energy from its victims (it accounted for at least some of the 'laziness ascribed to blacks by white southerners'). But the disease can also become ugly and dangerous. Sores erupt on the skin and form a thick black crust. Victims become morose, hallucinate, feel as if a fire burns in their heads and spines. Untreated, pellagra kills."

While Ninnie was a relatively early victim of this ravaging disease, there was a major epidemic of pellagra in the Mississippi Delta in 1927. That was eight years after Ninnie wasted away and died. By some accounts, there were up to 50,000 cases of pellagra in the Mississippi Delta alone.

Some of the *Oldtimers* remember that Ninnie was, indeed, a finicky eater. She shunned milk and eggs. She really hated green vegetables and would gag at the sight or thought of anybody in the family drinking a cup of pot "likker" off the collard, mustard, or turnip greens. Even though she was thin as a rail, she munched voraciously on the junk foods in the post office deli. She'd snack every day on the smoked link sausage, cheese, cakes, cookies, and soda pop. Those who knew her well heard her say she ate the link sausage because it didn't look like any animal in particular. She ate the cheese because it was a pretty color and wasn't as disgusting to her as cow's milk, which was often warm when consumed. It is an irony that poor Ninnie had a niacin deficiency since all of the members of the Byrd and Rounds family farmed and ate lots of boiled greens.

Seems that almost every family member—with the exception of Ninnie Rounds Byrd—ate and loved those mustard, collard, turnip, dandelion greens, and spinach. There never seemed to be enough of the tasty pot likker to go around at *Honey Island* breakfast, lunch, and supper tables. It was poured off the boiled greens glistening with the fat from the big piece of salt pork or ham hocks that had been cooked with a big onion and a hot pepper to flavor the greens. The dark green broth would be poured into a cup and sipped like tea. Or it would be poured into a bowl into which a big hunk of cornbread would be added. Ninnie turned up her nose at the greens and this liquid delicacy. And it cost her her life.

She got skinnier and skinnier. She began to suffer diarrhea, skin changes, severe nerve dysfunction, and mental symptoms. Ninnie's lovely face became disfigured when her lips swelled and turned black, preventing her from flashing her frequent and radiating smile. Her chest and back also blistered in big black crusty blotches. Under the black swatches there were sickening bloody red spots. The painful skin condition caused Ninnie sleepless days and nights. Her once sharp and witty mind began to leave her. She began to jabber unintelligibly while she foamed at the mouth. She moaned and groaned in pitiable pain. She would occasionally muster a blood-curdling shriek that frightened the children in particular.

The *Oldtimers*, including my grandmother who loved her sister, and my mother and two aunts who loved their aunt so much, erroneously thought poor Ninnie's condition was caused by too much exposure to the sun. That's the cause of the malady that was whispered about the island. Their assumption that the sun was the culprit was fueled by the fact that exposure to sunlight caused Ninnie such awesome discomfort. So they kept her in a dark room. She rotted away in twenty-four hour darkness.

Her husband, George, reluctantly moved her into the big house where her stepmother, Mary Lewis Rounds, could give her loving, around-the-clock care. George would now be able to continue his considerable duties as *Honey Island* postmaster while the young Byrd boys managed the farm without having to hear and see their mother die right before their eyes. The bed-ridden patient began to waste away more rapidly after the move, even though Mary Rounds tried to force-feed her warm doses of the pot likker she always hated. She soon curled into a fetal position and had trouble speaking and controlling her bowels or bladder and her once sharp mind. Some of the Rounds and Byrd children and grandchildren were initially allowed to see their beloved Aunt Ninnie in her invalid state. In the earliest stages of her terminal malady the little children would ask if Ninnie would get better. Their elders lied. After awhile, though, the children were kept away to keep them from having nightmares about this ugly disfiguration and death.

In 1917, Ninnie slipped away at age thirty-nine, leaving her husband a widower and her two teenage boys motherless. Her emaciated and blackened body was bathed and dressed. As was the custom of the day, Ninnie's remains were laid on a board between two chairs and put to lie in state in the living room. She was completely covered from head to toe with a crisp, white sheet. Sometimes the head of the deceased would be left uncovered by the sheet or bedspread shroud. In the case of Ninnie, her appearance would be too distressing to the mourners. Some of the Rounds menfolk had started to build a small wooden coffin for Ninnie weeks before she passed.

Since there was no mortician on the island, no facilities for embalming, and a trip into Belzoni to a proper undertaker would have allowed for virtually no attendance for a funeral in the city, Ninnie, like all those who *passed* before her had to be buried early on the day following her death. Rev. Rutger was called to officiate at her funeral in Jones Chapel. Like all funerals for Blacks of that era (and for a hundred years thereafter), her funeral was held at night so that workers who could not afford to miss a day's pay could get home, get scrubbed up, get dressed in their best clothes, and attend the service. She was buried in the Byrd family cemetery behind their farmhouse early the next morning with only a few family members and close friends in attendance.

Pity. Had Ninnie lived a century later, with the help of modern medicine she might have lived a half-century longer, or even more. After her death, George continued his work as postmaster. He stayed on until he was succeeded by Emanuel L. Gray on February 26, 1924. Gray was *Honey Island's* second and last postmaster.

Gray was married to George Byrd's sister, Hallie, in *Honey Island's* highly endogamous community. Hallie Gray joined her husband in his work at the post office for a while just as Ninnie Byrd had. In fact, she started work as an assistant to her husband after a little incident that caused a few titters around town. Emanuel Gray was a short, stocky, dark brown-skinned man. He walked with a noticeable limp, and some of the *Oldtimers* chortled that Mizz Hallie was at least a full head taller than her husband depending on whether he "reared up on the long leg or the gimpy one." Gray was known around town for his roving eye. That allowed the *Oldtimers* to observe that he never would have been able to catch up to any of the belles he fancied because of that bad leg.

His disability better enabled him to catch hell from the madame. Gray once hired the comely young Sally Turner as his assistant without bothering to tell his wife about his hire. When Hallie Gray found out about it, she showed up one day unexpectedly at the post office and gave Miss Turner, a woman considerably her junior, the gate. In no uncertain terms! Mrs. Gray herself then became her husband's postal assistant.

The little post office at *Honey Island,* Mississippi, was shuttered for good on March 30, 1935. After that date, the dwindling island population once again had to travel about twenty miles due east to the post office in Tchula for postal services. One could almost hear a death knell tolling for *Honey Island* when the post office my great-uncle had opened twenty-eight years earlier closed its doors forever.

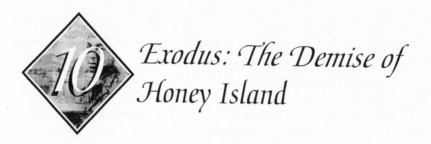

Exodus: The Demise of Honey Island

"... signed, sealed and delivered unto Ned Rounds, his heirs and assigns forever..."

"Forever" can be such a short time sometimes. So it was with the once-prosperous and independent Rounds Family of *Honey Island,* Mississippi. The contract drawn up by the attorney for Peter James Jr. that turned over 216 acres "more or less" to Old Ned Rounds for a thousand dollars cash on March 17, 1886, proved hollow. The deed written up on December 8, 1897, for Ned's purchase of an additional 160 acres of land turned out to be a bad deal all the way around for my great-great-granddad. Westly Rounds turned out not to be the wheeling-dealing, shrewd businessman his father had been. To meet the financial demands of a farm that required a smooth transition into a new century, to keep up with the taxes and interest payments on the loans, to meet the needs for updated farm equipment and implements, to compensate for the natural ravages of flooding and soil erosion, and to continue to support such a large family retinue, West needed frequent cash infusions. He borrowed and borrowed and borrowed as he got deeper and deeper and deeper into debt from exorbitant interest rates. Soon West lost the farm and everything salvageable on it through foreclosure.

The gravy days were over for the Rounds family and shortly after 1910, the family experienced a fast reversal of fortune and a slow trickle to northern cities. Then, in 1923, a mass migration of the Rounds Clan to points north—Memphis, St. Louis, Chicago, and Detroit, even to Wichita—began.

Westly Rounds' son, Ambrose, was one of the first to leave *Honey Island.* He abandoned the farm life by 1920 and moved to the big city—the Windy City. There, with the help of the education he had received on *Honey Island* and through the voracious reading habits he had inherited from his father, Ambrose—called Bud by his siblings and Uncle A by all of us younger folk—got a treasured job as a mail sorter at the post office. His relatives bragged about "Bud" being a "government man" now.

Shortly after Ambrose Rounds arrived in Chicago, he met a female worker named Sally at his postal job. Soon she was Sally Rounds. Bud Rounds was said to be so penurious that when he held a dollar bill you could hear George Washington screaming from Bud's tight grip. Still, he continued to send a little money to his papa and family on *Honey Island*. It was not enough, though, to keep West and Mary Rounds and the few children they still had at home in a style to which they had become accustomed just a few decades before. It was a rude tumble for the proud family, and West seemed to be overwhelmed by all of the demands on him.

When Ambrose made a couple of trips back home to Mississippi, he was appalled to find the family now living in near squalor. The outhouse and the water pump on the side of the house were still the Rounds family's only version of plumbing. Some of their neighbors had already met the challenges of the times much better than the Rounds family and had moved their bathroom facilities indoors. Some of West Rounds' neighbors now had electricity lighting up and heating up things in their homes. West did not. Some of the *Honey Island* farmers had spiffy new equipment to plant and harvest their crops. West Rounds did not. Some of the farmers on the island had managed to pay their taxes and other bills on time. West had not. The Rounds family in the mid-twenties were now among the "have-nots." They had been, since the 1880s, among the proud "haves."

Ambrose persisted and continued to send a little money now and again, but he soon began to realize that his best efforts were too meager to keep his *Honey Island* kinfolk from an ignominious end. Bud went back to Chicago after one of his visits to the land of his birth and found a modest apartment for his father, stepmother, and any siblings who wanted to abandon a hopeless homestead. On May 5, 1923, West and Mary and their children Inell, Eva, Bessie, and Ben boarded the Illinois Central at the Belzoni train station. Knowing they would never live on *Honey Island* again, they headed north. Upon their arrival in Chicago, they moved into the little apartment at 548 East 40th Street that Ambrose had found for them. Only a stubborn Minnie Rounds chose to stay behind.

Inez Rounds, the oldest of West and Mary's second round of children, married Henry Patterson of Deovolente, Mississippi after she got to Chicago. Everybody called her "Baby." She was interested in becoming a licensed beautician, and, after dropping out of school on *Honey Island* (at about the same age as Willetta had been when she fled to St. Louis), Inez and her mother, Mary Lewis Rounds, travelled all around the Mississippi Delta as itinerant hairdressers. Now that she was in Chicago, Inez enrolled in the beauty school operated by the venerable Lydia B. Adams. Lydia Adams was the Chicago version of St. Louis' Annie Malone and Madame C. J. Walker, although she didn't develop such a large line of beauty products for African Americans. She did run a thriving school of cosmetology in the late '30s and through the '40s at her school at 4655 South Michigan. Adams died at the age of ninety-four in 1993.

"Baby" created a beauty shop in her home at 4303 South Prairie Avenue. She had a steady stream of customers because her rates were reasonable and she did excellent styling of such popular hairdos as the *croquignole* and the *pompadour*. With the croquignole, a type of permanent, the client's hair was wound around rods from the ends inward and chemically treated. It comes to us from the French word for *crunch*. The pompadour called for the beautician to raise the woman's or man's hair in a roll over the forehead. Sometimes a bit of padding was the base for a woman's pompadour. Inez, listed on some documents as Inell, died in 1987.

Elmer Rounds, Eva's twin brother and twenty-two years old when the family evacuated *Honey Island*, was nicknamed Bully. Nobody among the *Oldtimers* remembers why. It certainly had nothing to do with his badgering any of the other kids his age when he was a boy on the Island. He was considered by all to be good-natured, even-tempered, and very wise for his years. He was tall and slim with a physique unlike the body forms of many of the other members of the Rounds family who tended, from the good life, to be variously called "pleasingly plump" and "full-figured" and "portly" and "stout." Old Ned's three hundred pounds might have appeared a bit hereditary, but diet had to figure in there somewhere.

Elmer also married a Mississippi girl. Ada Morgan was fresh out of Meridian, Mississippi, not far from *Honey Island*. They, too, met in Chicago in a little colony of expatriate Mississippians. She had one daughter by a previous marriage when she tied the knot with Elmer. As with so many other members of the Rounds family who left Mississippi, there were no children born of the union. The childlessness was an inexplicable phenomenon once the Rounds clan left the Delta where children grew like cotton and Spanish moss. Ada's daughter bore the interesting name of Lovie Morgan Johnson Radcliffe. Elmer Rounds was one of many family members—including his two brothers Ben and Perry—who worked at the Miller & Hart Meat Packing House. Elmer died in 1987 of what we would call today Alzheimer's disease. Back then the *Oldtimers* just called it "old age dementia," or they just noted sadly that Old Elmer had "gone out of his head" with old age.

Elmer's twin, Eva, is remembered as being pleasant and quiet. She married Jack Patterson who hailed from Deovolente near Eva's birthplace. Jack's cousin,

Henry Patterson, was also from Deovolente and Henry married Eva's sister, Inell, whom everybody called "Baby." Eva died in Chicago of bone cancer in 1981 at the age of eighty-one. She had worked as a piecework seamstress with her mother, Mary Lewis Rounds, at Sopkins. Later, Eva Rounds Patterson worked as a domestic in private family service.

Perry G. Rounds also got what was considered back-then a good job at the abattoir where his other relatives worked. He was twenty-years old when all hope was abandoned for saving the family homestead on *Honey Island*. Perry was considered by all to be mild-mannered and quiet, except when he was totally immersed in a hot and loud game of bid whist. Otherwise, Perry was very much like his father, West, and his grandfather, Ned. Perry Rounds died on June 24, 1938, never having married and fathering no children.

That was just about six months after his baby brother, Ben, passed. The cause of death was tuberculosis—that mysterious disease that can fatally infect any of the body's tissues—especially the lungs. The *Oldtimers* called the disease that carried Perry away *consumption*. The Rounds family and friends were rocked by grief from the deaths, within months of each other, of two hard-working, handsome, and lovable young men who had lived such short lives.

Ben Rounds was West and Mary's baby son. He was all of eighteen when the family packed up and left the homestead. Ben had taken to farming, but was much too young to take over from his dad and avoid the scheming of the loan sharks who had wrapped their tentacles around the Rounds' *Honey Island* legacy. Ben had to sell a precious ox he had raised from its birth before the move. At one time he had a photo made of himself and his mother standing next to the then thousand-pound beast. He had passed copies of that photo to all his loved ones. After he got to Chicago, Ben felt that a city slicker would never have pictures of himself with a pet ox floating around, so Ben quietly went around to all to whom he had given the photos and took them back. He didn't want anybody in Chicago to see him looking like a farm hick. A copy of that photo is included in the picture section of this book.

Ben, the big-boned, round-faced, good-natured, and gentle fellow lived a life in Chicago that was cut precious short. He got a job working with animals in Chicago, but this job involved their slaughter. He got a job with his two brothers, Perry and Elmer, at the Miller & Hart Meat Packing Company at Forty-fifth and South Ashland. He worked there for just about fifteen years when he was stricken with heart failure and died in 1938 at Cook County Hospital—the Homer Phillips Hospital of Chicago. Almost as sad as his untimely death was the fact that Ben had gotten engaged to the lovely Mary Ellen Turner just before he passed. The couple had met in Chicago after she learned that he was from *Honey Island* and he learned that she was from Vossburg, Mississippi. When she attended her intended's funeral, Mary Ellen was still wearing the engagement ring Ben had just given her. Ben died without ever producing an heir to carry the Rounds name. He did leave behind a brand new Buick he had just purchased on a time-payment schedule. Ben's older brother, Ambrose, was in the best financial position to take on the payments for the new car. And he did. Bud liked the classiness of the new Buick, so some years later he bought another Buick right off the assembly line.

Henry Rounds was a rather enigmatic and distant member of the family. Born in January of 1890, Henry moved to Chicago with his mother and father and siblings at the time of the mass exodus of the Rounds family from Mississippi in late 1927. Like his brother, Ambrose, Henry got a job at the post office in Chicago and was considered a "government man" by all who spoke proudly about him. He was an impeccable dresser. With no wife or children to support, my great-uncle Henry lavished the highest quality clothing on himself. It might seem like a small thing today, but Henry owned the first wristwatch in the family. At the same time, the family shielded a deep, dark secret about Henry. He suffered from a debilitating mental illness.

With a caring family's help and with dozens of loving arms wrapped around him, he was a man who would alternately, in no particular order of sequence, lapse into periods of deep depression, manic activities, irrational schemes, and illogical conversation. Some of the *Oldtimers* remember Henry was that way from boyhood until his death in the late '40s. In fact, a number of *Oldtimers* have vague memories that Henry had to sometimes be locked in a room by "Papa" West Rounds on the *Honey Island* farm. Sometimes Henry's clothes would be taken away from him to discourage him from escaping home confinement. There are some who remember at least one occasion in which Henry escaped and was returned by a neighbor to the custody of his parents. The babbling, incoherent Henry was, through the kindness of the neighbor who found him, wrapped only in a sheet.

There were some occasions on which Henry could engage the unsuspecting in lengthy conversations before he would veer off without warning into the realm of the absurd. He loved to talk about his "inventions." If necessity is, indeed, the mother of invention, some of Henry's mental creations were founded on a general societal need. The execution of his inventiveness warranted little Patent Office attention. For example, after he arrived in Chicago, Henry noted—and perhaps noted all alone—that a Chicago city ordinance prohibited spitting on the street. Henry also noted that the favorite launch points for the Windy City's plug tobacco-chewing and snuff-dipping passengers were the very buses and streetcars on which they traveled. Henry created sketches of a way to hitch a chain of spittoons around every bus and trolley car in Chicago!

During one of his more sane moments, Henry Rounds was able to take and score high marks on the postal service exam. After he got the job, it soon became evident to his supervisors that Henry had serious mental problems. In fact, getting all dressed up and being interviewed for highly respectable jobs was a regular pastime of my great-uncle Henry. His line of patter could be very impressive. Once he showed up for the job, it generally took only a short time for his employer and co-workers to find that he was stark-raving mad. At another time in another place, Henry might have gotten proper treatment for what was surely manic depression, usually called bipolar disease today. Had he been able to get professional help and medication when he was a child on *Honey Island,* Henry's life might have ended differently. As it turns out sadly enough, shortly after he posed for the photograph in this volume, Henry was committed to the Dunning Mental Institution where he spent the rest of his relatively short life restrained and confined in a depressing environment.

Many Rounds family members who knew and know Henry's sad story are in denial and practicing the famous Rounds selective memory about this story. None of those in denial can be convinced that there are few families untouched by mental illness. Little consolation can be bestowed on the Rounds descendants who are in denial by congratulating them on how well they handled a problem without discarding and abandoning the family member with the problem. Their filial fidelity sustained Henry for far longer than he might have lasted had he been shunned or tossed out into the world.

Minnie Lewis Rounds, thirty-three years old at the time of her stepfather's and her mother's departure for Chicago, had chosen to stay with her husband, Jonas Cummings, and their four children on *Honey Island.* They had one daughter of their union, Mabel, and Jonas brought three sons with him from his marriage to his first wife, Della. Minnie's stepsons, Thomas who was nineteen; Cleo who was seventeen; and Caesar, at fifteen; when West and Mary Rounds and their other children moved to Chicago, represented that *Honey Island* phenomenon of children being spaced exactly two years apart. Mabel Cummings couldn't resist the lure of the big city and she, too, moved to Chicago. Her mother and father continued to plant and pick cotton on their own little farm. They also brought in a modest produce crop and raised a few cows and hogs until Minnie died in September of 1975 at age eighty-five.

Minnie's brother, John Lewis, chose not to move as far north as Chicago and he settled in St. Louis. He married a Mississippi girl, Eliza Wells of Deovolente, the all-Black town not far from *Honey Island.* John and Eliza had one child together, a daughter, Beatrice. John Lewis, my great-grandfather West's stepson, was another one of the Rounds men who snagged a comfortable job in the post office. He worked at the main post office in downtown St. Louis until his retirement. He died in 1973 at age 81.

West began contemplating abandoning the beloved homestead in early 1926. That's the year before the Delta got deluged by the heaviest and most continuous rains anybody could remember. The entire Mississippi Valley got swamped following torrential rains that started just after mid-August that year. The Mississippi River, which fed the Yazoo right at the Rounds Homestead's back door, began to threaten. If the river became as swollen as it was in the fall of '26, more rain could cause a real catastrophe. According to Larry Banks, the Hydraulics Chief at the Army Corps of Engineers at Vicksburg, the river level gauge in October of 1926 posted an incredible forty-foot-high-water mark! Thirty-one feet had been the previous high water mark.

West Rounds, his family, and neighbors joined in giving a collective sigh of relief that the rains that had been virtually incessant for more than a month began to slack off, and then stop. But it was too early to rejoice. The first week in December, the skies were opening up again and pouring more water than West and other farmers in the area needed on their crops. The faithful at Jones Chapel Missionary Baptist Church began to believe that God was angry with them and the rest of the South for some reason or another and was letting His wrath show. Those who didn't go to church on *Honey Island* or its environs believed that Mother Nature—not God—was really ticked-off about something. Some of the *Oldtimers* remember that Christmas 1926 started getting a bit scary as they sloshed around in ankle-deep water from the Yazoo River, which had for most but not all years been a fairly quiet and unobtrusive neighbor. Some of the *Oldtimers* remember that the Yuletide season that year meant getting shoes and boots wet and muddy as family and friends went house to house exchanging presents and Christmas cheer. Even Tchula Lake's level made the Jones Chapel congregation glad that West and the other deacons had instructed the Masons who built the church/school to build it on stilts thirty-two years earlier.

Willetta Williams, West's granddaughter who was thirteen the year before the Big Flood, remembers that as a precaution, her kinfolk began to put perishable items like flour, sugar, and cornmeal in barrels on top of tables in the house. Small farm animals found roosts on rooftops and even trees. *Honey Island* hogs, horses, cows, oxen, and goats had no choice but to slosh around in the water. Willetta, in her late eighties today, still remembers how fierce the mosquitoes got with all that standing water. The discomfort the *Honey Island* residents felt inside their relatively insulated enclave, though, was minor compared to what was happening to Delta residents outside and beyond the island homesteads.

Black men in towns like Greenville, Yazoo City, and Belzoni were being literally snatched off the streets to work as conscripts filling sandbags to protect their towns. Some of the *Oldtimers* heard stories about some of their skin-mates getting beaten or even killed if they tried to resist being pressed into harsh labor on the levee patrol gangs. As the levee at Greenville, the only hope for *Honey Island*, weakened and showed no signs of handling even another inch of rain, historian and author John M. Barry notes that:

"Hundreds of blacks, held by guns, began risking their lives for someone they had to see as a white fool. Under the guns they filled sandbags, threw them into the breach, passed them down the line to men standing in the breach. The water poured through in a growing torrent, washing the sandbags away as fast as they threw them in. Under their feet the levee quivered, shook."

The levee at Mounds Landing broke apart violently at eight o'clock on the morning of April 21, 1927, sending a wall of water three-quarters of a mile wide and 130-feet deep raging through the land the Rounds family and their thousands of neighbors had settled three-quarters of a century before. Mattie Burns Williams remembers:

"That flood caused an awful mess in people's houses. And we had to deal with it in our homes because there was no place to go. Belzoni and Yazoo City were completely flooded out, too. Some folks went to stay with friends and kinfolk who lived on higher ground. But there wasn't much higher ground."

Jodie Thurman was a strapping young family man of twenty-seven when the crucial Mounds Landing levee blew and exploded from extreme swelling. Now a ninety-eight-year-old Baptist preacher, Rev. Thurman has served four Belzoni congregations and preached several times at Jones Chapel Missionary Baptist Church on *Honey Island*. He remembers the Great Deluge of more than seven decades ago as if it were yesterday:

"My family and me were living in the little town of Daybreak, just about a mile west of Belzoni. In fact, we were such a small little community that the name of the place doesn't even show up on most maps anymore. It was an all-colored community of hard-working, independent people.

"Anyway, you want to know about the flood. Well, we got a warning that the levee was going to break at any minute on that afternoon in April of '27. Most folks didn't take the warning all that serious. But all my kinfolk believed something like with Noah and that Great Flood in the Bible was gonna happen right there in Mississippi. I mean, after all, things was just as sinful in Mississippi as they was when Ole Noah was ordered to build that great big boat and gather up his family and all them critters. So, like Brother Noah, I gathered up my wife and five kids and waited to figure out which way to go to get outta danger of the flood.

"I had answered the call of the Lord just three years before the year of the big flood. So when we heard about the threat that we was about to get wiped out by water, I began to read Genesis 5-9 over and over again and waited to hear the voice of the Lord that has guided me for sixty-five years in the ministry.

"And then there came these men riding around in trucks in the driving rain with bullhorns. They didn't exactly look like messengers of God. And to tell you the honest truth, some of the language they was using to get us hustling to pack up what we could wasn't exactly inspired by Scripture. We knew how much it had been raining for what seemed like months, but it was still more than a notion to get ready to leave everything you owned and *get out of town and move on up to higher ground. Funny how there's a lot of old Negro spirituals that talk about getting to higher ground. It's like the songwriters knew that 'higher ground' could be the same thing as Heaven.*

"A freight train was sent to transport all the folks in Daybreak to Yazoo City where relief camps were being set up. I remember we all got packed in like sardines around five p.m. But we didn't make it into Yazoo City until around seven clock the next morning. Now that was normally about a thirty-mile ride—maybe about an hour and a half by car. Longer, of course, if you had to depend on a horse or mule.

"The water was so high when we were on that freight train that even with the doors closed water was seeping right in, getting our shoes real wet. We were standing in water at some times. And sometimes we felt like the train was actually floating like a boat. We heard later from some of our kinfolk and friends in Greenville that there were actually boxcars floating crazy through the streets and slamming into buildings and things right through the heart of town and causing a real ruckus when they crashed into buildngs. There was terrible high water all the way from the Sunflower River to Belzoni. When we made it to Yazoo City, the camp was filling up with people. We had to sleep on the ground the first night. The second night a shipment of Army cots had come in. And by the third night we were all sleeping under tents—and fighting the biggest flocks of mosquitoes we had ever seen in our lives.

"Early each morning the men were transported by truck to what you might call the front line of the battle to hold the water back. We filled sandbags like crazy. The womenfolk stayed behind to cook and take care of the children. Boy, you talk about backbreaking work. You ever thrown around a full-up sandbag? I've hoisted up pretty good-size children that weren't as heavy as the sandbags we were filling and throwing down the line. We worked from sunup till sundown every day. And we knew we were fighting a losing battle against that rising water. When the trucks took us back to the camp at Yazoo City after we had worked a full ten- or twelve-hour day, we were run down and beat out. We weren't up to much foolishness. The menfolk would just crash and pass out.

"There were some white men that would come around to us while we were laying bags to beat the band and they would try to get us to come to their plantations and farms after we had worked the line to lay sandbags around their places to save their property. We looked at them like they was crazy! But some of them were determined to steal us off to sandbag around their property. And I'm sure some of these white men would have forced us to go with them if it hadn't been for the soldiers who had been stationed around to keep law and order on the line.

"I will never forget that there was one white guy who owned a plantation near where we were sandbagging who came up with a clever little proposition he thought would tempt some us. He was like Ole Satan working the line, whispering promises in our ears. He wanted to put us to work after our regular shift was over. He even had some of his cooks lay out the most unbelievable spread of food we had ever seen in our lives. Set it right up on a real long table next to where we were working like dogs to hold off the water. Man, was that

a sight! Really made our mouths water up. More food than we would see in a month. And the food they were feeding us was pretty bad. Hard bread, cheese, fatback, and sometimes a real watery soup. Anyway, this white plantation owner told us if we came and worked on his place laying up sandbags we could have as much of that food as we could eat. And he said we could even take as much food as we could carry back to our families in the camp at Yazoo City. And he raised up a fist full of cash bills. Said he would pay top dollar for some hard-working colored boys who weren't afraid of a little extra work. But as I said... we were wore out. Some of the colored fellas said 'yes' at first, but at day's end, they changed their minds and said 'no.'

"Well, I tell you, that white man went into a rage and started calling all of us a lot of real bad names. He flew right into the faces of some of the men who had first told him they would come work for him and just yelled at the top of his voice at them. If it wasn't for the soldiers who stepped in, I think this white man would have struck some of the boys on the line.

"I never will forget it. He got so worked up that he just took his arm and raked all the food off that long table right into the water. All of that good food was ruined. As the white man stumped off yelling about how no-good colored folks was, something unusual happened: some of the colored men started calling him bad names right back. Not loud, you understand. But loud enough for each other to hear—and loud enough for some of the soldiers who were protecting us to hear, too. Those colored boys would never have had the nerve to do that if we were on dry land and there wasn't any flood.

"Now remember, we went to that camp in Yazoo City in late April of '27. We stayed there until late June! And then a train took us back to find our homes all but wiped out by the water. And inside what was left of our houses was three or four feet of awful, smelly silt. What a bad dream. But at least we had our lives. We began to hear about a lot of our people who were not so blessed. They didn't get out quick enough—and it cost them their lives."

Lue Annie Scott Rounds, who reached the age of ninety-two in 1999, and her husband Will Rounds Jr., were sharecroppers in a little community called Pluck when the flood wall ruptured at Mound's Landing. She remembers that everybody on the Pluck plantation had been warned about impending danger, just as Rev. Thurman and everybody else in the area had been warned. Mrs. Round's family took an unusual approach that was not too unlike Noah's approach:

"We took all the livestock we could—hogs, chickens, a goat and some ducks up into the hay loft 'cause we had no idea how high the water would get and we had no idea how long we would be away from home. And that's the scary part, not knowin' when you'd be coming back. We got some big washtubs and filled them with cattle feed, ears of corn, and a couple of tubs of water for the animals.

"All of the men in Pluck were gathered up by some white men who came around in trucks to get them to go and sandbag. As I remember it, the men didn't have any choice in the matter but most of them wanted to help save our places and the crops we had put in.

But the levee broke before our men got there, and they had to hurry back home to get ready to get on the train that was coming to pick us up."

As it turns out, Mrs. Rounds and her family ended up on the same refugee train as Rev. Thurman and his loved ones. The rescue and relief plan didn't put all the evacuees from around the *Honey Island*/Belzoni area in the same camp. While some of them were taken to the camp in Yazoo City where the Thurman family camped out, some of them, like Mrs. Scott's family, were taken on a roundabout journey. After traveling for a while, they ended up back near their flooded-out homes to a place called Goat Hill, very close to *Honey Island*. The hill was on a higher elevation than the Rounds homestead. They stayed there for three weeks—a shorter time than the refugees in Yazoo City. Mrs. Rounds continues:

"There were soldiers everywhere in their uniforms. They were there to keep the peace mostly because, to tell you the truth, it could get a little rowdy in that Goat Hill Camp. They had to keep telling some of the colored folks to settle down, especially at night when some of us with kids were trying to get some sleep. I guess the soldiers were also there to keep any of the men from sneaking away from the camp. After about the second week, there some of our men started to get a little worried and anxious about how things were going back home. And there were some serious concerns about whether there were looters who might steal what we had back home. So a few men did sneak out, but heaven only knows how they got back home. They would have had to do a lot of wading unless they could get a ride in a boat.

"At the end of that awful three weeks of sleeping on cots under a tent and battling the worst mosquitoes you could ever imagine, a train came to pick us up just like one had come to bring us to the camp. When we got home, water was pretty deep in the house. There was a lot of mud and silt as the water slowly dropped down. But, the animals we put up in the hayloft were all alive and looked to be in pretty good shape."

Mrs. Rounds also remembers an incident that had all the refugees laughing in her camp for weeks after they had returned to face the awesome, awful task of cleaning up after the flood.

"One of the young white soldiers took a real fancy to a young colored girl in the camp. He came to her tent early one morning and asked if he could come in. She told him 'no' in no uncertain terms. But the soldier boy wouldn't take 'no' for an answer and came into the colored girl's tent anyway. Well, honey, she picked up the night pot and flung the stuff that was in it right in his face and all over his nice uniform. When he came out of the tent all fixed-up we couldn't help but laugh and everybody had a good hard laugh. Everybody except the soldier boy!"

Annie West Rounds remembers that at least one plantation owner profited from the Great Flood of 1927. Thomas Lucas, who later had a frightening set-to with her brother-in-law, Thaddeus Rounds, saw the flood coming and decided that destitution could be the mother of prosperity. He sent wagons to fetch black refugees and bring them to his plantation to work as sharecroppers. The Lucas plantation was high and dry and unscathed by the massive flooding, so he sent mule-drawn wagons and even boats to flood-covered neighboring plantations. Rufus West Jr., took "Ole Mr. Lucas" up on his offer and quickly packed his wife and three children—including the then five-year-old Annie—into one of the Lucas wagons. Until they got to know Ole Man Lucas, they thought he was the Savior who had come to set them up in a new life on the Lucas plantation.

All was lost now for the several chapters of the Rounds Saga that involved the glories and disasters of *Honey Island, Mississippi*. West could take no more. He cast off the heavy yoke of trying to maintain what his tenacious father had started. And who can blame him?

West could have herded his destitute family and himself into one of the many relief camps the government set up for the white and black victims of The Great Flood of '27 and could have returned to try to make yet another go of it. But to this day, for many more than a hundred years, nobody with Rounds blood has ever accepted charity. We are too proud! West was certainly not going to set the precedent. So far as the family stories go, even before the 1927 deluge had subsided, West packed up and shut down the family farm. He moved north to join the relatives who had preceded him to Chicago.

West, no doubt, heard some of the horror stories of inhumane conditions in those relief camps. In fact, many of them were reportedly like concentration camps. Refugees were given meager rations, sometimes slept on the ground, and were not free to come and go as they pleased. The proud son of Ned Rounds wanted nothing to do with that scene.

The most horrible of the flood-spawned refugee camps in Mississippi didn't get any better until the NAACP sent Walter White to investigate and prod flood commissioner and presidential-hopeful Herbert Hoover to clean up the flood relief camps.

Ironically, while the water was just receding from Rounds' *Honey Island* property, the Ned Rounds descendants in St. Louis like Lillie B. Rounds Pfeiffer and her husband Wes were reeling from a devastating tornado which ripped through their Mill Creek neighborhood on September 29, 1927, damaging more than a thousand homes and causing $50 million damage. The Mississippi River flooding that year caused six times that amount in damage.

The Rounds family members who did not have the courage or the desire to get out of Mississippi became relegated to the miserable life of sharecroppers. It was a life that was entirely new to them. It was sadly denigrating when they remembered what comfortable lives they had lived on their own. *New York Times* correspondent Isabel Wilkerson writes of the mass exodus to Chicago:

"The new arrivals who stepped off the Illinois Central steam-engine trains at the 12th

Street Station, their cardboard luggage tied with string, were sharecroppers from Egypt, Miss., and Natchez and domestics and janitors from Jackson and Little Rock. (They) scanned the crowd for faces from back home, buzzing about the big money they would make at the steel mills and packing houses and rivet factories..."

Wilkerson also notes that:

"The migration, from World War I to the 1960s, redistributed six million Southern blacks who fled to nearly every major city in the North and West. They were fleeing the racial caste system that consigned them to the lowest rung and the racial violence that came with it. Factory jobs were plentiful and they were paid what seemed like unbelievable money to people accustomed to picking 100 pounds of cotton for a dollar."

Those Rounds family members who escaped just a bit north to Memphis or far north to Chicago, St. Louis, and Detroit were not only fleeing Mississippi's racial caste system of which Wilkerson writes, they were also desperately in the late 1920s trying to elude Nature's furies of water and wind.

"Chicago was built on the backs of black migrant workers. They worked the stockyards and the factories and the steel mills. Their hard work helped the country make it to the Technological Age."

—Harold Lucas, president
Black Metropolis Convention and Tourism Council of Chicago

In Chicago, West and Mary Rounds, after cutting their losses in Mississippi, led very different lifestyles. Mary kept very busy. She worked as a piecework seamstress at the old Sopkin's clothing factory. And what a sweatshop it was! Mary labored long hours at a big Singer sewing machine in less-than-comfortable conditions. She also created and sold handmade flower bunches. They were by all accounts quite beautiful and used as corsages, boutonnieres, and table centerpieces.

West Rounds, in contrast, did virtually nothing but sit around and read every newspaper he could get his hands on, day after day after day after day. When he wasn't reading, he simply stared blankly out into distant space. No doubt he was staring through Chicago roofs and walls, beyond Windy City concrete and smog, at a once-idyllic lifestyle. He, Westly Rounds, son of Ned, had once lived happily on the bucolic farmland his father had purchased for cash and promissory notes. To anyone who observed this sad-faced, pensive man he often appeared to be in a place somewhere between Depressionville and Melancholytown. He seemed to know that many folks he knew might judge him to be the person ultimately responsible for losing it all. He must have had trouble looking in the mirror when he trimmed the Kentucky-style moustache and goatee he wore to emulate his papa. Was it all his fault alone? Would his daddy have been upset with him for not hanging in there and finding a way to overcome all the obstacles of hardscrabble life? And surely, West must have looked over his shoulder occasionally, wondering whether some of the creditors and bill collectors he may have given the slip back home in Mississippi would ever catch up with him in Chicago.

But, it wasn't anything that West had done consciously that brought foreclosure to the family farm. Maybe he hadn't been the wheeler-dealer his pa was. Those who knew him have told me that he wasn't the most energetic or assertive guy they had ever met. He was very kind, but not at all aggressive; not at all assertive even. There were many other Mississippi Delta farmers before and after West who had thrown up their hands and then thrown in the towel. So very often that towel was soaking wet...from the all-too frequent flooding. The major deluges literally washed away so many *Honey Island* dreams, turning those dreams into indelibly ugly nightmares: nightmares of such intensities that no degree of transmigration to St. Louis or Chicago or Detroit or Wichita could erase them.

It is perhaps not such an odd fact that none of the *Oldtimers* volunteers information about the awful and relentless flooding they experienced. Maybe it was just too painful to talk about how the sometimes-domineering Mississippi River—just forty miles west of *Honey Island*—would act up and incite to riot the Yazoo River and all its tributaries, lakes, streams, creeks, brakes, bogs, and bayous. These servants of the Father of Waters would be forced to rise up year after year after year to show the farmers who had laboriously tried to tame the land just who the real boss was. The dams men built were damning. The levees they constructed were sheer folly when they tried to harness the great rivers in an attempt to determine the routes these waterways should obediently follow, in contrast to the way they wanted to go. It seemed to Ned and West and all their farmer/neighbors that the rivers were aided by a Higher Power who opened up the skies and fed the waters with too much rain to keep them happily inside their banks. When the rains came in torrents—in buckets for far too many days, crops and hopes were drowned under a watery denouement of destruction.

In all due respect to the power, notoriety, and romantic legends of the Mighty, Muddy Mississippi River, the Yazoo River's influence on the Delta area should never be ignored nor minimized. The Yazoo has been, for as long as it has been around, perhaps, a fickle, independent, irreverent, and radical river. Dams and levees and time itself have almost effectively lobotomized the Yazoo, but when Ned Rounds purchased property right on its banks, the Yazoo still had a mind of its own. In fact, from the time its parents, the Tallahatchie and Yalobusha rivers, give birth to it each day just north of Greenwood, Mississippi, and just south of Memphis, the Yazoo sets out determined not to play by anybody else's rules. She is a woman who does not like to look the same way every time we see her. While she is definitely the handmaiden of the Mississippi, it is still evident to those who live near her or with her that she has a distinct personality. Two hundred and seventy miles of levees stretched out from just south of Memphis to the Yazoo's mouth at Vicksburg now keep a check on the natural waywardness of the Mississippi and Yazoo, but these two independent bodies of water are never to be underestimated. And, aren't levees so much more temporal than rivers? Nevertheless, Ned and West would have wished for just a few more levees than were in place when their crops were so frequently jeopardized or destroyed.

Flooding of the type that only the Delta could know had taught the farmers to build their homes and churches and storehouses on stilts. Still the abundant waterways which ran around and through their Mississippi farmlands seemed, when they were in the mood, to find it necessary to deposit murky, smelly flood water and silt in living rooms, bedrooms, kitchens, and barns every few years. That's what happened so many times to Old Ned's property and the properties of all his kin and neighbors on *Honey Island*.

For example, devastating floods had come to the Mississippi Delta, *Honey Island*, and environs in late April of 1911. The Rounds Family and their neighbors were able to shake that one off since their land was covered with only about a foot of water. Then, early in April the very next year, *Honey Island* farmland was covered with nearly two feet of water. The Mississippi and Yazoo gave the farmers in the area of Belzoni two years of relief from inundation. But in 1920, on the seventh day of May, the Yazoo River was again two feet over flood stage, the highest water in twenty years. The following year, 1921, put a light cover of water—less than a foot on the Rounds' prized Lot #6 comprised of 107 acres, right on the Yazoo. There was some light flooding in low-lying sections of *Honey Island* in 1922 and 1923. The rivers may then have given West a false sense of security for the next three years. No flooding to speak of. Then there was a rare winter flood. Right after Christmas 1926, many *Honey Island* farms saw a foot of water in some low areas. That's when West began to think very seriously about getting the hell out of *Honey Island*. New Years' Day of 1927 brought the first hint of what was to come. It had been raining off and on—mostly on—since before Christmas. The Yazoo swelled more than three feet over its banks, spilling waist-high water onto the sixty acres West had managed to hold onto after a number of desperate land sell-offs to stay afloat.

There could be a frantic second planting of corn and cotton seed if the waters were gone by the end of May during a flood year, but a farmer who had tried to seed a crop in marshy ground—no matter how rich the rivers had made the earth—soon began to lose the will to fight a Malevolent Mother Nature or Omnipotent God, whichever came first in one's theology.

Larry Banks, the Chief Hydraulics Engineer for the Army Corps at Vicksburg, notes from his more than thirty years of studying the area on land and by plane that the *Honey Island* region was just about the highest land in the Delta, but it was never high enough to save it from the Mississippi and Yazoo rivers and all the bodies of water these two forces controlled. Just when the farmers in the Delta area got their heads above water and everything that was soaked dried-out, the relentless flood waters returned. Some of the *Oldtimers*, if prodded, can call up colorful stories of the overpowering floods. They particularly remember the Great Flood of 1927, the straw that broke the camel's back for Westly Rounds. That year—1927—was the year he decided he just couldn't take it anymore. That was the year when, with flood waters and the wolf lapping at his door, West made a monumental New Year's resolution. He would chuck it all and flee with his painful memories and his large family to Chicago.

The *Oldtimers* remember paddling around *Honey Island* in boats during the Big Flood. Almost every household had a boat that would seat four to six passengers. The boats were generally kept out back of every house and turned over to keep out rain when there was no flooding. They may also have been turned over to keep them from becoming storage depots that would have to be emptied when the real function of the boat was needed.

Some *Honey Island* flood victims could actually paddle from their backyards all the way to Belzoni to bring back supplies during the big flood seasons. Tchula Lake would take them a good part of the way. Those who knew the way could paddle out of the lake right across the road from Jones Chapel onto some water-covered roads they had traveled by wagon, horseback, or car during the dry months. Sometimes there would be as many as three oarsmen to provide the power and steering for those adventures. When a boat got tangled up in the bayou areas, a good man in hip boots could splash into the water to push, pull, and coax a hung-up vessel to freedom.

Interestingly enough, the *Honey Islanders* who survived the rigorous float trip to Belzoni were allowed to sleep overnight on the floor near the big furnaces in the basement of the Humphreys County courthouse before undertaking taking the arduous paddle back home. But as anybody familiar with the social, cultural, and political climate of the times might expect, the black overnighters were segregated from any white sojourners. And as one might also expect, the makeshift quarters for whites were closer to the big courthouse furnace than those areas designated for the "colored."

The *Oldtimers* recall, if the questions to them are focused, trying to salvage whatever they could from their flooded-out homes. They have painful recollections of sloshing around inside their homes with galoshes on. They have vivid memories of trying to stack furniture on top of furniture, knowing that their household furnishings on the bottom of the pileup would sometimes be damaged beyond reuse when the flood waters receded. They remember hanging corn and other staples from the rafters of home and barn and setting barrels of such treasures as flour on top of things in an attempt to keep the foodstuffs from contamination and rotting in the smelly, dark.

Willetta remembers that the 1927 flood—just before she fled her home for St. Louis—seemed to bring with it more snakes floating around outside the family home than she cared to encounter. The *Honey Island Oldtimers* didn't know all the proper herpetological names of the snakes that came out to swim and float in the high waters during major flooding. It was sufficient to put them all under the umbrella category of "water moccasins." Most of the islanders didn't really care to get close enough to a snake to give it a correct name. It was just not worth it to become chummy with a snake. Charles Hoessle, chief executive of the St. Louis Zoo, says all of the eight varieties of water moccasins, or cottonmouth snakes, that called the Mississippi Delta home were not poisonous. They found enough river rats, field mice, and unsuspecting birds, and even smaller snakes, to keep their slithering bellies full.

There were other snakes the *Oldtimers* remember seeing. There was the grey rat snake which could get up to seven feet long. Mostly during high water seasons, *Honey Islanders* would see speckled king snakes. They were black with yellow dots. They were more interested in eating other snakes than biting people. There were slithery mud snakes, black with red undersides. They were among the most prevalent and most harmless of the snakes in the Delta. What's more, there were tiny coral snakes that were non-venomous. Cane brake snakes loved to hang out around clearings in sugar cane and bamboo fields. Lest an islander with a basic knowledge of snakes around the area got too over-confident, there were, indeed, poisonous rattlesnakes on *Honey Island* during dry times and high water times. They always swam with their rattler tails sticking out of the water to keep them dry.

Perhaps the most theatrical snake that came onto the *Honey Island* stage was the puff adder. His act was always more entertaining than his bite was poisonous. When surprised, the puff adder —also called the hog-nosed snake—would inflate its hood and rear its viperous head just like a cobra and hiss and huff and spit and carry on like the meanest critter in the valley. Some of the *Oldtimers* remember that if one took a long stick and poked Mr. Puff Adder right in the middle of its dramatic thespian display of ferocity, the darned thing would quickly collapse and play dead. Applause was always due the performance. The *Oldtimers* didn't often stay around to do the stick thing, but the puff adder act has got to be the most amusing animal kingdom act one can shake a stick at. *Honey Island* residents, according to some of the *Oldtimers*, would leave the puff adder's act before intermission fearing that the liquid the viper sprayed during its self-protective charade was highly poisonous. Not so, says Hoessle who finds the Academy Award-winning puff adder performances enchanting.

— In fact, Hoessle is an inveterate advocate of more understanding and love for snakes. His thesis is that snakes, since the Garden of Eden, have inherited an undeserved bad rap. Hoessle believes the *Honey Island* residents, like other rural folk of their day, in the absence of television and video games and the like, would sit around and fabricate tall tales about their encounters with the critters of the woods. He chuckles about the stories the Islanders might have woven around a roaring fire in the fireplace about their chance meetings face-to-face with *Brother Puff Adder.*

It's a curious fact that the puff adder is a native of Africa. That means tales about its antics may have been passed down by word-of-mouth to the *Honey Island* residents through at least a couple of centuries. It would be even more of an irony if the puff adder had come to Mississippi aboard some of the slave ships.

More personally pesky than the snakes that came out of hiding during the flooding were the Delta's mosquitoes. *"Big as bats and twice as hungry,"* one *Oldtimer* remembers. I am ready to say "amen" to that observation after becoming the target of Mississippi's carnivorous mosquitoes in the Jones Chapel Cemetery. I felt the bites on my legs, in particular, for a month after they penetrated the *Cutter's* repellent in that graveyard.

During the 1927 flooding, the *Honey Island* mosquitoes, according to all accounts, became reckless and ferocious. To battle them, the islanders burned rags soaked in coal oil to create a smokescreen on their verandas. During the flooding, the buckets were tethered to float just outside homes. Young children, in particular, were rubbed down with coal oil to ward off the mosquitoes. Older folk also rubbed down in the smelly oil.

The biggest weapon on *Honey Island* was DDT, most often in those spray cans with the long tubular push-pump handles and big canisters up front. It produced thick clouds of pesticide during the high water periods. Some islanders even had the stuff sprayed on their bodies. It is only in recent years that DDT has been banned from use because of its toxic effects and its potentially carcinogenic properties. Nobody on *Honey Island* could have possibly known about the dangers of DDT at that time. Nobody in the world knew. Nobody on the island could have possibly have known even that DDT's full name is *dichlorodiphenyltrichloroethane.* Certainly nobody among the Rounds family nor in their community could have known back then that the health dangers of DDT were so severe that the Environmental Protection Agency would formally ban domestic use of the pesticide.

A May 20, 1992, report in the *Journal of the National Cancer Institute* found that exposure to DDT "can cause pancreatic cancer in humans under circumstances of heavy and prolonged exposure." Continued exposure to DDT has been linked to low-birth weight, breast cancer, and leukemia. What is even more disturbingly applicable to the use of DDT by *Honey Island* residents to control the thick mosquito population is a report released in an April 1976 issue in the *American Journal of Diseases of Children* reporting that human milk samples from low-income blacks residing in rural Mississippi *"are still highly contaminated with (DDT), even though the general use of DDT has been banned."*

Imagine how many *Honey Island* residents may have died from their attempts to protect themselves from mosquito bites. Imagine how many deaths attributed to "natural causes" may have been caused by continued exposure to the awful DDT. Imagine how many DDT-caused deaths were attributed to "unknown causes."

After the bites, camphorated oil, baking soda paste, calamine lotion, or more coal oil was applied to the skin to soothe the itch. The bodies of the Islanders sometimes looked as if a layer of extra-crunchy peanut butter had been spread on them, especially during flood season. There were many cases of yellow fever sickness and even deaths on *Honey Island* traceable to the dreaded mosquitoes.

During major flood seasons, while one watched out for snakes, it sometimes became a kind of sport for *Honey Islanders* to fish right from their front and back verandas. Big fat catfish and carp came swimming right past one's front door. It sometimes became a blessed convenience to be able to catch fish this way in order to get food on the dining room table.

The *Oldtimers* remember seeing their cows and mules and pigs and goats and horses trying to stay afloat during the flood years. It was absolutely necessary to salvage whatever dry bales of hay a farmer could salvage for the livestock, so boats were kept busy ferrying feed and fodder. Chickens often didn't make it when their feathers got too wet for too long. These fowl, just like fish, could be plucked from the water unless they found—as they often did—perches on rooftops of some of the lower level outbuildings. While they saw their livestock float away into the distance, residents would always find their neighbors' animal stock floating up to replace what they had lost. When the waters subsided, it was always a major undertaking to plod around in the mud to try to round up cattle that had survived and were now living at a neighbor's place. The highest ground on *Honey Island* was found at Matt Fields' place, Mark Clark's farm, and providentially, the land around Jones Chapel and the cemetery. Those three places were always good places to start looking for one's livestock when the post-flood roundup began.

What a mess. A horrible, recurring mess.

It sometimes seemed to the *Honey Island* farm families—especially during the devastating floods—that God was not at all on their side. They could not beat His system, His elements, and the money lenders that Jesus didn't particularly care for.

As he sat in the little apartment on East 40th Street in Chicago daydreaming and night-dreaming about the Rounds farm under floodwater and a sea of red ink, West seemed resigned to let the other members of the family go out each day to bring home the bacon. West, seventy-two years old at the time, often sat in a darkened room or on the porch out back of the apartment either reading or staring out into a space that was hundreds of miles away. It sometimes appeared that there were tears welled up in his old eyes. Was it just an ocular condition inherent with old age? Or were these tears he sometimes dabbed away with his crisply white handkerchief a never-ending stream that flowed like the Yazoo from his heart and soul to an outlet in his sad eyes?

Sometimes West would open up and interact with the family, especially the kids. He loved to play around the family's young people. He particularly loved to have anybody who was around —especially young children—comb and brush his silky white collar-length hair. As his hair was being groomed, he would often slip into a doze and slight snoring. He'd remain asleep until the groomer incorrectly figured that he or she could slip away with their aching arms and cramped hands. But if they made even the slightest move to escape the tonsorial task, Old West would quickly snort awake and insist that the combing and brushing continue until the compliant attendant felt that his/her arms were about to drop off.

While he stared or dozed or slept erratically, West was, no doubt, reminiscing about how the Rounds' land was systematically lost. In his daydreams or nightmares he could remember his father telling him in late December of 1888 something like this:

"Son, I'm gonna have to sell off a piece of our land to meet that note I signed. They gonna come after me if I don't have they money by the first of the year. Sheriff already been out here to give me a warnin' 'bout foreclosin' on me. If we don't pay up, we could lose everythin' I tried to build up here. And I don't have the cold cash to pay off the five-hunnerd dollar note that's comin' due on next New Year's Day."

Remember, Ned had actually signed in 1886 two promissory notes for five hundred dollars. One note came due on January first, 1887, a year after he had bought the two hundred and sixteen acres from Peter James Jr. Ned had somehow managed to come up with the cash to pay that one off. The second note was a bear that made way for the wolf to hang around outside the Rounds' door. Ned didn't have the money to satisfy the note that came due with its ten-percent per annum interest the following year.

Having somehow managing to hold on by his fingernails, the next major financial hurdle came after he had bought more land some years later. Two weeks after a note was due on January 19, 1899, Ned Rounds sold lots three and four to T. H. Craig and Company for five hundred dollars to cover the principal and interest. The deal was recorded in the Holmes County record books just two days later. Ned and his farm stayed afloat for four more years without any apparent financial perils. Then, at the end of 1912, the Rounds homestead needed a quick infusion of cash again. Perhaps it was to pay off another loan Ned took out. Perhaps to pay the taxes on the land. Perhaps to buy some new mules, farm equipment, or to buy seed. Most probably, it was all of the above. Although we are not sure of an exact death date for Ned, we think he died about 1907. He had certainly *passed* by 1908 when records indicate his land was in the hands of his children. We do know for sure that West made the next sell-off of Rounds land in 1913. Portions of lots five and six were sold to a Philip Liberto on January 3, 1913. For some reason that had to go even beyond the peculiarities of Mississippi record-keeping back in those days, the January third deal was not officially recorded until May sixteenth. Liberto bought the Rounds' land for $729.

Then something happened with the Rounds' finances that caused West to sell off still more farmland just a year later. The U. S. economy went into a tailspin in 1913, and the nation and West Rounds suffered through twenty long months of depression. This Philip Liberto was once again waiting to snap up another chunk of lots five and six. On April 13, 1914, he paid West $871.21 for still more pieces of lots five and six. Still chipping away at the Rounds property in an amount that seemed to suggest property taxes or a loan note, on January 2, 1915, West got nine hundred dollars from the ubiquitous Mr. Liberto for twenty-six acres in lots two and three, and twenty-five acres in lots five and six. Curiously enough, this first-of-the-year transaction was not recorded at the Holmes County Courthouse until May tenth.

As West stared out into Chicago space while seldom blinking, he must have thought often about what a monumental and downright awful year 1917 was. World War I was still raging in Europe and some of the *Honey Island* boys had gone off to do the dirty work of digging trenches and latrines in the European soil as black soldiers were expected to do. They were drafted that year because the Selective Service Act required that all able-bodied men ages twenty-one to thirty-one sign up for military duty, even though many recruitment stations still refused to register black volunteers. On June 5, the first official day of registration, 700,000 African Americans showed up to be counted, and maybe drafted.

For some reason West decided to cash in almost all of his chips during the War to End All Wars. On Christmas Eve of 1917, West sold off the biggest package of Rounds land to that date. He off-loaded the remaining portions of lots two, three, five and six to one Anna Sorrels for the incredibly fat sum of $5,516. In uncharacteristic Mississippi speed, the deal was notarized and recorded on the day after Christmas, 1917. A Holmes County land deal was made and recorded in just one day! West kept only sixty acres of what had once been four hundred and twenty-six acres of fine Rounds' land for him and for his family.

In the deal that might have been "the straw that broke the camel's back," West and his brother-in-law, Tom Simmons, had, two days earlier, taken out a mortgage of $5500 from Liberto. The amount was to be repaid in four installments, each due on the first of January over the next four years. When they didn't make the

1921 payment, they faced foreclosure.

The year 1917 was an interesting year for a black Mississippian to walk away from a land transaction with more than five thousand dollars. West could not have owed that much in taxes and back taxes. He certainly could not have owed that much in interest and principal on loans. Five thousand dollars would have represented a lifetime of paychecks for the average American and much more than that for a black southern farmer in 1917 America. Where did all that money go?

There were thirty-eight Blacks reported lynched around the nation in the year that West disposed of the bulk of the Rounds property. As many as one hundred Blacks were killed in an East St. Louis, Illinois, race riot, and ten thousand demonstrators staged a silent march through the streets of New York to protest the deaths. The all-black Fifteenth New York Infantry was refused restaurant and lodging services in Spartansburg, South Carolina, and beaten by a mob. To keep the African American soldiers from retaliating, the entire regiment was shipped off to the European Theater. Southerners in Mississippi and throughout the South vigorously protested the U. S. military bringing black soldiers to train at southern bases. Although a brief attempt by the military high command was made to satisfy the wishes of the southern protestors, the idea of trying to keep and train all-black troops on northern soil proved to be ridiculous and the idea was abandoned. Since his son, Ambrose, was known to send West Chicago newspapers to read, West must surely have known that in the city to which he planned to move, the house of a black man, S. P. Motley, was firebombed after he dared to move into a white neighborhood. Damage to the house was estimated at ten thousand dollars. That incident alone must have given West and Mary second thoughts about moving up north to Chicago. But they moved to the city by Lake Michigan anyway.

What happened to the more than five thousand dollars Westly Rounds made from the sale of almost all of the Rounds' farmland? *Oldtimers* remember vividly that West's father had set a tradition of not trusting banks. Ned preferred to hide money on his property and legend has it that he also liked to bury money. That's why Ned's *Honey Island* farm always gave the appearance that a family of giant moles had had a field day. Strangers came from miles around in the dead of the night to try to find any treasure troves Ned might have buried on his property.

West certainly wouldn't have buried all that loot on water-logged *Honey Island*. He would not have left that amount anywhere in Mississippi knowing that he would never return home. Or did West move to Chicago with the hope of quietly returning some day to claim a big chunk of loot? There is a much greater likelihood that he would have stuffed the money in a shoebox, a mattress, or in a hatbox in his apartment in Chicago. Even if West had owed two thousand dollars in property taxes and interests on loans, what could have possibly happened to the still-handsome sum of three thousand-plus dollars?

Might he have buried any profit from the land sale in the backyard of his apartment on East Fortieth Street? Did his son, Ambrose, who seemed to have the most interest in his father and stepmother's well-being, ever look for the money in their apartment after West's death? Did West turn the thousands of dollars over to Ambrose for safe-keeping? Did West buck family tradition by opening up a secret account at a Chicago bank? We do not know. And we may never know. West took that mystery with him when he died. Ambrose never acknowledged knowing about any money from the sale of Ned's land.

West died—or as it is still stated in Black traditions—he *passed* on May 5, 1928, at the age of seventy-four. His death certificate says he died of "organic heart disease." Did he die of a broken heart? From his sickbed he called out in a raspy voice as best he could to his wife of fifty years:

"Momma… can… can you come in here?"

Mary sprang from her sewing machine in the next room and ran to her dying husband's bed.

She knelt beside him so she could hear what he was able to whisper into her ear. She had heard this death rattle before in the chests and throats of the many family members she had attended who were at death's door.

"Yes, Poppa. I'm here, Darlin'…"

"Mama… I… I don't have… long now…"

"No, Poppa. I don't want you to leave me," Mary whispered as she squeezed West's cold hand tightly. *"Please don't leave me…"*

"I'm goin' now, Momma… But… but… you gotta… promise me somethin'…"

"Yes, Poppa… anything… anything…"

"Promise… promise…promise me." He coughed a little wet cough.

"Promise… me… you…you won't cry…won't cry… when… I… go home…"

"I'll try, Poppa… I'll try…"

And then… Westly Rounds smiled a smile so slight that only a wife of so many years could discern that it was not a grimace. She thought she felt an ever-so-small tightening of his hand on hers. Ned's son and successor closed his rheum-filled eyes… and left this world. Mary kept her deathbed vow to her husband. And in the coming days and months of mourning… nobody remembers seeing the broken-hearted Mary Hughes Lewis Rounds shed even one tear.

Westly and Mary had not lived in Chicago for an entire year at the time of his passing. Just before he died he seemed even more fatigued and withdrawn than ever. Even a bit disoriented, some thought. The internalized *Honey Island* memories were killing him, without a doubt. Funeral services were held two days later at the Ebenezer Baptist Church with Rev. Clark officiating. Old West was buried at Lincoln Cemetery in Chicago. Allowing only two days from death to burial was unusual. In that era and up until recent times, Blacks have been held for burial for as long as a week to allow relatives from far away to get to the funeral. The fact that West was buried so relatively quickly attests to the fact that there were almost no relatives and friends to come from any farther than St. Louis or Detroit in the traditional modes of transportation for African Americans of the day— automobiles, Greyhound buses, and trains.

Nobody in our family ever mentioned any money West may have spirited out of Mississippi. His widow, Mary, worked as hard after his death as she had ever worked during his life. She kept working her long shifts at the sewing sweatshop and selling her artificial flower bouquets. According to all accounts, she never mentioned being willed any bequest, nor did Mary ever mention finding any large sum of money hidden in the apartment after her husband's death. Five thousand, five hundred and sixteen dollars—the money reaped from the final recorded sell-off—was exactly my annual salary as a St. Louis public school teacher in 1965.

What a mystery! What Westly Rounds did with all that money remains to this day a baffling unsolved curiosity that will keep the Ned Rounds descendants speculating for as long as there are any of us left on this earth.

Mary Hughes Lewis Rounds lived almost thirty years longer than her husband. She remained active with her sewing till her eyes began to fail her just a few years before her death on May 15, 1959, at age eighty-eight. She died peacefully of old age with no unusual infirmities for her age. The Kersey, McGowan and Morrsell Mortuary at Thirty-fifth and Indiana handled the arrangements. Indiana Avenue in Chicago is now Dr. Martin Luther King Drive.

****

In the mid to late 1950s, after many of the Rounds descendants who had made Chicago their home were gone, I remember several summers riding up to Chicago with Aunt Gert and Uncle Walter. Aunt Gertrude didn't drive then, and never learned to drive. Neither did her mother, Hattie Coats. Neither did her sister, Willetta. My mother was the only one of the four who learned to drive—sort of. I must admit that I was always terrified when I had to drive with my mother. Still am today!

Uncle Walter had a big grey Packard. If I had to guess its year, I'd guess 1951 or 1952. It was a nice old car, but I remember that on every trip to Chicago, the darn thing would develop what was called "vapor lock." That would mean that we'd have to sit off on the shoulder of the highway, Uncle Walter would put up the hood, and we would just watch other cars sail by while the old Packard healed of its vapor lock. Seems like we had to pause two or three times on the road to Chicago about twenty minutes to a half-hour each time for the malady to pass. I heard a mechanic explain one time to Uncle Walter that these vapor locks were the result of the fuel to the gas line being blocked by bubbles in the gasoline. That caused, according to the mechanic, the engine to overheat. Those bubbles cost us hours of wasted time going to and from Chicago. I often wondered as a boy if everybody's car got vapor lock. If so, everybody must have gotten it just about the same time behind us and in front of us. And their cars must have gotten over their vapor locks, I thought, at just about the same time our car did because I saw so few people pulled over and waiting for this auto illness to pass. Maybe just grey Packards got vapor lock, I surmised as a youthful philosopher.

When we got to Chicago each time, we always stayed with Uncle A and Aunt Sallie. I remember Uncle A had really bushy eyebrows and I recollect he spoke in clipped and articulate language like the old newsreel sound bites I've heard of Presidents Roosevelt and Truman. In my earliest visits—when I was eight or nine—I was amazed to find out that my kinfolk in Chicago ate the same kind of food we ate in St. Louis. The dishes tasted exactly alike. The seasoning was astonishingly the same. But the sameness of the food! The fried chicken. The supper rolls. The collard and mustard greens. The mashed potatoes. The pound cake. Even the lemonade. Must mean there were family recipes created in the Delta that were now being served in St. Louis and Chicago. Since some of the relatives eventually moved farther north, I can imagine they were eating *Honey Island* style food in the Motor City, too!

Uncle A's and Aunt Sallie's home was meticulously clean. Both of them were always neatly dressed. Uncle A, like all the accounts of his father, West, and his great-grandfather, Ned Rounds, just loved to dress up in a starched-collar white shirt and a tie.

I really thought Uncle A was the kind of guy I wanted to grow up to be like. I remember that one time when I got to run errands with Uncle A, I saw a different side of him. He had a rather spiffy new car. I imagined that it never got vapor lock. I figured it didn't because my great Uncle Ambrose never seemed to drive it too far from his house. He always took the train when he came to visit us in St. Louis or when he went back to Mississippi. He didn't even drive the new car to work. It was kind of a prize and got treated very well. Uncle A gave me a nickel to put in the parking meter and I accidentally dropped it in some tall grass. I thought my great-uncle, with his appearance of prosperity, would say that the loss of the nickel was all right, that I shouldn't fret. I thought he would simply hand me another nickel, which would have been peanuts to him. I was wrong.

He had me picking through that tall grass like I was looking for a Kruggerand. I finally found the lousy nickel and we were able to move on. As my grandmother's brother, I suppose I shouldn't have been too surprised with Uncle A's penuriousness. After all, my dear grandmother, the granddaughter of the man who made banking on *Honey Island* a profession, always told me "Make a dime, save a nickel." I valued her advice then, and I thank her for that sound financial advice now. But I wish I hadn't had to save the nickel I dropped in the tall grass at that Chicago parking meter.

The nickel and parking meter incident was typical Rounds philosophy. And it represented the penny-pinching that sustained the Rounds men and women as they adapted to their new financial struggles and challenges in the North, following a period in our Mississippi history of relative prosperity.

 **Fleeing Honey Island**

Just after her grandfather West had given up hope of holding onto the last miserable, flood-ravaged vestiges of what had once appeared to be Rounds prosperity, my aunt Willetta Williams became the youngest of Ned Rounds' great-grandchildren to move away from *Honey Island* alone and settle in St. Louis. She wasn't the first to do so, though. West's daughter Lillie B. and her husband, Wes Pfeiffer, had preceded Willetta to St. Louis. Pfeiffer was not ever a *Honey Island* resident. He and Lillie had met in his hometown of Yazoo City.

My Aunt Willetta was her father's pride and joy when she was a little girl. Anderson Williams, although an oft-married man with a roving eye, seemed to have made his middle daughter the apple of his eye. When Williams and my grandmother Hattie were divorced, a light went out of the young Willetta's life. Then when her mother married John Coats on December 1, 1923, the ten-year-old girl began to dread her stepfather's lecherous eyes and his frequent attempts to touch her.

Something awful, terrifying, and unspeakable happened in 1927 in the Coats household. Whatever it was—and quite frankly, I've found it indelicate to ask my near-ninety-year-old aunt exactly what happened—it forced the young teen to take flight on short notice to her mother and two sisters. It was decided she would take a train to St. Louis and stay with her Aunt Lillie B. and Uncle Wes.

It was a tearful farewell between Willetta, her mother Hattie, and her two dear sisters. The women were a tight-knit family that never got real close to the Coatses. Dan and Dillie Coats were the only children of "Old Man Coats" still living at home. Dillie was a tall, plump girl of nineteen in the year that Willetta fled the advances of Dillie's father. She had kinky red hair and freckles. Dillie's brother Dan was two years younger than his sister, tall and thin with black curly hair and freckles, though he didn't have nearly as many freckles as his sister. Dillie later married the nephew of Anderson Williams—the father of Willetta and her sisters. Dillie and her husband, Willie Williams, had ten children—a full house for Dillie and Willie!

The three young Williams girls and their mother, my grandmother Hattie, had come to live on the Coats place in a little town called Warner Ridge, right outside *Honey Island*. Like so many other little sleepy Mississippi towns remembered by the *Oldtimers*, Warner Ridge is no longer on any maps.

The three sisters remembered that the Coats farm was not as nice as the one they had left before their mother remarried. It was a four-room, one-story place that wasn't particularly well-kept. The four girls and Dan shared one room, two girls to a bed and Dan in his own little bed. Willetta would miss her sisters, but not her step-siblings, when she was in St. Louis.

A traumatized Willetta, accompanied by her step-grandmother Mary Lewis Rounds and Cousin Bessie, got a ride to Belzoni in a neighbor's Model-T Ford. After the hour-long ride into town and to the railroad station, Mary purchased a ticket for herself and Bessie. Willetta—ever the independent family member—had her own money and bought her own ticket to freedom from sexual harassment.

Willetta could not have known how lucky she and the other *Honey Island* residents were that they didn't arrive in St. Louis earlier. The young girl and her *Honey Island* kith and kin had survived the devastating Great Flood of 1927. While the Islanders were waste-deep in flood water, a vicious tornado ripped through Willetta's new home-to-be. The 1927 twister smashed up the lives of hundreds of residents who were left homeless and without life's simplest amenities. Many of those who lost their homes and belongings in the devastating tornado of '27 were temporarily sheltered and given clothing and food at the Poro College, the business and cosmetology training school for African Americans. In what would be an interesting coincidence, Willetta would later attend classes at the "college." In fact, in still more coincidence—or as one might call it part of the Divine Plan—a lab that manufactured the beauty products for African Americans Mrs. Malone had created was located at 3100 Pine Street until 1918. That was just three blocks east of what would become Willetta's first St. Louis home. She would pass the abandoned building with the Poro name on it every day for years, until she enrolled in the beauty training program.

The question might be raised here of why Willetta, at age fourteen, didn't try to enroll in one of the city's public schools for "Negroes." For one thing, Willetta had come to really hate school after the experience of trying to learn anything amidst the cacophonous, even sometimes rowdy, sessions in the multigrade, one-room classroom at Jones Chapel. She had learned to strongly dislike the schoolmarm, *"Mizz Coats"*, for her harsh style. This feeling was cemented long before *"Mizz Coats" passed* and her lecherous widower husband came into Willetta's life and changed it dramatically and forever.

Willetta had also entered a city environment in which education for black students and white students was expected to go only to the end of the elementary school experience. Had the fourteen-year-old, fresh from Mississippi, chosen to go to school instead of a job, she would have, no doubt, enrolled in the Banneker School. It was within a short walking distance of her aunt and uncle's house on Pine. When Willetta first arrived in St. Louis, Banneker was located in a school house at Montgomery and Leffingwell. In an era in which schoolhouses for Blacks finally carried a name rather than a number, the school had just shed its name of *Colored School #5* and was named after Benjamin Banneker (1731-1804), an African American genius whose greatest claim to fame was his succession to the post of chief architect of Washington, D.C., after Pierre L'Enfant left the job in a huff and dispute over wages. Banneker was also an authority on mathematics, botany, and astronomy, and he was a regular pen pal of Thomas Jefferson on all these subjects. The Banneker School moved into a building at Lucas and Ewing avenues in 1932, just four years after Willetta moved to St. Louis. This school, too, was within a short walking distance of the Lillie B. and Wes Pfeiffer's residence on Pine Street. But Willetta would have nothing to do with school. She felt compelled to work, not only because she hated the thought of sitting in a classroom, but also because she thought she was old enough to pull her own weight and pay her aunt and uncle some rent for the privilege of living with them. What's more, her great-grandfather Ned and grandfather Westly had inspired a strong work ethic in their branch of the Rounds family, even though neither of these good men was a practitioner of manual labor.

The three Mississippians were given a warm welcome at the home of Lillie and Wes Pfeiffer. The three-story brick home the couple rented was at 3415 Pine Street at Channing, just a couple of blocks east of Grand Avenue. The area was called Mill Creek Valley, the community established in the 1760s after Joseph and Roger Taillon dammed up a little stream that ran through the area and formed Chouteau's Pond. Mill Creek's boundaries were Eighteenth Street on the east, Grand Avenue on the west, Olive Street on the north, and some railroad tracks on the south.

The Pfeiffers lived on the first floor of this house they rented. They sub-rented the second and third floors. Willetta remembers that the folks who lived on the upper two floors were quiet, often out of work, and more often unable to pay their rent. Next door to them on the east side was the Acetylene Gas Company at 3411 Pine. Odd commerce on a mostly residential block, and possibly hazardous commerce for a mostly residential block. You have to wonder a little if the potentially explosive tanks probably would have been allowed by the City's zoning laws to be stored so close to residences in any other neighborhood but a black community.

The five hundred acres which constituted Mill Creek Valley were beginning to show signs of deterioration and neglect. City Hall already had its sails set for leveling *Mill Creek* when Willetta moved to St. Louis. Just three decades after her arrival, demolition crews began to tear down everything in the already historic neighborhood. Homes, shops, churches, schools, saloons, groceries—all had to go, declared those in high places who championed urban renewal. The idea was to create a new little city inside the city for an idyllic mix of industrial and residential developments. The neighborhood is now a part of the St. Louis University campus, an athletic field, to be exact.

The *M.C.V.I.E.P.*—*Mill Creek Valley Instant Eradication Program*, as I will editorialize and dare to call it, turned out to be one of the biggest debacles in the history of a city. It often made major planning errors and would continue to make them for another forty years. There was no thinking ahead to what would happen to the thousands of displaced residents. Oh, there was the naive plan that low cost housing to the south and to the north of the Mill Creek Valley developed under the administration of Mayor Joseph Darst (1949-1953) would be available for the predominantly *"Negro"* population of the valley. The $62 million project, underwritten by grants and loans, was launched to provide two housing projects of one hundred units each and 150 acres for industrial businesses. Some black political leaders of the day cried foul. They suspected that this was a gentrification plan to provide houses and industry for Whites only.

Washington University's dean of the school of architecture, Joseph Passoneu, projected that the new neighborhood would provide *"a five-minute walk from schools, a ten-minutes' walk to work, a five-minutes' ride from the river, and a twenty-minutes' drive from open country."* The dream never happened and the nightmare was underway. The thousands of Blacks making the same income as Willetta and the Pfeiffers and their tenants didn't all fit in or choose to live in Mayor Darst's low income housing projects. Instead, when the wrecking balls began smashing their homes, they flooded the City's West End neighborhood—from Kingshighway to Goodfellow and Delmar to St. Louis Avenue, eventually creating an even bigger slum area than before. By 1965, these once-glamorous neighborhoods west of Mill Creek Valley began to look like bombed-out Berlin. Those who were still reeling from the ravages of the Great Depression, massive unemployment, and little or no experience in property care and management, set up new homes and Professor Passoneau's projections proved to be just that— projections, far from the reality of what actually happened. Consequently and sadly, when I drove my near-ninety-year-old Aunt Willetta to the old neighborhood in the early spring of 1999 to find her old stomping grounds, there was absolutely nothing left to evoke memories.

By 1980, before the intervention of St. Louis University and Harris-Stowe State College in the '90s, the Mill Creek Valley had not achieved the dream of city officials and architectural projectionists. The number of housing units was never reached and the industrial development has not come into the anticipated level. When those trucks pulled up to the building next door to the Pfeiffers and their new tenant and loaded the tanks destined to allow welding torches all over town to cut through metal, they were in essence, a harbinger of things to come.

When the wide-eyed, country teenager from *Honey Island*, Mississippi, first set foot in St. Louis, Willetta's Aunt Lillie B. was a hard-working, good-looking woman at the still young age of thirty-six. Her husband, a fair-skinned, lanky man always impeccably dressed, had a work ethic did not come close to that of his wife's. To put it plainly, Wes just couldn't keep a job. Under any circumstances. While Lillie B. held down steady work as both a domestic and a tobacco stripper at the Liggett & Myers tobacco plant on Vandeventer in South St. Louis, Wes went from job to job to job to job. Problem was he was a heavy drinker who could not resist the domination of demon rum...or gin...or beer. In fact, on paydays, Wes was known to leave work and not return home for two or three days at a time. When he would finally return home each time—desperately needing a bath, a shave, and a drying out, he would have only pennies, nickels, and dimes from his paycheck in his pocket.

Wes was, otherwise, a nice guy, his niece-by-marriage remembers. He was a gentle man, never violent. He was kind, but never dependable. Willetta often said she had never seen a woman love a man like Lillie B. loved Wes. And Willetta loved him, too, despite his glaring faults. Among his redeeming qualities, Wes was always neat as a pin. He was sometimes described as "sporty." His shoes were always polished to a high gloss. No matter how threadbare his trousers were, they always had a crease on them that one *Oldtimer* described as "sharp enough to cut you if you got too close!" The well-pressed trousers were a remnant practice from Wes' days as a steam presser at a Yazoo City cleaners. Wes was said to have pressed his own trousers two or three times a day. The presser job had left an indelible mark on Wes' face. The constant exposure to steam had opened up the pores on Wes' otherwise handsome countenance to deep proportions.

While Willetta settled into life on Pine Street, her step-grandmother Mary Lewis Rounds and Cousin Bessie stayed for a few weeks to visit with Mary's two sons by her first marriage before returning to *Honey Island* to be with Westly. He was not well, and Mary – even though she was glad to see her sons – was a bit anxious about leaving her husband of four decades. Her son John Lewis, his wife Liza, and their daughter Beatrice, lived near the Pfeiffers on Warne. They lived comfortably since John was in a profession that so many of the Rounds-Lewis men entered, the U. S. Postal Service. Willie Lewis, who sometimes used the name Willie Rounds, also lived nearby on Ewing. He "ran on the road" as a railroad short order cook.

The merger of the Rounds and Lewis families was a tight bond. There were strong ties between the *Honey Island*, St. Louis, and Chicago members. In the late '20s and into the '30s, Ben, Perry, and Elmer Rounds—the offspring of Westly and Mary Lewis Rounds—would hop in Ben's new car in Chicago on a Friday evening and motor down to St. Louis to visit their kin. The affable Ben always had a new car and he preferred Oldsmobiles and Buicks. In addition to his big moon-face smile, Ben was also kidded constantly about his big feet—and he was notorious for his heavy foot on the gas pedal when he hit the open highway. Ben, Perry, and Elmer would scurry from their jobs at the packing house when the whistle blew at three on Friday afternoon, bathe, change clothes, and hightail it to St. Louis. Sometimes, Elmer's wife Lovie would come with them. They'd all arrive at Lillie B. and Wes' house around ten or eleven that night ready for fun and frolic.

The big attraction of these weekend conclaves, in addition to the family camaraderie, was the popular card game "bid whist." Whist is an early form of bridge played with fifty-two cards and four players playing two against two. Some of the Rounds clan called the game "bid whisk." Whatever they called it, it was a wild weekend at the Pfeiffers with the teenage Willetta utterly fascinated by all the noise and raucous laughter at the card party. Sometimes the adults would let Willetta play. But she wasn't very good and was mostly used in a pinch.

Lillie B. and Wes would borrow a folding card table or two from neighbors, or a foursome could play at the kitchen table or even sitting on the floor in the parlor around a coffee table. Music from the Victrola was turned up really loud…rhythm and blues, bee-bop, jazz, and big band sounds blasting through the night. The food was brought out around midnight. Spaghetti, potato salad, fried chicken, fried catfish and buffalo fish, coleslaw, mustard greens, and cornbread. In the winter, pig parts were the main fare: chitlins, pig ears, pig feet, knuckles, snoots, ham hocks, and ham. And never mind Prohibition. There was plenty of bootleg booze to go around until the silly Volstead Act was repealed.

The bid whist house rule was "rise and fly" with the losers playing the losers and the winners pitted against the winners until dawn. Then all the players would collapse and find bedding wherever they could, at the Pfeiffers or at the homes of John or Willie, sitting in a chair, on the sofa, on the floor. Sometime around noon or one o' clock the next day, there was a resurrection of the card players. Over coffee and a light breakfast the sport became what Willetta remembers as a time for "tall tales and outright lies," with the men mostly engaged in rib-busting jokes and stories too ridiculous to be even remotely true. But absolutely howlingly hilarious. And then the religiously-played card games started up again and were played all day and all night long. The Chicago bunch gave hugs and kisses all around near noon on Sunday, packed up, and headed back to the Windy City winded from so much laughter over the weekend of family fun.

It was fortuitous that Willetta was able to see such a close-knot family and have that fun. Those memories would have to support her in the times of trials and tribulations she would face in the coming days.

Although the Pfeiffers did not specify any certain amount for Willetta to pay for room and board, she felt obliged to subsidize the household where the wife made minimum wage and the husband's paycheck could never be counted on to make ends meet. The alternative to work—school—was never a real option. Willetta's first job in St. Louis, beginning shortly after her fifteenth birthday, was repulsive to her, and consequently, short-lived.

Aunt Lillie B. had gotten her young niece a job alongside her at the Liggett & Myers tobacco processing plant at 4241 Folsom at Vandeventer in South St. Louis. The company had been incorporated way back in 1878, just a few years before Willetta's mother, Hattie, was born on *Honey Island*. Liggett and Myers soon became the largest manufacturer of plug tobacco in the world. By 1890, just thirty-seven years before Willetta came to St. Louis, St. Louis was also producing the lion's share of the world's chewing tobacco. The tobacco factory sounded a steam whistle to signal the start and finish of work shifts. I even remember that factory whistle when I was a young boy living on Vandeventer and on Windsor Place. That whistle was for Willetta and all the neighborhood residents who had ever heard a throaty bass sound from steamboats trawling the Mississippi and Yazoo rivers a sound from back home. The firm at which Willetta worked got its name from St. Louisan John E. Liggett, whose family had been in the tobacco trade since the 1820s. Liggett's partner was George H. Myers.

Before the Civil War, Missouri had been one of the biggest tobacco-producing states, but after the slaves were freed in 1863, Missouri farmers turned to the less labor-intensive business of wheat crops. The Emancipation Proclamation reduced Missouri's tobacco farming to a third of its ante-bellum output. Those statistics didn't mean a thing to a fifteen-year-old who had seen tobacco crops thrive all around the prosperous farms of her grandfather and great-grandfather on *Honey Island*. The Liggett & Myers plant was just a job to help pay room and board and be beside her aunt in a strange new city.

Willetta Williams smiled warmly, if not convincingly, as she was introduced by her Aunt Lillie to her co-workers. They were generally an unimpressive bunch of laborers who all seemed to be red-eyed and "high" on something or another, Willetta remembers. She also noticed that the workers' hands appeared to be puffy, swollen, and blackened. Even though the color was different, their hands were like those of a drowning victim she had seen pulled out of Tchula Lake. The new hire soon found out that the workers—both men and women—would, during this Prohibition era, take home with them the sweet and pungent swill of secret ingredients in which the huge tobacco leaves were "cured." The stuff made an intoxicating liquor. Elliott Ness in Chicago and the revenuers in Mississippi would have had a field day busting the Liggett & Myers workers who dared break the law.

The foremen at the L & M plant, though, turned a blind eye to the taking of the sludge from the plant's vats. Workers who got hooked on the alcohol and nicotine-laden drink they cooked up at home were likely to continue to show up for work again and again just for the opportunity to keep themselves and their friends in illegal tobacco booze. Some of the tobacco leaves cured at the L & M plant on South Vandeventer contained more than four percent of addictive nicotine. Some of the L & M workers were even known to sell the near-poisonous stuff at twenty-five cents a bottle to supplement their meager incomes when the government ludicrously tried to keep its citizens from drinking alcohol.

Aunt Lillie instructed Willetta on what the job entailed. With no gloves, the tobacco workers at the L & M plant were charged with removing a stack of wet, thick tobacco leaves from the vat and stripping the midribs—the central veins—from the leaf. The smell and the consistency of the sluice made the teenager just up from Mississippi violently ill almost immediately. After about two hours on the new job, Willetta could take no more. Choking and stifling the urge to throw up as best she could, she bounded through the door and out onto Vandeventer where she gasped for air. She tried her best to vomit the offensiveness of those darkened brown leaves. As the leaves were pulled out of the huge vats, they looked to her like so many rotting pieces of garbage in the kind of juices she had seen plug tobacco chewers and snuff dippers spit into the dirt and into spittoons on *Honey Island*. On occasion she had as a chore emptying her Grandpa Westly's spittoon and washing it out. The stuff at the L & M plant was the same stuff she poured out back in Mississippi when she was assigned that awful chore.

She would never in her wildest dreams and nightmares think of putting her hands into a spittoon to swish them around in the spit of a chewer. Nor could she imagine making a life-long profession of pulling those leaves from what appeared to her to be so much hot spit. Willetta had seen tobacco leaves lilting on their stalks in the sweltering breezes of the farm fields in the homeland, but she never thought she'd see the broad, thick leaves in this stage of their development before they were turned into the packaged product. After just those couple of hours, her hands were swollen and disgustingly browned. She thought she'd would never get that color and the smell from under her fingernails.

She began to walk north on Vandeventer holding her stomach; having dry heaves. She needed to get back home, to Pine Street, if not back to *Honey Island*. She hadn't bothered to tell the foreman nor Aunt Lillie that she wouldn't be able to take the job. She just needed to get as far away from that plant as possible. She wished she could have taken the bus home in this sudden sickness, but she didn't have a penny to her name that day. After a walk of two hours or so, she arrived back at home on Pine Street. Willetta was brave enough and sick enough to ask strangers for directions. Once back at home, the teenager began to try to scrub off the stains and stench of the job her system had tolerated for such short time. She later got letters from the plant manager asking her to return, at least get her pay for the work she had done. She felt that if she returned the foreman would try to entice her to come back to a job she truly hated. The workers were on a piecemeal salary scale and got paid for the amount of tobacco they had stripped from the stem, just like the cotton pickers in Mississippi and every other place in the South were paid. Willetta realized that she would have to be a lot faster and productive if she would ever make a decent salary at L & M anyway. She never went back for the pittance she had earned. She knew, to the embarrassment of her aunt, that she would never see the inside of that tobacco plant again. But she later would tell relatives and friends, *"Since I didn't die throwing up in that awful place, I figured I was ahead in life."*

Within a month, Willetta Williams had a new job. She got work taking care of an infant for a couple named Mitchell. Her employment was what tens of thousands of domestic helpers up from the South called—and still call—"staying on the place." The couple for whom the young girl from *Honey Island,* Mississippi, worked were of moderate income and lived in one of the units of a four-family apartment building in the 5200 block of Palm Street in North St. Louis. It was just east of Union Avenue. That specific location would be important later on in Willetta's story.

Her duties as a live-in involved taking care of the Mitchell's eight-month-old son. She to this day does not remember the young couple's first names because a domestic never even thought of addressing their bosses in such an employment arrangement by their first names. Conversely, some employers of domestics never really knew the surnames of their maids and butlers and gardeners and cooks, especially their black servants. A Christian name was sufficient for summoning them. In America, Blacks didn't need to know first names; Whites didn't need to know surnames.

The Mitchell's two bedroom apartment was relatively small, so Willetta had to sleep on a Murphy bed in the couple's dining room, right next to Baby Mitchell's bedroom. (It is hard to imagine, as Willetta told me her story that "Baby" Mitchell, if he is still alive, is seventy-one years old!) When the young nanny's bed was made up and pushed back into the wall, a sliding pocket door would be slid across the opening and nobody would be aware that there was a bed there. It looked just like any other door in the apartment.

Mrs. Mitchell would always take off right after her husband left for work.

She would go shopping, play bridge with friends, take in a matinee movie, and otherwise stay far away from the responsibilities of raising a child and keeping a home.

If Mrs. Mitchell happened to be at home at lunchtime, she would sometimes sit with the baby boy and Willetta at the kitchen table for a simple meal of a sandwich and cup of coffee. What a scanty excuse of a lunch, Willetta thought when she slipped into memories of the spreads in *Honey Island*. Mrs. Mitchell never touched food except to eat it. She had absolutely no cooking skills. Lunch could be a time for girl talk and some attention by the mother to her child. The teenager from Mississippi was never invited, however, to have a meal with the two Mitchell adults at suppertime. Although Willetta would prepare the supper meal, the Mitchell family would eat at the dining room table while their domestic help ate alone or with the baby in the kitchen. Willetta was a natural as a cook for the Mitchells. She had watched intently the cooking skills of her master-cook mother, Hattie, and the slightly lesser skills of her step-grandmother, Mary. The Mitchells loved Willetta's southern cooking, particularly her fried chicken and fruit pies. They were really impressed by the fare that was served every day at the Rounds, Williams, and Coats breakfast, lunch, and supper tables.

In addition to her jobs as nanny and cook, Willetta was expected to clean house and do the laundry. The twenty-four-hour job paid five dollars a week along with room and board and Willetta thought she was making a very good salary. She was even able to save a little money every week since her out-of-pocket expenses were rather minimal. She began applying the directive her wheeler-dealer great-grandfather Ned Rounds passed on to family members: *"Make a dime; save a nickel!"*

One day Willetta decided to buy a maid's outfit just like the ones she had seen the other domestics in the area wear. So she went to Nugent's Dry Good Store at the corner of Vandeventer and Olive, not too far from the Liggett & Myers plant, and bought herself a nice maid's dress and cap. They both cost her all of $1.50. That might sound to today's children her age like a pittance, but one must remember that sum represented more than a fifth of her weekly pay. The average income for a black tenant or wage worker in the South that year, 1929, was about $270 per year; the average for whites, about $450. A dollar-and-a-half was a lot of money when Willetta bought her first maid's dress and cap from Nugent's.

She kept her uniform washed and starched and ironed during her tenure with the Mitchells. She would change into her street clothes while the dress was being washed, starched, and ironed, always when the Mitchells were away. Other white families for whom black domestics worked supplied the uniforms, but the Mitchells, while they liked the idea of a uniformed nanny for their baby, never offered to pay for Willetta's outfit.

Nugent's was a popular place for black clientele. The working class could not only purchase dry goods in the store at a relatively reasonable rate, they could also pay their gas and electricity bills at the store. That saved postage, even though few realized that a trip to Nugent's to pay utility bills often cost more than the price of a postage stamp and envelope. The store at which Willetta felt comfortable shopping had been founded by Charles W. Nugent. He built a palatial Federal-Regency style mansion for his wife and sizeable family in 1906 at Number 3 Kingsbury Place. Nugent died just seventeen years before Willetta bought her maid's uniform from the store that bore his name. To graphically illustrate the kindred status of the poor and the rich, just as Willetta struggled to make it in her new world, the one-time millionaire family of the man who had started up the store from which she bought that uniform fell on hard times, too. When Charles Nugent died at age fifty-four of complications from a stroke, his wife Cora and the Nugent's eight children had to move out of their dream house on Kingsbury Place. The Nugent mansion changed hands several times after Cora and the children moved out and it was eventually torn down to save taxes in 1936. Willetta had been in St. Louis eight years when the headache ball began to demolish the Nugent mansion.

Willetta's employment with the Mitchells on Palm Street turned out to be a blessing of incredible coincidence to her Aunt Lillie. The apartment in which Willetta lived was just a few blocks from the Chevrolet plant on Union and Natural Bridge where Wes was ever-so-briefly employed as a custodian. He had had brief stints before the Chevy job as a custodian at Vashon High School and at the Liggett & Myers plant where Lillie worked. In each case he had been fired for failure to show up at work during his drunken binges. Willetta worked out a deal with the Pfeiffers that every Tuesday, payday at the Chevy plant, Willetta would push the little Mitchell baby in his buggy up to the plant gate. Because he realized his wayward ways, Wes would shove the paycheck through the gate to Willetta and her little ward. Wes seemed genuinely touched by the sight of nanny and baby coming to save him from a few days of drunken degradation.

If for some reason Willetta couldn't get to the Chevy plant on Wes' payday, her uncle would go to one of the neighborhood saloons to begin his binge. They were called saloons in those days, not bars or taverns. Some of the establishments right around the corner from the Pfeiffer residence were pretty stark in interior accoutrements. Some of the saloons even had dirt floors covered with sawdust. But, they all welcomed Wes, who would often drop his whole paycheck on draft beer and drinks on the house before he would disappear into whatever realm would keep him from returning to his home and devoted wife, Lillie.

Willetta had saved penuriously from salary she earned from the Mitchells. Since she had no rent or utilities to pay, no groceries to buy, and no large outlay for clothes to wear, Willetta was able to save most of her five-dollar-a-week salary. She sent a little money to her mother and sisters back on *Honey Island*. The recipients of her generosity were proud of her for making a fine living away from the comforts of her home in Mississippi. She gave them inspiration to move to another kind of land of milk and honey.

Willetta gave her savings to her Aunt Lillie for safe keeping. At just about the time the new nanny had saved about forty dollars, Willetta got a phone call from *Honey Island*. Her baby sister, Lena, was ill and wanted her to come home right away to see her. Willetta talked over her sister's illness with her employers and they encouraged her to make the trip home, assuring her that they could take care of their baby while she was gone.

Willetta was relieved to know that she would not be fired for doing her familial duty. She had heard of other domestics who were summarily dismissed if they needed to take care of family business, even in an emergency. Slaves in the Old South were almost never given days off for personal emergencies. Domestics in the New North weren't either, but the Mitchells were understanding. Of course, Willetta would not be paid for time she didn't spend "on the place."

Relieved that she had enough money saved for a round-trip ticket to Belzoni and that she had the Mitchell's blessing, Willetta approached her dear Aunt Lillie for train fare from the savings. The niece's request caught her aunt completely by surprise. Lillie broke into tears. Trembling violently, she collapsed in a heap on a kitchen chair and confessed to the then fifteen-year-old that she had spent all the money Willetta had given her. All of it. Wes was hopelessly out of work. The tenants renting out the second and third floors were also out of work, and Lillie sobbed that she had no alternative but to "borrow" Willetta's life savings to keep a roof over the heads of all those who lived on the three floors of 3415 Pine Street.

Willetta was crushed. Dismayed. Angry. Stunned. Heartbroken. Depressed by her beloved aunt's shocking confession. Amidst Lillie's promises of paying the money back, Willetta bolted out onto the street with tears streaming and once again took one of the long walks she would often take to sort things out and relieve her omnipresent frustrations. She dreaded having to write to her kid sister back on *Honey Island* and tell Lena that she didn't have a red cent to come to see her. In the Rounds tradition, Willetta hastily wrote back to her ailing sister but didn't tell all. She didn't tell her mother or sister that her aunt had spent every penny that she had worked hard to save over seven or eight months. As a consoling factor in adversity, Willetta had always remembered the words from the old Negro spiritual sung at funerals at Jones Chapel: *"I'm so glad trouble don't last always."*

She swallowed all her Rounds pride and went back to the Mitchells and asked if they would give her a salary advance, just enough for a round-trip train ticket.

They were happy to loan Willetta the train fare. Perhaps they thought that the advance would assure the return to her job of such an honest young girl. She swore to herself as she packed her little bag for the trip back home that she would never be so trusting of any individual in the world, especially where money was concerned. She must have inherited her great-grandfather Ned Rounds' general distrust of banking institutions. From the day of her Aunt Lillie's confession, Willetta squirreled away her savings in secret hiding places in her closet.

With her borrowed round-trip fare, Willetta took a streetcar to Union Station and boarded the Jim Crow car on the Illinois Central's *Seminole #9*. It would be decades later before a Black could legally board one of the cars which had been previously designated "white only." Some of the *Oldtimers* remember scrunching down in their seats as they passed through some sleepy southern towns where white racists might throw rocks and even fire a few shots at the "colored" cars. They remember the rednecks, far poorer than the relatively prosperous Blacks who called *Honey Island* home, who pelted the cars with stones and epithets. Willetta was lucky and never got hurt during her trips back and forth between her home in Mississippi and her new home in St. Louis. As she traveled to and from the South, she would sometimes reason that she might be in just as much peril in South St. Louis as in the Deep South.

Willetta would not have known at the time, but her specific seat and railcar on the Illinois Central had been determined for her and everybody else of her hue by none other than the U. S. Supreme Court a full thirty-three years before Willetta boarded the train at Union Station to go to visit her sick sister. In 1896 a black man named Homer Plessy whipped up the nerve and the gall to board a train in New Orleans and plop himself down in a railcar reserved for whites only. Plessy didn't keep the seat longer than a New Orleans minute. He was arrested and thrown in the slammer and eventually charged with trespassing and disturbing the peace. According to the arresting police officers, Plessy was in clear violation of an 1890 Louisiana law which authorized the segregation of the races on public transportation vehicles.

Plessy managed to get some lawyers who were willing to take his case all the way up to the highest court in the land. Justice Brown, writing for the majority of his *confreres*, opined that "separate but equal" public accommodations in transportation were a "reasonable" policy in this country—despite what the Fourteenth Amendment said. The majority of the members of the most distinguished fraternity in America did not want to tread, said Justice Brown, on the "co-mingling of the two races upon terms unsatisfactory to either." So, in other words, sit in the rail car where you and everybody else of your skin color should be happy, Willetta Williams. The "colored" car was the same kind of car as the whites were riding in. Your car is going to the same place the "whites only" cars are going. All the cars are going to the same place at the same speed. So cool it.

It was good for the country's future growth and development that all the justices did not share the opinion of the majority. Justice John Marshall Harlan wrote in dissent to the *Plessy* v. *Ferguson* ruling that *"The judgment this day rendered will, in time, prove to be quite as pernicious as the decision made by this tribunal in the Dred Scott case. The thin disguise of equal accommodations...will not mislead anyone nor atone for the wrong this day done."*

Despite the liberal and righteous thinking of the Supreme Court minority, Willetta wasn't about to try to board a "white only" rail car back to Belzoni to comfort the ailing Lena. In the year of her going back home, 1929, there were seventy-seven recorded lynchings of Blacks, seven of them in Mississippi. But hope also sprung eternal in that year. Dr. Martin Luther King Jr., a man who would be a powerful national voice for a radical change in public transportation segregation by race once and for all in the United States, was born in Atlanta.

BACK TO *HONEY ISLAND, NOT BY CHOICE*

The trip back to Belzoni was long. The train seemed to stop at every little town between St. Louis and Memphis and then Memphis to Belzoni. The length of the journey was heightened by Willetta's anxiety to get home. She arrived at the dusty little station to find her uncle George Byrd there to pick her up in his Model-T Ford. Its black sheen shone so brilliantly in the blazing sunlight that its paint job looked like patent leather. Willetta was sure he must have polished the dust off his prized flivver while he waited for her train to come in. Byrd was devoting most of his life to the farm now that he had given up the postmaster job about five years earlier. Willetta was happy her uncle now had the time to pick her up and she was glad to see him. But he did remind her—just seeing him standing there—of his late wife, her much-loved Aunt Ninnie. The widower was not the hugging kind and he stuck out his hand to give his niece a rather limp handshake. He managed what was almost a smile and, ever the gentleman, he took the little travel bag she carried, threw it in the back seat of the car, and held Willetta's door open for her.

The ride back to the Coats house in Warner Ridge didn't seem like a long one. There was much to talk about. The only distressing part of the conversation on the road south was that Uncle George confirmed that her sister was, indeed, real sick. Since George was never known to talk much, his volunteering the health update had particular significance.

When they got to John Coats' house, Willetta was first relieved to find out that the stepfather she had come to hate and fear was in Lexington, Mississippi. She was secondly relieved—after hugs and kisses from her mother and older sister—to learn that Lena's health was improving ever so slightly. Willetta rushed into the bedroom that Lena was still too weak to leave. As soon as the patient saw this sight for sore eyes, she managed to sit up in bed to give her returning sister a hug. They hugged and they hugged. Tears of a joyous reunion streamed down the faces of all the women. But Rounds-Williams women learned not to cry in the open or, if they did, they learned to stifle their tears. They had been through a lot together and couldn't imagine the tough times that lay ahead.

Lena had "*double pneumonia*" and bronchitis, contracted as a result of being a big hero around the little town. It seems the thirteen-year-old was walking home one wintry day by herself after visiting a friend. She came upon a neighbor man beating his wife on the couple's front porch. The enraged neighbor then violently dragged his wife by her hair into a near-frozen stream that ran in front of the couple's house, and pushed her head underwater. Lena, without giving it a second thought, ran headlong into the fray and into the chilly water. She wrestled with the man who reeked of alcohol in the cold air while trying to keep the victim's head above water. She managed to pull the gasping, screaming woman from her husband's clutches in a life-or-death tug of war. Lena and the victim won, probably because the abuser was so very drunk. With the assailant shouting slurred profanity at the two, the young girl ran with the battered woman back to the Coats house where Lena's mother Hattie helped comfort the abused woman, get her into some dry clothing, and get her warmed around the heat from the kitchen stove. Lena stayed in her wet clothes longer than the woman she saved while she helped get the woman situated and the kettle on to get a hot mug of tea for both of them.

It wasn't long after the lady went back to her house and probably more abuse from her husband that Lena began sneezing. The sneezing developed into a bad, hacking cough. Then, the next day there was an awful sore throat. Soon the young heroine was hoarse, had a high fever, and was too sick to get out of bed. Hattie tried all the standard home remedies and none of them seemed to work. The worried mother found a doctor somewhere, and his diagnosis was that Lena had pneumonia times two and severe inflammation of her bronchial chords, bronchitis. Hattie got a friend to drive into Belzoni to get the doctor's prescription filled. Lena managed to scrawl out a short message to her sister in St. Louis. It said:

"*Am very sick. Please come home. Love, your sister Lena.*"

Now the three tenacious sisters and their equally pertinacious mother were together again. The two Coats children were uncharacteristically scarce while the reunion was going on. Both of them stayed over with friends for a few days. That was quite alright with the close-knit Williams trio and their mother, who was beginning to come to the realization that she had made a big mistake in marrying John Coats.

The very presence of Willetta seemed to make a great difference in Lena's health. Within just a couple of weeks the patient was up, but not around. She tired easily and had to retire for naps throughout the day. The doctor's medicine seemed to be helping, too. He had prescribed two kinds of pills. One of them worked rather quickly in reducing the fever. The other, an antibiotic in the form of pink *"horse pills,"* were hard to swallow, but Lena managed to get them down.

Lena was glad to have gotten better, but she and Willetta knew—without ever saying anything to each other—that the day her complete wellness was declared, Willetta would have to return to her job in her newly-adopted city of St. Louis. The estrangement between her mother and John Coats was rather evident. He was now virtually living in Jackson. It came as no real surprise to anyone that he actually had another wife and another family there. The good Christian Hattie Rounds Williams Coats was fed up. She promised Willetta on the day all four women hugged and said goodbye that she and Lena and Gertrude just might move up to St. Louis some day soon to be with her. That possibility made the parting less painful.

Willetta returned to the employ of the Mitchells. The baby boy she cared for had started to make a word construction that sounded like: *"Wi-LEE...Wi-LEEEEE,"* and would break into a big toothless grin and giggle when Willetta came into his room or returned from an occasional day off. He loved his nanny and had missed her for the month she had been in Mississippi. And she loved her little ward. Mr Mitchell seemed nonplused by her return, but the Missus was obviously thrilled to get her full-time babysitter back so she could go off to play bridge and shop all day again. Mrs. Mitchell even broke the no-touch rule generally practiced between employers and domestics. She actually gave Willetta a little hug. She told Willetta: "The baby is always more glad to see you than to see me, so we're glad you're back!" Willetta remained with the Mitchells for almost two years. She worked off the loan for the train fare and saved her money all the while. There was that lesson again running through her mind as it was passed down from Old Ned. *"Make a dime, save a nickel."* But she never trusted anybody other than herself—and eventually only a bank or two—to keep her money for the rest of her life.

 *Life Again Back in St. Louis*

Upon her return to St. Louis after helping her sister Lena recover, Willetta moved back in with the Pfeiffers on Pine Street for awhile. While living with the Mitchells she was treated well, and she really enjoyed seeing the baby grow and learn new things like how to walk and gurgle a few intelligible words. At the same time, she missed being around black people and she missed being around family folk. When she lived on the place with the Mitchells, she missed all those wild and crazy and laughter-filled weekends when her kinfolk descended on the Pfeiffer's place from Chicago. She reasoned that she could actually help her Aunt Lillie B. pay the rent and make ends meet if she lived with her aunt and uncle on Pine. Even though Lillie B. had spent her life savings and had never been able to pay it all back, Willetta had saved a little more than a hundred dollars by now. She never let on to her aunt, and her Lillie B. was too embarrassed by her earlier act of desperation in spending her niece's nest egg to discuss the subject. Willetta offered to pay $1.50 a week for room and board. The offer was quickly accepted, and she moved back in with the Pfeiffers.

The Great Depression had reached a high point when Willetta packed up her kit bag at the Mitchells for the move back. She had heard of men with money jumping out of the windows of their towering office buildings. She had actually seen men and women in fairly decent attire selling apples and potatoes on street corners. She once took a bus down to the St. Louis riverfront and saw for herself the "Hooverville" and "Happy Valley" tent, shack, shanty, and hovel communities set up by the city's poorest of the poor. She was amazed that people within less than five miles of her home with the Pfeiffers were living in huts made of cardboard boxes. She had seen more beggars on the streets of St. Louis than she had ever seen before. *"Brother can you spare a dime?"* wasn't just a line from a then-popular song on the radio. That question had become a greeting on the streets of Depression-era St. Louis—especially in all-black neighborhoods.

Willetta couldn't have known the specific unemployment figures for 1931, but there were 99,666 St. Louisans out of work that year, 24 percent of the total work force. Those jobless figures represented 21.5 percent of the white work force and a whopping 42.8 percent of St. Louis' black working class. Things would get worse in the next couple of years for St. Louis workers, even as the unemployment rate for the nation as a whole had peaked. In 1933, while the national unemployment rate hovered at about 25 percent, St. Louis' jobless rate stood at over 30 percent. Eighty percent of the black population in St. Louis was unemployed that year.

Neil Primm, writing in his book, *Lion of the Valley,* noted:

"In November 1933, the entire force of eighteen black women in the filling and labeling department of the Conferro Paint and Varnish Company was laid off without stated reasons. As required by the NRA code, their wages had been raised from $9 to $14 a week shortly before they were discharged. An Urban League representative who visited the plant a week later saw that these experienced workers had been replaced by white women. In response to a League inquiry, company officials stated that they would not pay such high wages to blacks."

The National Recovery Administration, or NRA, was set up by the federal government to help the nation get back on its feet after the devastating Great Depression. It rather ineffectively tried to regulate and equalize salaries from 1933 to 1936 as set forth by the National Industrial Recovery Act established by congressional legislation. Minimum salary scales were set up and wages boosted. White employers refused to pay Blacks like my Aunt Willetta the higher wages—salaries that would allow them to make more money than some whites when competence and seniority were issues. Blacks were seldom represented at the code hearings to determine if discriminatory hiring and wage practices existed. In the laundries, steel mills, and tobacco processing plants like L & M of St. Louis and the rest of the nation, Blacks were almost always paid lower salaries than their white counterparts.

The fact that Con-Ferro's CEO, S. M. Koplar, could so openly defy the NRA and apparently get away with his obstinance speaks volumes about how weak enforcement of the Act was. The hiring practices of the paint and varnish company at 3228 North Broadway was emblematic of defiance rivaling the South's rebellious stand against Federal dictates regarding slavery. Willetta never heard of the Con-Ferro Paint and Varnish Company or of S. M. Koplar, but the company's story and stance would not have surprised her. Nor would the statistics that showed proportionately more Blacks than Whites out of work. Her racial kin were staying at home and looking for work everywhere she looked. Or, they were hustling this or that, conniving with this or that scheme—all to make a dime for some food for them and their families.

Of one thing Willetta could be sure in those depressing Depression times: She would **never** be out of work. And she never was for any length of time. There must have been something about that Rounds' work ethic that kept her and Lillie B. working even when all around them weren't.

Things with Wes Pfeiffer had seemingly gone from bad to worse. He still never kept a job past a couple of paydays. He was still squandering the little money he made. He was still going off on drunken binges, disappearing for two or three days at a time. He was still returning after his disappearances and throwing himself on the mercy of his beloved wife, Lillie, and "swearing on a stack of Bibles" that he had seen the error of his ways and was ready to repent and be saved from the jaws of hell and damnation. He'd even get dressed on a Sunday morning and walk repentantly to church with his wife and young niece to the St. Paul A. M. E. Church on Leffingwell and Pine just a short distance from their home. Then he'd lie to Almighty God in prayer and hymn on those Sunday mornings. And he lied to the two women he loved most and give them blessed assurance that Jesus was his hope. Soon afterward, he'd become a poor four flushing backslider again at the drop of a job.

The fortunes of the Pfeiffers and their niece appeared to turn around for the better when a ward-healing, cigar-chomping, three-piece-suit-sporting, spats-wearing, derby-domed black politician who lived next door to the Pfeiffers got Wes a job as a janitor at City Hall. Lillie B. and Willetta were ecstatic! They were elated even when Wes revealed that a certain amount of his salary would have to be paid back each week to the politician for getting him such a good, solid job. The politician, named Sparks, told Wes that if he played his cards right he could keep that job for the rest of his life. No Republicans would ever control City Hall, the politician predicted, and with Democrats in, nobody would bother Wes so long as he did his job, came to work every day, paid his bi-weekly kickback faithfully, coughed up the *lug* when the ruling party's hat was passed around, and managed to mind his own business and see some things and not see some other things. Of course, no term limit was placed on the weekly kickback. That would probably go on forever, too.

Hallelujah! A good job guaranteed to Wes for life! And at City Hall, Honey!

Wes actually lied to Lillie B. about how much the kickback was to be. He padded the number to give himself a little extra pocket money each week. He also lied to Lillie B. about when paydays would be. He was actually to get paid on the first and fifteen of each month. He told Lillie B. that City Hall pay was a little different from most jobs. City workers were paid on the *second* and the *sixteenth* down there, he said.

On the first scheduled payday that Lillie B. and Willetta expected, the second of the month, wife and niece waited for the man of the house to show up after work with his first paycheck from City Hall. Lillie's shift at L&M Tobacco was over at three, and she raced home anyway to get herself all dolled up and settled as if this occasion was no big deal. Aunt and niece paced. And bit their nails. And watched the clock. And crossed their fingers. And they prayed. Just like clockwork Wes' key was turned in the front door lock and the new City Hall Janitor, proud and beaming, made a little bow and presented his first City Hall paycheck to a wife who broke into tears and wild laughter as he spun her 'round and 'round the kitchen floor. Wes gave Willetta a big hug and repeated the swirling ceremony with her.

Those were to be the last such whoops of jubilation over a Wesley Pfeiffer City Hall paycheck. The hopeless, hapless Wes Pfeiffer screwed up yet another good job. Lillie had actually circled the *16* on the Wade Funeral Home calendar that hung on the kitchen wall. She had silently and audibly prayed and kept her fingers crossed beginning on the fifteenth of the month that there would be reason to repeat the kitchen celebration. She had even scraped up enough money to buy Wes a grey janitor's uniform at Nugent's for $2.75 and had embroidered his name *WES* just above the left shirt pocket. She had gone to buy the uniform for her newly-employed husband the day after the first paycheck came in. Willetta had traveled with her on the streetcar to buy the surprise gift.

On the evening of the fifteenth—just twenty-four hours from THE MOMENT OF TRUTH—Willetta had prepared a meal of Wes' favorites: meat loaf, mashed potatoes, and collard greens boiled in fatback. When Lillie got in, the two women discussed what a big smile they imagined Wes would paste on his face when his wife presented him with his new uniform. Willetta made a German chocolate cake and a big pitcher of lemonade just like her mother, Hattie, used to make to the joy of everybody who drank this remarkable lemon drink. In fact, although she had not found a new job quite yet, Willetta volunteered to buy all the food for the Feast of the Second Coming of a City Hall Paycheck. Willetta still didn't reveal to her aunt that she had all that money socked away secretly.

Lillie and Willetta looked at the clock. Wes must have run a little late with some extra chores down at City Hall. This wasn't his big payday. They joked about what if this happened tomorrow on the Big Day. They were happy this was the day before the payday. By 5:30 PM the two women who loved and put up with Wes' dereliction so often in the past went out and sat on the porch hoping to get a glimpse of Wes fresh off the bus around the corner. Fifteen minutes later they decided to walk down to the bus stop just to get a little exercise and walk Wes back home.

A couple of buses made their stops and Wes didn't get off them. The two women were still full of hope and diminishing expectations as they returned home without saying a word to each other. Wes did not come home at all that night. Nor the next night. Although the two women imagined the worst had happened to him, they were kind enough to each other not to share their silent alarm. That's how Rounds women were, are, and will be.

On the second night of Wes' disappearance, Lillie B. just couldn't take it any more and broke down into hysteria a couple of hours after she had turned in at midnight. She barged into the sleeping-not-too-soundly Willetta's bedroom and threw herself on her niece's bed. She asked the Lord Jesus and Willetta in pained sobbing where her husband could be, and if they thought he was lying somewhere dead. Should she call the police? Lillie asked. Neither responded to the query immediately. But Willetta tried gently to calm the quivering mass of tears and snot that was her auntie. And then the soon-to-be seventeen-year-old did something she doesn't understand why she did even to this day. She got out of bed, leaving Lillie crying there, threw on some clothes, and went out into the night looking for her errant or dead uncle.

She remembers that the moon was shining brightly that night and the extra light made her feel a little less scared in her manhunt. Crime wasn't so bad in the neighborhood. People still left their house doors and cars unlocked. There was a kind of feeling and unwritten neighborly agreement that the poor shouldn't rob the poor. Still, it wasn't very safe for a teenage girl to be roaming the streets in the wee hours of the morning. But Willetta was determined to find her Uncle Wes if he was to be found—dead or alive. Willetta knew her Aunt Lillie B. to have more pride than anyone else she had ever known. Lillie was too proud and too embarrassed to let the neighbors see her frantically going from door to door trying to find her husband from time to time. She just never could muster up the gumption to try to hunt her wayward husband down.

But here was her dear, dear, young niece at nearly three in the morning, searching alone and searching doorways and gangways and peering through the windows of darkened saloons. After walking as far east as Jefferson (about seven city blocks), two blocks south to Laclede, two blocks west to Grand, and two blocks north to Washington in a big rectangle, Willetta returned home without her missing uncle. She was tired, but her adrenalin was flowing. When the young girl returned home, tired but without Wes, she was somewhat surprised to find that Aunt Lillie B. had not waited up for her. The poor, tormented woman had collapsed and passed out from a lack of sleep. So as not to disturb her distraught aunt, Willetta covered her with a sheet and the bedspread and tipped out of her own bedroom. She slept—not too soundly—in the Pfeiffer's bed. The exhausted teen was sure she would not be disturbed there since the wilted Lillie wouldn't be able to wake up till much later that morning. If Wes would reappear somehow, Willetta would surely hear his entrance long before he got to the bedroom.

Next day—a Saturday—still neither hide nor hair of Wes. A long-time friend of his stopped by the Pine Street house that morning. Where the hell was Wes? The two cronies were supposed to walk to a buddy's house to check out some fishing rods and reels the guy wanted to sell. Where was Wes? his pal asked. Lillie B. was too broken up, too puffy-eyed, too emotionally ravaged to tell the whole horrible tale of her husband's most recent mysterious disappearance. Willetta took up the narrative. *"Wait a minute,"* Wes' friend told the two women. *"Just got a thought. Y'all just hold on. I'll be right back in a shake."*

Wes' friend was gone no more than fifteen minutes when he rang the doorbell and there, draped over his shoulder, was Wes, filthy, reeking of cheap wine and beer and vomit, and totally incoherent in his mumblings. It was a totally incongruous appearance for a man who in his highest state of sobriety was always clean as a whistle, sharp as a tack, and neat as a pin. Lillie B. shrieked *"Thank ya, Jesus"* and collapsed once again as she was wont to do in a heap on the hallway floor. Willetta dropped to her knees to comfort her sobbing auntie. Wes' friend stepped over the pile of anguished women and took Wes to the bed Willetta had just abandoned. Then the friend unceremoniously dumped the reprobate into the bed he hadn't slept in for two nights.

The teen who had had to grow up in such a hurry ran to get a little bottle of smelling salts. The Wade Funeral Home regularly handed out the little bottles at church services as premiums to anybody who looked like a prospective customer or who might know or be related to a prospective customer. The friend who had brought Wes home stepped over Lillie B. again, and as he closed the front door behind him said, *"Y'all owe me a good dinner sometime."* Then he slammed the door without ever telling the two grieving women where the hell he had found the remains of Wes.

After Lillie B. was revived from her hysteria, she went into the bedroom where Wes was snorting and snoring like a hog. He would alternately mumble something Lillie could understand and some gibberish she couldn't make out. He was alive. Thank God. But something came over the distressed wife this time. It was a feeling like no other she had ever had toward her husband. She approached him as if she didn't know him. And she hadn't known him for three whole days. If he ever sobered up, she knew she would have some things to say to him he had never heard from her mouth before. It would be ultimatum time. She would never go through this heartache again. Never. In this life or the next.

While Wes was sleeping a loud and distressed sleep, Lillie B. huddled with her young niece. They quickly hatched a plan, though obviously it was a plan that Lillie had already worked out in her head while Wes was missing; the operative next move if Wes ever came home alive again. She had already gone into the bedroom closet and got out his only good suit. Once after Wes had won a wad of money in a poker game, he bought himself a fairly expensive suit. While Wes was gone this latest time, Lillie had imagined that she would either have to bury him in that suit if he were dead or, if he was alive, she had other plans for the togs. When his ship had come in, Wes had also bought himself the most expensive pair of Stacey-Adams shoes he could buy. He didn't wear either item often. The suit stayed freshly pressed in its hanging bag. Every now and then when he ran out of things to do to keep him from going out and getting drunk, he would pull the virtually unworn shoes out of the box they came in and give them a good spit polish even though they didn't really need one.

Lillie B. handed Willetta the suit and shoes and instructed her to walk down to Jefferson and Market streets to the pawnshop and get what she could for the items. She instructed the teen to be tough with the pawnshop dealer and not take less than $25 for them. If the man offered her less, her aunt told her, turn around and walk out the door because the dealer knew he could get much more for the suit and shoes. Willetta was tough by now, and she returned proudly flashing a twenty and a five-dollar bill. Wes was still snoring, sleeping off his drunk.

Later that day the derelict began to wake up. He began crying out what a rat he was. Nobody disagreed. He sobbed that he didn't deserve forgiveness. Nobody disagreed. He said he would just kill himself. Although the two women in the house didn't want to see him go quite that far, neither offered to intervene if Wes really thought that was the best way to punish himself.

Lillie B. helped him take off his puke-splattered, alcohol-soaked clothing and helped him into the bathroom where she stood guard to see that he got washed up. She didn't utter a word. When he tried a sloppy attempt to put his arms around her and beg her forgiveness, she fended him off and pushed him away from her, making sure she didn't push him down to hurt himself.

"Baby, I don't deserve a good woman like you," he slobbered.

Lillie B. did not disagree with him.

"Baby Doll, I'm sorry. I'm sorry. I'm sorry. Will you please forgive me?" he pleaded.

Lillie did not answer him. She merely glared at him as her nostrils flared and she gritted her teeth to keep from exploding in a vindictive rage. She watched as he urinated a torrent of yellow reprocessed booze. She handed him his robe.

When he staggered out of the bathroom with little help from the wife who had always been there to help him before, Wes plopped down on the bed, almost falling backward as he sat unsteadily. Willetta was waiting with some hot soup in a mug. As Wes grimaced from the steaming hot soup hitting his tongue, his niece unsympathetically ordered him to down the rest. Wes complained the room was spinning and he needed to lie down again. Neither woman spoke to him. He splashed down prostrate. That night Lillie threw a blanket over her worthless but still loved husband to keep him from getting up in the middle of the night and disappearing again or falling down and hitting his head. Willetta slept on one side of him and Lillie slept on the other side, each on top of the blanket so it kept Wes pinned underneath. With the two women nearly gagging at the smell of Wes' putrid breath, Willetta and Lillie and Wes slept throughout the night. As Lillie lay there staring at a spot in the dark room where the ceiling light was, she had the hardest time of the three getting to sleep.

Next morning bright and early, Lillie shook Wes to an awakened state. Willetta jumped up and ran to her room to sleep another second or two. Wes sat up on the side of the bed and said:

"*Guess you're not speaking to me, huh, Baby?*"

"*Not just yet,*" she answered coldly.

"*Guess I really messed up this time, huh, Baby?*"

"*Yes, you did*" she replied icily. "*Go into the bathroom and take a bath and shave yourself,*" she ordered.

"*Yes, ma'am!*" he replied, and snapped a snappy military-like salute.

When he emerged from the bathroom, she had some clean clothes laid out for him. She also had his suitcase packed.

"*Where ya going, Baby?*" he slushed, barely able to stand. "*Guess you're leaving me.*"

"*No,*" she replied, looking him straight in the eye. "*You're the one that's leaving.*"

She told him that just as soon as he had gotten dressed and eaten the hot oatmeal and the bacon and toast Willetta had prepared for him while he was bathing, he was going to Gary, Indiana, to stay with some relatives while he dried out.

"*And while you're away,*" she said, "*I'm going to think long and hard about whether I ever want you to come back.*"

There was very little other conversation that morning. Willetta asked him if he wanted another cup of coffee, which was about the only thing said over the breakfast table. When the morning meal on this strange day was over, Willetta put on her coat, picked up Wes' suitcase, and went out the back door to wait for him in the alley. The niece thought her aunt and errant uncle might need a minute or two alone. Lillie's Master Plan called for Wes to exit the house and flee the city without any neighbors—especially a very angry politician next door—seeing him go into forced exile in Gary.

As Willetta, who had seen more things than most kids her age would witness in a lifetime, waited in the alley, Wes made a rattling-off of promises to Lillie B. about cleaning up his act. She didn't respond and wouldn't let him come near her for a goodbye hug and kiss. Wes rushed out, careful not to slam the door, and he and his young niece headed for the streetcar stop down the street and around the corner on Olive Street. The streetcar arrived soon, but not before Wes had tried to begin sentence after sentence to explain why he had been such a rat.

At the Greyhound Bus Station at Sixth and St. Charles in downtown St. Louis, Willetta handed Wes an envelope with the $25 inside. She watched as he purchased his one-way ticket to Gary. Lillie B. had insisted it be one-way until she and he could sort things out. Wes was certain he wouldn't be getting a farewell hug from his niece either. He somehow was able to flash back on the whirling hug he had given his wife and niece when he came home with his first paycheck from City Hall. There had been very little repartee on the streetcar or at the bus depot, but as he was about to board the bus to Gary, Willetta looked him in the eye and said:

"You hurt her, Uncle Wes. You really hurt her."

He turned on his heels without saying a word. His guilt and shame was written all over his face. For a teenage niece to have to arrange for his deportation was more than he could take. On the long Greyhound bus ride to Indiana Wes must have thought how he had caused such grave emotional abuse of his devoted wife. Maybe he thought about how he had helped rob a teenage girl of the things adolescent she should have been thinking about at her age: bebop, jazz, rhythm and blues, boogie-woogie, cosmetics, and boys. The music business was about to break wide open in 1933. That's the year Benny Goodman began to integrate his band and use "Negro" musicians for the first time on his recordings.

- NIGHTS OUT ON THE TOWN

There were lots of places for young "colored" folks to hang out and kick up their heels in the St. Louis ghetto in which most Blacks lived in the late '20s and through the years of that very silly national effort to prohibit by law the consumption of alcoholic beverages. Willetta remembers that "hootch" flowed as fluently during Prohibition as it did before and afterward. Just like at those card parties and the Pfeiffers where the gang came in from Chicago. She also remembers:

"You could get really sick or die if you got ahold of some of the really bad stuff. That stuff that was being sneaked out of the L&M Tobacco Company vats—that syrupy stuff that the tobacco leaves were being cured in—was making a lot of people really sick. And then folks were making that bathtub gin stuff…and you had to really careful about what you were drinkin'. It was true that bad hootch could make you go blind…or go dead."

We will never know how many boozers actually died from drinking too much of that stuff. Willetta remembers that people were drinking *"rotgut," "bathtub gin"* and *"moonshine"* laced with rubbing alcohol, turpentine, baking extracts, and anything else that looked even remotely like drinking alcohol.

A night out for Willetta and her young adult friends could include a movie at the *Critereon Theater* on Franklin Avenue—now Martin Luther King Drive—between Leffingwell and Jefferson on the south side of the street. Then after the movie, Blacks could go to a little hole-in-the-wall place down Franklin Avenue east of Jefferson run by Jesse Johnson. His patrons could get a tripe sandwich, a frankfurter sandwich, and on Friday nights, a good fish sandwich. One could get a nickel beer or a twenty-five-cent cocktail while Prohibition was in effect. One could get a drink and get pretty sick, too, until 1933 when the Thirteenth Amendment was repealed. Many cops who looked the other way while taking payoffs during the Volstead Act's enforcement noted that it was against the law to *sell* alcohol, not to *drink* it. And so, Willetta remembers that some of the speakeasies she visited dispensed their bootlegged booze in coffee cups and had their patrons pay for it at another time.

One popular night spot for St. Louis' Blacks looking for a good time on an evening out was the *Rosebud Bar*. It was located at 2220-22 Market Street and had been run by Thomas Million Turpin up until 1922, six years before Willetta moved to St. Louis. It operated for many years after that under a different management. In one of its heyday newspaper ads in 1902, the *Rosebud* boasted: *"...a first-class café in rear. Open all night day. All Prices. Private dining-room."*

Willetta remembers that by the time she got to St. Louis, the Rosebud was not exactly a "first-class" establishment. The current owners had let the place run down and, according to some of the *Oldtimers* who had by then withdrawn their patronage, the place had been taken over by "sissies," a term that is totally unacceptable today for the gay crowd. It was a shame Willetta had not seen the Rosebud when it was a center for many years of the best ragtime in town. Tom Turpin himself was a ragtime composer and had penned the very popular and very early classic, *"Harlem Rag."* Combos and bigger bands started jamming this tune just as soon as the piece was hot off the press in 1897. Scott Joplin used to hang out in his friend Tom's place when Joplin lived in St. Louis from 1900 to 1906. That was the second time the Texarkana, Texas, native lived in St. Louis. Joplin had lived a rather short walk from the Pfeiffer's house at 2658 Morgan (now Delmar.) The home was declared a National Landmark in 1975.

Although she never admitted to drinking any of the stuff, Willetta remembers that the most popular drink served at the Rosebud Cafe (the one time she admits spending an evening there) was sloe gin with a beer chaser. During the years of Prohibition, the young ex-Mississippian remembers the bartenders made a rather ineffective effort at keeping the booze under the counter until it was served.

On a few of the times when she and her dates wanted to go someplace fancy, there was the West End Waiters Club on Vandeventer between Enright and West Belle. It was, in fact, right across the street from Vandeventer Place. A block-long structure, the club building also housed shops, a hotel, and a restaurant. It is reported that in order to avoid violating the private place's covenant when he and his wife, Frances, stayed overnight with Mayor and Mrs. David Francis in 1888, President Cleveland moved across the street to the *West End Hotel*. No non-family members could stay more than one night in the posh Vandeventer Place.

By the time Willetta came to town, the club and hotel were the domain of an "all-colored" clientele. Only the cream of the City's black population and those who could pretend to possess class for even one evening could patronize the West End Waiters Club. On Sunday nights in particular, Willetta remembers that postal workers, politicians, teachers, and black entrepreneurs dined on some pretty fancy food, drank some good stuff, and kicked up their heels to the best big band music as they jitterbugged the night away in high style.

The Riviera Nightclub in the 4400 block of Delmar was another popular place for Blacks to take in the nightlife before there was any legal racial integration of the social spots in St. Louis. The Riviera was run by the most powerful Black politician in the City, Jordan "Pop" Chambers. Any politician or citizen, black or white, who wanted some clout exerted to get this or that done or win this or that election had to go through "Pop" Chambers. He was notorious for getting the job done—for a price. He took in "markers" and dispensed favors from his headquarters at the Riviera. In the '30s, Chambers biggest claim to fame is that he was able to wrest the votes from Blacks who had always voted Republican and swing those votes to a powerful Black Democratic voting machine. Willetta remembers going to dances and concerts at Chambers' Riviera where she and other Blacks out to enjoy top entertainment could hear and see the likes of Count Basie, Louis Armstrong, Duke Ellington, Cab Calloway, and "Ma" Rainey. Groups like the beauticians union and black postal workers and Pullman porters would hold dances and sponsor big band concerts there. The joint would really jump, she remembers.

Just before it closed in 1930, Willetta remembers seeing a few music shows, reviews, *black outs*, and vaudeville acts at the old *Booker T. Washington Theatre*. It was in the 2200 block of Market Street—about twelve city blocks east of Willetta's first St. Louis home on Pine Street. Willetta remembers hearing entertainer Ethel Waters sing there once. St. Louis historian John Wright notes that the *Booker T. Washington Theatre*:

"...seated one thousand and had both live entertainment along with motion pictures. A new show with a different theme—African, cowboy, Egyptian, etc.—appeared each week. Because it was a part of the Theatre Owners' Booking Association, the black vaudeville circuit, the theatre featured appearances by such black stars as Ethel Waters (1896-1977), Bessie Smith (1894-1937), and Ma Rainey (1886-1939)."

When Willetta was an advanced teen, she and some of her girlfriends and any single ladies could find good social opportunities at the Pine Street YMCA. This new Young Men's Christian Association Building for Colored had opened at Ewing and Pine nine years before Willetta arrived in St. Louis. It was literally just down the street from the Pfeiffer's house. The building had housing for "Negro" troops in the waning days of World War I, but Willetta remembers that soldiers who were passing back and forth through St. Louis after WWI would come to Friday and Saturday night dances at the "Y." The dances, she recollects, were chaperoned, so there was some decorum about the place. Willetta also took advantage of the "Y" gymnasium and often played a game she learned in St. Louis and got proficient at—volleyball. The games were never integrated by sex. Girls played girls and boys played boys. She remembered that a lot of Blacks, just up from the South, could find lodgings in the clean, well-kept dormitory of the Pine Street "Y."

Willetta recalls that a lot of people ate daily at the Pine Street "Y." They preferred the food there to going to any of the restaurants in town. There weren't that many restaurants with good food quality and variety that Blacks could go to in the early '30s. For seventy-five cents, Willetta remembers, one could get a really good lunch in those days. A Sunday dinner in the post-Depression era was $1.25, with more good food than one could eat.

There were any number of little joints that dotted the rather circumscribed territory Willetta and her racial kin covered on any given day. Some of them were nice little neighborhood saloons where even kids could hang out. Others were rather dangerous hangouts for a rather rough crowd.

Even more important to St. Louis' black population than where it was okay to go for food and entertainment was where "colored" citizens could not go. St. Louis was a town that discriminated openly against its citizens of color in matters of public accommodations for more than three decades after Willetta left the Deep South. She expected less racial discrimination than in the Delta, where she hadn't seen much bigotry. After all, it was a white man who had sold her great-grandfather, Ned Rounds, that prime riverfront property and had continued to live as Ned's neighbor for years on *Honey Island.*

Willetta knew, as every other black person knew in St. Louis, an attempt to get into all-white public places—even after Mayor Raymond Tucker signed an ordinance prohibiting racial discrimination in St. Louis' public places on June 1, 1961—could result in arrest for trespassing, jail, and worse. The fabulous Fox Theatre, which made its debut a year after Willetta moved just two blocks east of it, was totally off-limits for Blacks. The theater had more than five thousand seats, but none of them was open to Blacks when the theater opened its doors. Same for the St. Louis Theatre, which showed movies for four years before the Fox opened down the street on Grand Avenue. Same, too, for the Loew's Mid-City Theatre on Grand and the Loew's State Theatre not too far away. No Blacks allowed. Until the mid-1960s!

There was one period of time in which Blacks were given the rare opportunity to attend those all-white theaters and public accommodations in St. Louis. From the mid-1950s until the mid-1960s, African Americans were allowed into the all-white theaters and restaurants for one week during the entire year. That was an effort by the National Council of Christians and Jews to promote harmony in St. Louis. Blacks were allowed to attend the Fox and St. Louis and Loew's theaters, along with Howard Johnson's and other restaurants, from February 7 through 14. That was called Brotherhood Week. If Willetta or any of her relatives or black friends or work associates had tried to get into any of the 51-weeks-a-year-all-white establishments, handcuffs would be the next thing they wore.

When I, as president of my Sumner High School senior class, phoned the Chase Hotel catering office in 1961, I was curtly told that the hotel did not accept "all-colored" groups. When I headed the Upward Bound program at Webster University in 1967, I phoned the steamer *Admiral*'s reservations office to see if I could get booking for the two hundred students enrolled— predominantly black—and I had quite an experience. In those days before I appeared on television newscasts, the *Admiral* booking office had no idea of my race nor that I was a true great-great-grandson of Ned Rounds. Nor did I identify the racial composition of the Upward Bound group. I told the reservationist simply that I wanted to book an evening for two hundred "Webster College" students. The reservationist informed me that the *Admiral* would be thrilled to have our business. A caution was given: the boat had "the coloreds on Tuesday and Thursday nights," and the reservationist was certain I would want to avoid those nights for my Webster College group. I thanked the reservationist profusely and asked if we could have a Friday night. Reservations granted. Cleared. When I showed up leading a group of almost two hundred black high school students down the *Admiral* gang plank, I was sure the woman in the ticket window was going to have a heart attack. She stammered and stuttered and hemmed and hawed after I showed her our proper tickets. She then got some male superior who declared there must be some mistake. But there they were. Our tickets were in order and they begrudgingly allowed us to board.

Mustering up the *Pride of Ned*, I never ever again set foot on that scow boat in any of its incarnations, even when I was assigned to do TV news interviews on it. The interviewee either had to step onto terra firma or no interview. And that was in 1967! That may be another family trait not mentioned earlier. Ned Rounds' descendants never forget. And while we do not hold grudges because of our Christian upbringing, we do remember where we should hold grudges if grudges were ever to become an acceptable option.

 *Uncle Wes Returns from Exile*

Her aunt had given Willetta strict instructions to make sure that Wes got on the bus for Gary and not to leave the station until the bus rolled out of sight as it headed east. Willetta did exactly as she was told. She always did just that. Unless what she was told to do didn't suit her. Rounds independence.

A lot of things changed in Lillie B.'s and Willetta's lives after Wes was exiled to Gary. For one thing, the two women started going to another church. Lillie B. was afraid her next visit to St. Paul A. M. E. Church would cause some of the sisters and brethren to whisper mean things, nudge each other, and wag their heads about this poor, poor woman and her sweet young niece—and that wreck of a no-good husband and uncle the two had just thrown out of the house.

Yes, returning to St. Paul would be much too embarrassing for both of Wes' women. Lillie B. even thought, in her wildest dreams and nightmares, that perhaps since she had had such bad luck with her husband God didn't listen to the petitions at St. Paul as attentively as He might have inside the walls of another church. The two women unceremoniously moved their membership to the Galilee Baptist Church on Adams Street, just south of Pine. There they began praying to a Baptist God for Wes' salvation and redemption with a congregation that prayed and sang louder and more fervently than the A. M. E. flock had. Maybe God preferred the simple Baptist label to involvement with a congregation that called itself by the tripartite name of African Methodist Episcopal. Anyway, hopefully, the "Ballad of Wes Pfeiffer" had not traveled across town to the West End. Lillie B. could always tell a little fib that God would forgive about the whereabouts of her husband. She could always say he "ran on the road," the job description given

Pullman car porters and cooks and conductors. That was partially true of Wes. He often ran on the road right after he had blown a job.

Within a month of Wes' departure Lillie set up the sale of almost all the furniture and stuff she and Wes had amassed as a couple. There was nothing fancy to put on the block. No heirlooms. No precious possessions. The dejected quasi-widow didn't seem to want to look at much of anything that would remind her of her seedy husband. On a Saturday and Sunday Lillie held an open-house sale, and folks came from miles around to pick through her belongings and try to find bargains. There wasn't much money in the pockets of the would-be buyers during those years of generally hard luck, so chairs, beds, dishes, mementos, knick-knacks, and what-nots—even some of the dearly departed (to Gary, Indiana) husband's clothing—were sold off to poor folks looking for a bargain. Lillie B. realized a little more than sixty dollars for everything. Her belongings had to be sold for pennies on the dollar.

Her next task was to find a place for her and Willetta to stay. Since they were able to put down a month's rent with their separate savings, including the proceeds from the sale of the household stuff, they didn't have too much difficulty finding a furnished room they could share. They decided to move into a one-room apartment in the 3800 block of Windsor Place. It was a pretty and quaint little street of two long blocks between Grand Avenue on the east and Vandeventer on the west. It seemed all of Willetta's earliest years in St. Louis would be lived contiguously to those two broad and long avenues. Remember? The L & M plant was on South Vandeventer and the Pfeiffer residence was just east of Grand.

Windsor Place had been around since the 1880s when it was established on the north side of Bell Avenue as the living quarters street for the domestics who worked in the historic Vandeventer Place across the street. With its imposingly huge and elegant thirty-room mansions, Vandeventer Place became St. Louis' premiere enclave for the city's old money and the nouveau riche, too. They built monuments to themselves and to their industries and sometimes to their wives. St. Louis' upper crust often modeled their mansions after palaces and villas in Europe they had seen on the Grand Tour. One Vandeventer place household retained a household staff of more than thirty servants, including upstairs and downstairs maids, butlers, footmen, cooks, laundresses, gardeners, nannies, liverymen, and in the winter a full-time employee who kept fires burning in the two dozen fireplaces. Another Vandeventer Place residence had the city's first electric-powered home refrigerator, bought to preserve the wild game and fowl bagged by the owner of the mansion. Elaborate black wrought-iron gates on Grand to the east and Vandeventer to the west sealed the private street off from the passing world. In fact, this exclusive enclave was not called a "street." Just like in Mississippi, the word "place" was the operative word.

Willetta would often peer through these gates and wonder at the majesty of the mansions behind them. She could only fantasize about working in such an idyllic setting since it became well known to her, as it was to native black St. Louisans, that there was virtually no way for a "colored" domestic to gain employment here. The builders and owners of those Vandeventer Place mansions hired only white help, except for an occasional liveryman who was, it seemed either "high yeller" or black as coal. The first tier of St. Louis' private place residents hired German and Irish cooks and maids, English butlers, French and British nannies, and even some Chinese gardeners as a general rule. In many of the mansions in Vandeventer Place and in the similar places on Westmoreland, Portland, Kingsbury, and Washington Terrace, the mostly white domestics who served food had to wear white gloves. Each day as she walked to and from her new residence on Windsor Place, Willetta would fantasize about being a Vandeventer Place domestic.

The covenants the aristocratic owners of Vandeventer Place manses and the other private places signed were designed to guarantee the exclusivity of the compound. Every Vandeventer Place home, by covenant stipulation, had to have at least three sets of lace curtains for the windows. That regulation was intended to give threefold assurance that crispy clean curtains were kept in place to dress the windows because of the sooty conditions of the black and stifling St. Louis smog. To think, Willetta and her Aunt Lillie shared one room in a single-family dwelling right across Bell Avenue from the pretentious Vandeventer Place! Willetta could write to her mother and sisters in Mississippi that she was moving up in the world.

Sadly enough, rigor mortis had begun to set in on Vandeventer Place by the early 1950s when Willetta had moved out of the one-room apartment on Windsor Place and into larger quarters next door. Columnist Ron Elz noted in a recent article in the *West End-Clayton Word* that when he visited a great-uncle who lived at Number 70 Vandeventer Place in the summer of 1953 he was saddened to see:

"...the pot-holed street, weed-strewn parkway and few remaining great old houses, many in sad disrepair. An era was virtually vanishing and few seemed to care. Some speculators had descended like vultures on the carcass of Vandeventer Place to pick the bones clean from what remained of this once so important street in our history. The unwanted furnishings and interior and exterior architectural art was being plucked and secreted in dark storage in places such as the long-empty (since 1933) New Grand Central Theater building at Grand and Lucas Place."

That theater/storage house was not at all far from where Willetta now lived. She witnessed first-hand the total demolition of Vandeventer Place when she visited and later lived with her sister and my mother, Lena, Grandma Hattie, and my three sisters and me at 3842 Windsor Place.

In sharp contrast to the Vandeventer Place architectural grandeur, the homes on Windsor Place were modest—sometimes of the "shotgun" variety. Long and narrow. St. Louis author Tim Fox notes in his recently published book, *Where We Live: A Guide To St. Louis Communities*,

"the 'shotgun' style (was) *so named because if someone had fired a shot through the front door, the bullet would have passed straight through the living room, bedroom, kitchen and out the back door."*

Windsor Place was green, clean, and safe. Everybody knew everybody else up and down the street by first name and surname. There was an open-door policy among the neighbors, and nobody locked either front or back door. It's the gospel truth that woe be unto the youthful Windsor Place transgressor. If he or she committed an infraction down the street from his/her home, a neighbor lady was likely to chastise or spank the kid, then call his/her parent and have the punishment repeated at home.

Almost all the modest homes on the street originally built for servants had two features that provided countless hours of fun and games for the children on the long block. There was often a *trapdoor* just inside the front door. If one pulled up the spring-loaded trapdoor, there were steps leading down to the basement. Then there was a coal chute in back of every little home that provided kids with the opportunity to slide down into the basement and get their clothes and bodies black as soot.

Peddlers, purveyors, tradesmen, and "drummers" plied the streets and alleys around Willetta's and Lillie B.'s new little apartment on Windsor Place, all with their pushcarts or horse-drawn wagons. Drummers, by the way, had nothing to do with beating a drum. That's what the salesmen were called who sold this product or that as they strolled around. There was the "Watkins man" who sold the products of the Watkins Company. There were Watkins brushes, liniments, lozenges, cough drops, and the most popular line of the company's fare: Watkins extracts, vanilla and banana and almond flavored. The big bottle of vanilla flavoring gave pies and cakes a special flavor. The popular concoction shared its vanilla smell with the smell of alcohol. It had to be 25-percent alcohol. When some winos couldn't get hootch easily, they were known to tipple a little Watkins Vanilla Extract and get the same effect as drinking cheap wine.

There was a "rag picker," who collected old rags and clothing on his alley routes. He looked to all the world like he dressed himself in some of his collectings. He shouted a high-pitched nasal shrill that sounded like "Rayigggstoodaeey! Rayigggstooday! Rayyiggstooday!" It took a little bit of interpretation to know what he was crying out. Willetta soon learned that he was saying "Rags today!" She thought originally he was shouting "Yesterday!"

The alley traffic behind Windsor Place and environs included the "cutlery man." He rang a big xylophone-like gong that went "DING-DONG! DING DONG! DING DONG!" with the first syllable slightly elongated. He was there to sharpen the household knives on two big stone wheels cranked 'round and 'round by a foot pedal. Neighborhood youngsters loved to watch him work as the sparks flew from metal against stone. The smaller of the two honing wheels gave the sharpened knife blade a final polish before the attendant gave each hot knife a wipe with a rather unsanitary looking rag he whipped out of his back overall pocket. The cutlery man also sharpened axes, hatchets, and even shaving razors.

The ice man, Old Mr. Boyd, lived above his horse barn and storage shop at 3815 Bell, just up the street from our backyard. Bell, not to be confused with its extension just west of Vandeventer, West Belle, is the back street of Windsor Place to the south. Mr. Boyd, whose real name I only recently learned was Wesley W. Boyd, also sold coal. Ice in the summer; coal in the winter. He seemed to wear a constant grimace born of pain. To children of any other neighborhood, this craggy old man with the wisps of coal-soiled white hair would have appeared grotesque and menacing. But we kids in my neighborhood found him to be a gentle old soul who spoke in a wheezing whisper. He had a hunchback and walked with the upper half of his body almost parallel to the ground, obviously an occupational deformity from years and years of tossing thousands of pounds of block ice on his back with those big ice tongs, and shoveling what must have been many tons of coal into the area's residential and commercial coal sheds. In an ancient wagon pulled by an equally ancient white nag with a chronic swayed back, Old Mr. Boyd filled the ice orders by following the directions of the ice cards with their big black block letters. Customers placed these cards in their windows so the iceman would know how many pounds to haul up to the front door without having to get off the wagon. Customers wanted either 10, 25, 50 or, infrequently, 100 pounds of ice.

Old Mr. Boyd had to be in his seventies or eighties or nineties, we kids thought. Maybe even a hundred! On a blazing hot St. Louis day, just as kids had done with the ice man in Belzoni, we would beg a shard of ice from Old Mr. Boyd and pet the time-ravaged old mare. And just as in Belzoni, the sawdust had to be brushed off the ice before it could be licked to cool the tongue and body and soul. Somehow, the old, stooped ice man managed to hang onto his route and his ice and the aged white nag until the early 1950s. Willetta's young nieces and nephew, Joyce, Laura, Carol, and I got a chance to meet the ice man when we moved into a house at 3842 Vandeventer next door to the one in which Willetta and Lillie B. had lived. We moved to Windsor Place with our mother after she and my father, Van Hunter, were divorced in 1949.

There were still quaint hitching posts for horses and buggies and carriage blocks in front of every house when Willetta and Lillie B. moved into the house at 3840. Its owners, Dave and Anna Johnson, had cut what was once a single-family residence into little apartments. Dave "ran on the road." He was a Pullman porter, a prized job for black men in those days. It was a great job with a great deal of prestige. Black porters were always as impressive in their uniforms as today's airline pilots are. Pullman porters, postal workers, and teachers—in that order upward—were the three-tiered leaders in black employment in the '20s, '30s and '40s. Mrs. Johnson, the landlady, was a housewife and mother of three children, two girls and a boy.

Willetta and Lillie B. were made to feel quite at home as roomers in the Johnson family home. It was truly a communal affair at its best. The two tenants did not have to feel obliged to stay in their little bedroom. They had free use of the kitchen. They were perfectly welcome to entertain friends in the parlor with its two sofas whenever the Johnsons weren't entertaining and by pre-arrangement, of course.

Many meals were shared. Willetta, Lillie B., and Anna Johnson were all excellent cooks. It seemed that their specialties complemented each other. Willetta made great pastries and knew just the ingredients to make the best pot of greens in town: a good piece of salt pork, a big onion cut in half, okra, and a hot pepper. Lillie B. made excellent spaghetti and pot roasts and Anna made a mean pot of chili and the best soups in town. Put them all together and you had a real team of chefs with a diversity of specialties. The aunt and niece often ate with Anna and her children when Dave Johnson was traveling the rails between St. Louis and Memphis. The two boarders were thoughtful enough to let the Johnson family eat without them when the Pullman car porter was at home so the children could get Daddy caught up on everything they were doing in school and he could tell them the tales of his colorful adventures as a railroad man.

Even when Dave Johnson was at home, Sundays and holidays were special times in the Johnson household and everybody sat down for the main meal of the day or holiday together. In fact, Mr. Johnson seemed to encourage the incorporation of his two tenants in the family dining episodes. He knew he would get the creations of two additional cooks when they were included.

Lillie B. and Willetta and everybody else in the neighborhood generally did their *trading*, as grocery shopping was called in those days, at either the White Front Market or Schenberg's Market. Both were, of course, located on Vandeventer. Both operated before the word *super* was stuck on the front of the word *market*, although both stores provided everything a shopper could want in a one-stop effort.

Back then, a loaf of Wonder Bread or Taystee Bread cost fourteen cents; a dozen eggs, a quarter; a pound of butter, two bits (a quarter); a pound of the appearing-in-almost-every-dish lard, ten cents; a can of potted meat or sardines sold for a nickel, and you could buy just a packet from a box of saltines for only five cents. At White Front or Schenberg's you could buy a gallon of Pevely milk for forty-nine cents or you could sign up to have the Pevely milkman deliver milk fresh daily to your door in clean, clear bottles. Sometimes in the winter, if left out too long after the delivery, the rich cream in every bottle of milk would rise to the top, a little more yellow than the rest of the milk. The cream might actually pop the thin cardboard lid on the bottles up a bit if it froze hard enough. It became the favorite trick of kids to try to be the first to pour the milk in their glass or over their oatmeal. Some adults also vied for the first pour. If there were too many protests lodged about who was going to get the cream, somebody would shake up the bottle so everybody got a bit of the treasured cream.

As Willetta and Lillie B. shopped for groceries, very often they would sink into reverie and think how strange it was to be paying for all these produce and dairy items when almost all of them could be plucked, cut, shucked, snapped, picked, peeled, dipped, or gathered right outside their back doors on *Honey Island*. And all of it was free! Well, almost free, after the cost of seed and labor was considered. If you didn't have all these groceries outside your back door on *Honey Island*, you could just walk down the road a piece and get it from your neighbor. Free!

In the open spirit of sharing, just about anything in the Johnson icebox was communal property. But that Rounds' conscientiousness hung over the heads of Old Ned's descendants, and Lillie B. and Willetta were careful not to ever give even the appearance of being freeloaders and moochers. No stranger ever entered the door of any of the Roundses on *Honey Island*. The hosts always let a guest know how disappointed they were if they didn't have even a glass of lemonade or a cold cup of water from the well.

Life at the Johnsons was wonderful. But Lillie B. did miss Wes.

LIFE GOES ON/ WES COMES BACK
Willetta, true to her industrious and energetic nature, soon found a good job. Great Depression and NRA be damned! She started working in an apple factory at the end of north Vandeventer where the bus turned around to head back south. For this job the energetic young teenager had to dress in a hair net, a pair of Wes' slacks with the cuffs rolled up and a shirt that didn't get sold at Aunt Lillie's house sale, a heavy, dark brown apron, and some galoshes she had borrowed from one of her new co-workers. Willetta was determined to hang on to this job for awhile so she wouldn't get the reputation her Uncle Wes had for screwing-up employment.

The work was not at all back-breaking, just long hours standing on her feet. Her job was to shove six big apples into a machine that sequentially rinsed them, cored them, peeled them, and sliced them. She had never seen anything like this in Mississippi as she conjured up memories every now and again at the machine of her mother and aunts, her sisters, and herself sitting around the kitchen many Saturday afternoons on *Honey Island* rinsing, coring, peeling, and slicing apples and peaches for the delicious pies and cobblers that would be served in abundance the next day at Sunday supper. She recalled how much her grandpapa, West Rounds, loved apple pies and cobblers loaded with raisins and lots of cinnamon and nutmeg. She also remembered how he liked his apple treats served warm with a big slug of cheddar cheese or ice cream on top. Sometimes West Rounds would have cheese *and* ice cream on top. She wished she could have shipped her granddad one of those big 25-gallon tins in which the processed apples were sent out to customers. But West had died up in Chicago shortly after she had fled Mississippi for St. Louis.

As soon as the tins were loaded onto the trucks that moved in and out of the plant's docks, the apples—completely prepped for fresh-made pies—were shipped out to hotel kitchens that awaited their arrival almost daily. The biggest customers of the apple factory were the Lenox, Statler, Mayflower, and Chase hotels. No canned and preserved apples for their patrons!

The teenage apple packer learned a lot of things on the job. As the youngest of about a dozen "girls" who ranged in age from hers up to their sixties, the all-woman staff was quite willing to share everything they knew with the young girl who had just joined them. Everything! On any and every topic—profound, semi-profound, raucous, or racy—their chatterbox hearts could come up with. They richly increased her profanity quotient by at least tenfold. Every one of them could out-cuss a sailor. Their profanity was often stored up to be hurled at the little white foreman who imagined himself a local version of the infamous Simon Legree, the merciless slave master in *Uncle Tom's Cabin*. Who was he trying to fool? There was magpie malevolence just waiting for him to open his mouth. Every order he barked out was greeted with a barrage of epithets questioning the state of matrimony of his mother and father, his imagined but unfounded incestuous relationship with his mother, and his projected sexual proclivities. Yet the little guy continued to move from reading his newspapers and dozing inside his little cubicle/cage to verbally abusing the "girls" for not pushing through enough product. Then like clockwork, he'd go back and prop his feet up in his little office until it was time for him to come out and stir up the felines in their cages. The cacophony of cuss words was particularly strong from the girls when the foreman picked on the new hire for being too slow. Willetta never launched a verbal blast at the wimpish, foul-tempered foreman, though. When he yelled at her, she just smiled. She knew her new sisters could handle him quite adequately, thank you. She knew that if she really wanted to, she could join in the girls' chorus at the drop of…an apple.

Willetta learned a principle that had flowed in the veins of Rounds family members for generations: that if she was doing the best job she could—as fast and efficiently as she could—she didn't have to take verbal abuse from any foreman or employer. And she never did again…for the rest of her life.

****

A year and a half, many thousands of apples, and countless dreams of *Honey Island* had passed though Willetta's life, hands, and mind when her Aunt Lillie B. got a plaintive letter from Gary, Indiana. Wes Pfeiffer swore by all that was holy to him that he was dried out, spruced up, and ready to return to his darling Lillie B. For most of his life the most sacred thing to him had been a bottle of hootch or a mug of beer. Would she take him back? Lillie had really missed her husband and even his errant behavior. She would confide in Willetta often that there was a "hole in her heart" without Wes. She had written to him in his exile many times. Some of the relatives in Gary had kept her up to date on Wes' genuine effort to remain sober. He had done well, they reported. After eighteen months or so, Wes had earned the right for a reprieve and a pardon.

Lillie B. phoned Wes. *"Come on home, Baby. Come on home."*

They both broke into sobs they could not control. They weren't able to muster up any words.

So…they simply hung up.

Lillie asked Willetta to join her when they met Wes' bus down at the Greyhound station on a typically hot August afternoon in St. Louis. Both women had gone to church earlier that Sunday and Wes and his recovery were, no doubt, paramount in their prayers. They kept their church clothes on to meet the Greyhound bus at 4:45 that evening. As the aunt and niece watched the clock, each silently remembered watching the clock and waiting for Wes so many times before. There were flashbacks for sure, but each woman had that Rounds blood in their veins and that helped them put the bad stuff in their lives behind them and move on to a new day. There was also a strong family penchant for forgiving those who had committed trespasses against them. In most cases. And woe be unto him or her who had crossed the line beyond Rounds family forgiveness.

Wes' bus was only about five minutes late. Lillie's heart thumped, as Willetta's did, as the door of the bus opened. Wes must have either sat in the front of the bus in his excitement or he had bounded from the middle or back of the bus and knocked a few folks over to get out and back on terra St. Louis. The reunited couple hugged each other. Wes, as he had done on the occasion of bringing that first City Hall check home, picked Lillie B. up off the ground and whirled her around in a circle several times as she giggled and he closed his eyes in sheer teary joy. Willetta thought to herself that she mustn't remember the kitchen scene. She and her aunt had grown into such a sisterhood, she knew Aunt Lillie B. had to be trying to fight off thoughts of the kitchen whirl, too. Wes approached his niece with arms outstretched and a face and eyes that asked: "Do you forgive me, too?" Willetta raced into his arms and he gave her a tight hug, without the whirl that seemed to be reserved now for just his wife.

Wes looked good. He didn't seem so frail. His eyes were no longer bloodshot and he had obviously found some way to buy himself some new trousers (with razor-sharp cuffs, of course), a new shirt, sport jacket, and straw hat. Willetta carried the penitent's little bag while Wes walked between the two with a lanky arm draped over his two favorite women in the world.

The Pfeiffers and their niece found a nice two-bedroom apartment on Enright Avenue, between Sarah Street and the street that was omnipresent in Willetta's life, Vandeventer. It was a street that seemed to have some sort of umbilical attachment to young Willetta Williams. Was it attached to her? Or was she attached to it for the comfort zone it must have provided her? In many ways, Vandeventer was like a northern version of the Yazoo River in her life. Vandeventer was a lot straighter, but it, too, flowed north and south like the meandering river near her birthplace down South sometimes did.

Wes seemed to be a changed man. Nobody could quite say that he had found religion, but he was religious in his effort to stay away from the bottle. The shock of almost losing the woman he loved and who loved him seemed to have frightened him into a new life. He now took on what turned out to be the best job of his life! It was unorthodox. It was legal. Only a few people did what he did. It afforded him the opportunity to work indoors and out. It allowed him to travel around town all day long. Lillie had often analyzed that one of the reasons—just one of the reasons Wes hadn't kept any of his other jobs, was that he was a man who couldn't stay cooped up for any long stretches. But this was the perfect job for a man who had to stay on the move. What's more, this job paid twice as much as the City Hall janitor's job had paid, even if the custodian's gig only paid Wes for two weeks. The new job didn't automatically put money aside for a pension or health benefits. Wes would have to do that himself now. A real test for him.

Wes became a deliveryman for a thriving mom-and-pop catering service. A woman named Willie Edwards and her husband ran the food service out of their home in the 4300 block of Cook Avenue, near Vandeventer, of course. Wes could walk to work every day and walk home after he had checked in at the end of the day. Mrs. Edwards did most of the cooking that would be delivered to factory workers every day all over St. Louis. Wes would load up a big box of fruit-fried pies; hard-boiled eggs; collard, mustard and turnip greens; spareribs; meat loaf; fried chicken; fried buffalo fish; jack salmon or catfish on Fridays; potato salad; cornbread; and a host of cold cut and cheese sandwiches. The big, fat fruit pies were individually wrapped in waxed paper and cost ten cents apiece. The hard-boiled eggs at two cents each were boxed in the cartons they originally came in. The greens were delivered in the same kind of boxes that used to hold ice cream and now deliver Chinese food. You could get a little carton of greens for a dime, too. The meats were laid on pieces of white bread, wrapped in waxed paper and then in newspaper with the contents marked in big letters with a black crayola. They could cost twenty-five or thirty cents depending on which meat, fish, or fowl one picked. The cold-cut sandwiches were also a dime each.

After the huge box was packed tightly and Mr. Edwards had taken a meticulous inventory of what was being carried out, Wes would hoist the breakfast, lunch, or dinner victual box on his shoulder and almost run to catch the next bus so the hot food would stay hot for his customers. Wes was one of the Edwards' top salesmen. He could make a round trip on the bus and streetcar out to a factory and back for another packing quicker, it seemed, than any of the other dozen or more deliverymen on the Edwards' team. Wes had the advantage of knowing all the workers with whom he had worked before losing any of his previous jobs. They knew him and would be waiting in line for him to appear with their breakfast, lunch or dinner every day. He was such a good salesman, he was even known to sell a meal or two every day to the bus and streetcar motormen who got him around town to his regular customers.

The reformed alcoholic made twenty-cents on the dollar for all the food he peddled. And almost all his customers gave him a little tip for his delivery of great food. In a good week of work, he could bring home thirty or forty dollars. Lillie, by this time, was working as a domestic "in a private family." Willetta was still working at the apple factory. With the three steady incomes, the rent was never a problem like in the old days.

WILLETTA'S OWN APARTMENT

With the new money she managed to save, Willetta got herself her very first, all-on-her-own, all-to-herself little apartment. It was on Cook, near Vandeventer Avenue, of course.

Within a few years, her first relative/hosts in St. Louis were both dead. Lillie B. went first. Wes Pfeiffer phoned Willetta at her little apartment and told her that her aunt was very, very sick and he thought maybe she'd better go into the hospital. Willetta rushed right over. She could not help but think about how, as a little girl, she had watched her favorite aunt, Ninnie, waste away to become a miserable specimen of disfigurement and pain. Now she'd have to see the aunt who had extended a welcome mat to her when she was truly homeless and destitute, at death's door. When she got to the apartment on Enright where Wes and Lillie B. were living, Pfeiffer greeted Willetta at the door with a long and grave face. "It doesn't look too good, Honey," he told his niece. "She had a real rough night last night." Lillie B. opened her rheum-filled eyes in the darkened room, but she managed only a whispered greeting before she launched into an involuntary burst of dry coughing. The coughing featured a rattle and wheezing that did not at all sound good to Willetta. It really didn't take a medical degree to figure out that this was one sick lady.

Willetta packed up some of her aunt's personal belongings including a robe and makeup, while Uncle Wes phoned for a cab. When the taxi arrived in about fifteen minutes, Wes picked up his beloved wife just as he had carried her over the threshold at their first St. Louis home on Pine Street. This time he realized that this would be perhaps the last time he would ever carry her. Lillie B. was as limp as a dishrag, but she tried to flash a forced smile at her two most loved relatives. She could not keep her head up, and leaned on Wes' shoulder as she sat sandwiched between her husband and niece.

The cabbie, sensitive to the ailment of one of his passengers, drove to Homer Phillip's Hospital just as slowly as if he were driving in a funeral procession. The architecturally handsome hospital for black patients was more often called simply "Homer G's" or "City Number 2." The hospital was named after a prominent black attorney who helped swing a big bond issue for Mayor Henry Kiel in 1913. Phillips became a martyr in the black community after he was gunned down by an unknown assailant while he waited for a streetcar at Aubert and Delmar on the morning of June 18, 1931. Attorney Phillips, who lived in a predominantly white neighborhood, had been on his way to his office on North Jefferson, very close to Willetta's first home in St. Louis on Pine Street.

The hospital to which Lillie B. was admitted was then a magnificent new fortress of a structure dedicated in 1937. It was, at its grand opening, the largest facility in the world dedicated to the training of African American nurses and doctors. Blacks were proud to have it in their North St. Louis neighborhood. Its establishment meant that when medical services were needed in North St. Louis, its residents would not have to go all the way to South St. Louis to an ante-bellum facility known as City Number 1. That hospital was known for its filth and inefficiencies. The then-new Homer G. Phillips Hospital was a source of pride as it trained young interns to treat the full range of medical needs in general and emergency room situations in particular. The hospital, like the Rounds family prosperity in Mississippi, was to be short-lived. A mess of political squabbling, declining patient enrollment, and lack of City Hall support were blamed for the hospital's shuttering in 1979 after only forty-two years of service.

Had Homer G. Phillips Hospital not been open and had it not offered better and more modern services, Lillie B. would have most likely been taken to the old People's Hospital. It was then twelve blocks east of the Pfeiffer's house in the 2200 block of Locust. Before it moved into that facility on Locust, it was just two blocks east of the Pfeiffers on Pine Street. People's Hospital—another all-black facility—was generally for patients who had short-term illnesses. When Willetta's niece, Pearline Johnson, had an appendicitis attack in 1949 at the age of eleven she was taken to People's by a conveyance that would seem very strange to us today. Here's what happened that wintry day just two days before Christmas when Pearl got sick.

Willetta was living with her sister, Gertrude, her brother-in-law Walter, their two daughters Pearline and Evarine, and her mother, Hattie, at a house at 4202 A-West Evans, not far from Vandeventer, of course. Willetta had just observed her second decade in St. Louis and considered the city her hometown by now. Just as Ninnie and Lillie B. had been favorite aunts of a younger Willetta, Willetta was a favorite aunt of the Johnson girls. She was the favorite aunt of Lena's four children, too. Her popularity was, without a doubt, hinged on the fact that at that time she had never been married and had never had any children of her own. She was able to lavish a lot of love, attention, guidance, goodies, and convalescent care to the kiddies in the family as, between the six of them, they went through every childhood disease known to medicine and a few ailments not exactly charted in the medical books. So Pearl and Eva thought it a special treat to have their "Aunt Singie" in residence. When I first learned to speak, I started calling her "Doggie." Go figure. But "Doggie" was one of my most favorite people in the whole wide world. The name was not at all derogatory.

The eleven-year-old Pearl was just coming out of the bathroom after washing up for school that December morning. Her mother was putting out breakfast for her two daughters. Eva was nine at the time. Pearl began to cough violently. The paroxysms wracked Pearl's pre-pubescent body and she collapsed in a heap on the floor. She fell unconscious as her vermiform appendix split. Gertrude panicked. But "Mama" didn't. She carried the lifeless young girl to her bed and ran to get a cold compress for the patient's feverish forehead. Gertrude raced to the phone to call Dr. E. T. Taylor. His office was on Easton Avenue not far from the Johnson home. She implored him to rush right over. She screamed that her baby was dying. Dr. Taylor spent little time trying to console the hysterical mother, finished up quickly with the patient he was treating, and alerted his chauffeur that he would be making an emergency house call.

There was no doubt in Gertrude's mind whom she would call next. Willetta, that wonderful Florence Nightingale from *Honey Island*, of course. By this date, Willetta had found a job she didn't particularly care for, but it paid well and caused much less stress than the ever-so-brief job at the tobacco spit place or the atmospherically charged job at the apple coring/peeling plant. She was now a day nurse to an eighty-five-year-old woman whose two unmarried daughters took care of her by night. Calling them "unmarried" is the politically correct appellation today, but when recounting this story of Pearl's appendicitis attack, Willetta—well into her eighties by now—made frequent references to her two employers in the terms of the times: *old maids* and *spinsters*—no disrespect or derogation intended. In addition to providing basic care for the invalid octogenarian, Willetta, just as she had been expected to do two decades earlier when she cared for the toddler on Palm Street, was also hired to do light housekeeping, laundry, and cooking. Willetta had been at the house on Clemens Street about an hour when Gertrude's call came in.

When the telephone rang at the Clemens address, Willetta heard a hysterical Gertrude telling her she had to get home immediately! Immediately!! Then the panic-stricken Gertrude abruptly hung up on her sister. Willetta entered a more frantic state than was her general nature, and nervously searched for the work telephone numbers of her two employers. She couldn't find the numbers in her handbag. Then she remembered the sisters had taped the numbers at which they could be reached in an emergency on the refrigerator door. Willetta phoned the older sister who worked at the downtown Famous and Barr Department Store and blurted that she had a family emergency and the sister would have to come home quickly to relieve her. The woman left the department store in almost a flash, caught the next Page-Wellston bus, and was home in about half an hour. As Willetta watched the clock tick on, she had serious thoughts about abandoning her elderly ward and ultimately her job and getting to 4202 A-West Evans to find out what had caused Gertrude's laconic and hurried message of urgency. Then Willetta remembered what a bad reputation her Uncle Wes had with regard to jobs. She didn't want to be irresponsible. So she waited…and waited…and waited.

As soon as her employer turned the key in the door, Willetta gave her a quick greeting and bounded out the door to catch the Hodiamont streetcar. Willetta jumped off when the trolley arrived at Sarah Street, but waited only a few minutes for a Sarah bus to take her north to Evans. When it looked like no bus was imminent, just as she had run down Vandeventer after being repulsed by the tobacco job at L & M, she moved at a near jog north on Sarah till she came to Evans. She then headed west, out of breath, to 4202. When she opened the front door, Gertrude dropped to a kneeling position and told Willetta that her baby was dying. Entering Pearl's room, Willetta saw the grim-faced Dr. Taylor make a diagnosis and a prognosis rather quickly. Pearl's father, Walter, arrived from his job as a janitor at the Chase Hotel just in time to hear the verdict. Pearl needed to get to the hospital right away for surgery. It looked, said the physician, as if Pearl's appendix had ruptured.

In those days fifty years ago before 9-1-1 calls were an option, particularly in the black community, one did not call an ambulance. A call was made to the family's mortician. Funeral directors could get a hearse to a sick client's house much faster than a cab or ambulance. The Wade Funeral Home, not far away on Finney Avenue, had a car at the Evans address within five minutes, though it seemed longer. Mortician Granberry Wade came himself. He was a dashing and handsome and impeccably dressed young man and with Walter's help, Pearl was carried on a gurney into the hearse.

The long black car, with Granberry Wade driving, sped away towards People's Hospital. Since Willetta had already been awarded the position of Family Nurse, she alone rode with Pearl, holding the sick girl's hand all the way to the hospital. Pearl had regained consciousness by now, and managed a forced smile as her dear aunt assured her that she would be okay. Dr. Taylor followed in his chauffeur-driven Cadillac. Any unsuspecting person on the street might have thought this was a funeral procession—moving at a very fast speed.

This kind of emergency service was a hallmark of funeral homes of that era. Funeral directors also loaned families their limousines for other social functions— weddings, proms, family reunions. Their thought was obviously that if a family remembered their kindness and generosity, the right to the obsequies of family members was assured.

When Pearl's mini-procession arrived at People's Hospital, Willetta remembers how Granberry Wade and Dr. Taylor's chauffeur sprang into action. They parked their vehicles on the side of the hospital, and the stretcher on which the hearse took Pearline was shoved through a side door that led right into the operating room. It was a strange door with no steps. It was higher than the first floor and a little lower than a second floor. In the days before elevators were in every multi-story building, this entrance was referred to as a "coffin door." All early hospitals had them. Many residential mansions were also outfitted with these rather strange doors. As Willetta paced and waited for Old Doctor Taylor to emerge from surgery, she remembers that she almost fainted when the doctor exited the emergency room completely splattered in Pearl's blood. He comforted Pearline's worried aunt by assuring her that the girl would be all right, but it took Willetta quite awhile to get her heart back into a regular rhythm after seeing all that blood.

Pearl made a rather remarkable recovery. Doc Taylor had told Willetta that she would need complete bed rest for at least two weeks or so to keep from tearing her stitches. Pearl was up and around in about three days. Willetta brought her some lingerie that made her among the best-dressed patients at the hospital. That was a Rounds characteristic. One must always look one's best. The aunt had to convince the young convalescent not to try to move around so early after the surgery. The family brought Pearl's Christmas presents to her in the hospital.

I remember Old Doc Taylor when I was a young boy. He was the only doctor my grandmother would allow to see her for her rare illnesses. Doc Taylor could hardly walk. He looked like he was 117 years old as he shuffled in and out of our house on Windsor Place. I remember that he carried a big black bag and had a uniformed chauffeur who drove him around town in a big black Cadillac. I remember Doc Taylor came to see me one time when I had a bad case of the mumps. He whipped out his stethoscope and listened to my heartbeat, although I could swear that he was as deaf as could be. He checked around and asked me to cough. I'm not sure that he noticed that my grandma had smeared me with all that bloody, membranous crud from a hog jowl and wrapped up my face with cheesecloth. He said absolutely nothing about this home remedy brought up from *Honey Island*. He basically pronounced me alive and prognosticated that I would not die. Then he left. I understand that's the way the doctor operated. He made as many house calls as he had office visits. What ever would he have thought of HMOs?

To return to the Pfeiffers, Lillie B. could not afford a private room or even a semi-private room with just two patients in them, so she was put in a pneumonia ward where a young black intern soon diagnosed her case as pleurisy and pneumonia. The doctor didn't try to explain to either Willetta or Wes that pleurisy is an inflammation of the pleura—one of two serous membranes which lines the thorax and envelops the lungs. It was sufficient to their understanding that their loved one was in bad shape. Lillie B. lingered for a couple of weeks, not responding to the treatment. She got sicker and sicker, and weaker and weaker, and coughed more and more until the coughing fits rendered her almost unconscious each time.

Soon Lillie B. joined all the members of the Rounds family before her who had entered the Realm of Death. We have preferred for over a century to think that our dearly departed family member has entered the Realm of Heaven. Willetta was heartsick; Wes was devastated. Once again, as in many cases in the past, Willetta had to become a grownup. While Wes was just too devastated to deal with the good people at Wade Funeral Home, Willetta selected a dress she thought her aunt would like to be buried in and went to the funeral home on Finney Avenue—near Vandeventer—to pick out a coffin for her aunt's remains.

A couple of things happened then that did not surprise Willetta and wouldn't have surprised her Aunt Lillie B. For one thing, Wes started drinking heavily again. He didn't disappear for days at a time this time, but he often passed out on the bed he and his wife had shared and wouldn't come out of his room for days at a time. He was, after all, devoted to his wife as she had been devoted to him.

Then there was an ugly event. Lillie B. had carried a life insurance policy on herself for more than twenty years, ever since she had come to St. Louis from *Honey Island* to seek her fame and fortune, if not just a comfortable living and a good man. She had paid ten cents a week for the policy. She had not borrowed against it as many had at least tried to do during the Great Depression. She had spent all of Willetta's life savings some years before she died, but Willetta had guessed that after all her suffering and laboring on this earth, the poor woman wanted to be sure of a decent send-off to Eternity.

A month or so before she died in 1938, Lillie B. had summoned her dear niece and turned the insurance policy over to her. She then told Willetta that she felt that would be the least she could do after spending the girl's nest egg. Willetta dutifully kept up the ten-cents-per-week payments. Upon the death of her aunt she filed the claim. And it paid off, about $800. Wes knew that the policy had been turned over to Willetta on his late wife's suspicions that he just might go off on a binge and not pay the funeral home if he had been left with the policy.

On the day of the wake, when Willetta had gone by the apartment on Enright to see if her uncle were properly dressed and ready to be picked up by the funeral home, she found Wes in a mood in which she had very rarely seen him. He was in a mean spirit. He questioned his young niece about why he, the husband, had not been made the beneficiary of the policy and why Willetta hadn't turned any money over to him. In slurred speech, Wes Pfeiffer went into a fit of rage and lunged at the niece who had so often saved his paychecks from plunder, who so often had comforted his despondent wife during his frequent long absences from home, and who had helped usher him into exile in Gary.

She feared for her safety: flashbacks of John Coats and the foreman at the apple-coring factory and all the other men in her life who had not acted as the kind of gentleman her father and grandfather had been. She ducked his attempt to grab her, and then she unleashed years of pent-up anger. She bawled up her fist and decked her pathetic uncle, sending him sprawling onto the floor. She stared at the pitiful character rubbing his jaw and looking up at his niece in stunned silence. She helped him up, shoved him onto the bed, and fled the scene. The attendant from Wade's Funeral Home found Wes nursing a swollen jaw, escorted him into the black funeral home car, and took him to his wife's wake.

Willetta had realized about two hundred dollars after all the funeral expenses were paid to Wade. Somehow in her mind she justified the fact that her aunt had paid her back, with interest, for the life savings she had been denied when she needed train fare back to Mississippi to nurse her sick sister back to health. She thought about all the work she had done in the Pfeiffer household since she had arrived in St. Louis ten years before as a fourteen-year-old. She thought of all the adult responsibilities her aunt had thrown at her, robbing her of her teen years. The Rounds sense of fairness prevailed. She dropped by the Pfeiffer apartment the day after the funeral and, without coming inside the door, handed Wes a hundred dollars—half the money she had left. She was almost certain what would happen to the money.

Just a couple of years after Lillie B. passed, Wes died of what was suspected to be cirrhosis of the liver. The deaths of these two people ended a monumental chapter in Willetta's life. In the Rounds tradition, she kept on living a life of industry and family commitment. She persevered as a woman who had been denied a childhood, and who had met every challenge with tenacity and determination. A person less strong than she would have given up long ago and passed through life with no reputation of giving and sharing and loving. In a fitting tribute, several decades later, having been tested by all manner of trouble and tribulations, Willetta was unanimously awarded the position of matriarch of the Rounds descendants in St. Louis following the death of her mother and my dear grandmother, Hattie Rounds Williams Coats in 1978. My Cousin Pearl became the assistant matriarch. Willetta took the job willingly and performed our family's matriarchal responsibilities well. She had come a long way since she fled *Honey Island* in 1927.

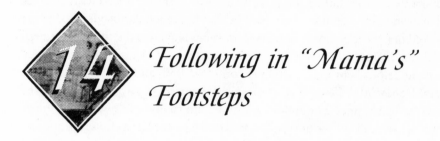 ‘Following in “Mama’s” ‘Footsteps

Taking over the reins of our large St. Louis family with all of the idiosyncrasies of the descendants of Ned and Ellen Rounds and those who married into the clan was no easy task, but Willetta’s success in holding us all together was based on the history of her predecessor.

Willetta was smart enough to look back to the year 1939—the year Hattie Coats moved to St. Louis from extremely unhappy conditions in Warner Ridge, Mississippi. She was escaping her marriage to the now infamous John Coats. He was the lecher who had forced Grandma Hattie’s middle daughter, Willetta, to flee *Honey Island*. My grandmother brought her daughters Gertrude and Lena— my mother—with her. Gertrude had married Walter Johnson, who was from a little town near *Honey Island*. Walter was an industrious man and would eventually provide a very comfortable living for himself, his wife, and their two daughters, Pearline and Evarine. He worked at Scullin Steel, and later at American Car Foundry.

The womenfolk in the Johnson family were all born on or very near *Honey Island*. When they moved to St. Louis they lived for awhile at 4202 A-West Evans, and then eventually settled in a lovely three-story brick home at 5119 Cates Avenue in a section of town that was then mostly white. When I was a young boy, I remember what a treat and what an apparently long ride it was when I caught the Hodiamont streetcar and went all the way out to my Aunt Gert and Uncle Walter’s house. I could not imagine that there were any other black folks in all of St. Louis with a house as big as the house on Cates. Three whole floors! Those in the family who are in the know, chuckle that Walter Johnson did so well here only after he "appropriated" that load of coal in Mississippi which he sold to buy his one-way train ticket to St. Louis.

Hattie Coats became the matriarch of the St. Louis Rounds descendants by unanimous consent and lived a beatified position in the family. The lives of her large and extended St. Louis clan revolved around her and her life revolved around them. She was known in the family for her Christian virtues and no-nonsense approaches to life. She spouted Biblical verse, country wisdom, and warnings about the wages of sin in her everyday conversations with all of us. As she evolved from Sister Hattie to Mother Hattie at her church and in the family, she took on the traditional elevated position started by Ned and Wes. As the venerated head of our family, she was not expected to work outside the home a single day of her life. She was totally supported, as Ned had been and Wes had been, by adoring and reverent offspring.

Hattie was born in 1881 according to the 1900 Holmes County U. S. census. Or she was born in 1886, as reported in the 1910 Yahoo County census. Or she was born in 1882, as she said when applying for her Social Security card on March 1, 1996. But we celebrated her "100th" birthday in 1976. You do the math. It will not come out quite right. The discrepancies are not at all surprising nor completely illegal. "Age" is not something one talked about or talks about with women descendants of the Rounds line. Shaving off a year or two here or there, or gently obfuscating statistical data now and again, is and has been a way of life for Rounds women for more than a century-and-a-half. Even today it is nigh unto impossible to get a Rounds woman to admit to being of a certain age.

They've always preferred that an inquisitor judge them by the way they look and act. Among the women over the age of sixty or seventy or eighty or even ninety who are descendants of Ned Rounds, the observer would have to look long and hard to find one wrinkle. Cosmetic surgery has not been, is not now, nor will it ever be on the Rounds women's agenda. Each of them will depart this earth with everything they came into the world with, unaltered and basically unblemished. The spryness of the Rounds women too is both legendary and incomparable. Hattie Coats, for example, was washing and ironing her own clothes and fixing her own meals if she wanted to into her nineties. I remember how, even when she was becoming infirm as she *approached* one hundred years of age, if one offered her assistance as she ascended or descended steps or stairs, she would flap her arms like a hen to ward off too much of a hand.

Hattie Rhoda Rounds Williams Coats neither smoked tobacco nor drank alcohol in her life (except a couple of drops of the alcohol-laced Dr. Tichenor's Antiseptic on a teaspoon of sugar from time to time). She reportedly signed a Women's Christian Temperance Union pledge against tobacco and alcohol use well before the calendar rolled around to 1900. In deference to her nineteenth century pledge, and out of respect for her position as matriarch, nobody ever drank booze in front of "Mama," as we all called her. In fact, at all the large family dinners over which she presided for decades, the menfolk have always made it a part of a humorous little ritual to sneak into the garage, backyard, basement, or attic—wherever a clandestine round of drinks could be served out of sight of the matriarch. There's no doubt in anybody's mind who has ever thought about it that she had to know what was going on with this ritual ruse. Why would so many male kinfolk disappear over a period of time in little clumps during those family get-togethers and return to the dining room or living room in even better spirits than they had left? And with regard to those little sneak-aways: it was a rite of passage for a boy to be asked to go out back with the men to have a drink out of a disposable paper cup and out of the line of sight of "Mama." It happened without the solemnity and sacredness or the preparation of, say, a bar mitzvah, but the "invitation" was almost as important to a young descendant of Old Ned Rounds as the Jewish ritual. It meant that the boy was now a man and was to be held at all other times, until the next family dinner, to a higher standard of responsibility.

Hattie Coats was the embodiment of the Jesus she worshiped so religiously at West Side Baptist Church. She was a pillar of that church and continued her membership even after the church split over the alleged infidelity of the minister. Hattie actually joined Antioch Baptist Church when she first arrived in St. Louis. She and her daughters and son-in-law would walk the relatively short distance to Antioch which was then and still is located at 4213 West North Market in the historic Ville neighborhood. After Hattie heard the Rev. Joe E. Crummie preach at the fairly new West Side Missionary Baptist Church located at 3966 Fairfax, she joined his church almost immediately. When the West Side congregation moved into a sanctuary formerly owned by a Pentecostal church at Page and Marcus, that edifice became Mother Coats' church home for the rest of her long life. It was a thriving congregation with a membership of 1,100 born-again Christians at the time of the Rev. Mr. Crummie's death on March 26, 1946.

On the first Sunday in November 1947, Hattie and her family and the West Side congregation got a new pastor when the charismatic Rev. Victor Hugo Wells accepted the call. Mother Coats and her family maintained a warm and friendly relationship with Rev. Wells. It was not at all unusual for the preacher and his wife to come to the Johnson home on Evans for some of the fried chicken and biscuits and all the other fixings which had culinary originations on *Honey Island*. Then, after twenty-two years as West Side's spiritual leader, the minister's feet of clay became apparent as rumor upon rumor began to swirl in and around the strong congregation. The rampant innuendos and whispered gossip about alleged infidelity forced Rev. Wells to step down from his post.

Grandma Hattie must certainly have had some flashbacks to John Coats, her second husband, but she neither took part in the gossip nor in a condemnation

of the preacher man. In fact, nobody dared even broach the subject around her.
The Rev. Wells stayed in touch with Mother Coats, and she was always ready to
receive him with her characteristic hospitality. Nevertheless, Hattie declined to
follow the leader to the new church he founded. The short-lived and tiny
congregation was, interestingly enough, called the *Totally Committed Baptist Church*.
It soon became evident that there were not enough members totally committed
to Rev. Wells and his message. Before too long, the few West Siders Rev. Wells
took with him trickled away from him and trickled back to the main church
when the Rev. Moses Javis accepted the call on March 21, 1971.

"Mama" practiced a certain amount of religious tolerance—but she never
quite made it completely down the road to total ecumenism. She accepted the
fact that her daughter, Lena, and Lena's four children, Carol, Laura, Joyce, and
I, had chosen to abandon the Baptist way for the Lutheran Church. But, she
would often quietly ask the four of us children when we were going to *really*
get baptized. What must she have thought as she stood in attendance at the
baptisms of her four grandkids at Holy Sacraments *Lutheran* Church on West
Belle just west of Vandeventer? What must have gone through Hattie's head when
she stood on four different occasions as her four grandchildren were *baptized?*
She must have shuddered a bit and mumbled a silent prayer as the congregation
stood around the baptismal font and the minister intoned as he sprinkled each
kid *in the name of the Father* (sprinkle a little water on the child's forehead being
careful not to get a drop on the youngster's clothes), *the Son* (sprinkle a tiny tad
more water, not much), *and the Holy Spirit* (sprinkle a modicum more holy water
and then quickly pat the kid's forehead completely dry with a fine linen cloth
handed the minister by an elder. Wouldn't want the newly-baptized to get a
cold.) *Amen.*

The Lutheran *"baptisms"* Grandma Hattie witnessed were a far cry from the
experience of total immersion she and the whole family, before my mother's
defection to Martin Luther's religion, had experienced standing waist-deep in
the cool Lake Tchula. She often but ever so diplomatically told us *sprinkled* kids
that she would *"pray that you will one day see the light of salvation and will go down
and under the waters of redemption in Jesus' name."* Then she would add the blessed
assurance that *"Jesus loves you (anyway), and so do I."*

As to my grandmother's cooking talents—she was revered in life and after
her passing for her really *greasing* in the kitchen. Just as people become renowned
for such simple things as their coffee or their martinis, "Mama" developed a
reputation for her superlative lemonade. How could something as simple as
lemonade be unusually good? Well, it was not unusual for her to use a dozen
lemons and at least two cups of sugar in the pitchers of lemonade she turned
out. During all of the summer months, any guest who passed over her threshold
was rewarded for the visit with a glass of that incredible ice-cold concoction.

Even deliverymen who rang the doorbell were offered a glass to cool them off before they continued their rounds. In fact, "Mama" took it as a real insult if a visitor of any kind did not partake of either something to eat or at least something to drink. That's the way it was on *Honey Island*, and that's the way it would be in St. Louis or anywhere else. The overly generous Rounds hospitality lived on.

We all used to say Mama cooked like she was still on the farm. We dared not mention the words "diet" or "fasting" around her. And never—no never—would we tell her that we were sorry, but we'd already eaten before coming over to visit her. That got you at minimum a glass of lemonade and a piece of her pound cake. She produced more caloric but delicious meals per day than many of today's health-conscious cooks turn out in a week. A piece of her pound cake was guaranteed to put on pounds around the waist and other body parts where fat was not flattering. She might have referred to herself as *"stout,"* which is, once again, that appellation commonly used among Ned Rounds' descendants to imply that one was just a few pounds shy of being fat.

Hattie Coats had some very cute and very quaint sayings she used to punctuate conversation. You could run into the room where she was always busy at some chore and yell: *"Mama, I just saw a man with a big ole monkey walking right down the middle of the street!"* Her expression of disbelief, more often than not, was *"Well, I know better!"* With that certain lilt she gave the expression it came out more like *"Well, Ina beddah."* Someone might tell her something that bordered on gossip like *"Mama, guess what? Suzie and Billy are breaking up after all these years!"* Since she didn't tolerate trashy gossip, she'd respond, *"Honey, hush."* But it wasn't said too harshly or as a real command. In fact, the way she said *"Honey, hush,"* kinda invited a little more information.

When she didn't understand exactly what you had said, she would say, *"Beg podd'n."* It took me a while to realize that she was saying *"Beg your pardon."* She'd say it with increased frequency when her ears were approaching their ninetieth year of listening to all manner of things.

Her version of "you'd better get your act together" was *"Mind out, now, mind out!"* Failure to heed that warning could result in swift punishment.

The quaintest expression "Mama" uttered often was her order to hurry up. It came out *"May case, boy, may case!"* For far too many years of my childhood I tried to figure that one out. What's a "may case," for goodness' sakes? Then one day it dawned on me. She was saying *"Make haste, boy, make haste!"* That just had to be an expression right out of the 1800s, 1700s, or even further back than that. In fact, the Psalmist David did implore God *"Make haste to help me, O Lord."* Hattie was probably speaking right out of the Bible as her parents had spoken to her and their parents had spoken to them.

She was always available to listen to every request for her ears and her incredible wisdom. She could be counted on to give wise counsel from her heart. She mediated little family disputes and always got the feuding parties to kiss—or at least, shake hands—and make up. She never tolerated one family member putting down another. She'd often take the case of the underdog to her personal court of appeals. We'd often say that even though she hated Beelzebub more than any Christian on earth, if anybody said anything bad about the Devil himself, she'd say something like *"Well you know, Honey, maybe Old Satan had a rough time of it as a boy."*

When my mother and father were divorced, "Mama" packed up her things and left the Johnson's house on Evans and came to live with my mother and sisters and me on Windsor Place. The shotgun duplex was owned by the Mitchell Family. Mrs. Mitchell was a pleasant, round woman with a particular treasure of gold showing in her dental work. Mr. Mitchell was a laborer whom it appeared was always wearing bib overalls. The Mitchells lived on the second floor with their children, some of whom were the ages of my sisters and me. I shall always remember that Mr. Mitchell was the apparent leader of a gospel singing group which met for prayer and song once a week—I believe on Thursday nights. One did not have to crane one's ear on the first floor to hear the smooth, harmonious, and syncopated rhythms of the choraliers who sang of crossing over the River Jordan and clinging to the Rock of Ages and riding the chariot on the golden streets of Heaven. One day, somewhere, Brother Mitchell received the Call from God to go preach Christ. Despite his minimal education and, no doubt, with his warming smile and some coaching instead of theological course, he became the head pastor of one of the biggest Baptist churches in St. Louis. As head of that huge flock, Rev. Mitchell exchanged his bib overalls for expensive tailored suits. Many speculated that it was his second wife—not Ethel—who propelled him into ecclesiastical prominence.

Grandma graciously made the move to Windsor Place so she could take care of us kids and so my mother could go to work every day and bring home the bacon my grandmother would use in many dishes. By making the move into our little house, Grandmama continued her lifelong tradition of never working outside the house. How strange it will seem to future Rounds descendants that neither Ned nor Wes nor Hattie ever did a day's work for any appreciable time for anybody else in their entire lifetimes. "Mama" did take in a little laundry when she suffered financial neglect while serving as Mrs. John Coats in Warner Ridge, but that still didn't take her outside her home.

How wonderful it was and how blessed we Hunter kids were that "Mama" was there to make breakfast every day, make sure we kids were dressed neatly, and see us off to school at Cole Elementary. There must have been some variety in the breakfast meal, but it seems in retrospect that we ate more than the national average amount of oatmeal. We ate so much oatmeal under her household administration, one would have thought we'd all eventually look like that Quaker guy in the black hat on the front of the distinctive cylindrical box. We must have had oatmeal every single morning of our young lives—summer, spring, winter, and fall. We almost never had cold cereal. No corn flakes nor corn pops nor brans of any sort. We must have been a vital support group for the company that made Quaker Oats. Those were the days when oatmeal seemingly had to boil for at least a couple of hours before it was ready to serve. I can still hear the "glop-glop-glop" of that oatmeal boiling as she stirred it in the pot ever so carefully and ever so often. Oatmeal rain or shine. Enough in our lifetime to tuckpoint several houses.

When we raced home for lunch every day, "Mama" always had our lunches ready as we listened to "Rex Davis and the News" on KMOX Radio. Then we listened as we ate lunch to bits of the popular radio soaps of the day, *"Our Gal, Sunday"* and *"The Romance of Helen Trent,"* two programs my grandma never missed. I remember how puzzled and amused she was that on *"Our Gal, Sunday"* they wrote one of the regular guys out of the program by sending him out to the garden to get some flowers. He never came back in from the garden! Ever.

"Mama" was so fond of KMOX newsman Rex Davis that I soon became a fan of his, too. I came to like and respect his work so much that, as president of my senior class at Harris Teachers College—now Harris-Stowe State College—I invited Davis to be the guest speaker at our class graduation ceremony in August 1965. I was thrilled that Davis accepted. But it was with one condition. He wanted it to be crystal clear that he himself was not a college graduate. I was particularly moved that here was a man who was the most respected radio newsman in St. Louis. And he didn't have a college sheepskin. We were honored to have him and he gave a great speech. "Mama" beamed when she got to meet and shake the hand of the man who had brought her the news on radio every single weekday since she had come to St. Louis. And Davis seemed just as interested in meeting my grandma.

But, I've gotten ahead of myself again. Back when I was a schoolboy at Richard Cole Elementary School, my sisters and I got out of school at 3:15 PM and were expected to check in with "Mama" by 3:20…at the latest. We had chores to do before we were allowed to go out to play. That was the beauty of having a neighborhood school less than five minutes' walk from home. I've often wondered how changed our lives would have been if we had had to get up an hour earlier each day to catch a bus to go way out to the Parkway District or some other faraway school district to achieve racial integration and had gotten home after 5:30 each day. What would "Mama" have thought about that plan? What would have happened to those chores and the hour or so of daylight we could have playing with our chums?

I was in charge of a couple of things for my daily chores. I was responsible for keeping all the wastebaskets in the house empty. God, it seems that no wastebasket ever got near the "full" line in our first-floor flat in Elmer and Ethel Mitchell's house on Windsor Place. While my sisters were washing and drying dishes and putting them away, I was kept more than busy keeping those wastebaskets completely empty. That was "Mama's" executive order, and I knew I'd better not break it. I'd get really peeved with my sisters for throwing any bit of trash in my freshly-emptied wastebaskets. But, heck, what were wastepaper baskets for? Wastepaper, of course.

Every Saturday afternoon I was expected to sweep, mop, and wax the linoleum floor in our kitchen. After the wax dried and Mama had inspected the job, I was trained to place newspaper down on the clean floor where the newspaper often stayed until I repeated the sweeping, mopping, and waxing the following Saturday. Unless we had company. The newspaper would come up until the guest left.

"Mama" made sure all four of us kids knew the right way and the wrong way to sweep. I didn't realize then, but certainly do know now, that there is a right way and a wrong way to sweep. First of all, one should never sweep anything under a rug to get rid of it quickly. If one is right-handed, one should hold the broom with the right hand firmly gripping the top of the broom and the left hand taking the subdominant role at a comfortable middle of the broom. The converse is appropriate for lefties. One should sweep away from oneself and never towards oneself. One should never sweep oneself into a corner and have to step over the dirt pile. If there were any line cracks in the linoleum or other flooring, that took strokes with the side of the broom along the crack. Most of all, one must never let the broom touch one's feet or the feet of anybody else in the room. It was felt that the one whose feet were touched would be going to jail soon or would have some kind of unspecified bad luck coming up. A quick antidote to the jail term could be effected by spitting on the broom. That ridiculous superstition was straight from *Honey Island*.

In addition to my house chores, I started a job at age nine working with my chum Michael Jones cleaning Old Mrs. Turner's house down the street on Windsor Place from stem to stern. She paid us each fifty cents for three hours work. Michael got fed up with the tough cleaning job and quit. But my mother and grandmother would not let me throw in my cleaning towel. So at the age of nine, I cleaned the entire house. The penurious Mrs. Turner raised my salary to seventy-five cents.

Later, when I was eleven, I quit working for Mrs. Turner and started at Teasley's drugstore on West Belle and Vandeventer, dusting shelves and stacking empty soda bottles. The most horrible part of this job was that I had to stack the soda bottles in the basement of the drugstore where every Saturday I saw the biggest sewer rats you can imagine. I still have nightmares about those surly rats unto this day! The best part about the drugstore job is that I made a buck and a half for three hours, twice as much as my housecleaning gig.

"Mama" expected all responses from kids, and younger adults, too, to be "*Yes, ma'am*" and "*No, ma'am*" or "*No, sir*" or "*Yes, sir.*" No adult was ever addressed by a first name by anyone subordinate in age. Now that I remember it, most women referred to their husbands by their last names for some reason. That practice came from *Honey Island*, too.

Punishment for breaking the house rules or the Golden Rule were meted out swiftly by "Mama," the Chief Justice of our home's Supreme Court. In fact, every infraction got my three sisters and me a formal arraignment at which we had to confess our sin aloud and acknowledge that we deserved the Court's punishment.

"*Julius! Did you push your sister outta that chair?*"

"*Yes, ma'am.*"

"*Do you think that was right?*"

"*No, ma'am.*"

"*Are you sorry you did it?*"

"*Yes, ma'am.*

"*You gonna do that ever again?*"

"*No, ma'am.*"

"*So what do you say to your sister?*"

"*I'm sorry.*"

"*I don't think she heard you.*"

"*I'm **sorry!***"

"*What do you think you deserve for being mean to your sister?*"

"*I have to go outside and get you a switch.*"

"*Get me a switch for what?*"

"*To give me a…a…whuppin'.*"

"*Well, make haste and get me a switch. A good-sized one.*"

"*Yes, ma'am.*"

The trial was over; the sentence levied. As I stomped out to the backyard stifling tears, it would seem that I could always catch a glimpse of the abused sibling victim with her hand over her mouth stifling a giggle. That was almost always the worst part of the whole proceeding—the victim and her *amici curiae*, the friends of the court—the other sniveling little snitches who turned me in.

There was always one part of the punishment that was as certain as my hide getting tanned with a switch from the peach tree out in the backyard on Windsor Place. The first couple of switches were never going to please The Executioner. She'd reject the first couple of peach tree specimens out of hand. "*Not big enough,*" she'd say, sometimes without even examining the thing. I now realize that was all part of the psychological game of dramatizing the scene and making it damned difficult to commit the same crime in the same way ever again. It was the same drill my mother and aunts and all the *Honey Island Oldtimers* remember that they had gone through under *"Mizz* Coats" at the *Panther Burn School*. The fact that there were never any real noticeable welts suggests that the bark was louder than the bite into the flesh.

When I reached the age of twenty-one and announced I was going to move out of town, out of the family nest, and up to the Big City—Chicago—some of the members of my immediate family and the folks around my life wondered how a young man who had never lived away from home would fare in such a Big City. But Hattie Coats never doubted that her grandson could make it as the first black copywriter at Foote Cone & Belding advertising agency in the Windy City. While my mother cried in distress, my grandma would sit down with me and offer me some sound and memorable advice. She didn't think Chicago was such a bad and distant place. Lots of Rounds kinfolk were living comfortably in Chicago, she'd tell me.

"First of all, I want my grandson to look real nice up there in Chicago. I want you to find the money to buy yourself three nice suits. You gotta look nice to feel nice. And when you feel nice you can do your best work. And if one of the suits gets rained on or something, you still got two more suits to make it for a couple of days while you get the ruined one cleaned and pressed.

"Then I want you to remember: 'Make a dime, save a nickel.' Got that? 'Make a dime, save a nickel.' Then, Son, I want you to be nice to the people up there. Even if they're aren't so nice to you sometimes. But just remember 'It takes a friend to be a friend.' Got that?

"Find yourself a church. You always been a church-goin' boy. And you gonna need God. And let me tell you, Honey. God is sometimes hard to find in big cities like Chicago. He don't like to come into towns like that often.

"Then, I don't want you to get beholdin' to anybody. Don't get caught up borrowing money from anybody so's you owe anybody a dime. You can't sleep well at night when you owe people anything. No loans! Now I already showed you how to wash and iron and sew your own clothes. 'Cause you never know what kinda woman you might meet up there and maybe marry up there.

"And you may need to lean on somebody's shoulder sometime or another, I reckon. But don't lean too long or you might freeze in the position of leanin.' And remember, Son, if you ever need a helpin' hand, try the one at the end of your own arm first.

"I know you gonna make it just fine up there, Son. And make your ole granny proud."

She gave me a big, strong hug after her loving marching orders. With the hug came her well-known slaps on the back which, if they had come from anybody else at any other time, would have hurt.

Wow! Just what I needed to hear. Faith in me. Confidence in my abilities. Hope for the uncertain future. Basic advice I could both understand and appreciate. Her wise words will ring in my ears forever. At every graduation speech I have given to kids over the last thirty years and every time I get to talk with young people anywhere, I've passed on "Mama's" basic message to me. My own daughters certainly have heard these words enough. Those words of Hattie Coats are words to live and grow by.

AROUND A ROUNDS SUPPER TABLE IN ST. LOUIS

The frequent family suppers "Mama" presided over were lavish affairs with a cornucopia of dishes prepared by the women who had enjoyed or at least heard about how big and abundant the suppers were on *Honey Island.* Our family dinners were the embodiment of the best of southern cooking. Not a soul ever thought of the dishes served as *soul* food, but the meals thrilled the soul. By the standards of many families, our family dinners were overdone. Not in the sense that they were overcooked. They were overly plentiful! Seven or eight times a year—not counting Thanksgiving and Christmas—we gathered, usually on short notice, to come on over to so-in-so's house for dinner. "Dinner," not "Supper." An acquiescence to the Rounds descendants' new northern vocabularies. Our big dinners were not just on Sundays after church. They could fall on any night of the week. An excuse was always facetiously given for the gathering, and caused a chuckle from all the invitees. Excuses like *"Can y'all come on over for dinner on Wednesday night? I got this turkey that's been taking up too much room in my freezer."* Or *"Honey, would you believe we just won this big ole ham in the church raffle and there's no way just the two of us can eat this thing, so y'all come on over for dinner tomorrow night."* Or *"So-and-So gave us a whole mess of catfish and buffalo fish and it's enough to feed an army, so we're gonna have a big fish fry Saturday evening and we need y'all to come over and put away some of this fish. About, say, seven o'clock?"*

The proper and expected response to these invitations was just four words: *"What can we bring?"* Then to deny the sheer spontaneity of the invitation, the caller would say without missing a beat *"Girl, your* (fill in the blank here) *macaroni and cheese / cornbread / fruit salad / greens / peach cobbler / pecan pie / spaghetti / fried green tomatoes / cloverleaf rolls / German chocolate cake / sweet potato pie / three-bean salad, etc., etc., etc., is so good. Just bring that. I've got everything else covered."*

Sometimes the inviter would say: *"Just bring yourselves and a good appetite."* A good appetite never went unfulfilled around our family's table. Only thing that could and always would go wrong is one family unit arriving with a certain key side dish after we had all started eating. Then there was the inevitable dish of one kind or another that would always be discovered in the refrigerator after the last family member turned in his / her fork.

While I always looked forward to the warm hospitality at the host house which was the site of most of the dinners—the home of my Aunt Gert and Uncle Walter on Cates Avenue—there was one, maybe two, aspects of the dinner visits I looked on with a small degree of dread and eventual loathing. From the time I was seven or eight years old, Uncle Walter for some reason felt compelled to take me into the kitchen to give me a private preview showing of his

Thanksgiving and Christmas special delicacies. He'd find me early on as the family guests were arriving and clap his arm around my shoulder. *"Son, got somethin' that's really good eatin' to show you in the kitchen."*

– "Oh, no," I'd think to myself. *"Not again. Not another one of those things...those road kill critters."*

Then he'd pull/push me over to the kitchen range, pull out a couple of potholders from the cabinet drawer next to the stove, and—here it was again. *"Aaaaaargh!"* I'd think to myself. Then a proud Uncle Walter would open the oven door and there *it* would be. A big ugly, skinned rodent, belly-up, with head and four denuded paws. And its teeth were still intact and shut tight in kind of a grimace. The critter would be at least a foot-and-a-half long—longer if the prehensile tail, still intact, were included in the measurement. This "road kill," as I would consider it, was enshrouded, or *enshrined*, as Uncle Walter would have seen it, variously in candied sweet potatoes or Irish potatoes, carrots and onions. On some rare occasions I have seen these things dragged in their pans or Pyrex dishes from Uncle Walter's oven with cornbread stuffing packed around them like a child in the sand. Zoologists would know the *"good eatin'"* as either a deceased member of the *Didelphis virginiana* family or *Procyon lotor* group. The former was called a 'possum (opossum); the latter was more commonly known as a raccoon (or just 'coon). In the Mississippi Delta a good "coon dog" could chase either of these creature up a tree and wait, barking frantically, for the hunter to get within shooting range to bring the catch down for cookin' and eventual *"good eatin'."*

I understand it to be the habit of the 'possum to roll over on its back and play dead if caught by surprise on the ground. Just like the puff adder of *Honey Island* and other places. This act was to keep away predators who do not eat things they have not personally and freshly killed and which may have been dead (and thus spoiled) for awhile. After learning about the ability of the 'possum to feign death, I have wondered ever since how many of the 'possums that ended up in Uncle Walter's oven had "played 'possum" just before being hauled in by a hound dog or a hunter who wouldn't be fooled by poor thespianism. I do know that Uncle Walter didn't have to go into any woods around Cates Avenue as he had trudged through the piney woods of the Mississippi Delta to haul in his prey. A big grocery store on Delmar and Goodfellow would post big crudely-letters signs frequently announcing to the passing world **"WE HAVE COONS"** or **"WE HAVE POSSUMS."** And the skinned critters, some of them seeming to be two feet long without measuring their tail, would be hung upside down by their tails on a clothes line in front of the store. Didn't they have to be refrigerated? Obviously not. The 'possums hung in *rigor mortis* on that clothesline in front of the store on Delmar just as they had hung by their tails during life to catch a few winks before possibly catching a few buckshot.

The first few times Uncle Walter had showed me his culinary treasure, I had averted my eyes in total disgust and fear. After all, I had seen big rodents scampering around in the alleys behind our houses that would have looked just like that had they been skinned, packed in potatoes, and cooked. I think my uncle liked to see that reaction from me. In subsequent years, I tried bravely to stare right back at the critters and even mustered up a feigned appreciation for his dishes. That act only brought his offer of fixing me up a little plate before the full dinner was served, so I stopped that mock praise.

If the sheer appearance of the 'possums and 'coons weren't repulsive enough, Uncle Walter had to throw in such details as telling me how much he liked the gristly part around the teeth. The ladyfolk never, no never, ate 'possum and sweet potatoes or 'coon and *taters*. But all the men in the family, especially if they had hailed originally from Mississippi or other parts of the South, bellied up to the table and picked the road kills' carcasses clean, often sucking loudly on those gristly parts to the disgust of young children and some of the women who knew what was being chewed on.

Many years later, sparked by many hours of watching my grandmother cook, I looked, out of sheer curiosity, in such venerated cookbooks as Rombauer and Becker's *Joy of Cooking* and, lo, and behold! There are recipes and cooking techniques for both raccoons and opossums! Included are some cautions that I am positive Uncle Walter never regarded. Among the cooking suggestions:

1. *"Small game should be dressed as soon as possible."* (What about those rodents hanging from the clothesline at that store on Delmar?)

2. *" Never handle any wild meat without using gloves because of the danger of tularemia infection."* (Although Uncle Walter was a meticulously clean cook aware of some basic sanitation rules, I don't think he ever even owned a pair of plastic gloves!) (And what the hell is **tularemia** anyway?, he might have asked *Rombauer and Becker.*) (Medical books scream out to us that the tularemia a chef can catch from just touching a wild animal with the disease is a sentence of two or three weeks in bed with a high fever!)(And don't tell me, Uncle Walter, or anybody else who fancies this delicacy that *baking the damned thing at high heat for more than an hour kills anything!!!)* (EXCEPT MY APPETITE!!!!)

Then the *Joy of Cooking* further disgusts the squeamish, of which I am chief, that *"Older animals should be cooked longer at higher temperatures."* (How does one know how old a damned 'possum or raccoon is????) (I've heard the expression "Ain't seen you in a 'coon's age. But how old is that???) The dubious *Joy of Cooking* further advises us of something that Uncle Walter obviously knew and that is: *"Some of the most delicious game sauces use blood as a thickener. To trap and preserve the blood, see page 810. To incorporate it into a sauce, see page 339."* The authors could have added "To find out why you would want to eat such unkosher crud, see a 'shrink'."

Then Rombauer and Becker advise: *"Small game may be substituted in most recipes calling for chicken."* Hey, Ms. Rombauer and Ms. Becker, I'm not all that crazy about **chicken** anymore!

Until I perused the so-called *"Joy of Cooking,"* I did not know how much work Uncle Walter had to do, both in Mississippi and on Cates to prepare the 'coon, in particular. The thing had to be skinned (unless the store did it for you). The 'coon's glands in the small of the back and on either side of the spine (to keep from poisoning the diner after really stinking up the house first) and the fat *inside and out* must be removed. The 'coon had to then be soaked in a solution of salt water and baking soda overnight. Next the 'coon had to be blanched in boiling water in an uncovered pot for about five minutes. (Speaking of blanching, I just might be able to pull off a blanch, despite my skin color right about now.) The blanching water then had to be poured off and new cold water added to the pot in which the 'coon was now cooked for about fifteen minutes. Then this real-life relative of the adorable "Rocky Raccoon" had to be stuffed with a sweet potato and apple dressing, and baked covered in a pre-heated 350-degree oven for forty-five minutes. But Uncle Walter, sans Rombauer and Becker, wasn't through yet! He had to take the lid off and continue to bake the thing for fifteen more minutes. Now, don't tell me that God wanted a young boy to be terrorized by this dish, and don't tell me that God wanted us to eat 'coon. Adam and Eve weren't even issued pans in the Garden of Eden. Cavemen surely didn't know about skinning an animal, yanking out its offensive glands, removing the fat *inside and out*, soaking the kill in salt water and baking soda in a refrigerator overnight, parboiling something that was killed the day before, baking the dish covered, and subsequently uncovered, for specific periods of time. I'm sorry, Uncle Walter, even though I hope you have secured some cooking responsibilities in Heaven by now. I, to this day, don't think we're supposed to eat stuff that so resembles an alley rat. And, who was the first person in history to decide that a sweet potato and apple stuffing was appropriate for these rodents?

Thank God there were lots of other things to eat at these big family dinners. I shudder to think what fate had befallen the turkey, duck, and the animals whose hams we ate. At least these dishes looked a lot less offensive and the diner across the table didn't have to see the gristly part around the teeth of any of these preparations being sucked on. 'Possum and 'coon. Two recommendations for vegetarianism, for sure.

The second kind of encounter I always tried to avoid while in the private company of dear old Uncle Walter was his rendition of the *"birds and bees"* story. With his telling of it, it might as well have been the *"'coons and 'possums"* story. I suppose he felt he had to act *in locus parentis*, since I didn't have a father in my life for almost all of it. The details were unintentionally X-rated and not to be presented in a G-rated text like this. But my late uncle's instructive lessons were as terrifying to the pre-pubescent me as the road kill dishes were during that same period of my life. His intentions were good, though—I guess.

At the family dinners, just as there was the rite of passage for the boys to be invited to sneak a drink with the menfolk, the boys as well as the girls knew they had reached at least quasi-grownup status when they were invited to sit at the adult table and eat with the big people instead of being relegated to one of the children's card tables in the basement or other outposts of the host house. Out of sight, out of earshot, was out of mind for the parents who had amply prepared the little smidgens and dabs of this and that for the kiddies and then left the children to their own devices. Devices like food fights!

There was a very strict pecking and serving order at all the family dinners. Mothers of young children fixed plates for their children first. These tots would be instructed to eat all the food on their plates—veggies, in particular. They were not to play with their food, and they were not to get up from their little tables until they were finished and properly excused. Then the youngsters who were approaching and who had just passed puberty loaded up their plates next and retreated to some teen nook of the house so they wouldn't be identified with the younger kids. And so that they could talk about stuff that adolescents talk about. Then "Mama," who always sat at the head of whatever dining table was longest, was served by any number of family waiters and waitresses.

Next in line were the menfolk who never, ever, when I was a kid, fixed their own plates under any circumstance. They were served by their wives or girlfriends. If the person they usually depended on to serve up their dinner was for some reason absent, a surrogate woman—a sister-in-law, an aunt, a daughter—heaped victuals of every course on the plate. The women who were the auxiliary preparers fixed up their plates next. Finally the hostess and her female helpers repaired to the kitchen where they who had nibbled on everything that was cooked that day "rounded out" their meals while they ladled on or dished out sweet and juicy gossip that would not be tolerated in "Mama's" presence. Then everybody came into the main dining room to hold hands in a big circle, bow heads, close eyes, and await "Mama's" exhortation. She prayed:

"Gracious God, we thank you for this food which we are prepared to receive. We ask you to bless those whose hands have prepared this meal, and bless those who could not be with us tonight to share the bounty of your most generous hand. Bless those who will go hungry tonight. And bless this food, O Heavenly Father to the good of our bodies and the service of thy kingdom. In Jesus' name we pray. Amen."

Everybody echoed in chorus: *"Amen!"* There would be many wet eyes at the end of the blessing and the mood would be solemn until Uncle Mose Perkins, Willetta's husband, would ritualistically add a postscript:

"Jesus wept. Moses crept. The Devil fell down the back doorstep."

To which everybody would say, *"Aw, Mose...you don't have to do that every time.*

That's not funny, Mose." As his wife, Willetta would give him a not-too-subtle dirty look each time while she shook her head in disgust, Moses Perkins would feign embarrassment and chuckle as he sat down with the other men to decimate the plate that Willetta had "fixed" for him. "Fix" was always the operative word when one spoke of food and a plate around my family.

The practice of the women "fixing" plates for their men, that tradition which had, without a doubt, started at the table of Ned Rounds on *Honey Island,* began to disappear around the time the Women's Liberation Movement began to sweep the nation in the late '60s. A few new-to-the-family independent women began fixing their own plates and sitting down. Their men began to catch on fast, if not reluctantly. That act of feminine defiance usually got initial responses of incredulity like *"Hey, Baby, you're not going to fix my plate?"* To which there were higher-pitched responses like *"Honey, you can fix your own plate, can't you? You're not cripple or anything, are you?"* To this day, all the men in the family get off their duffs and fill their own plates. Or they don't eat. And they always do.

After all those family dinners, and while the men slipped out for a not-so-secret drink, in the homes where there was a piano, I was always asked to play a "chune." Then Uncle Walter, a large man who always wore suspenders over his considerable, well-fed girth—would always request that I accompany him for his stentorian bellowing of what seemed like forty-three verses and choruses of *"Take My Hand, Precious Lord."* Just as I would prepare to give the big ending at *"Take my hand, Precious Lord...lead me on,"* this off-key basso profundo would pipe up—or groan up—a verse that nobody but he and God had ever heard. With words patch-quilted from any and all of the preceding verses and some to follow, Uncle Walter bayed, howled and made up lines that seldom if ever rhymed. If Frank Sinatra achieved fame by improvising *"Dooby-dooby doo..."* when he once forgot the words to *Strangers in the Night,* Uncle Walter, this *stout* and steadfast crooner, beat Sinatra out by decades when it came to the art of improvisational caterwauling. After he ran out of words in the English language in his imploring God to take his hand, his audience always gave him a respectable hand. Wiping the torrent of perspiration from his big round face with a big white handkerchief he always kept in his back pocket, he'd acknowledge the applause and plop down in a chair where he could be found snoring within five minutes of his unsolicited vocalist performances.

"Mama's" favorite hymn was *"Softly and Tenderly Jesus Is Calling"* and I was always moved to tears, as everybody else was, that this grand saint whose health was beginning to fail her after nine decades of vibrant life could muster up the strongest alto voice imaginable when she sang in a melodious lilt:

> *"Softly and tenderly Jesus is calling...*
> *Calling for you and for me...*
> *See on the portals He's waiting and watching*

Watching for you and for me."
Everybody would join in, interrupting their chatting and chores in distant
parts of the host house as if drawn by a powerful magnet to sing the chorus in a
number of harmonic configurations:

"Come home...come home...
Ye who are weary come home...
Earnestly, tenderly Jesus is calling...
Calling, 'O sinner...come home."

Then "Mama" would close her eyes and tilt her head back as if to call forth
the text of the hymn from her pew at Jones Chapel as many as seventy or eighty
years before this St. Louis dinner rendition.

"Why should we tarry when Jesus is pleading?
Pleading for you and for me.
Why should we linger and heed not His mercies?
Mercies for you and for me."

The chorus would swell as the number of singers would enter the ensemble
with the chorus. And then, verse three:

"Time is now fleeting, the moments are passing
Passing from you and from me.
Shadows are gathering; death-beds are coming,
Coming for you and for me."

This is where the back-up chorus came unglued. There were thoughts swirling
in the room that "Mama" would not be with us much longer. After all, death-
beds are coming. Then there was the chorus for the third time, as powerful as
ever. The fourth and last verse was coming:

"O for the wonderful love He has promised,
Promised for you and for me.
Tho' we have sinned He has mercy and pardon
Pardon for you and for me."

There was almost no need for any of us—piano accompanist in particular—
to even try to sing the final chorus. We were all simply wiped out before we hit
that final chorus. Tears flowed all the way around, except from Hattie Rhoda
Rounds Williams Coats. At the end of the hymn, she just made a fraction of a
second's grimace that dissolved into a warm little smile. We could only wonder
if there were some deep, dark memories attached to each verse—no, to each
word—of that hymn. I couldn't help trying to guess how many times "Mama"
had sung her favorite hymn. I calculated once that if she had sung it just ten
times a year at church, at home and in the fields, from the time she was seven
until her ninetieth birthday, she easily could have crooned *"Softly and Tenderly"*
more than 800 times! It is a small irony that hymnist Will L. Thompson (1849-

1909) composed the venerable piece just one year before Hattie was born, so that would have allowed Hattie Coats to sing *"Softly and Tenderly"* at least many hundreds of times from her pre-twentieth century renditions until her death three-quarters of the way to the next century.

Whew! Wow! There could be no more moving experience for all of us who loved and cherished and revered this saint among us; this venerable Christian soul who blessed us all by her very presence in the midst of our lives. And just think, you could combine all the ages of the kids present—including the youngsters who didn't want to be counted with the kids—and you would still not have the number of years since Hattie Coats had been singing her favorite hymn. After she sang, we all felt as if we had just gone to a five-minute church service that refilled any emptinesses we felt. We were family. Ned Rounds must have surely looked down on these gatherings and smiled with pride for all that he had created.

In her declining years, her daughters, especially Willetta with whom she spent her last years, took the excellent care of "Mama" they always had. She suffered a series of debilitating strokes in the last couple years of her exemplary life. All of her children, grandchildren, and great-grandchildren looked forward to the hours they could spend with this remarkable lady. We'd sit in the dark with her as her eyesight began to disappear with age, and we'd all hold her hand as if to hold onto her longer than her beloved Maker intended for her to stay with us. I was happy that she got to see the grandson she had guided through so many years get a job on television. Her spirit would always come alive, I'm told, even in her weaker, fading weeks, when she saw her grandson on the news. She'd wave a hankie at the set and say *"Hi, Honey!"* and blow kisses to the TV screen. That was my greatest reward.

While I was in Rome in 1978 covering the second death of a pope in eight weeks and sending back regular TV satellite reports to the Channel 4 viewers, my beloved grandmother slipped away to join the family and friends who had preceded her in death decades before. I have always wished I could have had just a few more words with her before she passed. But, how much more could she give me? My cup runneth over with her gifts of wisdom. Each of the St. Louis Rounds descendants, and those in Chicago and Detroit and others who knew her, feel equally touched. We all have pictures of her prominently displayed in our homes. I have two in my house. As I sat with Willetta in her kitchen just the other day to reminisce about life on *Honey Island* and since *Honey Island*, there on the kitchen table was a framed photo of "Mama" smiling on our efforts to recollect all the things she had taught us.

We miss you, "Mama."

 *Epilogue*

I do not want to harbor any hatred of Mississippi. This enigmatic state is, after all, the cradle of my existence; she spawned the people who gave me life and breath and foundation. Nevertheless, I cannot ignore the fact that the Magnolia State has been unrelentingly vicious in its treatment of Blacks in general and my family in particular since 1817. That's when Mississippi was admitted to the Union as a slave state. Ironically, the Mississippi state constitution in 1817 specifically required slave owners to take good care of their human chattel on penalty of having the state snatch mistreated slaves away from cruel masters. Then just three years after Mississippi lawmakers passed this seemingly humane law, the case of *State* v. *Isaac Jones* produced a court ruling that sent a mixed message about benevolence toward slaves. They said that the killing of a slave in Mississippi should not necessarily be considered murder.

That my African ancestors survived the nightmarish ocean passage from the homeland to the shores of America gives testimony to uncanny inner and outer tenacity. That my great-great-grandparents, Ned and Ellen, and all their contemporary kith and kin throughout America managed to survive being sold like cattle at a master's whim is remarkable. That slaves like my great-great-grandparents could be uprooted abruptly from shackles in one state to chains in another bears witness to their incredible physical, emotional, and mental strength. That my relatives and the millions of other chronically impoverished Blacks managed to endure the harsh regimen and criminal deceit of the Sharecropper era is clear evidence of exceptional backbone. That my kinfolk were able to flee Mississippi for points North, East, and West and forget their rise and fall from prosperity to destitution in the South shows true grit. And the fact that every single Rounds family member we know about has been able to set up a comfortable life outside Mississippi attests to extraordinary resilience and resourcefulness.

Historically, the Rounds Way has not been to whimper, whine, moan, weep, wail, gnash teeth, or complain about the hand we've been dealt. For as long as there have been records of our existence, we Roundsfolk have been among the original makers of sweet lemonade when life served us sour lemons. We have never cursed God! We have never cursed Fate! We have never even cursed Mississippi when we have experienced or remembered or heard tales of those excruciatingly hard times. Lord knows, Mississippi has deserved many more brickbats from the *Honey Island* descendants than the Almighty or Destiny ever warranted. While God and Fate are invisible and, thus, harder to hit, it would have been very easy for those of us who are sons and daughters of slaves and sharecroppers to spit in the direction of the very tangible Mississippi. But just as a mistreated child often tries to find some redeeming quality in an abusive parent, my Rounds ancestors and my relatives who remember the *Honey Island* experience unto this day have managed to roll with the often relentless barrage of punches Mississippi has thrown.

Some might accuse the Rounds clan of being too docile and submissive. To the contrary, we have consistently demonstrated how to triumphantly rise from the pitch darkness of bondage into the sunlight of freedom while burdened with a shackle on the leg, a millstone around the neck, a heavy load of cotton on the back, and the less fortunate on our shoulders. While the Rounds line has not yet produced a Nobel laureate, an occupant of the Oval Office, or a captain of industry, we also have not spawned any criminals, cry-babies, or charity-seekers. It was the harsh life in Mississippi that can be credited with teaching the Rounds family members the unshakeable credos of our existence today:

1. The only thing worse than failure is the failure to overcome failure.

2. Make a dime; save a nickel.

3. If you ever need a helping hand... first try the one at the end of your own arm.

My study of my family's history in Mississippi has been an eye-opening experience for me. The many interviews with Rounds family members, their former neighbors, and with today's Mississippians, both black and white have helped me understand why they all exude such reluctance, obstinance, and even abject fear of discussing their past or present lives. I now better understand the patina black and white Mississippians have manufactured to obscure, obliterate, whitewash and edit the history they've lived. It's been made crystal clear to me that my relatives who knew life on *Honey Island* have feared that their lifestyles down in the boondocks would be ridiculed as primitive, unsophisticated, or even backward. That's why they would evoke their now-famous selective memory whenever questions were asked about their Mississippi past. When ancient fears of intimidation, harassment, or worse have been rekindled by questions from an inquisitive relative/TV reporter, my own kinfolk, their former *Honey Island* neighbors and those who call Mississippi home today have deftly clammed up.

Historically, my kinfolk and their carbon copies in the south—with few exceptions—have not been openly rebellious against the system that so harshly oppressed them. There was, of course, the Jefferson Rounds who helped lead a small plantation revolt near New Orleans. He was among a group of slaves who flat out refused to work for a new government-appointed master after the original plantation owner had fled. And there was sharecropper Thaddeus "Ted" Rounds, one of my personal family heroes, who wouldn't take the nasty verbal abuse from a Mississippi plantation owner who called him the "N" word. As a consequence, Cousin Thaddeus had to flee the plantation by night and go into hiding lest he become a victim of a beating or lynching. But it seems the Rounds family's principal form of revolution has been to rise above the oppression, beat the odds, and continue to produce hard-working, God-fearing, honest, and independent citizens. Quietly.

I'm pleased to report that the once far-flung Rounds family is gaining strength and unity. At the 1999 Fourth Rounds Family Reunion held over the Labor Day Weekend in Memphis, one hundred and seventeen members of our clan from eleven states turned out. Alabama, Colorado, Georgia, Illinois, Kansas, Kentucky, Missouri, Mississippi, Ohio, Tennessee, and Texas were represented in a joyful conclave of many relatives who had not known about each other before Memphis. We made several resolutions in our formal and informal sessions. The most important, I think, is that we unanimously pledged to return to our home cities and launch a major effort to find out more about our roots in Mississippi and Ned and Ellen's birthplace in Kentucky. We acknowledged that time is of the essence! We must record the stories our beloved *Oldtimers* have to tell, we resolved, before these memories are lost forever. We also pledged to re-establish ties with the churches, schools, and any other remnants of our Mississippi past we can rediscover. And we promised that we would give our strong support to those ~~who~~ few hearty souls who are still living on the hallowed ground around *Honey Island,* keeping the faith and trying to make Mississippi a better place.

Even though there are few Rounds family members left on the old soil, there are some exciting things happening in the environs of Humphreys County, Mississippi and throughout the state today. There's a strong likelihood that Yazoo City will have its first black sheriff ever when voters go to the polls in the November 1999 election. And Rufus and Mattie Straughter, the cordial hosts who helped us get around in the Delta on our research mission are, I'm sure, human harbingers of a better day of justice and equality coming for black

Mississippians. Rufus ran unopposed in the August 1999 election and will return to a second term in the Mississippi State Legislature—the first black lawmaker ever to represent the county in which the first members of the Rounds family lived. Mattie won her Democratic party's nomination to a seat in the Belzoni Courthouse as Tax Assessor/Collector. Her chances are reportedly good for a victory in November. Her campaign should be helped by a spontaneous act at the Memphis reunion. When the family members were told about Mattie's aspirations, a descendant of Ned and Ellen Rounds from Lima, Ohio, passed the hat and a generous grassroots campaign contribution was collected and sent immediately to Mattie. In still another development from the Memphis reunion: Rep. Straughter now has a formal petition signed by more than a hundred Rounds descendants to take to the fall, 1999 legislative session asking that the nearly-forgotten name of *Honey Island* be restored to history books, maps, highway signs, and any future real estate developments on the hallowed soil on which the Rounds family shed blood, sweat, and tears. With that petition goes the hopes and prayers of a family that wants to see its history repainted on the Mississippi Delta landscape.

On the eve of the Memphis reunion, my eighty-five-year-old mother seemed to get really excited about attending the conclave and she particularly was looking forward to the possibility that a busload of family members would drive from Memphis down to her old homeland on *Honey Island*. A bit surprised by her unusual enthusiasm, I asked my mother why, in more than seventy years, neither she nor any other member of the St. Louis branch of the Rounds family had ever bothered to return for a visit to *Honey Island*. She responded quite simply: "*There's never been any reason before now to go back...*"

There *is* good reason now to go back. And we, the proud descendants of Ned and Ellen Rounds, *shall* return to *Honey Island!* Again, again, and again...

Honey Island: The Glossary

While definitions of the following words may be all too familiar to adults of the author's generation or those older, these terms are listed here to enlighten the younger generation and generations to come. Some of the words are already passing from our daily use. In some cases, that's not all bad.

A

acknowledgments, *n.*, in the funeral service, the time set aside for the church secretary or a family member to read selected cards, letters, and telegrams sent to the bereaved.

"acquire," *v.*, to pilfer or steal, but generally when there is a genuine need.

affrays, *n.*, legal language for a dispute between two or more parties, usually over property ownership.

antiseptic, *n.*, a germ-killer, as in *Dr. Tichenor's Antiseptic.*

appurtenance, *n.*, term used in land records to indicate anything attached to the property such as a house, barn, outhouse, smokehouse, fence, etc.

arpent, *n.*, a narrow strip of land equal to about one acre. Old French unit of measure.

asafetida bag, *n.*, in folk medicine, a small pouch full of foul-smelling herbs worn around the neck to ward off illness or evil spirits.

"Aunt," *adj.*, a diminutive term of endearment for an elderly slave woman or nanny who is too old to be called a "girl." Examples are *Aunt Jemima* of cake and pancake mix fame and *"Aunt" Sally sometimes sleeps in the same room with the master's children.*

B

baking soda, *n., sodium bicarbonate,* a multi-purpose white powder used on *Honey Island* as a leavening agent in cooking, deodorant paste, antacid, tooth powder, poultice, cleaning compound, and as an anti-odor ice-box sweetener.

bale, *n.,* a tightly compressed bundle of cotton or hay held together by a band of rope, hoops, or wire. Usually weighs fourteen hundred pounds.

bathtub gin, *n.,* an always potent, sometimes lethal alcoholic concoction that flowed freely during Prohibition. The mixture was often made up of grain mash, fermented juniper berries, and grain alcohol. Sometimes mixed in an actual bathtub.

bayou, *n.,* in the South, a marshy offshoot of a river or lake or a stagnant creek. From the Choctaw word *bayuk,* or small stream.

Beelzebub, *n.,* another name for Satan; the devil.

beeves, *n.,* the archaic plural of the word *beef.* Found written in some letters between Civil War leaders on both sides to describe the cattle they coveted and often raided on *Honey Island.*

bib overalls, *n.,* work trousers with a chest flap and shoulder straps often worn by field hands. Also called overalls or overhauls.

"big orange," *n.,* a rural term for an orange-flavored soda pop of any brand name.

black draught, *n.,* an awful-tasting elixir gulped by the tablespoonful by *Honey Island* residents and other southerners often in the springtime in an attempt to cure what ailed them.

black-eyed peas, *n.,* another name for cowpeas. Almost always cooked with salt pork and onions for humans. The dish is believed to spark fertility when eaten with hog's head on New Year's Day. Also used for cattle feed and soil fertilization.

blanch, *v.,* to scald or parboil produce or meats to facilitate the removal of stems, husks, seeds, or skin.

blockade, *n.,* a military maneuver to cut off supplies to an enemy especially, via a body of water like the Yazoo River or the Mississippi.

bluff, *n.,* a cliff or hill with a broad, steep, facade often overlooking a river.

boll, *n.,* the seed pod of the cotton plant, from an early spelling of *bowl.*

bootleg booze, *n.,* illegally-made alcohol produced for consumption; also called *hootch* and *moonshine.*

bootlegger, *n.,* the maker of illegal booze. From the practice of hiding the alcohol in one's boot.

"boy", *n.,* the term used to address a male slave, field hand, or sharecropper even after the subject had reached adulthood. A "boy" became "Uncle" after reaching old age.

buckshot, *n.,* rounded pellets encased in a shell fired from a gun to shoot wild game.

buffalo fish, *n.,* a favorite river fish of *Honey Island* residents and descendants. This carp-like fish has a strong taste and dangerous needle-like bones. Deep-fried in a cornmeal batter.

burn, *n.,* an ancient Scottish term for a brook or little river. *Honey Island* is located in what was once referred to as the *Panther Burn District.* See *panther.*

"buzzard's roost," *n.,* the third-floor, segregated seating for Blacks only in southern movie houses like the *Crescent Theater* in Belzoni frequented by *Honey Island* residents.

C

calamine lotion, *n.,* a commercially-manufactured solution of zinc oxide and ferric oxide rubbed onto mosquito and other insect bites to relieve itching.

camphor, *n.,* a white compound derivative of turpentine used as a counterirritant in medications ranging from lip balms to liniments.

camphorated oil, *n.,* one part camphor in four parts of cottonseed oil.

camphor ice, *n.,* the camphor compound mixed with beeswax and cottonseed oil.

candied yams, *n.,* sweet potatoes baked in sugar. Served as a side dish.

carp, *n.,* a popular, edible fresh-water fish enjoyed by *Honey Island* residents and regularly imported from *Honey Island's Eagle Lake* to St. Louis' *Meletio's Fish Market.*

caste, *n.,* a distinct social system based on race, class, or occupation.

castor oil, *n.,* a colorless, thick liquid from the castor bean used as a purgative or laxative.

catamount, *n.,* one of many names for the cougar, the panther, the concolour, or painter; members of the big cat family.

catfish lake; pond, *n.,* a closed body of water of variable size used to raise catfish in a controlled environment.

cession, *n.,* the act of giving up land or property parcels as directed by terms of a treaty.

chamber pot, *n.,* a vessel used generally in rural bedrooms to avoid a trip to the outhouse. Also called a *slop jar.*

chancery clerk, *n.,* a senior Mississippi courthouse clerk in charge of all deeds and county property records. The title varies from state to state.

chicken pox, *n.,* a contagious and infectious children's disease causing reddened eruptions on the skin. Also called *water pox.*

chigger, *n.,* a six-legged, blood-sucking parasite whose burrowing into human and animal skin can cause infectious diseases like typhus. Also called *jigger.*

china berry, *n.,* the yellow fruit of the china berry tree used in cooking and as a flavoring in curing meats.

chitterlings, *n.,* the northern mispronunciation of *chitlins.*

chitlins, *n.,* the small intestine of the hog that can be either battered and deep-fried or boiled. Also affectionately called *wrinkle steak.* A standard joke among *Honey Island* residents is that a nail should be thrown into the pot when cooking chitlins; when the nail is soft, the chitlins are done!

chlolesterophobia, *n.,* word coined by the author meaning the current fear and concern about the harmful effects of cholesterol. Of no concern to *Honey Island* residents.

chop cotton, *v.,* to thin the cotton rows, usually with a hoe, to allow the cotton-pickers access via field aisles. Gives rise to the statement "A tough row to hoe," said of a difficult predicament.

cloverleaf rolls, *n.,* rich dinner rolls whose tops take on the look of the cloverleaf because of the three balls of dough put into each baking tin's muffin compartment.

coal oil, *n.,* another name for *kerosene.* Created by the distillation of bituminous coal. Used for lamp fuel and as an unwisely-administered purgative, crude antiseptic for cuts, or toothache pain-killer by some *Honey Island* residents.

cobbler, *n.,* a thick and rich fruit-filled pie, usually with a thick crust only on top.

collard greens, *n.,* a leafy green vegetable of the *kale* family often boiled with a ham hock or fatback, onion, and other greens from the mustard, spinach and turnip families.

colored, *adj.,* a now derogatory term describing a person of African American descent. *n.,* an African American.

"colored only," *adj.,* the restrictive signs placed over the doors of restrooms, drinking fountains, and other facilities to designate segregated use by African Americans only.

commissary, *n.,* the company store on plantations and sharecropping farms where laborers could purchase foodstuff, hardware, and dry goods from the master. Cost of items would be levied against year-end money to be paid to field hands or sharecroppers.

concolour, *n.,* a seldom-used name for the panther, cougar, catamount, wild cat, mountain lion which once roamed the area on and around *Honey Island.*

conscript, *n.,* a military draftee or a slave abandoned by a master.

consumption, *n.,* a disease now called tuberculosis, which causes the victim to waste away.

'coon dog, *n.,* a canine trained to chase and hunt rabbits or "tree" raccoons and 'possums.

coral snake, *n.,* a poisonous viper of the South often banded in red, black and yellow.

cottonmouth, *n.,* a venomous snake of the southern swamps. Can grow to more than six feet in length. Sometimes called a *water moccasin.* Such *Honey Island* residents as my mother and aunts preferred not to call them anything but *"gone!"*

cougar, *n.,* yet another name for the panther, mountain lion, catamount, painter, or big wildcats of other names which once ran free in the Mississippi Delta.

county coroner, *n.,* the elected official charged with certifying death and determining the cause of deaths, especially in rural communities. Frequently replaced by better-trained *medical examiners.*

"crick," *n.,* a rural corruption of the word *creek.* Also a pain and stiffening of the neck.

cunctation, *n.,* procrastination; delay, tardiness. An abiding policy in Mississippi exercised by her citizens at all levels. Particularly noticeable by northerners who may work in a more punctual style.

curling iron, *n.,* a metal rod-like implement heated and used to curl or put waves in the hair.

cutlery man, *n.,* an itinerant vendor who went house to house when I was a boy, sharpening and polishing knives, hedge clippers, barber's tools, and other implements that needed honing.

cylinder head, *n.,* on a Mississippi River steamboat, the other end from which the piston rods stick out. The favorite engine part of Civil War forces to dismantle in order to totally cripple the steamboat.

D

Delta, *n.,* the rich, alluvial plain in the heart of Mississippi bracketed by the Mississippi River to the west and that river's tributaries to the north, east, and west.

DDT, *n.,* a liquid insecticide widely used in the South as an insecticide, especially to ward off pesky mosquitoes. Sometimes foolishly sprayed on the skin. Banned by the EPA in 1973 because of its suspected cancer-causing properties. Used heavily by *Honey Island* residents before that time.

dichlorodiphenyltrichlorethane, *n.,* the formal, spelled-out name of DDT. See preceding definition.

double pneumonia, *n.,* an acute inflammation of both lungs.

draught boat, *n.,* a boat that will seat about six passengers powered by rowing with oars. One person might operate a tiller/rudder to guide direction of the boat.

drugstore, *n.,* a shop in which pharmaceuticals and notions are sold. A pharmacy.

E

elixir, *n.,* a generally sweet tonic believed by users to be a "cure-all." Usually contains some measure of alcohol purportedly for medicinal purposes. Often taken in the spring of the year.

emancipation, *n.,* the act of giving those once held in bondage their freedom.

Emancipation Proclamation, *n.,* the formal declaration issued by President Abraham Lincoln in 1863 freeing the slaves in any states hostile to the Union.

endogamy, *n.,* the practice of marrying inside one's social, racial, religious, or economic group.

enumerator, *n.,* a scribe hired by the U.S. Census Bureau to record the demographic facts of a given population territory.

F

fatback, *n.,* the fat meat from the upper portion of a side of hog cured in salt and used to season vegetable dishes. In some cases a slice of fatback was used as the meat in a sandwich. See salt pork.

fasting, *n.,* the practice of abstinence from food for religious or medicinal reasons.

fellowship hour, *n.,* the social session following a church service which may last far longer than sixty minutes. A light repast and beverages always served.

firecracker, *n.,* a cardboard or paper cylinder filled with explosive powder and with a fuse used to light the pyrotechnic. Ignited in profuse numbers at Christmas around *Honey Island* and throughout the South. Fired on July Fourth in the North.

fodder, *n.,* feed for cattle, horses, and sheep. Can consist of corn, cornstalks, cane, hay, or soybean bushes.

G

"get happy," *v.,* the act of putting on a physical demonstration during a fundamentalist church service when one is said to be filled with the *Holy Ghost* or *Spirit.* This act can take the form of shouting, speaking in tongues, dancing, and/or clapping one's hands. See glossolalia.

gimpy, *adj.,* having a deformed, disabled, or irregularly sized leg or foot causing one to limp markedly.

glossolalia, *n.,* the speaking in tongues in unintelligible language when one becomes filled with the *Holy Ghost.* Said to evolve from the biblical incident at the Tower of Babel. See *get happy.*

goatee, *n.,* the v-shaped growth of hair allowed to grow under a gentleman's bottom lip. The underpinning of a moustache as worn by Ned and Westly Rounds and other southern gentlemen. Believed to have been first styled in Kentucky.

goobers, *n.,* the southern name for *peanuts.* Also called *goober peas.* From the African word for peanut, *nguba.*

goose grease, *n.,* fat taken from a goose. Used as a messy "cure" for the children's ailments of chicken pox, measles, and mumps.

government man, *n.,* a male who works for the U. S. government, most often to *Honey Island* residents and descendants, a postal worker, not a G-Man.

grease, *v.,* to be able to cook artfully or to be able to eat large amounts of food. Pronounced *greeze.* *n.,* any pomade or heavy oil used to make the hair shiny and laid back. *n.,* the drippings from hog fat.

greens, *n.,* leafy green vegetables of the turnip, chard, collard, mustard, and spinach families. Always boiled with fatback or ham hocks and other seasonings.

griping, *n.,* stomach cramping. Often treated with a purgative or laxative.

grits, *n.,* coarsely ground grain. Cooked and served at breakfast, lunch, and supper as a side dish in the South. Often served with a generous ladling of gravy; sometimes served with a cheese topping.

guinea fowl, *n.,* a chicken-like barnyard bird raised for its meat and eggs. Originally from Africa.

H

"happy," *adj.,* a state of joy and rapture caused by a filling with the *Holy Spirit* usually during a church service. See *get happy.*

"Happy Valley," *n.,* in the 1930s, any of the several squatters camps set up by the hopelessly poor to demonstrate their Depression era frustration with their lot. A tent city where those of similar economic status could "flock together."

"high yeller," *n., adj.,* a derogatory term for a person of mixed race and light skin. A mulatto.

hitching post, *n.,* a wooden or metal stave to which a horse, mule, or other animal may be tied.

hoecake, *n.,* a cornmeal pancake generally fried in a skillet.

hog jowl, *n.,* the jaw of a hog. Used for seasoning boiled dishes. The inner tissue scrapings of this piece of meat were also smeared on the infected skin to relieve eruptions caused by measles, mumps, and chicken pox.

homestead, *n.,* a piece of land cleared and upon which a house and crop fields are established. *v.,* to work to improve and harvest upon a plot of land.

hootch, *n.,* alcoholic liquor for consumption. Often illegally-made booze. See *moonshine.*

"Hooverville," *n.,* any of the tent-city encampments set up by the desperately poor during the Depression era. Named derisively after President Herbert Hoover.

I

ice box, *n.,* the forerunner of the refrigerator. A compartment chilled by blocks of ice to preserve food. Sawdust and canvas tarps were used to preserve the ice blocks.

ice man, *n.,* a now extinct vendor of blocks of ice used to preserve food products.

indoor plumbing, *n.,* toilet facilities inside one's home or other buildings. An advancement from outhouses. See *outhouse.*

intermarriage, *n.,* a wedding between persons of different races, classes, or religions. See *miscegenation.*

"Invitation, The," *n.,* the formal call by preachers to sinners to come to the front of the church during the fundamentalist worship service to confess their transgressions, "express their hope in Jesus," and join the church.

Irish potato, *n.,* a white potato; sometimes mispronounced *Arsh* potato.

Irish wake, *n.,* a ritual sitting with the dead mixed with equal parts mourning and alcoholic reveling in remembrance of the dearly departed.

J

jacks, *n.,* a game chiefly played on the ground or other flat service usually by girls using a small rubber ball and small metal objects with six points. Also called *jackstones.*

jackstones, *n.,* see preceding definition.

jack salmon, *n.,* a slender, edible fish of the croaker family. Also called *whiting.*

janitor, *n.,* a workman charged with keeping a building clean. A custodian.

jigger, *n.,* another name for the *chigger.* See *chigger.*

Jim Crow, *n.,* the practice or policy of discriminating against African Americans. From a minstrel show song written by one Thomas Rice (1808-1860).

jimson (weed), *n.,* a foul-smelling weed which is poisonous when ingested in anything but small quantities. Used for its purported medicinal properties. From a corruption of the word *Jamestown,* where it is first believed to have been used for certain medicinal purposes.

K

keening and crying, *v.,* weeping, wailing, and shedding tears for a deceased person's passing. From the Irish.

kerosene, *n.,* the product of the distillation of bituminous coal used as a lamp fuel, cleaning compound, and in very small doses by some *Honey Island* residents as a purgative. See *coal oil.*

kiln, *n.,* a compartment or small shack used for storing, curing, or drying food products.

king snake, *n.,* a constricting viper which feeds off other snakes and which terrorized my mother and aunts on *Honey Island,* especially during flooding.

Klan, *n.,* the Ku Klux Klan. A secret organization which has terrorized, assaulted, and intimidated African Americans and other minority groups since shortly after the Civil War. Founded in Georgia, but well known to the residents of *Honey Island.*

Ku Klux Klan, *n.,* see preceding definition.

L

lil ole, *adj.,* a corruption of *"little old."* A term of endearment and diminution.

liniment, *n.,* a liquid rubbing compound applied to relieve sore muscles and joints.

linoleum, *n.,* the most popular floor covering of *Honey Island* homes. Formed by burlap or canvas coated with linseed oil, powdered cork, and rosin. Its shiny surface is easy to mop and keep clean, making it a floor covering usable in every room in the house.

love offering, *n.,* a euphemism for a collection taken up specifically to pay the preacher during a worship service. May be one of at least three passings of the collection basket at a Baptist worship service.

lug, the, *n.,* a kickback paid to a politician by an appointee he/she had gotten a good job. Sometimes called a "donation" to the politico's campaign coffers or "favorite charity."

lynch, *v.,* to mutilate, disfigure, and hang a person without a trial often as a result of mob action. Perhaps named after Captain William Lynch (1742-1820) of Virginia.

M

mange, the, *n.,* painful skin disease transmitted to man and beast by parasitic mites. Causes loss of hair and skin eruptions.

manumission, *n.,* the act of freeing—as with a slave or indentured servant. See *emancipation.*

Mason-Dixon Line, *n.,* an imaginary yet politically recognizable line drawn between North and South. From the survey by Charles Mason and Jeremiah Dixon along the present Pennsylvania-Maryland border that was begun in 1763 and completed four years later.

Mason jar, *n.,* a glass jar with a rubber-ring airtight seal used for canning foods.

"marked," *adj.,* cursed by an evil force with horrific consequences. Said of women who miscarried after a frightening encounter with a corpse, snake, frog, rat, the Devil, or the like.

measles, *n.,* rubeola, an infectious childhood disease characterized by a cough and a skin eruption.

miscegenation, *n.,* No longer a politically correct term for the marriage or cohabitation of a man and woman of different racial groups.

moonshine, *n.,* illegally manufactured alcohol for consumption. See *hootch.*

mortician, *n.,* a funeral director.

mortuary, *n.,* a funeral home or parlor.

"Mu," *n.,* The Census Bureau's written abbreviation for a *mulatto.* See *mulatto.*

mulatto, *n.,* a person of mixed Black and White parentage. Sometimes designated to indicate the percentage of Black ancestry, as in a quadroon (one-quarter Black, such as the child of a mulatto and a White) or octaroon (one-eighth Black, such as the child of a quadroon and a White).

N

Negro, *n.,* a now unacceptable term for a person of African American descent.

Negro Spiritual, *n.,* a moving, often rhythmical song first sung by slaves, field hands, and chain gangs to give them hope and inspiration that a better day was coming.

nigger, *n.,* a highly derogatory name for a Black person. From the Spanish word *negro,* which means *black.*

nurse unit, *n.,* the crisply uniformed team of minimally-trained paramedics established to handle any medical emergencies during certain Baptist church services.

O

obsequies, *n.,* another name for *funeral services.* The word is seldom used in conversation, but almost always printed on the funeral programs in Black Baptist churches.

oil of wintergreen, *n.,* a mint-tasting solution of methyl salicylate used to flavor medicines, perfumes, and liniments. See *liniment.*

old age dementia, *n.,* the archaic, non-politically correct term for what we now call *Alzheimer's disease.*

old maid, *n.,* a politically incorrect term for a woman who has never married. See *spinster.*

Oldtimers, *n.,* a collective, respectful, and affectionate term used by the author in this book to designate all the wonderful former residents of *Honey Island* who were kind enough to share their golden memories and photographs with me.

ole, *adj.,* a corruption of the word *old.* Used in an affectionate way. See *lil ole.*

oleo margarine, *n.,* a butter substitute made from animal oils, refined lard, and sometimes cottonseed oil.

"on the place," *adj.,* the description of the residence, on a full-time or part-time basis, of domestic servants at the home of the person for whom they work.

outhouse, *n.,* toilet facilities located outside a main house or other building; a shack often with two holes, one for adults and one for children.

overalls, *n.,* See *bib overalls.*

overhauls, *n.,* a mispronunciation of *overalls.* See *bib overalls.*

overseer, *n.,* a person charged with the supervision of slaves, field hands, and sharecroppers. Sometimes known for cruel treatment of the workers.

overshirt, *n.,* a long shirt, usually made of burlap or flour sacks, often the only clothing provided for slaves. Similar in style to today's night shirts.

P

Packard, *n.,* an automobile manufactured during the 1940s and 1950s.

painter, *n.,* another name for a panther, cougar, etc. See *panther.*

pallbearer, *n.,* a person, usually one of six or eight, selected to bear the coffin at a funeral and graveside ceremony.

palmetto, *n.,* a palm plant with fan-shaped leaves. Thrives in marshy, hot areas like *Honey Island.*

parboil, *v.,* to boil meat or produce in scalding water to facilitate the removal of skin or husks. See *blanch.*

pass, to, *v.,* (1) to cross the color line. "She is now living in Boston and *passing* for white." (2) *v.,* to die. Never used by southerners with *away.* "He *passed* this morning."

pawnshop, *n.,* a store where an individual can sell items to the storekeeper for quick cash. The individual can buy back his property later (usually for more cash than he received) if the item has not already been sold by the pawnbroker.

peanut brittle, *n.,* a candy made of burnt, skillet-cooked sugar liberally sprinkled with fresh peanuts. Served when the concoction cools and hardens.

pellagra, *n.,* an insidious and often fatal disease caused by a vitamin deficiency. It manifests itself by large black scabs on the skin with bloody patches under the scales.

penny postcard, *n.,* a postal card which costs just one cent. They cost twenty cents each in 1999.

piecework, *n.,* a job which pays the worker for each item produced rather than a straight salary.

pine tar, *n.,* a brownish-black solution obtained by the distillation of pine wood. The thick liquid smells like turpentine and had many applications on *Honey Island* in elixirs for treatment of everything from skin eruptions to coughs.

place, the, *n.,* a farm, plantation, or home which is the workplace of domestics, field hands, or sharecroppers. A domestic who lived in the home of an employer was said to be *"living on the place."*

"play possum," *v.,* to pretend to be ill or dead. Taken from the practice of the opossum of feigning death to avoid being eaten by animals who won't eat carrion.

pleurisy, *n.,* a devastating, sometimes fatal, malady caused by the acute inflammation of the lining of the membrane enveloping the lung or thorax.

poacher, *n.,* one who lives on land that the inhabitant does not own by deed or formal papers. Also, one who hunts or fishes or farms on land without permission, license, or deed.

poll tax, *n.,* an illegal levy required before an individual was allowed to vote; imposed most often on Blacks in the South to discourage them from voting.

pomade, *n.,* a scented ointment used for dressing and sometimes pressing the hair.

pone, *n.,* a fried or baked corn meal cake. See *hoecake.*

postpartum anovulatory cycle, *n.,* the period shortly after giving birth in which a woman is less fertile. This cycle helps contribute to the phenomenon which caused *Honey Island* children in most families to be born two years apart.

pot likker, *n.,* the liquor which remains after greens have been boiled with ham hocks or pork fat, onions, and other seasonings. Believed by *Honey Island* residents to contain all the vitamins from the cooked greens. Often eaten as a full meal with cornbread.

poultice, *n.,* a concoction of herbs, spices, or medicines placed in its moist composition in a cloth and applied to a sore, cut, inflammation, or irritation on the body.

"prove up," *v.,* to clear and improve virgin land. Often a condition of acquiring and owning the land for free under government contracts including homestead laws.

puff adder, *n.,* a thick-bodied snake originally from Africa which, when agitated, puffs up its body and hisses in a cobra-like way. When confronted or touched with a stick, the viper quickly deflates and "plays 'possum." See *playing possum.*

purgative, *n.,* a medicine taken to purge the system. A laxative. See *castor oil.*

R

rag picker, *n.,* a person who gathers rags from refuse and sells them to make a living.

reb, *n.,* an abbreviated term for a rebel. Used to designate a Confederate soldier. Also *Johnny Reb.*

redeye gravy, *n.,* a gravy made from pouring hot water or hot coffee on the grease that remains in the skillet after frying ham.

Reconstruction (era), *n.,* the historical period following the end of the Civil War in which the South was punished by some Congressional legislation and guided in an attempt to rehabilitate the Confederacy.

redneck, *n.,* a derogatory term for a white person with rural roots. Often used to connote persons who are racists or crude in their habits and manners

rhubarb, *n.,* an edible leafstalk plant used to make pies. The extract from the plant is also thought to have medicinal powers. Some *Honey Island* residents used the root as a tonic or astringent.

rock candy, *n.,* crystals of hardened sugar. Used medicinally in hot tea or whiskey for sore throats and colds.

rotgut, *n.,* bad whiskey often made from fermented corn. See *hootch, moonshine.*

"run on the road," *v.,* to travel on a moving train as one's occupation. Said of cooks, porters, baggage handlers, engineers, and conductors.

S

sanctified, *adj.,* filled with the *Holy Spirit* causing one to live a life without sin.

scalper, *n.,* one who buys properties or land plots cheaply and quickly sells them at inflated prices.

sedition, *n.,* the act of stirring up or promoting disorder or rebellion against one's government.

sedition speeches, *n.,* rabble-rousing oratory aimed at toppling a government.

secessionist, *n.,* one who advocates pulling out of an established government.

shaman, *n.,* a medicine man who deals in the supernatural and folk medicine.

sharecropper, *n.,* a *tenant farmer.* A farm laborer who works the property of another in exchange for a percentage of the crop sales. See *tenant farmer.*

shotgun house, *n.,* an extremely narrow house.

shuck tea, *n.,* a beverage made from boiling corn shucks in water. Used, perhaps ineffectively, to treat measles and other ailments on *Honey Island.*

slop jar, *n.,* a chamber pot used to avoid the trek out to an outhouse. See *chamber pot; outhouse.*

smokehouse, *n.,* a shack or barn in which meats and produce are cured, smoked, or dried.

soul-dead, *adj.,* said of a person who has no chance for salvation or eternal life because of his/her inability or resistance to opening his/her heart to Jesus.

soul food, *n.,* southern cooking characterized by a cornucopia of fried and boiled foods, multi-purpose used of pork and chicken along with tubers, roots, legumes, leaves, corn, and heavily-sugared fruit dishes served on the side.

Spanish moss, *n.,* wispy, creeping plant which drapes trees in the southern region of the country.

speculator, *n.,* one who buys quantities of land and properties on the chance that they can be sold at a good profit.

spinster, *n.* a politically incorrect term for a woman who has never married. See *old maid.*

"splitting a post," *v.,* two or more people dividing up and walking on either side of a telephone pole, hitching post, parking meter, or the like while strolling in the same direction. Thought by the superstitious to bring bad luck.

squatter, *n.,* one who occupies land with no formal papers identifying ownership. One who believes that possession is, indeed, nine-tenths of the law. See *poacher.*

stage plank, *n.,* a rectangularly-shaped, thin, iced, gingerbread cookie. Takes its name from the wooden slats used to make stagecoaches.

staying on the place, *v.,* a servant or domestic's taking up permanent or part-time residence in the home or plantation of an employer or master.

stout, *adj.,* full-figured, plump, pudgy. A term used by the Rounds Family and others as a courtesy to keep from referring to a person as "fat."

straightening iron, *n.* an implement used to straighten hair. See *curling iron.*

streetcar, *n.* a motor coach used in public transportation which is usually track-bound and powered by electrified tracks or overhead cable system. Becoming extinct.

sweat shop, *n.,* a manufacturing plant in which the laborers generally do piecework during extremely long work days in an often uncomfortable setting at extremely low pay. See *piecework.*

sweet potato pie, *n.,* a dessert pastry made with the sweet potato or yam in a crust.

switch, *n.,* a slender tree limb used for giving whippings to errant boys and girls.

switching, *n.,* the act of using a switch to administer corporal punishment. See *switch.*

Sunday-go-to-meeting clothes, *n.,* one's dressiest outfit. Worn for church services and any other dress-up event.

Suspiciere mississippianus, *n.,* a term coined by the author to describe the noteworthy suspicions Mississippi residents seem to have about talking to anybody from the North in person or on the telephone. The suspicions seem particularly acute when a male northerner attempts to speak with a southern woman about anything.

T

taters, *n.,* a corruption of the word *potatoes.*

TB, *n.,* the shortened term for tuberculosis. An infectious disease which can affect any part of the body, especially the lungs. See *consumption.*

"tetched," *adj.,* a corruption of the word *touched.* Used singularly to describe someone who is crazy or, more politely, mentally ill. "I think he is tetched in the head!"

tenant farmer, *n.,* a euphemism for *sharecropper.* The position created in the South after the Civil War to keep former slaves in virtual bondage to avoid upsetting the economic system of the South. See *sharecropper.*

"Three R's," *n.,* a folksy term for Reading, 'Riting, and 'Rithmetic—reading, writing, and arithmetic.

township, *n.,* a geographic division of a county for administrative or political purposes.

trade, *v.,* to shop at or do business with a particular store. "We trade at *Joe's Grocery Store.*" *n.,* to do business with.

tularemia, *n.,* a disease causing several weeks of fever and malaise usually transmitted to humans by insects, squirrels, or rabbits.

typhus, *n.,* a disease transmitted to humans by lice, fleas, or mosquitoes causing the victim to become bed-redden, afflicted with a nervous disorder, and covered with blotchy red spots.

U

umbelliferous plant, *n.,* plant family which produces carrots, celery, parsley, and parsnips.

"Uncle," *n.,* in the Old South, the name given to a Black man who had, because of advanced age, passed the category of being called "boy." See *boy.*

"unfaircropping," *n.,* word coined by author to mean the traditional and annual cheating sharecroppers were given when they went to claim money for half their crop.

"ursher," *n.,* a common and almost acceptable mispronunciation of the word *usher.* Used very often in African American Baptist and Pentecostal churches.

V

vaudeville, *n.,* entertainment, usually in a theater, made up of a variety of acts following each other in rapid succession.

vendors lien, *n.* the legal document or right of a seller to apply payment for a claim.

victuals, *n.,* food. Sometimes pronounced *vittles.*

W

wake, *n.,* the occasion during which mourners sit with the dead either in the home of the deceased, a funeral home, or at a church. See *Irish wake.*

Walker Method, The, *n.,* a method of hairstyling patented by Madame C. J. Walker, the millionaire African American cosmetologist.

water moccasin, *n.,* a harmless viper also known as a cottonmouth. See *cottonmouth.*

water pox, *n.,* See *chicken pox.*

Watkin's Extract, *n.,* the once-popular baking product of the Watkin's Company. Bakery goods could be flavored with vanilla, banana, or almond extract.

W.C.T.U., *n.,* the Women's Christian Temperance Union, an anti-alcohol, anti-smoking feminists group. My grandmother signed "the pledge" before the turn of the twentieth century.

white lightning, *n.,* homemade whiskey. See *hootch; moonshine.*

"white only," *n.,* the signage for restrooms, drinking fountains, rail cars, etc. to indicate that non-whites would not be admitted, served, nor seated. See *"colored only."*

wrinkle steak, *n.,* a light-hearted euphemism for *chitlins; chitterlings.* See *chitlins.*

Y

"Y," The, *n.,* The Young Men's Christian Association (YMCA) or the Young Women's Christian Association (YWCA).

Yankee, *n.,* in the South, a northerner. From *Jan Kees* (John Cheese), a colonial term used by the Dutch for English settlers.

Yankee beans, *n.,* a southern term for green beans.

"yeller," *n.,* a corruption of the term *yellow.* Used in derogation to describe the skin of a person of mixed race.

Yoruba, *n.,* a West African tribe from an area that is now southwest Nigeria. This tribe was heavily tapped to provide slaves for America's southern plantations.

Bibliography

Archer Jr., Chalmers. *Growing Up Black in Rural Mississippi*. New York: Walker and Co., 1992.

Ausman, Megeare, historian, Corporate Information Services, US Postal Service, Washington, DC. Personal Communication, July 21, 1998.

Banks, Larry. Chief Hydraulics Engineer, Army Corps of Engineers, US Army Corps of Engineers, Vicksburg, MS. Personal Communication, October 1, 1998.

Ball, Edward. *Slaves in the Family*. Boston, MA: G.K. Hall & Co., 1998.

Barry, John M. Rising tide. *The Great Flood of 1927*. New York: Touchstone, 1997. 387-388.

_____Rising tide. *The Great Flood of 1927*. 200-201.

Becerra, R.M., Iglehart, A.P., *Folk Medicine Use: Diverse Populations in a Metropolitan Area*. Social work in health care. 21(4) 37-58, 1995.

Benefo, Tsui, Johnson, J.D. *Ethnic Differences in Child-Spacing Ideals and Practices in Ghana*. Journal of Biosocial Sciences. 26(3) 311-326, 1994.

Bergman, Peter M. *The Negro in America*. New York: Harper & Row, 1969, 169.

_____*The Negro in America*. 210.

_____*The Negro in America*. 275.

_____. *The Negro in America*. 297.

Berlin, Ira; Glymph, Thavolis; Miller, Steven F.; and Reidy, Joseph P., eds. *Freedom. A Documentary History of Emancipation 1861-1867. Series I, Vol. III. The Wartime Genesis of Free Labor: the Lower South*. Cambridge: Cambridge University Press, 1990.

Beschloss, Michael R. *Taking charge: The Johnson White House Tapes, 1963-1964*. New York: Touchstone, 1998.

Botkin, B. A. ed. *Lay My Burden Down*. Athens, Ga.: Georgia Press, 1989. 97.

_____ *Lay My Burden Down.* 116.

_____ *Lay My Burden Down.* 239.

_____ *Lay My Burden Down.* 252..

Brown, R.E. *Breast-Feeding and Family Planning: A Review of the Relationships Between Breast-Feeding and Family Planning.* American Journal of Clinical Nutrition. 35(1), 162-171, 1982.

Carpenter, Barbara, ed. *Ethnic Heritage in Mississippi.* Jackson, MS: University of Mississippi Press, 1992. 45-70.

Cross, Jean. *In Grandmother's Day: A Legacy of Recipes, Remedies and Country Wisdom from 100 Years Ago.* Englewood Cliffs, NJ: Prentice Hall, Inc. 1980. 207.

Civil War CD-ROM. *The War of Rebellion; A Compilation of the Official Records of the Union and Confederate Armies.* Version 1.5. Carmel, IN: Guild Press of Indiana, Inc., 1997.

Cunningham, Lyn Driggs; Jones, Jimmy. *Sweet, Hot and Blue. St. Louis Musical Heritage.* Jefferson, NC: McFarland & Co., Publ. 1989, 20.

Decatur Herald and Review. "Justice Denied." Moore, D. 1955.

Deeds. Humphreys County, Mississippi, 1880-1890.

Deeds. Land purchase. Holmes County Courthouse recorded by James Woods, July 30, 1886.

Drewal, Margaret Thompson. *Yoruba Ritual Performers, Play, Agency. African System of Thought Series.* Bloomington, IN: Indiana University Press, 1992. 38-47.

Elz, Ron. "In Our Town." *West End-Clayton Word.* July 9, 1998, 6.

Fox, Tim. *Where We Live: A Guide to St. Louis Communities.* St. Louis, MO: Missouri Historical Society Press, 1995. 112.

Franklin, John H. *From Slavery to Freedom.* 8th edition. New York: McGraw-Hill Companies, 1999.

Garabrandt, D.H., Held, J., Langholz, B., Peters, J. M. Mack, T.M.. "DDT and related compounds and risk of pancreatic cancer." *Journal of the National Cancer Institute.* 84(10)764-771, 1992.

Helms, J. *Land Tenure in Territorial Mississippi,* 74-86.

Hoessle, Charles. Director, St. Louis Zoo. Personal Communication, 1998.

Howie, P.W. "Breast-feeding. A natural method for child spacing." *American Journal of Obstetrics and Gynecology.* 165, 1990-1991, 1991.

Humphreys, M. *Water Won't Run Uphill: the New Deal and Malaria Control in the American South.* 1933-1940. Parasitologia. 40(1-2), 183-191, 1998.

JET Magazine. October 13, 1955.

Jones, James Weldon. *God's Trombones: Seven Negro Sermons in Verse.* New York: Penguin, 1990.

Llanza, Michael. *Agrarianism and Reconstruction Politics: The Southern Homestead Act.* Baton Rouge, LA: Louisiana State University Press, 1990. 84-85.

_____ *Agrarianism and Reconstruction Politics: The Southern Homestead Act.* 88-89.

Mbiti, John S. *African Religions and Philosophy.* 2nd edition. Oxford: Heinemann Educational Books, 1969. 145-161.

Mississippi Department of Economic and Community Development. Division of Tourism. *The South's Warmest Welcome.* 1998.

New York Times. "A Great Escape. A Dwindling Legacy." Wilkerson, Isabel. February 15, 1998. 8-9,18.

Newsweek. "Slavery's Real Roots." Ellis Cose. October 26, 1998. 75.

Primm, James Neal. *Lion of the Valley.* St. Louis, MO: Pruett Publ. C., 1981. 342-343.

_____ *Lion of the Valley.* 513.

Rombauer, Irma S., Rombauer Becker, M. *Joy of Cooking.* New York: Bobbs-Merrill C.

Inc., 1975.

Rounds, Annie West, St. Louis. MO. Personal Communication. 1998.

Rounds, Thaddeus, Chicago. IL. Personal Communication. 1998.

Scott, Lue Annie, Isola, MS. Personal Communication. 1998.

Skates, John R. *Mississippi: A History.* New York: W.W. Norton & Co., 1979.

St. Louis Post-Dispatch. "Marchers Achieve Only Hollow Victory from 1963 Protest." Bill McClellan. September 3, 1993, Section 1-C.

St. Louis Post-Dispatch. "Major Events in the Civil Rights Movement," compiled by Jerry Brown. May 18, 1997. Section News analysis, 6-B.

St. Louis Post-Dispatch. "Civil Rights Veterans Recall Early Days." Yvonne Samuel. March 29, 1998. Section: Editorial C-3.

Straughter, Mattie, Belzoni. MS: Personal Communication. 1998.

Thurman, Rev. Jodie. Belzoni. MS: Personal Communication. 1998.

Turner, Joe Nathan, St. Louis, MO: Personal Communication. 1998.

Turner, Sally, St. Louis, MO: Personal Communication, 1998.

US. Bureau of the Census. Holmes County, Mississippi, June 1, 1880. Henry Christmas, Enumerator.

Uris, Leon. *Trinity.* New York: Doubleday, 1976.

Walton, Anthony. *Mississippi: An American Journey.* New York: Alfred A. Knopf, 1996. 167.

Washington, Booker T. *Up from Slavery.* New York: Doubleday, 1933.

Wiencek, Henry. *The Hairstons: An American Family in Black and White.* New York: St. Martins Press, 1999.

Wolff, M.S. *Pesticides- How Research Has Succeeded and Failed in Informing Policy: DDT and the Link with Breast Cancer.* Environmental Health Perspectives 103 (Suppl 6) 87- 91, 1995.

Woodard, B.T.; Ferguson, B.B.; Wilson, D.J. *DDT Levels in Milk of Rural Indigent blacks.* American Journal of diseases in Children. 130(4)400-403, 1976.

Wright, John A. *Discovering African American St. Louis: A Guide to Historic Sites.* St. Louis, MO., Missouri Historical Society Press, 1994. 23.

_____ *Discovering African American St. Louis: A Guide to Historic Sites.* 27-28.

_____ *Discovering African American St. Louis: A Guide to Historic Sites.* 41.

Index

About the Author...

Julius K. Hunter is an award-winning, thirty-year veteran of broadcast news in St. Louis whose assignments have taken him around the nation and world. Legendary newsman Walter Cronkite once referred to Hunter as a "consummate pro."

During his three decades of journalistic pursuits, Hunter has written a weekly column on little-known facts about St. Louis history for the **St. Louis Post-Dispatch,** and he has hosted a weekly three-hour talk show, "At Your Service" on **KMOX Radio.** Among Hunter's many other accomplishments are his exclusive one-on-one television interviews with five incumbent U.S. Presidents: Ford, Carter, Reagan, Bush and Clinton.

Hunter is popular on the lecture circuit and conducts frequent addresses and seminars on broadcast ethics; the effects of television viewing on our mental, emotional and physical health; the importance of early childhood reading; and the use of effective public relations techniques. A former Lutheran church organist and choirmaster, Hunter's avocation is music. He has conducted several choral and instrumental ensembles on a regular basis. He recently wrote the lyrics and music for the alma mater anthem now sung at his alma mater, Harris-Stowe State College.

"Honey Island" is Hunter's fifth published work which includes a children's alphabet book, a broadcast news college textbook, and two books on St. Louis' great and historic mansions and the Midwestern industrial giants who built them.